Third Edition _____

Politics and the Budget

The Struggle Between the President and the Congress

HOWARD E. SHUMAN _____

Prentice Hall, Englewood Cliffs, New Jersey 07632

Library of Congress Cataloging-in-Publication Data

Shuman, Howard E.
    Politics and the budget : the struggle between the President and
the Congress / Howard E. Shuman.—3rd ed.
      p. cm.
    Includes bibliographical references and index.
    ISBN 0-13-682378-5
    1. Budget—United States. 2. Budget—Political aspects—United
States. 3. Separation of powers—United States. I. Title.
HJ2051.S49 1992
353.0072'231—dc20
                                          91-28652
                                             CIP

Acquisitions editor: Karen Horton
Editorial/production supervision and
   interior design: E. A. Pauw and Karen Buck
Cover design: Bruce Kenselaar
Prepress buyer: Debra Kesar/Kelly Behr
Manufacturing buyer: Mary Ann Gloriande

Printed in the United States of America

10 9 8 7 6 5 4 3 2 1

ISBN 0-13-682378-5

Prentice-Hall International (UK) Limited, *London*
Prentice-Hall of Australia Pty. Limited, *Sydney*
Prentice-Hall Canada Inc., *Toronto*
Prentice-Hall Hispanoamericana, S.A., *Mexico*
Prentice-Hall of India Private Limited, *New Delhi*
Prentice-Hall of Japan, Inc., *Tokyo*
Simon & Schuster Asia Pte. Ltd., *Singapore*
Editora Prentice-Hall do Brasil, Ltda., *Rio de Janeiro*

To the memory of Frank Hamilton Shuman and Paul Howard Douglas, two sons of Illinois whose constructive works at the cutting edge of events improved the lot of mankind

Contents

5

Fiscal Policy: Government Responsibility for the Economy   152

6

The Politics of Money and Credit   182

7

The Nixon Constitutional Crisis and the 1974 Budget Act   211

8

The Reagan Budget Revolution   249

9

Gramm-Rudman-Hollings and the Reagan Budgets   277

New

10

President Bush, the Congress, and the Five-Year Budget Agreement   304

New

Preface

At the end of almost two decades of experience under the Congressional Budget and Impoundment Control Act of 1974, the results are a classic example of the law of unintended consequences. It was passed during a state of euphoria by votes of 80 to 0 in the Senate and 401 to 6 in the House. Before it had been in effect for a full year, Senate Budget Committee Chairman Edmund S. Muskie (D.-Maine) and ranking minority member Henry Bellmon (R.-Okla.) wrote that

> it equipped Congress for the first time with the institutions and procedures needed to assert control over the Federal "purse strings."[1]

But congressional and presidential spending expert Louis Fisher expressed some doubts. The act, he said, "received an extraordinary amount (and it seems to me a somewhat suspicious amount) of praise."[2] He was suspicious for a variety of reasons:

> Applause came from all sectors: Democratic and Republican, liberal and conservative, the press and business community, even from the President himself. Seldom has legislation enjoyed such sweeping and unreserved support. We might have taken that as a gentle warning, suggesting that something was amiss.

> When the legislation passes unanimously in the Senate and encounters only six negative votes in the House, there is further ground for apprehension.[3]

The Congress had designed the act to retrieve the power over the budget that it had so easily and sometimes joyously delegated to the president. Instead, however, the act enhanced the president's budget power. It was passed to bring the budget under control, but the budget is now out of control. Its purpose was to discipline the Congress, but there has been little congressional discipline either over the substance or procedure of the budget.

During the 1970s, when Muskie and Bellmon joined together to enforce its letter and spirit, the act worked quite well. But in the 1980s it was the victim of an untested economic theory known as "supply-side economics." Its advocates asserted that a tax cut of $750 billion over five years would, as Secretary of the Treasury Donald T. Regan argued before the House Ways and Means Committee in 1981, stimulate savings and the economy and thus "finance the red ink by freeing new money for investment."[4] Instead of increasing savings and investment, however, much of the newly freed money went into financing the massive increase in the annual deficits and public debt occasioned not only by the tax cuts but also by a major rise in spending for defense, entitlements (such as Medicare, Medicaid, and Social Security), and interest on the debt. This in turn brought unprecedented deficits in both the balance of payments and the balance of trade. The accompanying deregulation of financial institutions set off an orgy of speculation in junk bonds, corporate takeovers, and excessive risk-taking by banks and savings and loan institutions that were under pressure to raise profits to pay for the increase in debt financing. This added an estimated $500 billion to the debt and deficit.

In 1985, in an attempt to address the problem, the Gramm-Rudman-Hollings Act was passed. It did not, however, tackle the substance of the problem but sought a solution by adding to the process, which was excessive. As David Stockman, Reagan's first budget director, said in an interview with *The New York Times:*

> There's an excess of machinery and dispersion of authority (in Congress and the executive branch). There's a massive overload on the decision process of the Federal Government at the highest levels.[5]

Its sponsor Senator Warren Rudman (R.-N.H.) referred to it as "a bad bill whose time had come."[6] Process was added to process, and the act choked on itself. In an attempt to hide its failure to meet the target figures for deficit reduction and to escape the mindless across-the-board cuts called sequestration that the failure occasioned, a series of deceptions, circumventions, and budget legerdemains were used.

There was the "Miss Rosy Scenario" in which the president submitted a budget based on generously optimistic estimates for economic growth, increased revenues, reduced spending, and a lower deficit. Rather than provide the billions in new taxes or spending cuts needed to rectify the president's estimates, the Congress accepted them.

There was the blue smoke and mirrors syndrome in which pay raises or post office deficits were transferred from one fiscal year to another to improve the deficit outlook, future sales of government assets were counted as budget revenues even though no such sales took place and thus no revenues were received, and the real cost of financing the public debt was masked by using a "net" interest figure that subtracted interest receipts of the Social Security and other trust funds (see Table 10–3, n. 1).

There was the "Rip Van Winkle Effect." His twenty-year nap was in fact a long, inebriated snooze. Whenever he broke his pledge to stay on the wagon, he said, "We won't count this one." Qualifying under this rubric were the losses from the savings and loan scandal and the cost of the war in the Persian Gulf, which were put off-budget and not counted; the eight or more tax increases from 1982 through 1988 that not only raised employment, health, excise, sin, and estate taxes but corporate and individual income taxes as well during a period that the president's motto was, "Make my day, no new taxes"; and the sleight-of-hand maneuver, which insiders referred to contemptuously as "the son of Gramm-Rudman-Hollings," by which the deficit reduction targets were delayed for two years, given a $10 billion annual "cushion," and revised upward when the real annual deficit exceeded the Gramm-Rudman-Hollings figure by such a massive amount that it could no longer be hidden.

Finally, in 1990, the president and the Congress began to face reality. The July *Mid-Session Review of the Budget* raised the president's rosy January budget deficit figure of $100.5 billion for fiscal year 1991 to $231.4 billion. But even the new figure excluded the costs of the savings and loan bail-out and Desert Storm. The president, much to the chagrin of his party in the House of Representatives, abandoned his "no new taxes" campaign pledge and entered into negotiations for a budget agreement with the congressional Democrats.

The result was the effective repeal of Gramm-Rudman-Hollings and the prospect for a truce in the budget strife. The general provisions of the agreement included:

1. A five-year $492 billion deficit reduction through tax increases and spending cuts over what it would otherwise be.
2. The Omnibus Budget Reconciliation Act of 1990, which changed the tax and spending laws to reach the new deficit reduction target.
3. The abandonment of any effort to control the *overall* annual deficit by the Draconian methods of sequestration or closing down the government. The

president would report in the annual budget an estimate of the overall deficit. But any increase over the targets due to updated economic and technical estimates or changes in budget concepts and definitions would not require a sequester. The president and the Congress were called upon to control only those items that were controllable.

4. Any breach in the ceilings for discretionary spending, which the president can control in his budget and the Congress can control by appropriations, would be rescinded by a minisequester.
5. Any new legislation to increase entitlements or reduce taxes would be subject to pay-as-you-go procedures. The increased spending or tax cuts would have to be offset by an equal decrease in spending or increase in taxes.
6. The Congress once again delegated authority to the president and gave him and his OMB the power to enforce the provisions.

This was the five-year pact under which the budget would function from 1991 through 1995. As its budget ceilings were written into law and its enforcement provisions were arbitrary, most of the budget action would be automatic. Very little would be left to presidential and congressional discretion. If it worked, it was more apt to reduce presidential-congressional friction over the budget than the deficit itself.

The five-year agreement signaled the end of an era. An understanding of the struggle that led to this agreement, its legislative history, and its provisions is the occasion of this third edition of *Politics and the Budget: The Struggle Between the President and the Congress.*

Given the experience under the 1975 Budget Act, it is clear there is no such thing as the "budgetary process." The budget is not put together in a mechanical, predetermined, orderly way as the elementary textbooks on how to pass a bill or on the budget process would have one believe. It is not a process but a tale of conflict and struggle. At the end of a congressional session when the continuing resolution or the Christmas tree tax bill or the five-year budget agreement is before the House or Senate the atmosphere is that of a barroom brawl.

If upon reading this book, the reader concludes that the budget is the number-one political and priorities document of the government; that it is now initiated and dominated by the president after a historic struggle with the Congress; that it consists not of spending alone but of a half dozen major elements including taxes, credit, debt, and (rarely) surplus; that it is greatly influenced by the economic estimates (routinely optimistic) and monetary policy; and that it is not produced by a process but by political clash and conflict; then the reader will have grasped the salient points of this book.

I want to thank my wife Betty Shuman for her patience and forbearance while this book was being written and edited. I also wish to thank Prentice Hall reviewers Professors Allen D. Hertzke from the University of Oklahoma, John Crow from the University of Arizona, Mary Timney Bailey from the University of Cincinnati, and June Speakman from Claremont McKenna College for their help and criticisms. I am especially grateful to

Professors Hertzke and Speakman for their suggestion that Chapter 3 on the Congress include not only a description of the appropriations committees' role in passing the budget, but the role of the authorizing, budget, and taxation committees as well. In the previous editions these topics have been treated in other chapters. I have followed their suggestion even though it has resulted inevitably in a rather long chapter. Finally I want to thank Professor James P. Pfiffner of the Department of Public Affairs of George Mason University whose comments and criticisms of succeeding manuscripts over almost a decade have been invaluable.

Senators Paul H. Douglas and William Proxmire provided me a front row seat in the eye of the political hurricane for more than a quarter of a century. It was a vantage point where few are privileged to sit. Neither senator could be flattered, bought, or bullied to do an ignoble public act. Both combined massive intelligence with great strength of personal character. They have added luster to the titles "elected official" and "public servant." As the chief of staff to each, they paid me to do what I most wanted to do. I am deeply indebted to them for the experience I gained which I hope is appropriately reflected in *Politics and the Budget: The Struggle Between the President and the Congress.*

NOTES

1. Senate Committee on the Budget, *Congressional Budget Reform* (Washington, D.C.: U.S. Government Printing Office, 1976), p. iii.
2. Louis Fisher, "The Congressional Budget Act: Does It Have a Spending Bias?" (Paper delivered at the University of Oklahoma, February 1982), p. 1.
3. Ibid.
4. *Congressional Quarterly,* 21 February 1981, p. 335.
5. Quoted from April 1984 speech. In *The New York Times,* 7 October 1985, p. A14.
6. *The Washington Post,* 5 October 1985, p. A6.

1 —————————————————————————

The President's Budget:
The Country's Number-One
Political and Priorities
Document

—————————————————————————

INTRODUCTION

When the *Budget of the United States Government* is signed by the president, it is done at a ceremony elaborately staged and carefully crafted by the president's political followers. The reason great care and attention are given to the budget's release is that its significance is far greater than the several thousand pages of detailed figures and dry text that compose the budget documents.

The budget sets the priorities for the nation. It sets the stage for both the congressional and presidential elections, which occur every two and four years. It sets forth the massive dollar benefits that flow from the federal government to virtually every public and private institution in the country, and to every individual. The spending benefits now total more than one-fifth of the Gross National Product (GNP). But the budget also details the taxes, the debt, and the credit, which are as important to many people as the grants and outlays are to others.

The fiscal policies the budget sets forth, the economic estimates on which the budget is based, and the accompanying monetary policies will greatly affect the fortunes of the nation—the services cities and states will provide their citizens; the profits or losses of commerce and industry; the ability of farmers, small businesses, and consumers to borrow money; and the number of jobs and the level of unemployment for the work force. The budget's programs and policies will also affect the safety of the country and the security of the people.

The Founding Fathers assigned most of the powers over the budget to Congress, and Congress exercised those powers for the first century and a quarter of the history of the United States. In 1913, the Congress began to delegate budgetary powers to others, primarily to the president. Power or responsibility over monetary policy, the debt, the budget, and the economy were gradually assigned to others. In 1974, the Congress attempted to retrieve some of the authority it had so generously given away. The broad outlines and some of the details of that saga are set forth in this chapter.

THE RELEASE OF THE BUDGET

The scene: The Oval Office of the White House. *The time:* The first Monday in February. *The key player:* Sitting at his desk amidst a flurry of clicking cameras, klieg lights, and reporters' questions, the president signs the *Budget of the United States.*

No other routine public event rivals the release of the budget and the events that precede and follow it. They get more sustained attention year in and year out than the Super Bowl, the World Series, the U.S. Open Tennis Tournament, and the Masters Golf Tournament combined.

These moments of theater and public relations are no accidents. They are preceded by days of planning and thought—the events carefully scripted, the production highly controlled, the leaks to the press carefully calculated.

By design the final unveiling usually takes place at noon. In fifteen consecutive years in the 1970s and 1980s, the budget was released at noon nine times, at 10:00 A.M. five times, and at 5:00 P.M. once.[1] Noon is the first choice of the president's press secretary and the director of the Office of Management and Budget (OMB). Their job is to promote and enhance the president's political fortunes. When the signing is too early it interrupts the multitude of morning news and editorial conferences held by the Washington press and TV bureaus within a stone's throw of the White House press room. A 5:00 P.M. conference is inconvenient for reporters and too late for the evening TV news. A noon announcement, however, gives the wire service photographers time to develop their film and the TV reporters and camera operators time to edit the footage for the evening news carefully. Noon has other advantages, too. It is not too late for the event to make the final edition of the afternoon papers. The newspapers' White House correspondents have typed the words of their embargoed copies of the budget into their computers before the actual signing. Now they can update their stories with a presidential picture or quote. Key members of Congress and staff also get copies of the budget before the embargoed release time. Further, a noon release is still timely for the next day's morning papers, which will carry pages of text, tables, and charts, all taken from the carefully scripted and self-serving documents placed in their hands by the administration.

The choice of the day Monday is also an artful political move. It was selected twelve times in fifteen recent years.[2] The choice of noon on Monday gives government officials, briefing officers, reporters, and congressional allies a weekend to pore over the massive pile of materials.

The signing ceremony is the climax of days of action and activity. On the preceding Friday, hordes of reporters gather at the White House and at the budget director's office to pick up their copies of the budget and accompanying documents. In Washington press corps parlance, this is known as "shopping bag day" because it takes a shopping bag to carry the documents.

In years when the budget news was bad, when the estimated deficit was excessive, or when the White House wanted to avoid leaks or to punish the press, the procedures have varied. In 1983, for example, embargoed copies for a Monday noon release were handed out to reporters not on Friday but on Sunday during the Super Bowl, when the Washington Redskins were playing. This was in retaliation for massive leaks the previous year, when the press failed to abide by the embargo. This was inconvenient for reporters as it gave them less than twenty-four hours to prepare their stories. In 1987 reporters were given no lead time and did not get copies until the Monday 8:00 A.M. release time, an ungodly hour for them. In the same year, amid reports that the president's budget was so irrelevant that it would be "dead on arrival," the administration sent the first copies to Capitol Hill in an ambulance to mock its critics.

The budget is far more than the three-page "Budget Message" signed by the president. There are at least seven major documents. In his first full-year budget, President Bush published them in a single, condensed 1,600-page volume, which reduced the price from $94.50 to $38 and the weight from fourteen to seven-plus pounds. But in most years, whether they are printed separately or consolidated in one volume, the key budget documents are as follows:

The *Budget of the United States Government* is a textbook-size paperback of 600 to 650 pages, printed in black and white. It has more than 350 pages of text, almost 200 pages of detailed budget accounts, and up to 75 pages of summary tables.

The *Budget in Brief* is a ninety-five-page booklet, done in multicolored print, that contains the president's message. This is the document prepared by the president's partisan public relations experts and written to appeal to popular opinion. The multicolored pie charts shown on the evening TV news and the sidebar quotes in the morning papers are lifted from it. It is prepared to advance the president's political fortunes, but it follows the advice of his sophisticated advisers—namely, that in this world one must be political without appearing to be so.

The *Appendix Budget of the United States Government* is a 9-by-12-inch black-and-white book of more than two thousand pages. Here are found the budget details, the sophisticated tables, and the distinctions among outlays, budget authority, and obligated and unobligated balances. These terms fascinate budget experts and detail the substance so important to the recipients of federal largess. More than that, the details of the *Appendix* symbolize the power and influence the president now has over the budget. The *Appendix* contains page after page of language proposed for the congressional appropriations bills and routinely included in them. While the Constitution gives power over the purse strings to Congress, the president now not only initiates the budget but had a substantial role in writing the appropriations bills.

The *Special Analyses Budget of the United States Government* presents in three hundred pages a dozen or so analyses designed to highlight specified program areas or to provide significant budget data. Here one may find a discussion of tax expenditures, aid to state and local governments, or civilian employment in the executive branch.

Major Themes and Additional Budget Details is an almost six-hundred-page book highlighting major programs and policies.

Historical Tables is a useful three-hundred-plus-page cornucopia of budget data designed to reconcile budget figures dating back over a half-century or more.

Management of the United States Government is the OMB's self-serving document of 130 pages describing its "valiant" efforts to improve management, cut out waste, and reduce costs.

Not only are the budget documents carried away by reporters in shopping bags, but the Government Printing Office ships a truckload to Capitol Hill and distributes hundreds of copies to budget officers and policy-making officials in Washington and throughout the world.[3]

Following "shopping bag day" on Friday, there are a dozen dress rehearsals for the president's Monday budget release. These take place on Saturday in the press rooms of the great departments and agencies of the government scattered along Pennsylvania, Independence, and Constitution avenues from the White House to Capitol Hill and in the Pentagon across the Potomac.

Deep in the bowels of the Pentagon—which is not just a five-sided building but five separate five-sided buildings snuggled within each other like a nest of different-size pie pans—military reporters and the staffs of the House and Senate armed services committees and defense subcommittees of the appropriations committees meet to be briefed. Here and in the congressional hearings the following week a torrent of additional budget information is released.

Of key interest is a twenty-one-page briefing manual giving details on the growth of the military budget, its proportion of the total budget, and its percentage of the GNP.[4] Hawks and doves alike pore over the figures and argue their significance for almost a year.

But the document that the contractors line up for and that the House and Senate staff members squirrel away is the "P-Book" (*P* is for *procurement*).[5] Incredible as it may seem, nowhere in the (3,000 pages of the budget itself is there a detailed list of the dollars-and-cents funding for specific weapons systems. While the 166-page P-Book provides the raw data on which the articles in the *Armed Forces Journal, Aviation Week and Space Technology, Sea Power,* and another half-dozen military and contractor journals are based, it has a more important function. The details it contains are transferred by telegram and fax machines from the Rayburn and Russell buildings on Capitol Hill to the prime contractors and subcontractors throughout the country. The P-Book is the moving force, the bread and butter, and the jobs and payrolls for countless communities in every state of the Union. Some unkind Pentagon critics call it the "pork" rather than the "procurement" book.

At the Pentagon the P-Book is rivaled only by the R-Book, the detailed statement of the Pentagon research and development (R&D) projects to be funded in the coming fiscal year.[6] When the Pentagon briefing adjourns on Saturday morning, reporters and congressional staff members who are experts on the research budget may seek to supplement their knowledge and scamper over to the White House to hear the head of the president's Office of Science and Technology brief them on research and development for the government as a whole. Added details are picked up at the National Aeronautics and Space Administration (NASA) or the National Science Foundation budget briefings.

These sessions take place all over town—at the Environmental Protection Agency and at the departments of Transportation, State, Justice, Energy, Commerce, Agriculture, and others. The list of reclamation projects so vital to western states and western senators is provided at the Department of the Interior briefing, the state-by-state breakdown of community development block grant funds is published by the Department of Housing and Urban Development (HUD), and the table of civil works projects is put out by the Army Corps of Engineers. These data are important not only to reporters and congressional staff, for they also provide the reason for the existence of the lobbyists housed at the Hall of States building at the foot of Capitol Hill who represent the country's mayors and governors.

The presidential signing ceremony is not the final but only the penultimate act of the budget drama. The climax of the drama comes in the news coverage that evening and the following day by the networks and the daily papers. On a typical budget release day, a third or more of the ABC, CBS, and NBC nightly news times is devoted to the budget.[7] Even a lame-duck president's "last hurrah" budget attracts massive amounts of newsprint. The budget's power to attract printer's ink was seen in the treatment given to President Reagan's fiscal year 1990 budget. As it belonged to a lame-duck president, it was foreordained to be modified, amended, or abandoned. Nonetheless, *The Washington Post* reported it with seven stories and an editorial that filled three right-hand columns above the fold on page one, six full columns on two inside pages, and the lead story on the "Arts Budget" in the "Style" section.[8] *The New York Times* gave the story only slightly less space.[9] A month to the day later, President Bush's revised budget, which was short on details and not a several-thousand-page revision of the Reagan proposal, got even more ink. The *Post* gave it a six-column headline and three stories on page one plus three full inside pages of coverage.[10]

THE NUMBER-ONE POLITICAL DOCUMENT

Why is there such overweening interest in these dry-as-dust documents couched in turgid bureaucratic prose and prepared to be pored over by the green-eyeshade brigade? Why is such care taken by the president and his allies to make a production of the document's release? And why do intelligent, well-educated reporters and editors spend such an inordinate amount of time and treasure on the pursuit of these documents' details?

The reason is that the *Budget of the United States* is the country's number-one political document. Presidential elections are fought over it. Congressional sessions are devoted to it. More than at any other time, the 1980s and the 1990s are the era of the budget.

From Roosevelt to Reagan, presidential candidates have criticized the budget, run against it, and promised to balance it. Franklin D. Roosevelt campaigned for a balanced budget at the depth of the Great Depression in 1932; it was never achieved in his twelve years in office.[11] President Carter promised to balance it in his fourth year. He failed.

At the first presidential debate in Baltimore in the 1980 campaign, candidate Reagan said the budget plan he had submitted was "based on projections—conservative projections, out for the next five years—that indicate that this plan would by 1983 result in a balanced budget."[12] On October 24 he added that "this program [the Reagan plan] will give us a balanced budget by 1983, and possibly by 1982."[13] After only a few weeks in office he backed off, however, and emulated Carter's promise to balance the budget in his fourth year. Yet before the end of the first year of his presidency he abandoned these claims altogether, claiming a balanced budget was never more than a goal. For fiscal years 1983, 1985, 1986, and 1989, the deficit exceeded $200 billion a year. During his presidency the national debt tripled, from $914 billion to over $2.8 trillion. Candidate Bush promised, "No new taxes. Read my lips." Eighteen months into his presidency he reneged on that promise.

The fact is that while almost every president has campaigned on a balanced budget, in the ten presidencies in the more than half-century from 1932 to 1992, only Truman and Eisenhower achieved significant surpluses.[14] Even though promise almost always exceeds performance, the budget and budget policy are critical ingredients of presidential campaigns.

The budget as a political issue is no less important to House and Senate members. The ratings of incumbents put out by conservative, liberal, business, labor, consumer, religious, and other groups are based on key budget votes.

One watchdog group, the National Taxpayers' Union (NTU), is in a class of its own. It does not pick key issues but rates representatives and senators on the basis of every single vote affecting spending. In 1990 the NTU based its ratings on 244 such votes.[15]

Other groups are less universal and more selective in their ratings. From the right side of the political spectrum is the Conservative Caucus. One year its ratings were based on eight issues, three of which affected the budget—votes on indexing taxes, the item veto, and the debt ceiling. In addition, a representative or senator scored well with the American Conservative Union if he or she voted "right" on eighteen key issues, eleven of which were budget items.

The liberal or progressive lobbies also use budget votes as touchstones. *Network*, the publication of the Catholic Social Justice lobby, ranked senators on eleven key votes, asserting that "a voting record helps to assess, in part, the nation's commitment to justice." Nine of the eleven votes it counted were votes on budget items, from food stamps to fiscal year budget targets. Congress Watch, a Ralph Nader consumer organization, counted twelve budget votes in its list of thirty key issues. Eight of the eleven votes the American Federation of Teachers use to rate members were on budget issues. The Public Employees Department of the AFL-CIO counted seven budget votes in its total list of nineteen. The liberal Americans for Democratic Action based their praise or condemnation on twenty key votes, ten of which were on the budget.

The budget is not only the number-one *political* document of the country; it also is the chief *priorities* document. More than any other event or institution, it establishes national priorities. The policies and priorities of the New Deal, the Fair Deal, the New Frontier, the New Beginning, and Reaganomics were carried out primarily, although not exclusively, through the budget. When presidents proclaimed the Urban Crisis, the War on Poverty, and the Energy Crisis, or proposed to enhance the country's research and scientific base in order to compete with the Russians in space after *Sputnik*, they shifted priorities by allocating funds to their proposals and policies through the budget.

ELEMENTS OF THE BUDGET

The budget is a many-sided instrument. There is a hexagon of budget elements and a smorgasbord of budget benefits.

Spending   The spending side of the budget is perhaps the most important. It certainly receives the most attention. Public policy is often determined by how much is spent. The spending side of the budget pinpoints who gets the money. It is the major instrument by which the American people, through their elected legislative officials, make choices.

Some spending choices are deliberate. Others are made by accident. Some are intelligent and carefully designed. Others are unconscious, automatic, mindless, unintended, or made by default.

To the public, the word *budget* means spending. The same meaning is also applied in most of the textbooks on the politics of the budget or the budgetary process, which almost exclusively emphasize the spending side of the budget. Other important aspects, however, are either treated lightly or ignored. Crucial as it is, spending is only one side of a many-sided budget instrument. As man does not live by bread alone, so the budget is not composed of spending alone.

Revenues   The revenue side of the budget—the amount taken in by personal, corporate, excise, and payroll taxes and tariffs—almost equals the amount spent. The question of who pays the freight is equal in importance to the question of who gets the benefits.

In general the needy get benefits or welfare through direct payments that are proposed each year by the president, authorized under a specific program, appropriated by the Congress, and paid with a government check. In addition, they receive some benefits in kind such as surplus food. Both forms of aid are very visible. Further, much but by no means all spending for the needy is closely examined or reexamined yearly by both executive and legislative officials.

On the other hand, welfare for the well-to-do generally takes a different form. More often than not, it is the result of a permanent tax law that allows income *spent* in a particular way such as interest on a home mortgage or tithing to a church) to be deducted from taxable income. Similarly, income *received* from certain sources or in certain ways (for example, from an oil or gas well, from income earned abroad, or from a family inheritance) is not taxed at all or is not taxed to the same degree as the same amount of money earned as wages or as a salary would be taxed. The benefits from not paying taxes are often as great as or greater than the benefits from receiving direct government payments. The issues of who pays the taxes and how much is paid are fought over, lobbied about, and as important politically as the issue of who benefits from a government check or contract.

This point may be illustrated by housing subsidies. A study done by Alvin L. Schorr of the Department of Health, Education, and Welfare (HEW) showed that the value of housing subsidies for those with income in the upper 20 percent was twice that of the subsidies for those with incomes in the bottom 20 percent. The subsidy received by the top 20 percent was measured in terms of the tax savings occasioned by deductions of property taxes and interest paid on mortgages by homeowners, whereas the subsidy received by the bottom 20 percent was measured in terms of direct housing subsidies for public housing and the housing portion of welfare payments.[16] Later studies show equal or greater inequities.

The political effects of the various types of government benefits are different, too. There is an onus attached to the direct payment received by the poor that is not felt or even acknowledged by those who legally take the tax deductions. Standing in line for a handout of surplus cheese is considerably more demeaning than taking a deduction on line 18 of form 1040 for the "paper loss" from a tax shelter to make sure that little or no income taxes are paid.

Deficit or Surplus The amount of the deficit or, in rare years, the surplus is an intrinsic part of the budget. It is a function of the difference between spending and revenues. It has widespread effects on the amount the government can spend, the level of interest rates, the rate of inflation, and whether the economy prospers or recedes. It is argued over politically and is the subject of several partisan congressional votes each year. It has equal standing in the formulation of the budget resolution with both revenues and spending.

The cumulative amount of the deficit as reflected in the public debt has a profound effect both on priorities and on political events. It may crucially affect housing policy through the level of interest rates, the cost of living increases for Social Security beneficiaries and federal retirees, and the availability of loans for farmers, consumers, and small businesses. Both professors and politicians ignore it at their peril.

The Credit Budget An important part of the budget that historically has been overlooked and unexamined is the credit budget. It has been ignored by academics and avoided by politicians, and is unknown to most public policy critics. The problem of controlling federal credit existed subrosa until the June 1980 hearings of the Special Subcommittee on Control of Federal Credit of the Senate Budget Committee.[17] Those hearings resulted in part from a March 1980 letter from Senator William Proxmire (D.-Wis.) to Chairman Edmund Muskie (D.-Maine) proposing that an aggregate ceiling on federal credit programs be established, that a real credit budget be developed, and that both be acted on under budget resolution and Appropriations Committee procedures.[18]

Popular publications such as the *U.S. News and World Report* publicized the problem.[19] The hearings, chaired by Senator Howard Metzenbaum (D.-Ohio), spawned a plethora of further proposals and activities. As a result of those initial hearings, the credit budget began to take its proper place on the political and budget agenda. House and Senate members introduced bills to create a credit budget to be acted on under the Budget Act in the same way as the aspects of spending, taxes, and the debt. One result was that ninety-two pages of special analyses have been devoted to the Federal Credit Programs in recent budgets.[20] The credit budget is now in effect (See Appendix B).[21]

The extension of federal credit takes many forms and is carried out by 150 programs.[22] The forms include direct loans (such as student loans), federal guarantees of private loans (such as electrification loans), loans by privately owned government-sponsored enterprises, or GSEs (such as the Federal National Mortgage Association, or FNMA), and access to tax-exempt credit through tax-exempt bonds. All of these involve a subsidy of one kind or another, for they "provide more favorable terms than borrowers could otherwise obtain in the private market."[23] In fiscal year 1992 more than $2 trillion in federal direct loans, guaranteed loans, or loans by GSEs was outstanding, which was more than the total estimated government spending for that year.[24]

The politics of the budget and the purposes of government are advanced as much by the extension of federal credit as by direct spending, agency grants, or tax expenditures.

Economic Estimates   A critical component of the president's budget is the economic forecast upon which the budget figures are based. Almost every president's budget in every year has been based on optimistic forecasts. Estimates of revenue are higher than the revenue the treasury will receive. Spending estimates are lower. Economic growth is exaggerated. The rise in the cost of living and in unemployment is minimized. The deficit is narrowed by billions of dollars.

The budget routinely carries sections entitled "Economic Assumptions," "Economic Outlook," "Economic Forecast," and "Sensitivity of the Budget to Economic Assumptions."[25] As President Reagan complained in his State of the Union Address while explaining how the budget in his first year had gone from a projected balance to "one of the biggest deficits in history,"

Another example of the imponderables that can make deficit projects highly questionable: A change of only one percentage point in unemployment can alter a deficit up or down by some $25 billion.[26]

If politics is the art of the possible, the way economic assumptions are used to provide rosy budget-spending, revenue, and deficit projections is the art of exaggeration.

Monetary Policy   No budget can be described without giving attention to the monetary policy that accompanies it. The ability to create money and to regulate its expansion or contraction is not a function of the president but of the Federal Reserve System, which is a creature of the Congress but is independent of the executive. Its policies, along with the fiscal policy carried out by the budget, vitally affect the availability of credit, the level of interest rates, the cost of financing the national debt, the level of prices, and the amount of employment and unemployment in the country.

In virtually every political democracy in the world, the money supply is determined by the minister of the treasury, the chancellor of the exchequer, or the director of the central bank acting under the direction of the government. In the United States, however, the power to coin money and to regulate the value thereof is a constitutional prerogative of the Congress. The function has been delegated to the seven members of the Federal Reserve Board, who are appointed by the president with the advice and consent of the Senate, and to the Federal Reserve's Open Market Committee, which is composed of the seven board members and five private citizens. The private citizens are not selected by the president but by the commercial banks and other members of the business community. The Federal Reserve Board has a veto over the appointment of these board members, but they serve without the advice and consent of the Senate.[27]

While no budget could exist without a monetary policy component, the unique nature of the Federal Reserve gives every president an opportunity to blame the misfortunes and mistakes of his budget on an agency over which he has no direct control. Because most House and Senate members are unaware that the Federal Reserve is their agent, it serves as a whipping boy for both the president and the Congress.

BUDGET BENEFITS FLOW EVERYWHERE

The economic and political benefits of the budget are received by every person and institution in the country. They favor the corporate members of the 500 largest industrial corporations, ranked by *Fortune* magazine according to their sales, and flow to the lowliest citizen. The benefits form an enormous bounty.

A Fortune 500 firm may benefit from the oil depletion allowance, the subsidy for the minerals it buys, or a defense contract. Its executive airplanes are subsidized and supported through the public funding of airports, air traffic controllers, and the weather reports necessary for these planes to fly.

The firm may get a guaranteed loan, as did Chrysler. Trucks and railroads are subsidized through the Highway Trust Fund or the Federal Railroad Administration. International firms such as Caterpillar Tractor, the Bechtel Corporation, and Texas's Brown and Root gain enormous benefits from budget decisions. Their overseas employees pay no taxes on the first $70,000 of income earned aboard. Their goods are shipped on vessels operated with maritime subsidies. The harbor from which the ships leave is dredged by the Army Corps of Engineers. Caterpillar Tractor bulldozers are used at overseas construction sites to clear land for military installations, NASA tracking stations, or a foreign-aid project paid for by the American taxpayer.

The international shipments of some Fortune 500 firms are financed by an Export-Import Bank loan that is below the market interest rate. They get a tax expenditure (or subsidy) from the deferral of income from a controlled foreign corporation.

Businesses along Main Street, America benefit as well. They may have a loan from the Small Business Administration (SBA). Their bank deposits are protected by the Federal Deposit Insurance Corporation (FDIC). The downtown parking garage, new luxury hotel, or shopping mall may have been financed by an Urban Development Action Grant (UDAG). The new federal building that counts as a "local" contribution to help make all this possible is paid for by the federal government. The money the local bank lends out is "created" under the fractional reserve system of the Federal Reserve through its purchase of bonds that finance the national debt. The local national bank and federal savings and loan also have valuable charters from the federal government.

The farmers are favored too. They buy their land under a Federal Land Bank loan; finance their houses with a Farmers Home Administration mortgage; get a loan on their crops from the Commodity Credit Corporation; send their wheat abroad under Public Law 480, get their phone and electricity from the Rural Electrification Administration (REA) cooperative, which obtained a low-interest loan from the government; receive advice from their county agent or land grant university, whose services are paid for in part by Washington; get reliable crop forecasting information from the Department of Agriculture; and are paid a subsidy for growing sugar cane, sugar beets, tobacco, cotton, peanuts, corn, or wheat or for milking a herd of dairy cows.

Cities are no less favored. The playhouse theater is built with money from a Community Development Block Grant (CDBG). Its theater company is financed with a National Endowment for the Arts grant. The local police force is trained at a Federal Bureau of Investigation (FBI) school. The city airport, hospital, interstate highway, and local roads are built with federal money. The water is supplied by an irrigation project financed by a subsidy from the Department of the Interior. The local park, tennis courts, and swimming pool are built with federal funds. The sewer lines to the new city annex at the edge of town are paid for in part by Washington. The public housing is built with tax-free municipal bonds and gets an annual subsidy for operating expenses from HUD. Food stamps, school lunches, job training, and the day care center are federally financed. For every $100 cities and states raise through the local and state sales and property taxes, the federal government has provided $40 (see Table 4–2). State and local governments receive about 16 percent of their income from the federal government.

Not only do citizens benefit indirectly through the services and subsidies the federal government provides to states, cities, and the economic system in general, but they benefit directly as well. Their houses may be financed with mortgages guaranteed by the Federal Housing Administration (FHA). Student loans may provide college tuition for their children. They may live in a subsidized Section 202 housing unit for the elderly and save with or borrow money from the local federal credit union. If they are more opulent than most people, their boat may be docked at the public wharf and their sailing misadventures may be protected by the Coast Guard. They may get a federal tax deduction for mortgage interest paid. The magazines they read are subsidized by the Post Office, as is the mail delivery of their local paper. The library is built or extended with federal money, and the TV and radio news they hear is provided by stations that have received a valuable charter from the public and are regulated by the Federal Communications Commission (FCC). They can rely on the information sent to them by their local stockbroker because stock issues are regulated by the Securities and Exchange Commission (SEC). If they become unemployed, or if one spouse dies and leaves the survivor with school children or retires at age sixty-two, unemployment compensation, aid to families with dependent children, or a Social Security check are available directly from the federal government.

The political and economic benefits flowing from the federal budget are ubiquitous and peripatetic. The bulk of the benefits go to those with power and wealth, who have the political clout to get them and keep them. Yet some who most vehemently denounce the government's nefarious ways are among the biggest beneficiaries of its largess. As the English journalist and member of Parliament Henry LaBouchere said about Prime Minister William Gladstone, "I don't object to Mr. Gladstone always having all the aces up his sleeve. What I object to is his insistence that the Good Lord put them there."

CONTROL OVER THE ECONOMY

The budget has another function that is highly political and only partially successful. It is the instrument through which an administration may attempt to direct, control, or finely tune the economy. This role was implicit during the days of the New Deal and was made explicit with the Employment Act of 1946 as amended.[28]

Through budget and other policies the government is charged with providing maximum employment, stable prices, sustained economic growth, and increased productivity. While these are the subject matters of economics, which Thomas Carlyle called the "dismal science," they are the chief political issues routinely before the country. They are thus vital to the politics of the budget.

Since 1946 the budget has been charged with heroic tasks. It has been called on to fine-tune the economy. It has been flaunted as an instrument that could both stimulate jobs and recovery and dampen price rises and inflation. It has been asked to provide a countercyclical fiscal policy, to redistribute income, and to carry out numerous other economic and political functions.

While the federal budget has an enormous effect on both politics and the economy—year in and year out it accounts for 20 percent, more or less, of the GNP—it has had only partial success as an economic regulator.[29] On one hand, since the Employment Act of 1946 the United States has suffered from no deep depression or financial panic, phenomena that previously were endemic to the society and had occurred about every twenty years. On the other hand, the nation has been beset by a series of generally mild and short-lived recessions, sustained inflation since 1967, and prolonged and stubborn recessions in the early 1980s and 1990s.

The concept of a countercyclical fiscal or budget policy was popularized during the 1930s. Until then, except during wartime, it was accepted as dogma that the federal budget should be balanced every year. Maintaining such a policy during periods of panic and recession, however, had devastating effects, deepening and prolonging the malaise. The countercyclical budget policy proposed that the budget be balanced not each and every year but over the business cycle. Deficits in bad years would thus be offset by surpluses in good years. This would both help provide stable economic conditions and satisfy the moral and political arguments against heavy deficits made by those who held to the old-time budget religion.

There was no alternative to large deficits during the Depression and World War II. But in the five decades since 1946 there have been only eight budget surpluses, three of which (in 1949, 1960, and 1969) were so small compared with the GNP and the federal budget itself as to be negligible.[30] Since 1969 the budget has been out of balance every year. Neither a balanced budget nor a surplus is in sight in the decade of the 1990s. Countercyclical budget policy is a success in theory but a failure in practice. It provides the deficits in bad times but has been unable to provide surpluses when the economy has been either booming or enduring periods of runaway inflation.

Presidents have also failed to provide reliable budget estimates and to fine-tune the economy. There are several reasons for this. Historically, politics and economics were not separate disciplines. Adam Smith, David Ricardo, and Malthus wrote not on politics or economics but on the principles of political economy. Political economy is not a science. It is a social science, a form of art, and an imperfect discipline. Unlike engineering or physics, it is influenced by impetuous rather than mechanistic forces. Attempts to estimate, project, and fine-tune the economy are made with fragile and ephemeral tools. For other than very short-run estimates, reading chicken entrails, relying on the Oracles of Delphi, or examining tea leaves may be as reliable. As James J. Kilpatrick has noted, budget estimates are "about as solid as soap bubbles."[31]

A second problem is that of timing. For example, in the early years of the Kennedy administration a major public works bill was passed, ostensibly to stimulate the economy, reduce unemployment, and provide jobs. Because it takes months and even years for public works projects to be planned, designed, engineered, and built, the big bulge in outlays for those projects occurred in 1965 and 1966—at precisely the wrong time. By that point increased spending for the Vietnam War had kicked off inflationary forces. These public works projects thus had a deleterious effect that was opposite to their original intent.

Similarly, the unprecedented 1981 Reagan tax cuts, designed to stimulate both investment and the economy, had no perceptible stimulating effect in the first two years of their existence. When the economy began to recover in 1983 it was not clear whether the recovery was the result of normal cyclical forces or the earlier tax cuts.

Third, because increased government spending to stimulate the economy or to pick up economic slack has to be authorized by the votes of a congressional majority, it is difficult to target the funds. Regional influences, mutual "back scratching," and an unrepresentative Senate too often cause public works projects to be built in places where high unemployment is not found.

Finally, relative failure and limited success result from the slowness of budget procedures. Budget preparations begin more than ten months before the president releases the budget in February. Its fundamental features are fixed in concrete the month before it is released. The fiscal year for which it is proposed does not begin until the following October. The fiscal year ends the following September 30, or twenty months after the budget is first released. The cycle takes two and one-half years from beginning to end. During this period the president does make routine and cosmetic changes in the budget, and Congress nibbles around the edge. But political promises or campaign rhetoric to the contrary, the budget is too unwieldy and imprecise an instrument with which to fine-tune the economy. This does not mean we should abandon countercyclical fiscal policies or the effort to provide maximum employment, sustained economic growth, and stable prices through fiscal and monetary means. What is needed is more honesty in the use of numbers and projections, more humility about the ability to fashion results, and more courage and discipline by both the politicians and the practitioners of the "dismal science" to make hard and tough choices.

THE SHIFT OF BUDGET POWER: FROM THE CONGRESS TO THE PRESIDENT

The budget of today is the president's budget. Even when the budget is said to be "dead on arrival," as has been the case in many recent years, the president's proposals set the agenda. With only one-third of the votes in one House of Congress, he can sustain a veto of a spending bill that exceeds his requests. He can succeed with as few as 34 of 535 congressional votes, or less than 7 percent of the members. The veto, or the threat of it, combined with the president's command of the "bully pulpit," which allows him to speak with a single voice against the diffused and disparate voices of the Congress, enables his priorities to prevail.

The president sets the political and priorities agenda. The president initiates or prevents major tax changes. The president finances the debt. The president borrows the money. The president calls the tune. He exercises the power. The president views the budget he sends to the Congress "as an opportunity to state his convictions, not compromise them."[32] Too often the Congress merely ratifies those decisions. That the budget is now initiated and dominated by the president is the result of struggle, usurpation, delegation, abandonment, abdication, and atrophy. The one power the Congress did not delegate or lose to the president, namely the power to create money, it delegated to the semipublic, semiprivate Federal Reserve System.

Like the person who wrestles with his or her conscience and the conscience always loses, the Congress has struggled with the president over who should exercise its constitutional budgetary prerogatives, and the Congress has almost always lost.

The fundamental struggle over the budget is thus between the president and the Congress. The politics of the budget are dominated by the saga of that struggle.

Minor struggles also take place, but they take place elsewhere. Within the executive branch there is struggle between the president or his agent, the (OMB), and the various agencies. Agencies also fight agencies. The president, the OMB, and the agencies in turn have conflicts with interest groups.

Within the Congress there is a natural conflict between the House and Senate, between the political parties, and between and among committees for power and jurisdiction. More often than not, interest groups are the allies of particular congressional members or groups who in turn do battle with other congressional groups and *their* interest group allies.

Finally, the struggle over the budget takes place between and among regions of the country and sectors of the economy. One finds conflict between the Sunbelt and the Northeast-Midwest states, between farm and city, between defense and civilian needs, between consumers and business, between business and labor, and between the diffused interest of the general public and any and all of the narrow and particular interest groups that exercise power far beyond their numerical strength.

LANDMARK EVENTS IN THE SHIFT OF POWER

The Founding Fathers gave to the Congress virtually every power over the budget. These powers are enumerated in Article I of the Constitution:

> Sec. 8. The Congress shall have Power;
> —to lay and collect Taxes, Duties, Imports and Excises;
> —to pay the Debts, and provide for the common Defense and general Welfare of the United States;
> —to borrow Money on the credit of the United States;
> —to coin Money and regulate the Value thereof, and of foreign Coin. . . ;
> —to raise and support Armies, but no Appropriation of Money to that Use shall be for a longer Term than two Years;
> —to provide and maintain a Navy. . . .

Under Article I, Section 9, the Congress, not the president, was granted power over the purse strings:

> No Money shall be drawn from the Treasury, but in Consequence of Appropriations made by Law, and a regular Statement and Account of the Receipts and Expenditures of all public Money shall be published from time to time.

Article II, which delineates the power of the president, is silent on these spending, tax, credit, debt, and monetary issues. These enumerated powers were granted to the Congress and not to the president for a variety of reasons. There was the fear of a too-powerful executive. The Revolutionary War was the culmination of the colonists' battle with the British monarchy and its representatives, the royal or proprietary colonial governors. As Charles and Mary Beard wrote in *A Basic History of the United States:*

> In contest with royal and proprietary governors and in the ordinary management of legislative business, Americans by the hundreds learned to practice and think about the arts of government.[33]

Members of the lower house of the colonial legislatures exercised extensive political power over their own affairs. The power of the purse was their most formidable weapon, and they could "fix the kinds and amounts of taxation to be laid on the people" and "control the voting of money to pay salaries, including the governor's and audit the disbursement of funds."[34]

As Justice Oliver Wendell Holmes wrote in the opening sentences of *The Common Law*:

> The life of the law has not been logic; it has been experience. The felt necessities of the times, the prevalent moral and political theories, institutions of public policy, avowed or unconscious, even the prejudices judges share with their fellow-men, have had a good deal more than the syllogism in determining the rules by which men are governed.[35]

At the time of the Constitutional Convention, the colonial experience extended back almost 180 years, or for almost as many years as have passed since then. That experience of struggle and conflict with the colonial governors not only prepared Americans to govern themselves, but it also provided a strong bias in favor of the legislature as opposed to the executive.

During the nineteenth century, except for short periods of war, the Congress dominated the American government and its budget and budget procedures. In the twentieth century there has been a steady delegation by the Congress of its power over the budget to the president. This has ordinarily not been the result of conspiracy or usurpation but of the deliberate delegation, atrophy, or shunning of power by the Congress. Although the process has occasionally been acrimonious, as in the Nixon years, which were an exception to the rule, the flow of power from the Congress to the president is "the product of considered legislative decisions, neither acts of impulse by the Congress nor presidential coups d'etat. The Congress has to consent, because it has to pass the laws.[36]

The first major delegation was made not to the president, but to an independent regulatory agency. In specific terms, the power to coin money and to regulate the value thereof, which critically affects the budget, was transferred by the Congress to the Federal Reserve System in 1913 under the Federal Reserve Act. As stated earlier, the Federal Reserve is a quasiprivate, quasipublic institution that according to the Federal Reserve Act is to act independently of the president but as an agent of the Congress.

After that initial experience, the Congress began to delegate its powers over the budget and the economy directly to the president and his agents. The power to pay the debts and to borrow money on the credit of the United States was delegated by the Congress to the Treasury Department under the two Liberty Bond Acts of 1917. Until that time the Congress had authorized the treasury to borrow a specific amount of money under a separate act each time the treasury needed funds. During World War I, however, the treasury was granted general authority to borrow funds up to a ceiling or "debt limit."

Today the annual increase in the public debt limit is made possible by amending the second Liberty Bond Act of 1917. Instead of seeking congressional authority to issue each new bond or certificate of indebtedness, the treasury, under the amendments to the 1917 act, issues new instruments of indebtedness dozens upon dozens of times each year. On any one day, about two hundred fifty issues of treasury bills, bonds, and notes plus an even larger number of issues backed by the full faith and credit of the United States are outstanding.

From 1971 until 1982 there was a permanent debt ceiling of $400 billion and a temporary ceiling that reached $1.3 trillion of indebtedness. In 1982, the two were combined, and the total was made permanent. Since then additional amounts of temporary indebtedness totalling hundreds of billions of dollars have been added to the temporary ceiling as the annual deficits have burgeoned. In the five-year budget agreement of 1990 the permanent debt ceiling was raised to $4.145 trillion in order to avoid further action until after the presidential and congressional elections of 1992.

Power over the budget itself, through the creation of an annual presidential budget and the establishment of the Bureau of the Budget, was delegated by the Congress to the president under the Budget and Accounting Act of 1921.

Next, in several dozen independent actions, most of them taken since 1932, the Congress has also granted to a variety of executive or independent agencies vast authority "to borrow money on the credit of the United States." There are myriad federal programs under which an agency makes direct loans or guarantees loans to public and private institutions and to ordinary citizens. Loans and loan guarantee programs exist for farmers, small businesses, veterans, college students, exporters, banks and their customers, renters, and home owners as well as water users and power producers such as the Tennessee Valley Authority (TVA), the Rural Electric Cooperatives (REC), and the Grand Coulee Dam on the Columbia River. The authority flows from the congressional power over credit, but is now exercised by public and private agencies over which Congress in fact exercises little control or oversight.

The Congress has lost control of the purse strings in other ways as well. The Constitution limits the allocation of funds to "raise and support" armies to a two-year period. That is one thing, but the money to "equip" armies or to "provide and maintain" a navy is quite another. The Congress now appropriates two-year funds to the military for research, development, test, and engineering (RDT&E); three-year funds for procurement of planes, tanks, and weapons; and five-year funds for ships. Likewise, a "regular Statement and Account" of certain military, foreign aid, national security, or intelligence funds is *not* "published from time to time" as the Constitution requires. And the specific purposes for which such funds are used are sometimes unknown to members of the key military, intelligence, or appropriations committees of the Congress.

Through the Employment Act of 1946 and its amendments and through the Full Employment and Balanced Growth Act of 1978, better known as the Humphrey-Hawkins Act, the Congress gave the president vast responsibility over the economy and shared with the executive the authority to set goals, propose measures, and initiate action over production, prices, and employment.

In an attempt to limit presidential spending power and to bring a certain discipline to itself, the Congress passed the Congressional Budget and Impoundment Control Act in 1974. In practice it has limited some of the presidential power over impoundments and has established important congressional institutions and procedures. But under a unique and innovative interpretation of its "reconciliation" provisions, Ronald Reagan—acting in the tradition of Alexander Hamilton in fiscal matters and Andrew Jackson in the use or threatened use of the veto, and backed by working majorities in both the House and Senate during his first two years—legally and constitutionally enhanced the powers of the president over spending. Similarly, while the Congress retains the power to lay and collect taxes, the president and not the Congress most often takes the initiative to raise or lower them.

Finally, in 1985 the Congress passed the Gramm-Rudman-Hollings Act, a Draconian measure in which the Congress attempted to delegate its and the president's fiscal responsibilities to an automatic and mindless procedure called by the inelegant name *sequestration*. It was abandoned in 1990 but the Congress delegated new powers to the president.

The shift of power over the money supply, debt, credit, spending, taxes, and the economy came about as a result of experience and public need. Except for the short-lived Nixon impoundments, power was not so much seized by the president as deliberately and consciously handed to him or others. Like the Constitution itself, however inspired the precise language or specific provision, the various shifts of power had their origins in events and history.

Each act and each transfer of power were preceded by economic problems, panics, wars, depression, or constitutional crisis. The Federal Reserve Act was the child of the depressions and panics of 1893 and 1907 as well as the Progressive movement and was the culmination of the conflicts over hard or easy money, gold against silver, and creditors against debtors, fought out between the forces of William Jennings Bryan and William McKinley. One can trace its origins to the First and Second Banks of the United States and to the age of Andrew Jackson.

The Budget and Accounting Act of 1921 had its origins in the shift from routine budget surpluses for most of the last third of the nineteenth century to heavy budget deficits during the first fifth of the twentieth. Preceded by a series of studies and commissions and occasioned by a vast expansion of the size of government itself, it was nurtured by the Progressive movement and the movement for "scientific management" among both business and political reformers. It was an outgrowth of the economic needs of the country occasioned by the flowering of the industrial society and the necessities of World War I.

Similarly, the transfer of power over the public debt from the Congress to the treasury was the child of necessity. Outlays grew from less than $750 million a year before fiscal year 1917 to more than $18 billion two years later, and deficits rose from less than $100 million before 1917 to more than $13 billion in fiscal year 1919. The Congress and its two tax and debt committees—the House Ways and Means Committee and the Senate Finance Committee—would have been in session twenty-four hours a day, 365 days a year, if the Congress had continued the practice of approving each and every treasury issue of bonds to pay the debt. The life of this law was experience, war, and necessity.

The Employment Act of 1946 was the result of crisis, namely the economic trauma of the Great Depression. Born of the fear of another depression, Congress was determined that, contrary to the economic philosophy of laissez faire, the government should exercise what authority it could through fiscal and monetary policies to prevent depressions and to alleviate the misery brought to human beings by less severe and less prolonged downturns in economic activity called panics and recessions. The Humphrey-Hawkins Act was the product of the new condition of "stagflation." High levels of unemployment in harness with high levels of inflation plagued the United States and the world from 1971 (especially after the oil shock of 1973) into the 1980s.

The Budget and Impoundment Reform Act of 1974 was the creature of crisis. The crisis had two components. One was the struggle for power between the Congress and President Nixon, the only major transfer of power—this time from the president to the Congress—occasioned by an attempt to abuse power. The other component was the Congress's guilt over its inability to discipline itself and to bring the budget under control.

The Gramm-Rudman-Hollings Act and the 1990 five-year budget agreement had their origins in the massive deficit compiled by the Reagan administration and in the attempt by both the president and the Congress, Republicans and Democrats alike, to avoid responsibility for creating it and blame for the failure to deal with it.

Not only were all the transfers of power the result of perilous times or new conditions, but all the Liberty Bond Acts were preceded by a period of study, appointment of commissions, and political bargaining until a solution was reached. All of the decisions were based on the assumption that the federal government must take on new responsibilities and functions. All but the transfer of power to the Federal Reserve Board and some aspects of the Budget Act of 1974 either directly or in practice enhance the role of the president at the expense of the Congress and Article I. The president now initiates and hence sets the priorities on spending, taxes, borrowing, and control over the economy, powers that the Founding Fathers deliberately gave to the Congress out of fear of a too-strong executive.

THE FRAGILE NATURE OF THE FEDERAL BUDGET

Contrary to the rhetoric of its framers, the modern presidential budget is not the product of business efficiency, scientific management, or rigorous policy analysis. Neither can the budget theory of incrementalism be used to predict next year's budget on the basis of last year's budget. The "feast or famine" nature of military budgets, the explosion of spending on entitlements, and the savings and loan scandals have buried that theory.

The budget is an inexact and unscientific collection of guesses, predictions, and off-the-cuff estimates. Its scientific basis is only marginally superior to that of astrology, pop psychology, or palm reading. It is rather the result of impetuous forces, fortuitous events, and unanticipated consequences. Its outcomes are accidental, uncertain, and unpredictable.

How can the budget be otherwise? Decisions made in formulating the president's budget are estimates of events that will take place eight to thirty months after its release. Who can predict the state of the economy and its effects on revenues, outlays, and interest rates three months ahead, let alone more than two and a half years into the future?

Who predicted the savings and loan scandals and their hundreds of billions of dollar effects on future budgets? Who foresaw the unexpected end of the Cold War, the destruction of the Berlin Wall, the breakup of the Warsaw Pact, and their budgetary effects? How does one plan for the budget effects of a San Francisco earthquake, Saddam Hussein's invasion of Kuwait, the HUD scandals, the toxic waste clean-up costs, or a recession midway through a presidential term?

How is it possible to calculate the results of the struggle between a conservative Republican president and a liberal Democratic Congress, between a malapportioned Senate and a House based on precisely equal constituents, and between powerful executive branch agencies driven by the economic interests of their patrons and the centralized OMB, which often does not share the goals and priorities of the agencies and has powerful interests of its own?

Who can predict the timing of revenues and expenditures? The authority to spend appropriations for weapons systems are spread over three to five years. For other programs there is not only "multi-year" authority but also "no year" authority, which means the funds can be spent over as many years as necessary to bring about the objective of the appropriations. And there is "contract" authority, which means the government can let contracts for the appropriated amount that will be paid as the work is completed.

Some appropriations are "open-ended," or essentially unlimited, unless the authority is rescinded. A declining GNP, a rise in unemployment, or a housing slump can devastate the best laid revenue estimates of the treasury and Council of Economic Advisers.

The budget is thus not based on science or incremental theories or public administrators' devices or a process contrived by politicians or pundits. Its outcome is the result of chance, struggle, friction, constitutional requirements and institutions, raw politics, economic power, personal persuasion, geographic clout, public opinion, and forces and events that have their origins in the conflict of ancient religions, geological stresses, human greed, and institutional folly, no one of which can be estimated with any reasonable precision.

NOTES

1. *Budget of the United States Government: Fiscal Years 1971 to 1985* (Washington, D.C.: U.S. Government Printing Office).
2. Ibid.
3. As a sign of the times, double-digit inflation hit President Reagan's first full-year budget (Fiscal Year 1983) with a vengeance. The price of the 4 paperbound volumes of the budget was $37.50, up 24% from the previous year.
4. Office of the Assistant Secretary of Defense (Public Affairs), *Department of Defense Budget for Fiscal Year 1983* (Washington, D.C.: U.S. Government Printing Office, 1982).
5. Office of the Assistant Secretary of Defense (Comptroller), "Procurement Programs (P-1)," in ibid.
6. Office of the Assistant Secretary of Defense (Comptroller), "R,D,T,&E Programs (R-1)," in *Department of Defense Budget for Fiscal Year 1983*.
7. "CBS Evening News," carried 3 budget stories at the top of the show that ran for 7 minutes, 52 seconds, of the 23-minute, 32-second, news portion of the program. NBC ran 6 minutes, 42 seconds, of budget stories, and ABC ran 7 minutes, 46 seconds. Sources: CBS News and *News Digest*, 9 February 1982. The following night the NBC, ABC, and CBS network news programs dedicated 10 minutes, 31 seconds; 7 minutes, 58 seconds; and 6 minutes, 43 seconds, respectively, to budget and budget-related stories. Source: *News Digest*, 10 February 1982.
8. *The Washington Post*, 10 January 1989.
9. *The New York Times*, 10 January 1989.
10. *The Washington Post*, 10 February 1989.
11. Roosevelt's 12-year deficit total was $201 billion, of which $174 billion occurred in fiscal years 1942–1945. *Budget of the United States Government: Fiscal Year 1987*, pt. 6e–45.
12. Baltimore Convention Center, 21 September 1980. President Carter did not take part.
13. TV speech.
14. Truman had surpluses in 4 of 6 peacetime years. In Fiscal Year 1948 it was $12 billion, or 40% of the $30 billion outlays that year. In 7 years he achieved an overall surplus in his budgets. *Budget of the United States Government: Fiscal Year 1987*, pt. 6e–45.

15. NTU release, 22 March 1990.
16. Alvin L. Schorr, "National Community and Housing Policy," *Social Service Review* 39 (December 1965): 434–435.
17. Senate Budget Committee, Special Subcommittee on Control of Federal Credit Hearings (Washington, D.C.: U.S. Government Printing Office, 1980), 19 and 23 June and 1 July 1980.
18. Ibid., pp. 123–124.
19. 7 July 1980.
20. Special Analysis F, *Budget of the United States Government: Fiscal Year 1990* (Washington, D.C.: U.S. Government Printing Office, 1989), pp. F-1–92.
21. *Concurrent Resolution on the Budget*, Appendix B, "Appropriate Levels of Total Credit Activity," 101st Congress, 2nd Sec. 3(a)(6).
22. Special Analysis F, *Budget of the United States Government: Fiscal Year 1990.*
23. Ibid., p. F-39.
24. *Budget of the United States Government: Fiscal Year 1991,* (Washington, D.C.: U.S. Government Printing Office, 1990), p. 232.
25. Ibid., pp. A-3–7, A-100.
26. *Congressional Record* (daily ed.), 28 January 1982, S-85.
27. *Federal Reserve System, Purposes and Functions* (Washington, D.C.: Board of Governors, 1979).
28. See Secs. 2(a); 3(a)(2)(A); and 7.
29. *Budget of the United States Government: Fiscal Year 1991*, p. A-332. From fiscal year 1965 to fiscal year 1991 outlays ranged from 17.6% (1965) to 24.3% (1983) of the GNP.
30. The other 5 were in fiscal year 1947, 1948, 1951, 1956, and 1957.
31. *The Washington Post*, 13 July 1986, p. B8.
32. Ibid., 12 December 1982, p. A4.
33. Charles A. Beard and Mary R. Beard, *A Basic History of the United States* (New York: Doubleday, Doran, 1944), p. 79.
34. Ibid., p. 80.
35. Oliver Wendell Holmes, *The Common Law* (Boston: Little, Brown, 1923), p. 1.
36. James L. Sundquist, *The Decline and Resurgence of Congress* (Washington, D.C.: The Brookings Institution, 1981), p. 35.

2

The President Proposes:
The Politics of the Budget
in the Executive Branch

INTRODUCTION

The Budget and Accounting Act of 1921, by which the Congress delegated power over the budget to the president, was a historical watershed. Many believe that the modern presidency began with it. The law required that each year the president develop and publish the *Budget of the United States Government*. The act established the Bureau of the Budget and provided for its director. Since then, the Bureau of the Budget has been transformed into the Office of Management and Budget (OMB), and its original awesome powers have been considerably enhanced. The act also set up the General Accounting Office (GAO), which is now called the "watchdog for Congress." It is responsible for overseeing how the executive branch spends money. Its reputation for excellence and integrity has grown over the years, as has its size.

It must not be thought, however, that there was little or no history of presidential budgeting prior to the 1921 act. While the Congress dominated the budget procedures before 1921, many presidents and treasury secretaries influenced spending. One president, William Howard Taft, actually sent two presidential budgets to the Congress. The events that preceded the 1921 act were not unlike those that preceded other major delegations of power in budget history. There was a series of crises—panics, deficits, burgeoning budgets, and war. Study commissions were set up, public opinion stimulated, and a consensus reached. The major thrust was to bring economy and efficiency to budget matters, to apply new standards of scientific management, and to substitute facts and intelligence for political and bureaucratic pressures.

Today there is a timetable for budget action in the executive branch, which starts ten months or more before the president's budget is released. Public administrators and budget experts have provided several principles and procedures by which scientific management can be carried out, but an examination of budget making in practice reveals that a variety of other influences have overwhelmed the effort to provide objective budgeting by scientific means.

HISTORICAL WATERSHED: THE BUDGET AND ACCOUNTING ACT OF 1921

The budget, budget policies, and budget procedures are dominated by the president. Even when the president's budget is said to be "dead on arrival," it sets the priorities, shapes the goals, and charts the course of the government, the economy, and the country. As former Vice-President Hubert H. Humphrey stated:

> When the budget comes down to Congress, it is as though it were Holy Writ newly discovered. It is wrapped in the gold paper of the Executive Office of the President; it is tied and bound and finally crowned with the sealing wax of the presidential seal. It is opened and revealed to the waiting publicans with an almost religious mystique.[1]

While not as true as it once was, for several weeks in January and early February of every year the president still commands and monopolizes public priorities. Three institutionalized presidential occasions—the State of the Union Address, the release of the budget, and the publication of the *Economic Report of the President*—not only dominate domestic party politics but strengthen and augment each other as one by one they are thrust on the public and the Congress. Of the three, the president's budget has the greatest substance and the most enduring effect. From the day it is released, as the knowledgeable Humphrey said:

> Congress is on the defensive, able merely to attack, adjust, minimize, expand, or contract what has been presented by the President. But the *initiative* for planning, for determining the amount and timing of expenditures, is in the hands of the President. Congress, no matter how well run, how wisely populated, seems to haggle, delay, argue, debate while the country and the President wait.[2]

It was not always thus. The watershed was the Budget and Accounting Act of 1921. "The modern Presidency," according to Brookings scholar and active practitioner James L. Sundquist, "judged in terms of institutional responsibilities, began on June 10, 1921, the day that President Harding signed the Budget and Accounting Act."[3]

The act did several things. First, it established the Bureau of the Budget under the control of president but operating out of the Treasury Department and provided for its director. Second, it required the president to send a national, or president's, budget to Congress at the beginning of each new legislative session. Third, it created the GAO as an arm of the Congress, with the power to examine and audit appropriated funds. Finally, it put the GAO under the direction and control of the comptroller general and the deputy comptroller general, who are appointed by the president with the advice and consent of the Senate for terms of fifteen years and who may not be reappointed.

Since 1921 the Bureau of the Budget has not only become the OMB but has also been transferred from the treasury to the Executive Office of the President. The appointment of its director, often called the second most powerful official in the government, is now confirmed by the Senate. The OMB clears all legislative proposals made by the executive branch departments and agencies to the Congress and coordinates their recommendations on whether the president should sign or veto a bill. Since 1981 it has supervised the formerly independent regulatory agencies, often with a heavy hand. Because of its enormous powers, the OMB is often referred to by its critics as the "nay sayer" of the federal government.

The GAO has carved out a monumental reputation for its independence and integrity. Under the stewardship of Elmer B. Staats, the fifth of only six comptrollers general since 1921, its functions were expanded to oversee not only financial accountability by the executive agencies but the quality and performance of programs in every department. The GAO reports on virtually every aspect of government activity with a quality and authority exceeded by no other government office.

While the Budget and Accounting Act of 1921 revolutionized budget procedures and is the keystone of modern budget practices, one must neither exaggerate its initial effects nor diminish what went on before its passage. It has generally been understood that from 1789 to 1921 each agency sent its "Book of Estimates" either directly to the appropriate congressional committee or perfunctorily to the treasury for transmission to the Congress, that no general budget policy was set by the president, and that there was no revision or comment by either the treasury or the president on the estimates. This was said to be a mindless method of forming a budget that was generally in balance because a surfeit of customs and excise receipts greatly overbalanced the totality of the individual agency requests sent informally to Congress.

As Louis Fisher writes:

> It is convenient to identify pivotal statutes, but all too often they become the secular counterpart of the Creation. We assume that nothing existed before, that all was void and darkness. This perception dominates the literature on the Federal budget.[4]

Fisher explodes that myth and shows that numerous presidents before 1921 examined the budget in detail. As he points out, a number of them actually complained about, campaigned against, or proposed cuts in the budget. For example, President Jefferson and his Treasury Secretary Albert Gallatin had a systematic budget review and a five-year plan. James Monroe complained that reports were sent to the Congress before he saw them. John Quincy Adams proposed padding the budget estimates because he knew from experience that the Congress would cut them. Andrew Jackson's fight over the Second Bank of the United States resulted in federal funds being deposited in state banks at his and the Congress's insistence. During the 1837 panic, Martin Van Buren insisted in his budget message on cutting the budget (the wrong policy). William Henry Harrison campaigned against the "unhallowed union of the Treasury with the Executive Departments," but his successor John Tyler urged budget cuts in his second budget message. James K. Polk was an active budgeter who tried to control department and agency spending, set the level of federal expenditures, and was outraged at the actions of a dishonest Army quartermaster. Polk, who historians now rate as one of the better presidents, reviewed the work of both cabinet and bureau chiefs, and warned against padding the budget estimates. In 1912, President Taft sent a presidential budget to the Congress, a document that was ignored but that represented a pre-1921 precedent for a presidential budget. As Fisher concludes:

> Unless we appreciate the development of the 1789–1921 period, and comprehend the political and economic forces that were part of the momentum building up to the Budget and Accounting Act, we may wrongly conclude that Presidential spending power began with a statute and can be ended with a statute. Yet this is not so. The power is an accumulation of numerous statutes, financial panics, wars, a splintering of congressional controls, and demands from the private sector for economy and efficiency.[5]

ORIGINS OF THE 1921 ACT

The major events that culminated in the Budget and Accounting Act of 1921 began three decades earlier. The first was the shock of budget deficits. For twenty-seven years, from 1867 through 1893, the budget was in balance and ran a surplus. This was followed by deficits in each of the six years from 1894 through 1899 (three under Grover Cleveland and three under William McKinley). Theodore Roosevelt had three deficits in seven years (1904, 1905, and 1908), and Taft has deficits in the first two years of his term (1909 and 1910).

The second was the general rise in the level of government spending, which occasioned great concern in the Congress and throughout the country. For thirty-one years, from 1867 through 1897, federal budgets were always below $400 million a year. For the nineteen years from 1871 through 1889 they were under $300 million. The costs of the Spanish-American War, the digging of the Panama Canal, increased pensions, and the assumptions of new powers and duties by the central government brought a dramatic increase in expenditures. In the years from 1899 to 1912 they jumped from the $200 to $400 million level of the last third of the nineteenth century to $500 to $700 million a year.[6]

Third, these concerns led to the appointment of a series of congressional and presidential committees or commissions. The Cockrell Commission (1887–1889) was headed by an unsung senator from Missouri, Thomas M. Cockrell, who served in the Senate from 1875 to 1905. Like the World War II Truman Committee (headed by another then-unsung senator from Missouri), which exposed waste in military contracting, the Cockrell Commission exposed some of the worst inefficiencies in the executive branch, which political scientists and public administrators were generally loath to admit. The Cockrell-Dockery Commission (1893–1895) was another congressionally initiated effort to bring efficiency and economy to the executive branch. It anticipated by more than a decade the concerns of a later day. Next, in 1905, belatedly reacting to the problem of growing outlays and reduced revenues, Theodore Roosevelt appointed the Keep Commission. Like its late twentieth-century successors, it not only examined duplication and waste but centered on the elimination of paperwork as a means of reducing the federal deficits. Cutting red tape and paperwork and getting rid of duplication, fraud, and waste, however, are among the traditionally exaggerated methods of reducing the federal budget. For almost a century the real savings from such cuts have been ephemeral and seem to vanish in the mists of time.

Most importantly, President Taft requested $100,000 from the Congress in 1910 to establish a Commission on Economy and Efficiency to launch a fact-finding investigation on how the government could be conducted more efficiently and more economically. Its report, entitled "The Need for a National Budget," proposed a number of procedures that were not adopted until a decade later. These included the president's systematic review of the estimates of the departments and agencies and the presentation of an organized, coherent annual public budget document to the Congress. When Taft did this on his own initiative in 1912 and presented to the Congress not only the usual "Book of Estimates" but also a national budget organized by functions, the latter was rejected by the Congress, which acted on estimates from the executive agencies based on the usual procedures. Taft's action, while courageous, was premature. There were several political reasons for its rejection. First, there were budget surpluses in fiscal years 1911 and 1912, which brought about a diminution in the concerns about the budget problems. Second, 1912 was an election year in which the Democrats controlled the House and in which the Republican Taft, whose party support was split by Teddy Roosevelt's third-party Bull Moose candidacy, lost the presidency to Wilson. Taft's budget, although an important historical document with long-term effects, became a part of the unread literature of the times. In February 1913, after his defeat, Taft sent the Congress another presidential budget, but it too was ignored. History should credit this conservative and conventional president with a unique and unconventional initiative. But there is also great historical irony in Taft's advocacy of the presidential budget, for he opposed the concept of a strong presidency. His conservative fiscal views led him to champion what became the chief political weapon of the powerful twentieth-century president. It was a modern example of the unintended consequences of political acts.

A fourth important force that led to the 1921 act was the Progressive movement and the rise of a belief that scientific management could be substituted for the graft and corruption that the Muckrakers—principally Lincoln Steffens, in *The Shame of the Cities*, and Ida Tarbell—had exposed in municipal government. There was also the establishment of the New York Bureau of Municipal Research, which Jesse Burkhead believed was of great significance in the development of the "good government" movement of the turn of the century.[7] Dwight Waldo, in his classic book *The Administrative State*, wrote that:

> The Bureau Movement was a part of Progressivism, and its leaders were leaders of Progressivism. They were tired of the simple moralism of the nineteenth century, although paradoxically they were themselves fired with the moral fervor of humanitarianism and secularized Christianity. They were stirred by the revelations of the Muckrakers, but despaired of reform by spontaneous combustion. They were sensitive to the appeals of and promises of science, and put a simple trust in discovery of facts as the way of science and as a sufficient mode for solution of human problems. They accepted—they urged—the new positive conception of government, and verged upon the idea of a planned and managed society. They hated "bad" business, but found in business organization and procedure an acceptable prototype for public business. They detested politicians and were firm in the belief that citizens by and large were fundamentally pure at heart, desirous of efficient and economical government, and potentially rational enough to "reach up" to and support a vigorous government, wide in its scope, complex in its problems, and utilizing a multitude of professional and scientific skills. They proposed to educate citizens to and assist them with this responsibility. They were ardent apostles of the "efficiency idea" and leaders in the movement for "useful" education. These last three notions—civic awareness and militancy, efficiency, and "useful" education—together form the core of the Efficient Citizenship movement.

They caught the vision that "true democracy consists in intelligent cooperation between citizens and those elected or appointed to serve. . . !"[8]

A fifth influence was exerted by the enemies of the Muckrakers: the Senate's "millionaires' club" and those Teddy Roosevelt called the "malefactors of great wealth, who looked upon the deficits as the result of fraud, inefficiency, and the lack of business management in government." The leader of the club, Nelson Aldrich of Rhode Island, claimed that the Congress had passed no less than $50 million in wasteful appropriations in the deficit year of 1909. The Muckrakers and the public administrators joined with the National Chamber of Commerce and the business community to support both scientific management and business efficiency in government. In the end the business community was more influential on this issue. As Burkhead said, "In the development from the end of World War I to the passage of the Budget and Accounting Act of 1921, the voices of the reformers were lost in the outcry for economy and efficiency."[9]

A final factor was World War I and the related explosion in government spending. Between fiscal years 1913 and 1919, outlays increased twenty-five-fold, from $715 million to $18.5 billion. Taxes paid for less than one-third of the war. The deficits rose to $9 billion in fiscal year 1918 and to $13.4 billion in 1919. From 1913 to 1919, wholesale prices more than doubled. Inflation as well as borrowing and taxes financed the war, each accounting for about one-third of the total.

These facts and events increased support for an executive budget. Strong medicine indeed was advocated. The item veto was proposed. Presidential impoundment of funds was advocated. Some sought to limit the Congress's power to raise any presidential estimate and to force the Congress to content itself with cutting them. The public administrators led by W. F. Willoughby sought to turn the Constitution on its head. Willoughby, a member of the Taft Commission on Economy and Efficiency, argued that "there are cogent grounds for holding that the legislature should be largely, if not wholly, excluded from the direct determination of the appropriations of funds."[10] Hearings were held by a special House Budget Committee in 1919 at which Willoughby was not only a chief witness but a consultant to the committee. Even in those days the executive branch sought to hijack congressional powers.

What little opposition there was to a national budget came almost exclusively from those who had had experience in the legislative branch. A former chairman of the House Appropriations Committee, Democrat John F. Fitzgerald of New York, expressed the traditional congressional view succinctly:

Many who are arguing the adoption of a budget in the United States are really in favor of a revolutionary change in our whole system of government. What they favor is practically the elimination of Congress from very much of the work which it now does.

Another of the few voices speaking out against a new national budget to be dominated by the president and the executive branch was that of "Uncle Joe" Cannon (R-Ill.), the former speaker of the House of Representatives whose wings had been clipped in 1910 by the "Fighting Liberal," George Norris of Nebraska. Relying on Article I of the Constitution, which grants every power of the purse to the legislative branch, Congressman Cannon wrote in *Harper's Magazine* that

> when Congress consents to the Executive making the budget it will have surrendered the most important part of a representative government.[11]

The Select Committee recommended the establishment of a Bureau of the Budget under the president, and in 1920 the Congress passed the first Budget and Accounting Act, which President Wilson vetoed. The bill provided that the Congress could remove the comptroller general and/or the deputy by means of a congressional concurrent resolution that did not require the signature of the president. Wilson argued that the power to appoint includes the power to remove and vetoed the bill as unconstitutional. The Budget and Accounting Act of 1921, which President Harding readily signed, provided for the removal of these officials by a joint resolution of the Congress which, like a bill, requires the president's signature. On grounds that the president and the president alone must take responsibility for the budget, the act did not provide for the confirmation of the director of the Bureau of the Budget.

Because of these political and economic forces, the Congress deliberately transferred much of its massive constitutional power over the purse strings to the president. Willoughby's view that the Congress should be largely if not wholly excluded from the system did not entirely prevail, and the Congress kept the right to review the president's budget and both to raise and lower it. The Congress refused to give the president the item veto and prevailed over the public administrators and scientific managers who canonized the executive and downgraded the legislative by retaining the power given by Article I, Section 9, that "No money shall be drawn from the Treasury, but in consequence of Appropriations made by Law."

What were the conditions, the accumulation of forces, the milieu, and the events that resulted in the watershed 1921 act? Jesse Burkhead summarized these circumstances and those that he believed were necessary for any substantial reform. First, he said that "pressures for federal reform were strong only when federal outlays increased faster than the increase in economic activity, and only when this differential rate of expansion produced stringency in federal government finance." These conditions were clearly present when the 1974 Budget Act, the 1985 Gramm-Rudman-Hollings amendments, and the Five-Year Budget Agreement of 1990 were passed. Second, Burkhead said that it was not enough that there were known improvements that could be made with a minimum of effort to ease the taxpayer's burden and to make programs more effective, because "administrative reforms do not proceed until a near crisis is reached." Third, he said, "The divisions between executive and legislative authority in the constitutions and practices of governments in this country had to be greatly altered before budget systems could be established." In this respect reform was "revolutionary" and "a product of and a contribution to a fundamental change in the structure of government," namely a shift of power from the Congress to the president. Fourth, reform required a coalition between the reformers, public servants, and administrators on the one hand and the business community on the other. "Both of these divergent groups subscribed to budget reform under the heading of 'economy and efficiency,' that phrase which seems to have such powerful appeal in American politics."[12]

President Harding, who called the Budget and Accounting Act the greatest reform in government practices since the beginning of the Republic, appointed a strong first director of the Bureau of the Budget, General Charles G. Dawes, and gave him extraordinary presidential backing. An imperious man, Dawes was quick to establish his authority. In a June 1921 meeting opened by the president and attended by the heads of all departments, agencies, and bureaus, Dawes took charge. He announced that his requests for information to be used by the president from any bureau chief or other administrative officer would "take precedence over the Cabinet head of a department, or any head of an independent organization." He proclaimed that while the budget representatives in the department would present the views of the department to the budget director, "the call of the Director of the Budget for their presence and advice takes precedence over the Cabinet head." He compared the president and his right to information with the head of a business corporation who "has the right to get information where he pleases and from any source in that corporation, whether it is from a washerwoman scrubbing the floor, or his first vice-president."[13]

While Dawes knew how to establish authority and wield power, he was either dissembling or extraordinarily naive about the objectivity or political impartiality of the budget actions of the president and director. More likely, he was a victim of the blindness that leads powerful people to believe that their strongly held, even self-serving or self-righteous views are devoid of politics. But Dawes proclaimed in his June 1921 speech to the federal establishment that

> The Budget Bureau must be impartial, impersonal, and nonpolitical.
>
> The Director of the Budget in the matter of governmental business administration has no responsibility under the law save for the administration of his own bureau. He is simply an adviser of the President and Congress in the matter of correct business administration.[14]

THE OFFICE OF MANAGEMENT AND BUDGET

In the more than seventy years since President Harding signed the Budget and Accounting Act and Director Dawes established its authority at the right hand of the president, the Bureau of the Budget has gained in power and prestige. Since those early days when it gained central responsibility over the departments and agencies for drawing up the estimates and for clearing all legislation proposed to the Congress, it has accumulated additional influence and authority through legislation, executive orders, and reorganization acts. In 1933 it gained "the power to make, waive, and modify apportionments of appropriations, a responsibility previously fixed in the individual department heads and bureau chiefs."[15] In 1939 it was transferred to the Executive Office of the President, and the director's office is now in the old State, War and Navy Building, now called the Executive Office Building, which sits next to the White House, a physical presence that enhances the authority of the OMB and its directors. It was given the power not only to prepare the budget but to "execute" it, to clear executive orders, and to promulgate codes of management to the departments and agencies. In 1950 it gained additional power over apportionment through an amendment to the Anti-Deficiency Act designed to prevent what is known among Washington insiders as "closing down the Washington Monument." One of the tricks of the bureaucratic trade is to spend or apportion most of an agency's annual funds in the first three-quarters of the year and return to the Congress for "emergency" supplementals when funds run out. In the past, the Congress has been put over a barrel to provide emergency ammunition for "our boys fighting overseas," to keep embassies open, and to fund half-finished buildings or roads. The 1950 amendment was conceived when, in 1947, the Post Office spent all but 1 percent of its funds in the first three-quarters of the year and threatened to stop delivering the mail if its request for further money went unheeded.[16] In 1981, in a trial of strength with the Congress, President Reagan vetoed a continuing resolution and in fact did close down the Washington Monument. In 1990 President Bush closed the Washington Monument in the same manner (see Chapter 10). Since 1950, in concert with the Council of Economic Advisers, the agency has also expanded its authority over fiscal policy.

In 1970, by a reorganization plan, the Bureau of the Budget became the OMB. Its mandate was enlarged and

> its authority to act in the President's name extends to the entire Federal administrative establishment, as well as to State and local governments and Federal contractors. It keeps its finger on every pulse of Federal activity.[17]

Under the Budget Enforcement Act of 1990, the president and the OMB were given the power to set and adjust the overall deficit targets annually and to determine and enforce the discretionary spending ceilings and the pay-as-you-go provisions of the five-year budget agreement. This included the power to initiate the sequesters under the discretionary spending limits and the pay-as-you-go provisions. The OMB became the official scorekeeper. It was now both the judge and the enforcer of budget action, a massive delegation of power from the Congress to the president and his agent, the OMB (see Chapter 10).

In a recent year the OMB's own budget request was for $53.4 million and 600 permanent positions. Some $32.4 million, or 60.6 percent of the total, and about an equal proportion of its personnel were to be devoted to its historical function of preparing, developing, and executing the budget. The remaining $21 million was budgeted for management, information and regulatory affairs, and the director's office.[18] On the whole the OMB has a reputation for being a lean and efficient agency, for subjecting its employees to extraordinarily long hours of work, and for being a lightning rod for agency, departmental, congressional, and public criticism that dissenters are often too timid to hurl at the president. It has been called the "nay sayer," the "Abominable No Man," and "the Office of Meddling and Budget."

THE PRESIDENT'S BUDGET-ORGANIZATION CHART AND DEVICES FOR EFFICIENCY AND ECONOMY

No sooner is the president's budget issued on the first Monday in February than preparation for the next year's budget begins. The formal organization chart, timetable, actions, and functions by which the budget is developed are one thing; the facts, politics, and actual practices are quite another.

Formally, the first phase, called the development stage in the organization charts, takes place from early April until midyear (see Table 2–1). Economic assumptions and revenue estimates are made in concert with the Council of Economic Advisers and the Treasury Department, respectively. The president and his budget director meet and talk over the general budget outlook, policies, and projections. The OMB issues general guidelines to the agencies for their planning review. As spring merges into summer, the estimates of revenues and spending are refined, the economic outlook is revised, and recommendations are made to the president on fiscal policy, program issues, and budget levels. By the first of July, general guidelines, policies, and targets are established by the president and the budget director and conveyed to the agencies.

The second stage occurs in July, August, and a part of September. After six months of review, the agencies make their budget decisions. They compile and submit their formal budget estimates to the OMB.

In the third stage, the agency budgets are formally examined by the OMB. Materials are presented, hearings are held, and formal OMB decisions are made on agency budgets. These budget decisions by the OMB have the formal, if not the personal, approval of the president and are referred to

TABLE 2–1 Executive Branch Budget Timetable

Timing	Action to Be Completed
April–June	Conduct spring planning review to establish presidential policy for the upcoming budget
July–August	OMB provides agencies with policy guidance for the upcoming budget
September 1	Agencies subject to executive branch review submit initial budget request materials
September–January	OMB and the president review agency budget requests and prepare the budget documents
October 15	Independent agencies not subject to executive branch review submit initial budget request materials
November–December	Legislative branch and the judiciary submit initial budget request materials
December	Cabinet officers' and agency appeals to the president
1st Monday in February[1]	President's budget submitted to the Congress
January–February	OMB sends allowance letters to agencies.
July 15	President submits mid-session updates of the budget estimates.

Source: OMB Circular No. A-11.
1. This was previously done 15 days after the Congress convened in January, then on January 3, and now, after the passage of the Omnibus Budget Reconciliation Act of 1990, no later than the first Monday in February, which by 1990 had become the traditional release date.

as the president's decisions. By making decisions formally in the name of the president, the OMB enhances its power over the agencies.

In the final stage, the agencies revise their budgets to conform to the president's decisions. The departments and major agencies may appeal directly to the president on a few major issues, after which the final budget is agreed on. The director of the budget, the Council of Economic Advisers, and the Treasury Department once again review the economic outlook, revenue estimates, and general fiscal policy. Revisions and reestimates may be made as a result. The several thousand pages of the various budget documents are prepared and sent to the Government Printing Office. The president's budget message is drafted. The vast public relations panoply of the government is set in motion. The president sends the new budget to the Congress no later than the first Monday in February.

Under the impartial, impersonal, and nonpolitical provisions of scientific management that public administrators have devised and that budget directors from Dawes to the present day have publicly embraced, the annual development of the budget should give the agencies extraordinary opportunities to apply the principles and exercise the tools of economy and efficiency. There are many principles of scientific management that the practitioners of budget building have devised and that can be applied at the agency level. A discussion of some of the principles most often mentioned follows.

Planning, Programming and Budgeting Systems   A government agency should systematically review its program, evaluate alternatives, and inject a consciousness of cost into its planning and programs. Preparing the budget provides the discipline necessary for such a review. As Frederick C. Mosher stated,

> Planning involves first the conceiving of goals and the development of alternative courses of future action to achieve the goals. Second, it involves the reduction of these alternatives from a very large number to a small number and finally to one approved course of action, *the program*. Budgeting probably plays a slight part in the first phase but an increasingly important and decisive part in the second. It facilitates the choice-making process by providing a basis for systematic comparisons among alternatives which take into account their total impacts on both the debit and the credit sides. It thus encourages, and provides some of the tools for, an increasing degree of precision in the planning process. Budgeting is the ingredient of planning which disciplines the entire process.[19]

Planning, Programming and Budgeting Systems (PPBS) was an important tool devised in the 1950s for the agencies to use during the annual development stage of the budget. Its purpose was to substitute rationality for the drift toward incremental budgeting. Instead of focusing on the cost of inputs, it emphasized the outputs. The steps and goals were elaborate. As James P. Pfiffner wrote, "One of the most salient features of PPBS was its strong centralizing implications. In contrast to the traditional process in which budget decisions are built on estimates sent up the hierarchy, PPBS reversed the flow of decisions."[20] The Department of Defense remains its only principal user.

Cost-benefit Analysis   Another tool of the so-called budgetary process is the cost-benefit analysis. In some agencies, such as the Army Corps of Engineers, a formal cost-benefit ratio is provided for each proposed public works project. If the benefits and costs are equal, the cost-benefit ratio is one. Historically, the Army Engineers have underestimated the costs and exaggerated the benefits to the degree that most independent critics believe a cost-benefit ratio of at least two is needed for projects to break even. But it is better and more revealing to do the analysis and provide even optimistic detailed data than not to do an analysis at all.

Discount Rate   The discount rate is a method for valuing future benefits. If investment in the private sector brings an average return of 15 percent, for a public project to be economical it should bring an equal return. Otherwise, the funds might better be left in the private sector for economic activities that would be both more economical and more benefi-cial. Especially in periods of high interest rates, when the government itself is paying double-digit amounts for borrowed funds, unless there are overrid-ing national security or social policy reasons, it is an even more inefficient use of resources for the government either to borrow funds at, for example, 12 percent or to tax income that could earn 15 percent and then invest the money in a dam, harbor, or public building for which the return is 6 percent. Budget policy development should give each agency an opportunity each year to determine if an appropriate discount rate is being applied to its projects or expenditures.

Zero-based Budgeting   According to the glossary *Terms Used in the Budget-ary Process*, which the comptroller general was required to compile under Title VIII of the Congressional Budget Act of 1974, zero-based budgeting (ZBB) is defined as

> a budgeting technique that generally attempts to analyze budget requests without an implicit commitment to sustaining past levels of funding. Under this system programs and activities are organized and budgeted in a detailed plan that focuses review, evaluation, and analysis on all proposed operations—rather than on increases above current levels of operations, as in incremental budgeting. Programs and activities are analyzed in terms of successively in-creasing levels of performance and funding, starting from zero, and then evaluated and ranked in priority order. The purpose is to determine the level, if any, at which each program or activity should be conducted.[21]

One purpose of ZBB was to avoid "incremental" budgeting whereby some arbitrary percentage increase is more or less blindly added to last year's appropriation. Incremental budgeting has now been institutionalized in the Current Services Budget, which is required under the 1974 act, where it is defined as "a budget that projects estimated budget authority and outlays for the upcoming fiscal year at the same program level and without policy changes as the fiscal year in progress." Under ZBB, an agency would be asked whether the program should exist at all, whether it is carrying out its original or amended purpose, and whether an alternative program might do so more efficiently with less money and bigger returns.

ZBB's central thrust is to allocate budget resources through a system of ranking programs and alternatives. It involves an elaborate system of pre-paring budget requests for "decision units" that are then placed in "decision packages" according to incremental spending levels. There are also "deci-sion package sets" and "decision unit overviews" for the "decision package sets," language that evolved from the jargon of space systems and behavior-ism popular at the time of ZBB's inception.

ZBB emphasizes management's responsibility to plan, budget, and evaluate, and it places new programs on an equal footing with existing programs through its ranking system.

Other Techniques   Agency budget offices use other devices to review budgets and determine priorities. One method is to require budget presentations that list priorities by increments, for example, what programs would be cut if funds were reduced from 100 to 90 and then to 80 percent, or what particular programs, projects, or weapons systems would be added from the shopping list if funds in real terms were raised to 110 or 120 percent of previous amounts?

All of the aforementioned devices, and many others, are widely advocated, allegedly widely used, and of considerable benefit in examining and reviewing budgets of public agencies in which the private business need to raise revenues to meet outlays and the disciplines of the market are lacking. The purpose of these techniques for budget review is to prevent padding, incremental budgeting, mindless outlays, and nonobjective and political decisions.

THE BUDGET IN REALITY: A CASE STUDY

Budget building in fact is very different from the organization charts and the theories of PPBS, ZBB, and cost-benefit analysis. The view that budgeting is a nonpolitical act buttressed by the twin pillars of economy and efficiency is a myth. It can be exploded by examining the budget preparations of any bureau, agency, or department. Examine, for example, budget building at the Bureau of Reclamation in the Department of the Interior during the last year of the Carter administration and the first full years of the Reagan and Bush administrations.

The Bureau of Reclamation (BuRec) was created by the Reclamation Act of 1902. Originally called the Reclamation Service, it was first established under the Geological Survey. The Reclamation Service became the Bureau of Reclamation in 1923. For a short period of time under President Carter, it was called the Water and Power Resources Service, but its name was changed back by Secretary of the Interior, James Watt.

The bureau provides water—life-giving water—to the seventeen contiguous arid western states, chiefly for irrigation, for municipal and industrial purposes, and for the generation of hydroelectric power. In the 1990s, appropriations of more than a billion dollars a year have been requested by the Bureau. It also has the authority to spend funds contributed by non-federal entities for some construction projects as if they had been specifically appropriated.

The reclamation water program involves one of the biggest subsidies by government. Funds for irrigation projects are given to the BuRec, which builds the projects. The local water users—usually western water districts—agree to pay back a portion of the amount on highly preferential terms. No repayment is required for up to ten years after construction is completed. There is then a forty-year repayment period, sometimes extended for up to ten more years, for the principal, with no interest required. On the whole only "about 85 percent of all direct project costs are reimbursable."[22] This means that 15 percent of the principal is also forgiven. This does not include the foregone interest, which may push the subsidy to over 90 percent. The economic effect is the same as a nonreimbursable direct grant.

Power projects have a similar ten-year forgiveness and fifty-year payback period, but both hydroelectric power projects and municipal and industrial water users pay some interest, although in practice the time at which interest becomes due is often extended by adding a new project feature. Depending on when they are authorized, power projects historically pay from 1 to 6.75 percent, although the average rate on outstanding projects is less than 3 percent. This too amounts to a nonreimbursable direct grant from the taxpayers of fifty states to the specific beneficiaries in seventeen.

These enormous irrigation subsidies were justified by the original requirement that water provided to any one landowner would be limited to 160 acres. The subsidies were to promote the family farm and the development of typical American communities with churches, schools, locally owned businesses, and a stable social base to serve them. In practice, both farmer and spouse could qualify, as well as their sons or daughters, so that 320 to 640 acres and sometimes more were irrigated. This was sufficient to provide a substantial income and, in the case of fruit orchards, a relatively high return. Over 90 percent of irrigated farms are less than 320 acres in size. Unfortunately, in area after area the 160-acre limitation was not enforced. Large land companies such as those owned by the Southern Pacific Railroad, Standard Oil, J. G. Boswell Co., Boston Ranch, and the Kern County Land Company; corporate farms in the new Westland and Central Valley projects in California; and individuals who leased vast acreages many, many times larger than the 160-acre limit, all benefited from the federal water and the subsidy. Instead of promoting family farms and stable, conservative, adjoining communities, the failure to enforce the original policy brought with it migrant workers, shantytowns, substandard labor and health conditions, and social problems. Further, on some projects, especially on the Upper Colorado, initial sums as high as $2,000 an acre were provided to produce hay and forage crops at high altitudes on land worth $100 an acre or less. Some projects were no more efficient than growing bananas on Pike's Peak.

A 1976 federal court ruling to enforce the 160-acre provisions and the Carter administration's efforts to reform the program brought great hostility from those in western states. In 1982 the Congress passed and President Reagan signed a bill that made substantial changes for farms over 960 acres, which meant only 3 percent of all farms, but that essentially ratified existing practices for all others. Senator Barry Goldwater (R-Ariz.), "Mr. Conservative" and the spokesman for competition, free enterprise, less government, reduced subsidies, and laissez-faire policies, charged during the debate on an amendment to the bill that would have sharply reduced the subsidy that "our friends from the water-wealthy East want to deny water to the water-poor West."[23] As *The Los Angeles Times* reported:

> Western farm and water groups have spent millions of dollars in legal fees, political donations and public relations campaigns to win congressional relief from restrictions in the 80-year-old reclamation law.
>
> The bill would raise the 160-acre limit (320 acres for a married couple) on farms eligible for the subsidized water to 2,080 acres. More importantly, it would allow unlimited leased acreage to be eligible—at a higher price than before—and would remove the requirement that the farmers live on the land.
>
> Another special section of the bill would exempt outright the huge corporate farms in the Kings River area of California's Central Valley from any acreage limitation. Although they do not get subsidized federal water, they store their water behind a federal dam and were specifically ordered to comply with the 160-acre limit when that 1944 dam was authorized by Congress.[24]

A determined floor fight by Senator Howard Metzenbaum (D.-Ohio) and Senator William Proxmire (D.-Wis.) limited many of the changes that were criticized by *The Los Angeles Times*. In essence, existing water claimants are politically more powerful than future water claimants. Politically strong clients with economically weak claims are more powerful than politically weak clients with economically strong claims. The 1902 Reclamation Act was under siege. With this background, let us examine how the Reclamation Bureau's budget was built and reviewed by the Carter administration for the election year of 1980 (fiscal year 1981), and by the Reagan and Bush administrations in their first full budget years, fiscal years 1983 and 1991, respectively. Were the features of the budgets examined on the basis of the scientific principles propounded by the public administrators, or were they built on the foundations propounded by powerful political forces with influences in both administrations?

Carter and BuRec

As the OMB's Executive Branch Budget Timetable (see Table 2–1) requires, the BuRec began its budget policy development early in 1979 for the 1980 presidential election year (fiscal year 1981). It and other bureaus in the Department of the Interior sent their budget instructions to field offices in February. Then in March the department sent its policy guidance to the various bureaus, such as the National Park Service, the Bureau of Reclamation, and the Fish and Wildlife Service. The instructions included an overall policy view as well as technical details on how to prepare the budget. The emphasis for the Bureau of Reclamation, as was appropriate for an election year, was not on cutting projects or funds but on constructing projects on an "engineering-efficient" schedule. The guidance in effect told the bureau to construct the projects as fast as possible. This fact was not lost on key employees.

By May 15 a two-hundred-page program strategy paper was prepared for the Department of the Interior's budget officers. The baseline was something called the "minimum level," defined under ZBB by the OMB as the level below which it would be impossible to operate the program. This vague definition caused some initial soul-searching in the department, which finally defined the minimum level as the much higher level of the previous year's appropriations. Under ZBB this is called the "current level," two levels above the "minimum level" in the decision package. This contradiction went unchallenged at every stage and supports the view that some budgeting for the limited amount of "controllable" funds in the budget is incremental.

From May 15 to early August the Budget Office of the Department of the Interior reviewed the proposals and required the program officials to defend them. One or two of the accounts were picked out and examined in detail. This occasioned some field trips and produced valuable budget information, but the intense review was narrowly limited to a small part of the funding.

By early July, budget and program options were prepared for the secretary of the interior. By mid-July each assistant secretary had met with the secretary for a two- to three-hour session. In the meeting with the assistant secretary for land and water resources, the time was divided equally between the program merits and the political issues. Most secretaries see these meetings as a chore, because the assistant secretaries almost always want a greater amount than the secretary feels comfortable recommending to the president. During the next two weeks, or by early August, the secretary had closeted himself with his political advisers and made his decisions. The result was a "decision memo" from the secretary to the assistant secretaries and bureau heads that was prepared by the budget officer on the instructions of the secretary. This was the basis for the department's formal budget estimate for the OMB, due by September 15. It was also a restatement of the secretary's May 15 paper, taking into account the secretary's decisions. These decisions can be influenced by anything from dislike of an assistant secretary to a telephone call from an old friend pleading for a specific program.

During the period from September 15 to Thanksgiving, the OMB reviewed the budget, held formal hearings on the details, and heard the informal appeals from Interior Department bureaus that wished to restore funds that the OMB had tentatively proposed to cut. The OMB itself had recommended a sizable cut of about 15 percent in the Interior Department's proposed budget, which the department had anticipated by including a generous padding allowance when it was presented.

In early December, President Carter met with Secretary of the Interior Cecil Andrus to hear his appeal on the recommendations of the OMB. Five items were on the agenda. A two-page issue paper prepared jointly by the Interior Department and the OMB outlined the issues and presented separately but side-by-side the OMB's and the Interior Department's positions. Present were the president, his assistant for domestic policy, the director of the OMB and two or three key staff persons, the secretary of the interior, his budget officer, and key staff members—about twelve people in all. On the five key issues the secretary won two and lost two, and a fifth issue was resolved by compromise. There was virtually no discussion of the merits of possible decisions, only of their political and institutional consequences. The secretary got more money for both the urban park fund and land and water resources, largely on the recommendation of the president's domestic policy adviser, who pointed out that the urban park fund was the only item in the president's urban policy to pass the Congress and that the land and water conservation fund was extremely popular with environmentalists, a key constituency.

NONPOLITICAL DECISIONS

To what degree were the budget decisions in this entire procedure based on the nonpolitical goals of promoting economy and efficiency? First, two of the largest reclamation projects, the Upper Colorado and the Central Arizona projects, were originally initiated because of strong political pressures. President Eisenhower approved the former in part as a reward to Utah's then senior Republican senator, Arthur V. Watkins, for the role he had played in the censure of Senator Joseph McCarthy (R.-Wis.). The Central Arizona Project was due in great measure to the diligence of former Senator Carl Hayden (D.-Ariz.), who had served in the Senate for forty-two years and chaired the Senate Appropriations Committee. Neither project could be justified on any reasonable cost-benefit analysis or economic basis. Any nonpolitical review would have resulted in major cuts in both of these projects. Neither was touched.

Throughout the nine months of procedures, the Department of the Interior kept one eye on its "clients"—the Western Governors Conference, the National Farm Bureau, and the Farmer's Union. The other eye was on crucial subcommittees of the Appropriations, Energy and Natural Resources, and Interior committees of both the House and the Senate. Their energy and water subcommittees are dominated by members from western and lower Mississippi River states.

Was there an "iron triangle"—that is, a mutual lobbying and back-scratching relationship—between BuRec officials, user and lobbying groups, and key congressional members? Yes, absolutely and at virtually every stage, from original formulation in the seven regional offices to the secretary's decision memo to the appeals meeting at the White House Oval Office.

Was the final budget incremental—that is, largely based on an arbitrary or percentage increase over the previous year's budget? Yes.

Was it padded at various levels to cover anticipated cuts? Yes.

Was ZBB used—that is, an examination of the programs *de novo* to determine if they were economically justified or cost effective, or if there were other, more efficient means of achieving the goals? With the possible exception of two minor items that were reviewed intensively, there was no semblance or pretense of ZBB.

Was an appropriate discount rate applied to the projects? No such rate was or is applied to reclamation projects.

Was the agency concerned at any point specifically about the revenues that would be available to pay for the projects? No, and generally no agency is so concerned. As Burkhead wrote:

> An agency budget is an expenditure budget or an expenditure-appropriation budget, but it is not an income-expenditure budget. An agency budgets on the assumptions that revenues will be available to cover its estimated expenditures; the agency is not directly concerned with how these revenues are to be provided.[25]

The Bureau of Reclamation does have a trust fund into which goes the repayment of its loans. Reclamation proponents sometimes attempt to justify projects as self-liquidating because of the revolving fund, but the projects do not effectively pay back even the principal. The fact that an agency budget is an "expenditure" budget highlights one of the weaknesses of government. In standard business practice, those who spend money are required to raise it, as a discipline to prevent excesses. In government, the central budget office or the chief executive officer must at some stage be concerned about revenues, but this is not true of most agencies, bureaus, and departments, and supplies no discipline against them when they build their budgets.

Reagan and BuRec

The Reagan administration's first full-fiscal-year budget for the Bureau of Reclamation was prepared under similar circumstances. The secretary, the undersecretary, the assistant secretary for land and water resources, and their deputies and personal assistants had all supported the "sagebrush revolt" and had campaigned against the 160-acre limitation. In a year of recession and stringent proposed budget cuts elsewhere, the request for federal funds for the Bureau of Reclamation rose by 23 percent. This first full-year Reagan administration budget reflected the promises of the presidential campaign. No one could claim perfidy in this area. President Reagan had carried every reclamation state. Six new Republican senators from these were elected, four of whom replaced Democrats. Twenty-two Republican senators now represented the seventeen reclamation states. They included the chairman of the Senate Appropriations Committee and of its Energy and Water Subcommittee (Mark Hatfield, R.-Oreg.), which funds the projects. One of the major political concerns of the bureau was that none of its even regional offices was located in Oregon, the state of the person with the greatest influence over its budget. Another key senator was the then chairman of the Energy and Natural Resources Committee (James McClure, R.-Idaho), which authorizes the projects. In the House, ten of the twenty-three Democratic and, more importantly, twelve of the sixteen Republican members of the Interior and Insular Affairs Committee, which has jurisdiction over reclamation projects, were from the seventeen reclamation states.

The failure of the Reagan administration to propose cuts in a single reclamation project—including some of the most heavily subsidized, economically inefficient, low-priority government projects—during its first years in office while it was making decisive cuts in other programs it considered to be inefficient and wasteful was not lost on the critics of the president. The Bureau of Reclamation is a political sacred cow.

Bush and BuRec

When the Bush administration took office on January 20, 1989, President Reagan had proposed the fiscal year 1990 budget for the government and the Bureau of Reclamation. While the Bush administration proposed some amendments to the overall Reagan budget, changes to the bureau's budget were not among them.

From the fiscal year 1991 budget of Bush's second year, it was clear to the leaders of the Department of the Interior, the White House, and the OMB that a new set of priorities prevailed. The political milieu was vastly different than it had been a decade earlier. What had been an incestuous relationship between the BuRec and its superiors was now an adversarial one. The bureau stood firm and defended the status quo, forgoing the offensive position.

Political conditions had changed almost everywhere but at the Bureau of Reclamation. Its sister water development institution, the Army Corps of Engineers, which in the past had been the servant of narrow local interests, had broadened its base of support to meet the new situation in the areas outside the seventeen reclamation states where it prevailed. It accepted cost sharing, was sensitive to environmental concerns, and sought public support far beyond its previously limited group of clients, mainly local chambers of commerce and those seeking large government subsidies and largess.

But unlike the Army Engineers, in the face of new conditions the bureau retained its antediluvian positions. It did not reach out to environmentalists and broader community and regional interests but restricted its base to its traditional clients, the organized water users who benefited enormously from water subsidies. Against enormous public unpopularity, it also clung to its bias for big dams. The bureau resisted cost-sharing and the new limits (960 acres) on the amount of land that could receive heavily subsidized water. And its top echelons were still peopled (*manned* would actually be more correct, for few women were found at its upper rungs) with those from the ancien régime, who were adamant, ossified, and beholden to its historically narrow and determined base.

Meanwhile, two of the bureau's showcase projects, the Central Arizona Project (CAP) and the Central Utah Project (CUP), were in great trouble. Water from the Colorado River is divided between the Upper Colorado and the Lower Colorado River basins. The division point is at Lee's Ferry, Arizona, fifteen miles south of Glen Canyon Dam, where all the rafts and wooden dories enter the river for the two-week, two-hundred-mile journey through the Grand Canyon. CAP is a Lower Basin project, while CUP takes its water from the Upper Basin.

There are two problems. More Colorado River water is dedicated to the Upper and Lower basins than the average annual flow provides. There is constant friction between the two basins over who is to get what water. In addition, neither project is able to pay its way, even with the present massive subsidies.

CAP, the Carl Hayden project, was in serious financial difficulties. Built in a period of historic inflation, it suffered from a cost four times the original estimate, or a 300 percent overrun. Instead of a water cost of $15 an acre-foot, it came in at $60 to $70. The number of potential water users who had signed up for the project was 25 percent below the break-even point, even with large subsidies. The costs of operation and maintenance, let alone capital, could not be covered even at 75 percent of capacity. Even in Arizona, ground water could be pumped more cheaply. In addition to the cost of the water, potential users were also reluctant to enter into forty-year contracts when the limited amount of water was based on the seniority of the contract.

Instead of anticipating and facing these problems forthrightly, the dominant forces in the Bureau of Reclamation hoped to repeal recent reforms and to relieve prospective big water users of having to pay market rates for water to irrigate more than 960 acres. One proposal was to provide another retirement present, this time to Congressman Morris Udall (D.-Ariz.), who had championed CAP, by offering additional subsidized water to both the large cotton farms and to Indian tribes previously short-changed by the program.

CUP suffered from some of the same problems, especially those of cost, environment, and limited water from the Colorado River. Under contracts first authorized by the Upper Colorado River Project of 1956, some water costing several thousand dollars per acre would irrigate forage crops on high altitude land worth only $100 per acre.

One other factor was affecting the Bureau of Reclamation's long-time position: the change in personnel of key congressional committees. George Miller (D.-Calif.), a champion of the reclamation laws' original goal to protect the small farmers, would succeed Congressman Udall as chairman of the House Interior Committee. A powerful proponent of heavy water subsidies, especially for the giant corporate farms in his congressional district, was Tony Coelho (D.-Calif.), the Democratic whip and a member of both the Interior and Agricultural committees, who resigned his seat. In the Senate James McClure (R.-Idaho), the ranking Republican on both the Energy and Natural Resources Committee and the Interior Subcommittee of Appropriations, and a supporter of western water users, had announced his retirement. Senator Bill Bradley (D.-N.J.), who had a very different view of reclamation policy and represented citizens from a populous eastern state who help pay for the water subsidies for the arid western states, chaired the Water and Power Subcommittee of the Energy Committee.

In fiscal year 1991 the Bureau of Reclamation was in a defensive position against the forces of change. It was no longer omnipotent. It could and did stonewall, but it could no longer prevail as the champion of big dams and highly subsidized water for corporate users, nor could it with impunity flout the environmental requirements of the law. It lost the offensive. Neither the BuRec, nor its allies held the citadels of power any longer. This new situation was reflected in its budget request.

None of these budget decisions during three administrations over more than a decade was made on the basis of scientific or objective criteria. Instead, pressure groups, politics, and personal power ruled. The practices of both Republican and Democratic administrations indicate that nonpolitical budgets based on business practices of economy and efficiency are largely unknown outside the rhetoric of textbooks on scientific management and public administration.[26]

SOME PRINCIPLES OF EXECUTIVE BUDGET MAKING

PPBS, ZBB, cost-benefit analysis, and other techniques of scientific budget management are not applied for a variety of reasons.[27] Some systems are quite elaborate. One experiment with ZBB at the Department of Agriculture consumed 180,000 worker hours. PPBS was introduced by "whiz kids" insensitive to existing institutions and personnel. Top agency management felt threatened by the new quantitative tools. Trained personnel were lacking. Aaron Wildavsky has said that "no one knows how to do program budgeting"[28] and that "I have not been able to find a single example of the successful implementation of PPBS."[29] Both Wildavsky and Arthur Hammond concluded that ZBB was unworkable: "Some butterflies were caught, no elephants stopped."[30]

If budgets are not always made objectively by applying the principles of PPBS, ZBB, and cost-benefit analysis, how *are* they made? Is budget making an art or a science? Is it mechanistic or evolutionary? Woodrow Wilson's attack on Montesquieu's mechanistic views on the nature of government could well apply to the budget:

> The trouble with the theory [checks and balances] is that government is not a machine, but a living thing. It falls, not under the theory of the universe, but under the theory of organic life. It is accountable to Darwin, not to Newton. It is modified by its environment, necessitated by its tasks, shaped to its functions by the sheer pressure of life. No living thing can have its organs offset against each other as checks, and live. On the contrary, its life is dependent upon their quick cooperations, their ready response to the commands of instinct or intelligence, their amicable community of purpose.[31]

Rolling History   Each new budget is a function of the past. As President Reagan's first budget director, David Stockman, complained, "The budget is a sort of rolling history of decisions. All kinds of decisions, made five, ten, fifteen years ago, are coming back to bite us unexpectedly."[32] As Bayard Taylor has written:

> For every sentence uttered, a million are dumb:
> Men's lives are chains of chances, and History their sum.[33]

Relatively Uncontrollable   The decisions of the past have led to budgets that are "relatively uncontrollable." They are deemed "uncontrollable" when

> the program level is determined by existing statutes or by contracts of other obligations. Outlays for these programs generally depend on factors that are beyond administrative control under existing law at the start of the fiscal year. For example, the definition of beneficiaries eligible for programs like medicaid and civil service retirement is established by law [and usually can be altered only by a change in the law]. Prior year contracts and obligations are also legally binding.[34]

In recent fiscal years, about 75 percent of the budget has been officially considered to be "relatively uncontrollable." Of the remaining "relatively controllable" items, two-thirds are in the military budget, while only one-third can be found among civilian programs.[35]

Among the most important "relatively uncontrollable" programs are Social Security; military, civil service, and railroad retirement; veterans' benefits; Medicare and Medicaid; unemployment compensation; public assistance, assistance to students, and food and nutrition programs; interest on the national debt; farm price supports; and prior-year contracts. Payments for prior-year contracts for defense weapons, publicly assisted housing, and other civilian programs account for the remainder of the 75 percent of the budget, which is more or less paid out automatically in any particular year. But programs do not become "relatively uncontrollable" by accident. Powerful political forces had them enacted in such a way as to prevent review and to require payment without going through the formal two-step authorization and appropriation procedure.

Excluded from Review Certain outlays lie completely outside the purview of the OMB. Outlays for the Congress, the courts, and the Federal Reserve Board are among them, and rightly so, for the first two are independent, equal branches of the government and the third is the agent of the Congress. From time to time it is argued that the funds for the independent regulatory agencies should merely be transmitted to the Congress without executive department review on the grounds that they are creatures of the Congress and subject to specific statutory duties. How can they be independent, it is asserted, if the president controls their money? The deregulation of the Home Loan Bank and the refusal of the Reagan administration's OMB to provide funds for needed examiners were most important reasons for the savings and loan scandals.

No Control over Revenues A principle that affects budget making is the fact that the OMB has little effective control over revenues. This is a closely guarded prerogative of the treasury and the Internal Revenue Service and a function of the tax laws. Instead of the central budget office influencing the revenues, the revenues influence the limits of the central budget office's actions.

Politics of the Bureaucracy Further, the budget is influenced by the internal politics of the bureaucracy. Most agencies have a sense of mission. They believe in their programs and are proud of their achievements, limited in their self-criticism, and chauvinistic in their views. What knave or rogue among them would criticize the Marine Corps, the Space Agency, the Federal Bureau of Investigation (FBI), the National Science Foundation, or the Land Grant Colleges. Whistle-blowers in the Air Force or zealous inspectors general in any agency are not only scorned by their fellow workers but fired by presidents. There are built-in inducements to increase the programs, spend the money, and turn a blind eye to criticism. The self-esteem of the heads of agencies and departments is based in part on the size of their agencies or departments. The executive level position, the civil service grade, and promotions are based on how many people are supervised and how much money is in the given program. In addition, one of the facts of life in the bureaucracy is that it is extraordinarily difficult to fire anyone for inefficiency or incompetence. Further, as it is not the administrators' responsibility to meet the payrolls of their agencies, there is little inducement for them to limit their staffs. This promotes bigger staffs and bigger budgets, thus limiting a critical review.

A Community of Interests   A corollary of the situation described above is that the OMB, while the nay sayer of the bureaucracy, also serves the president and his administration. As Paul H. Douglas wrote in *Economy in the National Government:*

> the basic aim of the Bureau is the same as that of the administrative agencies, namely to see that administrative policies are carried out fully and adequately. . . . Recently there has been an interchange between the Bureau and other agencies. Why should a budget reviewer stick his neck out and make a cabinet member dislike him by being overly strict? After all that particular secretary may hold the key to his getting a better job in the agency he is reviewing.[36]

There is not only a conflict but a community of interests between the OMB and the agencies.

Implied Blackmail   A seldom publicized aspect of budgeting is implied blackmail. The late J. Edgar Hoover of the FBI would, when his agency budget was under review, visit key persons in the White House, at the OMB, and in the Congress to inform them that, while his files indicated that close associate "A" or "B" had a juvenile arrest record or an alleged homosexual affair or had been questioned about his income tax return, he, J. Edgar Hoover, was not about to make this public. The White House aide, the OMB director, or the House or Senate member with a vote on the Justice Department or FBI budget got the message—loud and clear: "Cut my budget, brother, and I'll leak the alleged, even dubious information." It was a clear form of political budget blackmail.[37] Another FBI ruse was to disconnect all the domestic wiretaps the day the FBI director testified before Congress for his budget funds so that he could testify under oath without fear of perjury that no domestic wiretaps existed. They were reinstalled within hours of his appearance.

Some Departments Are More Equal than Others   Another problem in budget making is the insufficient review of the "relatively controllable" budget items, two-thirds of which are for Pentagon programs. But the OMB has never assigned sufficient personnel to examine the military budget. Of the almost six hundred employees at the OMB, about seventy-five budget examiners are assigned to the National Security and International Affairs Group. They review the budgets for the Department of Defense, the Department of State, the Central Intelligence Agency (CIA), the Agency for International Development (AID), the Export-Import Bank, the International Communications Agency, and other defense and international agencies. Less than fifty examiners are assigned to the Defense Department. Thus 8 percent of the OMB personnel are assigned to examine 67 percent of the "relatively controllable" budget items.

Historically, the Defense Department has been treated differently than other agencies. Instead of calling its officials to the Executive Office Building to be examined by the OMB, the OMB examiners marched over to the Pentagon, where they shared the interrogation. Instead of acting as judges, they held a "joint review." Lyndon Johnson's budget director, Charles Zwick, testified before the Joint Economic Committee in early 1969 that "Defense is a big department. We obviously do not get into as great detail in that Department as we do in some other departments." Richard Nixon's budget director, Robert Mayo, testified that no more than fifty of the then five hundred budget professionals were assigned to review the Pentagon budget. As former Congressman William Moorhead said, "The Budget Bureau trembles before the Defense Department while all other agencies tremble before the Budget Bureau." It is a fact that OMB examiners treat the Pentagon budget with kid gloves.

There are massive opportunities for savings in the Defense Department. Some 89 percent of all defense contracts are negotiated rather than let under competitive bidding. Overruns on weapons systems, taking full account of inflation, are routinely double and triple their estimated costs. The causes of this are political, not scientific. There is a revolving door between the Pentagon and the military-industrial complex. Civilian secretaries, undersecretaries, and assistant secretaries at the Pentagon, under Republican and Democratic administrations alike, routinely move from executive positions in the top defense firms to the Pentagon and back to the defense firms. The one hundred largest defense contractors employ more than two thousand former military officers of the rank of colonel or navy captain and above. While there is no "conspiracy," there is a "community of interest" among these groups.

As William Greider wrote in "The Education of David Stockman," during the biggest peacetime military build-up in history (a doubling of the defense budget and a total expenditure of $1.4 trillion in five years):

> The only Cabinet Officer Stockman did not challenge was, of course, the Secretary of Defense. In the frantic preparation of the Reagan budget message . . . the OMB review officers did not give even their usual scrutiny to the new budget projections from Defense.[38]

Stockman's hope was that when things settled down a bit he could go back and analyze the defense budget more carefully:

> Hell, I think there's a kind of swamp of $10 to $20 to $30 billion worth of waste that can be ferreted out if you really push hard.[39]

But the best-laid plans of a budget director who believed that he could cut weak claims by strong clients were frustrated:

> Generally he did not lose his temper, but on a pleasant afternoon in early September, Stockman returned from a meeting at the White House in a terrible black mood. In his ornately appointed office at OMB, he slammed his papers down on the desk and waved away associates. At the Oval Office that afternoon, Stockman had lost the great argument he had been carefully preparing since February: there would be no major retrenchment in the defense budget. Over the summer Stockman had made converts one by one, in the Cabinet and among the President's senior advisers. But he could not convince the only hawk who mattered—Ronald Reagan. . . .
>
> Autumn was cruel to David Stockman's idea of how the world should work. The summer, when furious legislative trading was under way, had tattered his moral vision of government. Politics, in the dirty sense, had prevailed.[40]

In the United States there are both hawks and doves. But in this case of Pentagon spending it was not a choice between hawks and doves, for there are divisions among the hawks. There are those who believe in an adequate, efficient, lean and mean defense. There are also those who would give the Pentagon everything it asks for. It was a choice between fat hawks and lean hawks. The fat hawks won.

The reasons for a double standard for the Pentagon are legion. During World War II, the explanation of why almost all military recruits were routinely trained at southern bases was that the weather was moderate or warm, allowing year-round training. But the war was fought in northern Europe, where the climate from November through March was harsh. Decisive conflicts like the Battle of the Bulge were fought in the coldest winter weather. The real reason the training camps were in the South was that the Pentagon clients, the ranking members of the Armed Services Committee, were from the South—Virginia, South Carolina, Georgia, and Mississippi–along with a disproportionate share of the professional officers. Troops were trained in the South not in preparation for battles in warm climates but because the political power over the Pentagon budget resided there. This tradition continued in the postwar period. There were Representative Carl Vinson and Senator Richard Russell both Democrats from Georgia, Representative L. Mendel Rivers (D.-S.C.) and Senator Strom Thurmond (R.-S.C.), and Senator John Stennis (D.-Miss.). Rivers of Charleston, South Carolina, succeeded Vinson as chairman of the House Armed Services Committee. His ninth congressional district included Charleston, where the Ashley and Cooper rivers join to flow into the Atlantic. His district's military installations included the Charleston Air Force Base, the Charleston Army Depot, the Charleston Navy Shipyard, the Marine Corps Air Station at Beaufort, the Parris Island Marine Corps Recruit Depot, two naval hospitals (at Charleston and Beaufort), a naval station at Charleston, and the Naval Supply Center, the Naval Weapons Station, the Navy Fleet Ballistic Missile Submarine Training Center, and the Navy's Polaris Missile Facility at Charleston. It was said that Charleston was the place where the Ashley, Cooper, and Mendel rivers joined to form the Atlantic Ocean. Other wags claimed that if they added any more military bases, South Carolina would sink into the sea.

When Senator Stennis became chairman of the Senate Armed Services Committee, an "appreciation dinner" was held in Jackson, Mississippi. Flown down at taxpayers' expense to express their regard and esteem were the secretary of defense, the chairman and three members of the Joint Chiefs of Staff, the secretary of the navy, the head of NASA, the commander of U.S. forces in the Pacific, the commandant of the Coast Guard, and the "father" of nuclear submarines. All members of the Armed Services Committee were on the guest list. The military flew in the entertainment. The Air Force's Strolling Strings came in from Washington, and the Pensacola Naval Air Training Command Choir and the 14th Army Women's Army Corps Band from Fort McClellan, Alabama, provided the dinner music. In more recent times Senators Sam Nunn (D.-Ga.), John Warner (R.-Va.), Daniel Inouye (D.-Hawaii), and Ted Stevens (R.-Ala.), were the chairman and ranking minority members of the Senate Armed Services Committee and Defense Appropriations Subcommittee, respectively. All represented states especially favored with defense installations.

In the real world, there are few nonpolitical budgets based on economy and efficiency.

Pressures of Public Opinion   Another element of budget making is public opinion on and public pressures for a program. In the late 1940s and 1950s, spending for President Truman's "Point IV" foreign-aid program; for engineering, science, and mathematics after the Russians launched *Sputnik* and to meet the "Russian menace" or to fight the Cold War had strong public support. John F. Kennedy campaigned in 1960 against the "missile gap," which, although mythical, resulted in increased Pentagon spending. In the early 1980s, President Ronald Reagan argued for the MX missile on grounds that "a window of vulnerability" existed. At critical budget decision periods the Pentagon leaked intelligence reports exaggerating Russian military capability. This routinely occurred during the early December "appeal" periods for the Pentagon budget to the president and during the week of critical congressional debate on the Pentagon's authorization or appropriations. Insiders referred to it as the annual "The Russians Are Coming" intelligence report.

The War on Poverty and the "urban crisis" of the 1960s paved the way for massive budget increases and permanent entitlement programs. The "balance of payment crisis" has been used by the Export-Import Bank not only to get funds from both the president and Congress, but to get authority to lend them out at heavily subsidized, below-market rates. But economists dispute whether a small unfavorable balance of payments constitutes a crisis. When Britannia ruled the waves in the nineteenth century, she ran a perpetual unfavorable balance of payments. As no one kept the figures, there was no apparent crisis, and England's domestic economy and overseas empire prospered. Public pressures, real and manufactured, have more to do with whose budget is increased, whose programs get priority, and who gets the gravy than do all the PPBS and ZBB techniques put together.

Sacred Cows   There are also certain historic sacred cows—the untouchable budget items—that are insulated against effective budget slashes because of their political and economic clout. Among them, in addition to Social Security and the FBI, are the Veterans Administration, the Army Corps of Engineers, the National Institutes of Health (what budget examiner or foolhardy members of the Congress will propose to cut funds for cancer research or heart disease?), the Highway Trust Fund (it has both a fifty-state lobby and an insulated, automatic budget), and the Clinch River Breeder Reactor, a $3.2 billion boondoggle that survived several strong attacks because it was in the state of the Senate majority leader at the time.

The Unofficial Leak   In Washington there is also an art form entitled the "unofficial leak" that affects executive budget making. In the days and weeks before the president's budget is finally put to bed—from Thanksgiving to early January—the unofficial leak about proposed presidential or OMB cuts is to Washington what spring training is to baseball. Each affected agency arms its favorite Washington reporter with inside information. The leak has three purposes: (1) to go over the heads of the president and the budget directors and to arouse public opinion in general against the proposed action; (2) to alert the agency's and the program's clients and lobbyists to fight the cuts; and (3) to inform the agency's congressional supporters about the action before it is final. Here is a sampling of some real prebudget headlines: "New Budget Would Slash School Aid," "New Cuts Reported for Cities, Housing," and "Huge Cutback Proposed in Foreign Aid," each accomplished by an article giving the source as "a copy of the OMB proposal obtained by this newspaper." Notwithstanding the fact that foreign aid is the single most unpopular program in the country, the foreign-aid story asserted that the reduction "is drawing fire from Congressional critics and State Department officials who are fearful of losing control of foreign policy to budget cutters." The article alleged a strenuous fight by the secretary of state to restore the cuts and claimed that officials were meeting to map strategy to resist them.

Other leaks told the public that Secretary of Commerce "Baldridge Angrily Assails Stockman Budget Slash," that the "Task Force on the Arts and Humanities . . . will recommend [to the president] that the activities of the endowments continue without substantial alteration," and that "Proposed U.S. Space Budget Cuts" imperiled the "Study of Halley's Comet."

The head of the Bureau of Labor Statistics was delighted when, during an early December appearance before the Congress to reply to a friendly senator's planted question ("Were the proposed budget cuts impinging upon the Bureau's ability to perform a professional job?"), the commissioner of labor statistics unloaded a page of facts and figures before the unsurprised committee in an "I'm glad you asked that question" manner. The testimony ended with the disclaimer, "I, of course, am here to support the President's budget."[41]

In a hearing before the Senate Appropriations Subcommittee, which funds the Justice Department, Senator Ernest F. Hollings (D.-S.C.) reminded Attorney General William French Smith that he and FBI Director William Webster had supported the president's proposed 6 percent cut in the FBI budget the year before:

> Judge Webster [the FBI director] comes up here, and his eyes are saying "yes, yes, yes" and his mouth is saying, "no, no, no," Hollings said. Webster laughed, but did not comment. Smith later convinced the Office of Management and Budget to restore those cuts.[42]

As *The Washington Post* editorialized during one of the prebudget-release blitzkriegs:

> The outlines of the president's budget—due for unveiling next month—have begun to emerge as one department head after another leaks reports of the OMB's insistence on massive reductions in their respective budget. Some gamesmanship is surely involved in these performances. The Cabinet secretaries who are now protesting had already proposed large cuts on their own. OMB's grab for more allows the secretaries to gain some needed credibility with the special interest groups who normally support their departments.[43]

Optimistic Projections   Yet another tool or principle of OMB and presidential budget making is the use of optimistic economic projections. Economic growth is exaggerated. Inflation is underestimated. Unemployment estimates are below those of the private forecasters. Revenues are "enhanced." Spending cuts are overstated. The savings alleged from cutting fat, fraud, and waste are unprecedented. This is done regularly and routinely by every president and every budget director.

Perhaps the most shameful example of jiggering the figures occurred during the first months of the Reagan administration. Here's the story as told by William Greider in "The Education of David Stockman":

> An OMB computer, programmed as a model of the nation's economic behavior, was instructed to estimate the impact of Reagan's program on the federal budget. It predicted that if the new President went ahead with his

promised three-year tax reduction and his increase in defense spending, the Reagan Administration would be faced with a series of federal deficits without precedent in peacetime—ranging from $82 billion in 1982 to $116 billion in 1984.

Even Stockman blinked.

Stockman set about doing two things. First, he changed the OMB computer. Assisted by like-minded supply-side economists, the new team discarded orthodox premises of how the economy would behave. Instead of a continuing double-digit inflation, the new computer model assumed a swift decline in prices and interest rates. Instead of the continuing pattern of slow economic growth, the new model was based on a dramatic surge in the nation's productivity. . . .

But, second, Stockman used the appalling deficit projections as a valuable talking point in the policy discussions that were under way with the President and his principal advisers. . . .

How much pain was the new President willing to impose? How many sacred cows would be challenged at once? Stockman was still feeling out the commitment at the White House, aware that Reagan's philosophical commitment to shrinking the federal government would be weighed against political risks.[44]

THE POLITICS OF EXECUTIVE BUDGET MAKING

The president's budget is the "priorities document." While some minor shifts in priorities take place in the Congress, for all practical purposes much of the budget is set in concrete from the day it is released. With respect to conflicts with the Congress, the president has what Teddy Roosevelt called the "bully pulpit." He speaks with one voice. His most mundane pronouncements are reported as if written on stone tablets and brought down from Mount Sinai. Once released, it is "The President's budget." All loyal executive branch hands stand up and salute.

While there is the pretense of objectivity in its preparation, in fact there is very little. The great departments of government are not custodians of the public interest or guardians of citizenship like the security forces who guard the gold at Fort Knox. They are the advocates, solicitors, and barristers of the interest groups; the patrons of the powerful; the defenders, protectors, and champions of the clients of their departments. The Department of Agriculture is the partisan of organized agriculture. The Labor Department is not a judge or referee but the advocate of the unions. The Commerce and State departments fawn at the solicitations of their mighty clients, the national and international chambers of commerce, banks, and oil companies.

When the budgets of the great departments are put together and the decisions as to who will get the subsidies, privileges, licenses, grants, and loans are made deep in the bowels of the bureaucracy, there is no "judicial" public process in which a disinterested judge examines the evidence and then makes an objective decision. There is no public hearing when the amounts for sewers or housing subsidies or Energy Department grants are set. Neither Common Cause, the Consumers Federation, the Taxpayer's Union, nor John Q. Public sits at the counsel table.

Unless information is deliberately leaked, these functions are performed in secret. They are not "adversary" but ex parte "advocacy" proceedings. While phone calls, private luncheons, and informal consultations are held with the clients of the departments, public interest groups are kept in the dark. As Hubert Humphrey said:

> Whether there is a Democrat or Republican in the White House, the budget has remained more secret than the plans for an atomic bomb. . . . As the proposals move from the various departments and agencies through the Bureau of the Budget (the name changes, the function remains the same) to the President, it is a subliminal process.
>
> The press in Washington, which can expose almost everything that happens in our country, from the private life of a belly dancer to the secrets of the Central Intelligence Agency, seems deaf, blind, and dumb when it comes to the preparation of the budget.[45]

Unlike every city council, New England township government, or county board of supervisors, where budgets are made openly, the federal budget is made in private. According to Humphrey:

> Simply, the bureaucracy can be the enemy of what is proper and necessary in a federal system. This is not to malign the motives and public interest of civil servants so much as it is to question the nature of the institution that has developed.[46]

What if there were a public procedure with open decisions openly arrived at? Would not this too be dominated by the high-priced lawyers, the interested lobbies, the narrow advocates of the "selfish interest groups"? There is that danger, but steps could be taken to offset it.

First, through long-term appointments, strict civil service protections, and regular promotion, steps could be taken to insulate a cadre of budget officers and budget examiners to sit in public sessions to hear agency requests. To avoid incestuous relationships, rotation among departments should occur routinely.

Second, the Congress by law could require agencies to present to the budget officers certain vital information, such as cost-benefit analyses, the way in which the benefits are spread among various income groups (for example, does money appropriated for low-income farmers in fact go to them or to corporate farms?), the specific goals of each program, and alternative methods of reaching those goals. The foremost question to be asked is, "Is this program needed at all?" The next question is, "Where does it stand in the list of priorities?" The point is that scientific management should be given a chance to operate. The executive branch should be able to do this in a relatively simple and practical way without the excessive complexities of PPBS or the complexities and jargon ("decision units" and "decision packages") of ZBB.

Third, a public adversary proceeding could be established. Agency budget proposals should be examined through the critical testimony of nonpartisan, outside, disinterested parties. Businesses, universities, state and local governments, foundations, the Library of Congress, the General Accounting Office, and former public servants could provide the necessary criticism and evidence. The interest groups should be allowed to attend, but the proceedings should be kept between the agency advocates on the one hand and experts with no known conflicts of interest on the other.

Such a procedure could greatly enlighten and upgrade budget procedures. While the examiners' decisions might be discarded by the president, the information would be on the record, the public would be enlightened, and the Congress would be fortified. Most important, the debate would precede the decision rather than "sentence first, verdict afterwards," as the Red Queen said to Alice in *Alice's Adventures in Wonderland*.

NOTES

1. Hubert H. Humphrey, *The Education of a Public Man* (Garden City, N.Y.: Doubleday, 1976), p. 193.
2. Ibid.
3. James L. Sundquist, *The Decline and Resurgence of Congress* (Washington, D.C.: Brookings Institution, 1981), p. 39.
4. Louis Fisher, *Presidential Spending Power*, p. 9. Copyright © 1975 by Princeton University Press.
5. Ibid., p. 10.
6. *Statistical Appendix to Annual Report of the Secretary of the Treasury on the State of the Finances, FY 1979* (Washington, D.C.: U.S. Government Printing Office, 1980), pp. 6–7.
7. Jesse Burkhead, *Government Budgeting* (New York: John Wiley & Sons, 1956), p. 13.
8. Dwight Waldo, *The Administrative State* (New York: Ronald Press, 1948), pp. 32–33.
9. Burkhead, *Government Budgeting*, p. 26.
10. W. F. Willoughby, *The Problem of a National Budget* (New York: Appleton, 1918), pp. 39–40.
11. Joseph Cannon, "The National Budget," *Harper's Magazine*, October 1919.
12. Burkhead, *Government Budgeting*, pp. 28–29.
13. Charles G. Dawes, *The First Year of the Budget of the United States* (New York: Harper & Brothers, 1923), pp. 8–9.
14. Ibid. For a more intensive review of the factors that led to the Budget and Accounting Act of 1921, see Burkhead, *Government Budgeting*, esp. pp. 9–29; A. E. Buck, *Public Budgeting* (New York: Harper & Brothers, 1929); Frederick A. Cleveland and A. E. Buck, *The Budget and Responsible Government* (New York: MacMillan, 1920); Fisher, *Presidential Spending Power*, pp. 9–31; Henry Jones Ford, *The Cost of Our National Government* (New York: Columbia University Press,

1910); Judith H. Parris, *The Office of Management and Budget: Background, Responsibilities, Recent Issues* (Washington, D.C.: Congressional Research Service, Library of Congress, Report No. 78-158 Gov., 27 July 1978); Sundquist, *Decline and Resurgence*, chap. 3; Leonard D. White, *The Federalist* (New York: MacMillan, 1948); and Willoughby, *Problem of National Budget.*

15. Parris, *Office of Management and Budget*, p. 16.
16. Fisher, *Presidential Spending Power*, p. 155.
17. Parris, *Office of Management and Budget*, p. 26.
18. *Budget of the United States Government: Fiscal Year 1992* (Washington, D.C.: U.S. Government Printing Office, 1991), pt. Four-278.
19. Frederick C. Mosher, *Program Budgeting* (Chicago: Public Administration Service, 1954), pp. 48–49.
20. James P. Pfiffner, "Budgeting and the 'People's Reform'," *Public Administration Review*, March-April 1980, p. 196.
21. Comptroller General of the United States, *Terms Used in the Budgetary Process* (Washington, D.C.: General Accounting Office, 1977), p. 29.
22. Office of the Federal Register, National Archives and Records Service, General Services Administration, *The United States Government Manual 1983/84* (Washington, D.C.: U.S. Government Printing Office, 1983), p. 322.
23. *Los Angeles Times*, 16 July 1982, part I, p. 5. Copyright 1982, *Los Angeles Times*. Reprinted by permission.
24. Ibid.
25. Burkhead, *Government Budgeting*, 261.
26. This section is based on the author's detailed discussion with an Interior Department budget officer with personal knowledge of the facts.
27. See Pfiffner, "Budgeting," pp. 194–197.
28. Aaron Wildavsky, *The Politics of the Budgetary Process* (Boston: Little, Brown, 1979), p. 197.
29. Ibid., p. 196.
30. Quoted in Albert C. Hyde and Jay M. Shafritz, eds., *Government Budgeting* (Oak Park, Ill.: Moore Publishing Co., 1978), p. 244.
31. Woodrow Wilson, *Constitutional Government in the United States* (New York: Columbia University Press, 1917), p. 56.
32. Quoted in William Greider, "The Education of David Stockman," *Atlantic Monthly* 248 (December 1981): p. 51.
33. Bayard Taylor, "Napoleon at Gotha," *The Poetical Works of Bayard Taylor* (New York: AMA Press, 1970), stanza 1, p. 171.
34. *Fiscal Year 1987 Budget*, pt. 6a–29, 30.
35. *Fiscal Year 1990 Budget*, pt. 10–26, 27.
36. Paul H. Douglas, *Economy in the National Government* (Chicago: The University of Chicago Press, 1952), p. 64. © 1952 The University of Chicago Press.
37. The author has knowledge of such attempts by Hoover.
38. Greider, "Stockman," p. 35.
39. Ibid.
40. Ibid., p. 53.
41. Congressional Joint Economic Committee, "Hearings on November Employment Situation," 4 December 1981, transcript pp. 43–44.
42. "Justice Asks $130 Million for Drug War," *The Washington Post*, 10 December 1982, p. A10.
43. "The Coming Budget Showdown," *The Washington Post*, 10 December 1981, p. A30.
44. Greider, "Stockman," p. 32.
45. Humphrey, *Education*, pp. 192–193.
46. Ibid., p. 194.

3 _____

The Congress Disposes: The Budget, Legislative, Appropriations, and Tax-Writing Committees

_____

INTRODUCTION

There is as much action on Capitol Hill when the budget is received as there is when it is released by the president. Members of the House and Senate are briefed by their committee and personal staff in order to respond to both the facts and the politics of the document.

The legislative environment in which the budget is acted on is characterized by certain features. The Senate is an unrepresentative body in which the low populated states are supreme because Article I, Section 3, of the Constitution gives each state two senators regardless of size. Article V prevents that provision from being changed. In the House, as a result of the one-person, one-vote decisions of the Supreme Court, political power has shifted away from the rural areas, not so much to the big cities as to the suburbs. Members from the latter now often join with rural members to form working majorities, regardless of party. To fashion majorities in both houses of the Congress, spending has often been universalized to attract votes, and this has made it difficult to target budget funds to areas most in need.

Four types of committees deal with the budget. First, there are the budget committees, one in the House and one in the Senate. Both were established under the 1974 Budget Act.

Second, there are the legislative or authorizing committees, which are the permanent standing committees of the House and the Senate. Funds must first be authorized by a legislative committee and then appropriated by an appropriations committee. The legislative and tax-writing committees also provide funds through entitlements, which are funds (such as Social Security, Medicare, veterans' benefits, and interest on debt) that are paid if certain conditions are met by the recipient. Spending under entitlements is generally referred to as "relatively uncontrollable" spending. Unless the law authorizing them is changed, the funds go automatically to qualified recipients.

Third, there are the two appropriations committees of the House and Senate. They lost relative power to the budget committees under the 1974 Budget Act, but, as has so often happened, they have regained power in recent years.

Finally, there are the tax-writing committees, the oldest and often the most powerful of all. The House Ways and Means Committee and the Senate Finance Committee *originally* handled all three budget functions: taxing, spending, and credit.

The timetable for budget actions involves all of these committees from the moment the budget arrives at the Congress. The House and Senate budget committees set the overall figures, either at their discretion or in line with previous statutory or budget agreements. Under the rules of both houses, the legislative committees must pass the authority to spend before the appropriations committees can allocate the funds, although in practice the letter of the rule is not always followed. On their own initiative, at the president's request, or at the direction of the House or Senate under the reconciliation provisions of a budget resolution, the legislative, appropriations, and tax-writing committees may reduce or increase spending or revenues under their jurisdiction.

All of this is supposed to be accomplished between the first Monday in February, the last day for the president to submit the budget, and October 1, when the new fiscal year begins. Neither the president nor the Congress has been diligent in meeting these deadlines, often in part through the fault of the other party. In the past the government has often functioned after September 30 under one or several continuing resolutions (CR) until all the appropriations and tax bills were signed into law. This period has extended from a few hours or days up to ten weeks or more. In rare instances some agencies have run for a full fiscal year under a continuing resolution.

Under the Omnibus Budget and Reconciliation Act of 1990 and its Title 13, the Budget Enforcement Act of 1990, both budget procedures and their enforcement are vastly different from those that existed under the 1974 act and the 1985 Gramm-Rudman-Hollings amendments (see Chapter 10 for details). How the Congress and its committees function in this new budget environment is the subject of this chapter.

THE BUDGET GOES TO THE CONGRESS

The Congress receives the president's budget amidst a flurry of activity. When the budget is released members pore over it, digesting the figures that affect their personal, state, and legislative interests. Their personal staffs and committee experts spend hours writing summaries and memoranda. House and Senate members who chair the key committees get briefings from their staff experts. Before the end of the day the budget is released members of the House and Senate budget committees will have on their desks thick, mimeographed reviews from the Congressional Budget Office (CBO). Facts are set forth, criticisms are leveled, and highlights are outlined. Summaries of economic assumptions, budget aggregates, major rises or cuts in spending, tax changes, deficits, and the effect on the public debt of the president's proposals are ready so that members can sound informed and intelligent when asked to comment by their state or the national press. Partisan summaries prepared by the Democratic and Republican staffs of both the House and the Senate standing committees are also delivered to members to provide appropriate political ammunition.

The chairman and ranking member of each of the thirteen House and Senate appropriations subcommittees get not only verbal briefings but thick briefs from their staff experts on critical aspects of the budgets they oversee. The Republican and Democratic policy committees in each house send out voluminous reviews of the president's budget to all their members.

Before the ink of the president's signature is dry on budget release day, members of the House and Senate have in hand a list of the public works projects funded in their state or district, tables of weapons systems and research projects from the Defense Department's P- and R-books affecting local firms, and budget language and dollar figures for Veterans Administration or other public buildings proposed for their constituents. Lists of money or projects for housing, space tracking stations, harbor dredging, dairy payments, school milk and school lunch programs, impacted school aid, waterways, airports, hospitals, railroads, national parks, medical research, and dozens of other items will be on the desks of Senate and House members or their staffs, ready to be faxed or phoned to key local interest groups. The sheer accumulation of budget data and detail absorbs most budget watchers well into the first week of the budget's release. What does the budget mean for the country, the state, and the congressional district? How does it affect the farmers, businesses, mines, and factories at home? For what projects or programs can the member take credit? Is spending too high or too low? How will the totals affect interest rates, housing costs, and credit? What does the budget mean for national security, foreign trade, and the country's relations with the rest of the world? Most important, what does it mean for the Senate or House member's political survival, his or her reelection, and the political climate in which he or she will run? Is the member publicly defending the president's budget but privately moaning about its political weaknesses or regional inadequacies? Or is he or she publicly condemning the budget and its priorities while privately rejoicing about how much it will help his or her bid for reelection.

Reaction is swift, hearty, and partisan. There are few introverts in the House or Senate, and members, by nature more verbose and articulate than ordinary citizens, neither hesitate to react nor hide their opinions.

But the initiative still lies with the president. His budget and his views are the subjects of the lead paragraphs in the early budget stories. Congressional criticism trails as an afterthought at the end of the article. The president speaks with one voice, while the views of the critics are diffused in a cacophony of comment.

In the fight to have the budget approved, modern presidents take the initiative by making forays into friendly territory (the capitals of Indiana or Iowa for Republicans, and the conventions of the U.S. Conference of Mayors or the AFL-CIO for Democrats), where they flay the opposition and defend their budgets and priorities. In a speech before the Indiana legislature on the day after President Reagan fired his budget at Congress, he challenged his national opponents to "put up or shut up." Earlier in the day, in a speech in Des Moines to a joint session of the Iowa legislature, he threw down the gauntlet and said:

> The budget we have proposed is a line drawn in the dirt. Those who are concerned about the deficits will cross it and work with us on our proposals or their alternatives. Those who are not . . . will stay on the other side and simply continue their theatrics.[1]

The president and his administration retain the early advantage even as Congress begins the public review of the budget proposals. Within the first week, the president's secretary of the Treasury, budget director, and chairman of the Council of Economic Advisers appear before House and Senate appropriations and budget committees, the tax-writing committees, and the Joint Economic Committee. The secretary of defense and the joint chiefs of staff testify before the armed services committees and deliver their posture statements. Every astute member of Congress knows that the prepared testimony of the cabinet officer is reported by the press while the congressional questioner is largely ignored, and that the cameras focus on the administration witness, not the legislative interrogator. Friendly House and Senate leaders may be pictured leaving the White House or welcoming the budget director to their committees, but the momentum lies with the president and his team, who speak in harmonious tones against the discord and babble of several hundred disparate voices on the Hill. Just as Hernando Cortez conquered Mexico with a few hundred disciplined soldiers who subjugated thousands of scattered defenders, so a forceful and determined president backed by his cabinet press secretaries and defended by his congressional partisans can overwhelm the Congress in its confused, disordered, and chaotic state.

THE LEGISLATIVE ENVIRONMENT

What are the legislative conditions and circumstances in which the Congress reviews and passes the president's budget? The Congress finds it exceedingly difficult to target limited funds to areas where a problem or need exists. If unemployment is exceptionally high in Detroit or the central cities of the industrialized East, there is almost no way to fashion a program to direct funds there. Similarly, funds in programs to aid regions of chronic depression, such as the northern parts of Maine, Wisconsin, and Michigan, most of West Virginia, the Ozarks, and southern Illinois, are diffused. Because by political necessity coverage must be extended to garner a majority of votes for passage, areas covering 80 percent or more of the country become eligible for the limited amounts of money. Funds for highways, railways, farm subsidies, science education, and law enforcement are universalized, so that often the money goes out by formula to make sure an appropriate amount goes to each state or area, regardless of need. In programs without such formulas, politically astute agency heads take care to ensure equitable regional disbursement. The maldistribution of funds through either excessive diffusion or allotment of disproportionate benefits to limited regions is the result of at least two fundamental conditions.

The first is the effect of Article I, Section 3, of the Constitution, which states that "The Senate of the United States shall be composed of two Senators from each State, elected by the people thereof, for six years and each Senator shall have one vote." While the original provision of this section calling for the selection of senators by state legislatures was changed by the Seventeenth Amendment in 1913, the stipulation calling for two senators, each with one vote, is riveted into the Constitution. Article V, the amending article, provides that "no State without its consent, shall be deprived of its equal suffrage in the Senate." As no small state, and certainly not all of the fifty states, would consent to a change to representation on the basis of population, this provision cannot be changed or amended.[2]

What this means is that after the Supreme Court decisions in *Baker v. Carr* (1962)[3] and *Reynolds v. Sims* (1964)[4] providing for "one person, one vote" in elections to city, county, and state legislative bodies as well as to the House of Representatives, the Senate of the United States remains the only legislative body in the country where equal representation does not now apply. The malapportioned Senate could be called a constitutional gerrymander. To understand the Senate one must understand this constitutional fact. The smallest seventeen states, with thirty-four senators—one-third plus one—have only 7 percent of the population. The largest seventeen states, with thirty-four senators, have 70 percent of the population, which gives a ratio of ten to one. The Senate is the small states' Mecca. This fact dominates its affairs, procedures, politics, and budgeting. It has led to coalitions between the South and the mountain states of the West, to an upside-down distribution of funds on a per capita basis, to a situation in which citizens of the most populous states pay a disproportionate share of the taxes and receive an equally unfair share of the benefits, and to the name "tin cup states" for those with tiny populations who receive generous funding. Alaska, New Mexico, Hawaii, and Nevada rank first, second, third, and eighth, respectively, in the per capita federal funds their citizens receive. With respect to population, Alaska ranks forty-ninth, and New Mexico, Hawaii, and Nevada rank thirty-seventh, fortieth, and thirty-ninth, respectively. On the other hand, Ohio, Michigan, New Jersey, Illinois, and Pennsylvania, all among the ten biggest states in population, rank from thirty-fifth to forty-eighth in the per capita federal funds their citizens receive.

In the Senate the populous industrialized states have been held hostage by the small, arid, mountain or rural states. Bills concerning taxes, subsidies, and programs favorable to the large states or central cities are defeated by Senate votes of sixty to forty, when the forty votes represent 65 percent of the people and the sixty votes only 35 percent of the people. Article I, Section 3, was the price the country paid for the Union, and while it is universally accepted, it still extracts a heavy payment from the many for the benefit of the few.

In the House, a different situation exists. There a fundamental reason for the diffusion of funds is the outgrowth of the two famous Supreme Court decisions providing equal representation. In *Baker v. Carr*, the Court determined that apportionment was not merely a political issue but one that the courts could decide. Until then members of the gerrymandered states legislatures refused to reapportion according to population and hence vote themselves out of a job. In California, for example, some of the sparsely populated mountain counties had as many state senators as did Los Angeles. The state legislatures in turn drew up gerrymandered congressional seats that favored rural and conservative areas. The second case, *Reynolds v. Sims*, provided that people rather than trees or acres or cows should be represented in popularly elected legislatures.

But *Baker v. Carr* and *Reynolds v. Sims* did not shift power in the House of Representatives from rural to city areas, for there was a simultaneous migration of mostly blacks from poor, rural southern areas to the central cities. This was accompanied by a vast surge of mostly white citizens from the cities to the suburbs. Because of these migrations and reapportionment, political power shifted from rural areas to middle-class suburbs. In the House, the combination of rural and suburban members and those who vote with them can generally defeat the targeting of funds to urban pockets of distress. It was this coalition that allowed President Reagan to pass unprecedented budget and tax cuts in his first year, even though the Democrats ostensibly controlled the House.

A different example is provided by the coalition needed to pass the so-called depressed areas bill in the House. The Senate bill originally targeted the funds to limited regions of special need. But to find enough votes to pass it in the House, the program had to be expanded to cover not only the pockets of poverty in West Virginia, northern Wisconsin, eastern Kentucky, northern Maine, and southern Illinois, but also all the poor rural counties of the South and West, or over half the country. Since then coverage under the program, administered by the Economic Development Administration, has been expanded and once included 80 percent of the counties of the country.

One further situation affects the House of Representatives. The movement of population, as reported by the 1990 census, from the Northeast and Midwest to the South, Southwest, and West, has changed the composition of that body. With a net shift of 16 House seats from the Northeast and Midwest to the South, Southwest, and West, the latter states now have a majority of the 435 seats. California, with 52 seats (a gain of 7), has 12 percent of the total. Its votes can provide almost a quarter (23.8%) of those needed to pass legislation in the House.

The dominance of the small states in the Senate, the rural-suburban coalition in the House, and the movement of population to the South, Southwest, and West create the fundamental political atmosphere in which the budget is considered.

THE BUDGET TIMETABLE

Since the five-year budget agreement was reached in 1990, the Congress and its committees have acted under the budget timetable that is shown in Table 3–1 and examined below.

THE BUDGET COMMITTEES

The CBO Report

Under the budget acts and the Rules of the House and Senate, the two budget committees have specific duties. The budget is referred to them, as it is referred to every committee that must act on any portion of it.

The first and principle duty of the two committees is to prepare the Concurrent Resolution on the Budget and submit it to the House and Senate. They do this by gathering information and holding hearings. By February 15 the Congressional Budget Office provides them with its report on the president's budget. In particular the CBO will evaluate the economic estimates on which the spending, revenues, deficit, and public debt figures in the budget are based. Historically, the president's estimates are optimistic, and the CBO's figures have been more accurate. The CBO has a reputation for giving disinterested and objective figures to the committees, whereas the Office of Management and Budget (OMB), under every president, has provided more or less rosy estimates.

TABLE 3–1 Congressional Budget Timetable

Timing	Action to Be Completed
5 days before budget release	CBO's sequester preview report
1st Monday in February	Deadline for president to submit budget and revise GRH targets and caps
February 15	CBO's annual report to budget committees
Within 6 weeks of budget release	Standing committees submit views and estimates to budget committees
April 1	Budget committees report budget resolution
April 15	Congress completes budget resolution. If not, chairman of House Budget Committee files 302(a) allocations;[1] House Ways and Means Committee is free to proceed with pay-as-you-go allocations[2]
May 15	Appropriations bills may be considered in House
June 10	House Appropriations Committee reports last bill
End of previous session to June 30	If an appropriation bill violates caps, OMB sequesters 15 days after enactment
June 30	House completes action on annual appropriations bills
July 15	President submits midsession review
August 10	President's notification on military personnel exemption
August 15	CBO's sequester update report
August 20	OMB's sequester update report (with adjustments to caps and GRH targets)
October 1	Fiscal year begins
10 days after end of session	CBO's final sequester report
15 days after end of session	OMB's final sequester report (with adjustments to caps and GRH targets)
30 days after end of session	General Accounting Office's compliance report

Source: Senate Budget Committee
1. Budget Act. Overall allocations of outlays, budget authority entitlements, and credit among House committees.
2. Legislation providing the offset (the pay) to be reported before legislation providing new entitlement spending (the go) could be reported.

Hearings

Hearings begin in the budget committees even before the president submits the budget. The committees will hear from the director of the CBO, who provides some or much of the information to be submitted in the February 15 report. They will also hear from the chairman of the Federal Reserve Board, who will discuss the general economic situation with special regard to money, credit, and interest rates.

Once the budget is submitted, the committees will hear from the director of the OMB, the secretaries of the Treasury and defense and sometimes the secretary of state, and the chairman of the joint chiefs of staff, plus whichever other officials they feel should provide information. The House and Senate alternate from year to year as to which committee hears which witness first.

The Budget Resolution

The primary job of the budget committees is to prepare the budget resolution, which is in fact the congressional budget. It is a concurrent resolution, which means that it affects only Congress. If it changed any law or affected the president or any executive branch agency, it would have to be in the form of a joint resolution or an act, which under Article I, Section 7, of the Constitution, must be signed by the president. Instead the concurrent resolution is a plan or a directive, jointly agreed to by the House and the Senate, that is to be followed by both chambers (for an example, see Appendix B).

The concurrent budget resolution has three functions. First, it tells both houses and their committees the *overall* recommended or appropriate levels for the following six items for five years:

Revenues
New budget authority (BA)
Outlays (O)
The deficit
The national debt
Federal credit activities

Second, the resolution allocates the overall figures for budget authority (BA), outlays (O), and credit to twenty "functions," including national defense, international affairs, science, energy, environment, and agriculture. Note that these allocations are made by function and not by agency or department, even though the appropriations committees will appropriate by agency or department. These functions have numbers. Defense is 050, natural resources and environment is 300, and health is 550. They are often referred to by their numbers instead of their names.

Third, the concurrent resolution includes reconciliation instructions directing specific House and Senate committees to report legislation that changes existing laws to cut spending or increase revenues by specific amounts in order to meet the overall revenue and deficit figures for the fiscal year (see Appendix B, "Reconciliation," for specific examples of reconciliation instructions for House and Senate committees).

Within six weeks after the president submits the budget, the committees with legislative functions submit to the budget committees their estimates of the amount of revenues, new budget authority, outlays, and credit within their jurisdiction. These Budget Act Section 301 (d) estimates are especially intended to give the budget committees information on costs of new programs or authorizations that may pass in the coming year. Historically, however, these estimates have been of little practical value, for they have been routinely exaggerated and arrive too late to affect the budget resolution figures in any major way.

Floor Action

The Budget Act calls for the budget committees to report the budget resolution to the House and Senate by April 1 and to complete action by April 15, an illusory annual goal. In a very good year the resolution may be reported by April 15 and action completed in a month.

Depending upon the amount of contention surrounding the budget and the relationship between the president and the Congress, the resolution may be either passed quickly or subjected to extensive debate. Once the resolution reaches the floor, action in the House is much faster than in the Senate because of the difference in their rules.

The Conference Committee

When each house has passed a budget resolution, the two resolutions go to a Joint Conference Committee that compromises the differences. This committee is the "third house of Congress" about which little is known, little has been published, and much of what has been published is of limited value.[5] Most academic studies are a "bean counters" festival. The number of amendments won or lost by each house has simply been tabulated, with little understanding that if the Senate prevails on a major issue it may have given in to the House on twenty-five minor provisions. Neither the House nor the Senate is the routine victor in the conference committee on the budget resolution.

After the committee's conference report is adopted by both houses, they must abide by the provisions of the budget resolution.

Waivers and Points of Order

The authority of the budget resolution is enforced through a series of House and Senate rules and amendments to the Budget Act by which, in general, points of order may be made against legislation that would breach the spending limits of the resolution or add extraneous matter (riders) to a reconciliation bill. Waivers from the budget committees are required for the House or Senate to consider legislation making any changes in budget authority, outlays, revenues, credit, or the debt limit until the budget resolution is passed. In general 60 percent of those present and voting are needed to override points of order or to provide a waiver in the absence of budget committee approval.

Under the discretionary spending ceilings and the pay-as-you-go provisions of the five-year 1990 budget agreement (see Chapter 10), the budget committees will function as the major enforcement mechanism for the Congress. After the budget resolution is passed, much of the committees' time is spent in exercising these watchdog functions.

Reconciliation

In the last two months of the fiscal year, much of the budget committees' time is also taken up in overseeing and passing the reconciliation bill that contains the changes in the laws provided by the legislative committees under the reconciliation provisions of the budget resolution. These changes, which are necessary to provide new revenues or to cut spending to bring the overall figures of the resolution into balance, are among the most contentious political issues dealt with by Congress. Raising taxes, cutting spending, and reducing entitlements are difficult matters to deal with at any time, but especially just prior to the new fiscal year or under a continuing resolution after the new fiscal year begins, which is often just before an election. It is perhaps the most difficult function the budget committees perform.

The Nature of the Budget Committees

On the whole, the budget committees have been a success. Both are permanent standing committees of their respective houses. The ratio of majority to minority members in each reflects that in the House and Senate as a whole. But in other ways they have been quite different from each other.

Once appointed, members of the Senate Budget Committee are permanent and rise by seniority. This makes the assignment reasonably attractive, although the committee is not considered one of the five or six most important in the Senate. In the House membership on the Budget Committee is temporary. Members may serve for only three out of five consecutive terms, or for six out of ten years. At the end of six years they must leave the committee unless they have been elected chairman in their fifth or sixth year, in which case they may stay on as chairman for two more years. At the beginning of the One-Hundred-Second Congress in 1991, a rules change was made at the request of Minority Leader Robert H. Michel (R.-Ill.) to allow Willis D. Gradison, Jr. (R.-Ohio), to remain on the committee into his fourth term, as he had just qualified as the ranking minority member. A member who has served for only a partial term is eligible to remain for a full third term. Leon Panetta (D.-Calif.) was a member for six years, was off the committee for four years, and then returned as chairman in the One-Hundred-First Congress in 1989. In addition, the Ways and Means Committee and the Appropriations Committee are each given five positions on the House Budget Committee, divided into three seats for the majority and two seats for the minority, and the Rules Committee gets a minimum of one seat. The majority leader of the House serves on the committee for as long as he holds the position, notwithstanding the six-year rule. Almost one-third of the total seats are thus accounted for by these designated members.

The Senate Budget Committee has no subcommittees. It is argued that since the committee is established to deal with overall budget problems, it should not establish subcommittees dealing with specific subjects that might attract members hoping to promote the parochial interests of their states. The House Budget Committee, however, has established six task forces that are virtually indistinguishable from subcommittees; some of them—Defense, Foreign Policy, and Space; Community Development and Natural Resources; and Human Resources—might indeed attract members with related interests in their districts.

In the early days of their existence, especially during the Reagan "budget revolution," membership on the budget committees was very attractive, and they were the centers of action and publicity. Recently, membership has become less attractive. In periods of tight or no-win budgets, members who are inclined to say "yes" to as many people as possible, both constituents and fellow members, have become the nay sayers of the Congress. Further, during years of budget summits negotiated by the president, his chief of staff, and his budget director on the one hand and the leaders of Congress and the chairman and ranking members of the budget committees on the other, there is very little but perfunctory work for the remaining members. Finally, under the 1990 five-year budget agreement, the budget committees may have very little to do. The president has the authority to determine the overall deficit, which by its nature is a moving, flexible target. The limits or caps on discretionary spending are established by law. Taxes, direct spending (entitlements and other relatively uncontrollable outlays), and the pay-as-you-go provisions can only be changed under legislation that offsets an increase in spending or a decrease in taxes by an equal spending cut or tax increase. Thus budget policy for the five years is largely set by law, leaving very little discretion to the budget committees.

The House Budget Committee has been highly partisan. In the Senate, especially before 1981 and from 1983 to 1989, it has been collegial, partly because of the type of people who led the committee but also partly by intent. The former staff director of the Senate Budget Committee, John T. McEvoy, attributed its style to the personalities and experience of its first two leaders:

> In [Senators Edmund S.] Muskie and [Henry] Bellmon, we have two former governors of the minority party in their own states, who dealt with legislatures, overwhelmingly of the other party. They both had to learn how to come to agreement with people whose views they did not accept, or they would have had no programs.[6]

Muskie had been a Democratic governor of the Republican state of Maine, and Bellmon had been the Republican governor of the Democratic state of Oklahoma. They would agree to a budget resolution and then stand toe to toe on the Senate floor to beat off both liberal and conservative members whose amendments would destroy their consensus.

This tradition, with some exceptions, was carried out by Muskie's and Bellmon's immediate successors, Pete V. Domenici (R.-N.Mex.), who became chairman in 1981, and Lawton Chiles (D.-Fla.), who succeeded Domenici in January 1987. In recent years, and especially during the budget summit negotiations of 1990, the Senate Budget Committee, under Democratic Chairman James R. Sasser of Tennessee and Domenici has been more partisan than in the past, but still far less partisan than the House Budget Committee. The early harmony was ruptured in 1981–1982, after Muskie and Bellmon had left the Senate, not so much by the personalities than by the determination of the White House to force through its fiscal programs and the Republican Party discipline that accompanied it.

The House Budget Committee has been more divided and partisan in part because the Republicans have essentially refused to take a constructive role in the process. As McEvoy wrote:

> Delbert Latta (R.-Ohio), the ranking member of the House committee is a man well known—and this is not a criticism of him—as a political gut fighter in the House. There is no reason to believe that it was an accidental choice when he was put on the House Budget Committee.[7]

THE LEGISLATIVE OR AUTHORIZING COMMITTEES

The legislative or authorizing committees, which are also known as the standing or permanent committees of the Congress, have two tasks with respect to the budget: They authorize spending, and they appropriate funds. Starting in the House in 1837 and in the Senate in 1850, money was appropriated under a two-step procedure. First, the Congress had to pass a bill, signed into law, to authorize a program and its funding. Second, it had to pass a bill, signed into law, to provide the actual money.

In the early Congresses there were no standing or permanent committees. The House functioned in the tradition of the British Parliament by working in the Committee of the Whole. Legislation was debated and issues were decided by the whole House. Then an ad hoc committee was appointed to write into legislation what the House had decided. When the ad hoc, or drafting, committee finished its work, it was dismissed. In the Third Congress there were about 350 such committees.[8]

The Senate, with only twenty-six original members, needed no standing committees, for the entire body was smaller than many present-day committees. As it grew, it too appointed ad hoc committees to draft legislation.

Finally, in about 1816 in the Senate and somewhat later in the House, except for the Ways and Means Committee that had an earlier creation, standing or permanent legislative committees with jurisdiction over specific subjects were appointed. Members became experts in the subject matter of their committees although membership was nothing like as permanent as it is today and changed dramatically from Congress to Congress. In addition, the system of seniority had not developed in any serious way.

Today there are twenty-two standing committees in the House and sixteen in the Senate. They might also be called the legislative committees, as the remaining select or special committees of both bodies generally do not have legislative authority. Woodrow Wilson, in his book *Congressional Government*, written in 1885, referred to congressional committees as "little legislatures," and wrote that "it is not far from the truth to say that Congress in session is Congress on public exhibition whilst Congress in its committee-rooms is Congress at work."[9]

Some committees are more equal, or more important, than others. The tax-writing committees and appropriations committees in both Houses have historically been among the most powerful and most sought-after assignments. The Armed Services Committees in both houses, the Senate Foreign Relations Committee, and the House Rules Committee are also among the most powerful or desirable.

Some committees attract the power-oriented member, some the issue-oriented member, and others the reelection-oriented member, or those with a combination of interests and motives. Members from farm states flock to the agriculture committees; those with major military installations to the armed services committees; big city members to the banking committees, which handle housing; the Senate Labor and Human Resources Committee, and the House Education and Labor Committee; western members to the House Interior Committee and the Senate Energy and Natural Resources Committee, with their jurisdiction over water, minerals, and public lands. Those senators with presidential ambitions seek seats on the Foreign Relations Committee to develop their expertise in this area. Thus committee membership can satisfy members' interest in exercising power over their colleagues, over issues and policy, over their chances for reelection or bringing home the bacon to their district or state. Many committees are dominated by members with parochial and personal as well as national interests. Nonetheless, they are essential for dealing with the vast subject matter of legislation, for without specialization virtually nothing could get done.

One must distinguish between authorizing funds and appropriating funds. Very simply, the standing or legislative committees *authorize* spending for an agency or program and set the maximum amount, whereas the Appropriations Committees *appropriate* the funds, up to the total authorized. This is the general rule, but the appropriations committees are also legislative committees and thus can and do authorize spending; likewise, the legislative committees can and do provide spending through legislation that either by-passes the appropriations committees or leaves them with little but a perfunctory role. Here, however, we are concerned with distinguishing between the authorizing and appropriating committees in general.

The armed services committees, for example, authorize a new weapons system, a research and development program, and the total number, the number per service, and the pay and allowances of military personnel. The interior and public works committees authorize water projects. The foreign relations and foreign affairs committees authorize foreign aid. The agriculture committees authorize farm programs. There have been years in which the authorizing bills for housing, clean air, and space, to name a few, have not been passed although the funds have been appropriated by the appropriations committees.

The legislative committees not only authorize spending but also borrowing and contract authority. However, in almost all cases borrowing and contract authority must be approved by the appropriations committees before the funds are borrowed or the contracts let. In addition, legislation also authorizes an agency or department and gives it certain functions. Authorizations may be for a year only (military pay), for several years (a weapons system), or permanent (interest on the debt). The dollar amounts may be either specific (definite authority) or "such sums as may be necessary" (indefinite authority).

In addition, the authorizing committees provide for entitlements, such as Social Security, Medicare, veterans disability, and military and civilian pensions. Essentially, under these programs an individual who meets specific requirements (for example, having reached age 65, paid Social Security taxes for more than 10 years, or sustained a service-connected disability) is entitled to certain benefits. Neither the OMB nor the appropriation committees have any effective jurisdiction over the amount of money paid out in entitlements, although money for entitlements is found in the budget and in appropriations bills. In most cases, however, only legislation from one of the standing committees can change the amounts to be spent. The major function of the OMB and the appropriations committees with respect to entitlements is merely to add up the costs and approve them.

Because of entitlements, previous contracts, interest on the debt, and other mandatory payments, the amount of "discretionary" spending, or spending that the appropriations committees have real authority to change, makes up only slightly more than 40 percent of the president's budget request.

The legislative committees have therefore authorized, by one device or another, all the funds appropriated by the appropriations committees as well as the larger amount of funds that are spent outside the appropriations committees' primary jurisdiction through entitlements and other budget devices. Thus the power over the budget wielded by committees other than the Appropriations Committee is very great indeed.

THE APPROPRIATIONS COMMITTEES

Duties and Functions

The appropriations committees have five main duties. Their first business, when the president's budget arrives, is to examine the "discretionary spending" ceilings (also called caps, or allocations) for both budget authority (BA) and outlays (O) imposed by the 1990 budget agreement (see Table 10–11). While the ceilings for defense, international, and domestic appropriations are set by law for fiscal years 1991, 1992, and 1993 and for these combined categories for fiscal years 1994 and 1995, the caps may be modified by the OMB when the president's budget is released. This can happen because of changes in concepts and definitions, inflation, and, in fiscal years 1993 and 1994, credit reforms. The committees may not appropriate more than the ceiling amounts, which define their work for the year.

Second, the chairmen of the appropriations committees make their Section 302(b) Budget Act allocations. They divide among their subcommittees the total allocation of outlays, new budget authority, and new credit authority made to the appropriations committees by Section 302(a) of the budget resolution. The chairmen further allocate these amounts between "discretionary," or controllable, amounts and all other amounts. This promotes a major struggle between the chairmen and the subcommittee chairmen and among the subcommittees themselves. How much of the total each subcommittee receives, and which win and which lose in this allocation, define the subcommittees' work for the year.

Third, the job of producing and passing into law the thirteen regular appropriations bills for the new fiscal year as well as any supplemental bills for the existing fiscal year begins in each house. Hearings will be held by each of the thirteen subcommittees. Mark-ups by both the subcommittees and the full committees will be held. Floor action will be taken, but the Senate subcommittees will wait for their companion House bill to pass the House before floor action is taken in the Senate. After a conference committee between the two houses is held and the conference report is passed by both houses, the bill will be sent to the president for his signature.

Fourth, if any bill fails to pass before the beginning of the new fiscal year on October 1, the appropriations committees will act on a continuing resolution, which is a temporary appropriations bill, until the regular bill is passed and signed into law. There may be a series of continuing resolutions if deadlines cannot be met. In some years some agencies, especially those dealing with foreign aid or health and human services, have been run for an entire fiscal year under a continuing resolution.

Finally, the appropriations committees oversee the agencies and programs under their jurisdiction. The committees' hearings and the investigations and reports of the General Accounting Office are the most effective means by which this major function is carried out.

A Short History

Not until the Civil War period did appropriations committees exist. The Ways and Means Committee in the House (from 1789) and the Finance Committee in the Senate (from 1816) handled both taxes and spending. Further, separate "expenditure committees" were established from time to time to fund the major departments: the Army, Navy, State, Treasury, and Post Office.[10]

The power to appropriate is found in Article I, Section 9, of the Constitution:

> No money shall be drawn from the Treasury, but in Consequence of Appropriations made by Law; and a regular Statement and Account of the Receipts and Expenditures of all public Money shall be published from time to time.

During the first two Congresses, appropriations were made in a single bill. The very first bill, in 1789, appropriated $639,000. It provided $216,000 for the civil list, $137,000 for the Department of War, a sum not to exceed $190,000 for the Treasury to discharge the warrants that the late Board of Treasury had issued, and $96,000 for pension for invalids.[11]

By 1837 in the House and 1850 in the Senate, the rules provided for a two-step appropriations procedure that still exists, although its provisions are often avoided or evaded. The Senate rule then read:

> No amendment proposing additional appropriations shall be received . . . unless it be made to carry out the provisions of some existing law, some act or resolution previously passed by the Senate during that session, or moved by a standing committee . . . or in pursuance of an estimate from the head of some of the departments; and no amendment shall be received whose object is to provide for a private claim, unless it be made to carry out the provisions of an existing law or a treaty stipulation.[12]

Points of order may be made against amendments to add funds where there is no authorizing legislation.

From their origin until the present day, the power of the appropriations committees has ebbed and flowed in relation to both other committees and the executive branch. There have been conflicts with the president over his power to transfer funds from one object to another, to use unexpended balances passed for one purpose or another, to carry funds forward from year to year, to limit the ability of departments to spend more than they receive, and to enter into contracts in excess of appropriations.

Conflicts occurred in both houses between the appropriations and the legislative committees. Both the legislative committees and the departments in the executive branch chafed under appropriations committees' restrictions on their freedom to spend. By 1885 all but six of the fourteen regular spending bills in the House were removed from the Appropriation Committee's jurisdiction. In 1899 the Senate clipped the wings of its Appropriations Committee in almost precisely the same way. Under a resolution called up by Republican Senator Nelson Aldrich of Rhode Island:

> the rivers and harbors bill continued to be referred to the Committee on Commerce, and the bills on agriculture, the Army, the Military Academy, Indians, the Navy, pensions, and the Post Office went to the appropriate legislative committees. This left the Committee on Appropriations with six appropriations areas. . . : Deficiency, Diplomatic and Consular, District of Columbia, Fortifications, Legislative, and Sundry Civil.[13]

For the next thirty-five years in the House and twenty-three years in the Senate, the power to appropriate was exercised by at least nine committees.

The event surrounding the passage of the Budget and Accounting Act of 1921 once again consolidated the power of the appropriations committees over most funding. In 1920 in the House and 1922 in the Senate, the rules again required that "all general appropriations bills shall be referred to the Committee on Appropriations."[14] To make this loss of power over the purse palatable to the legislative overlords, the Senate provided that three ex officio members from each legislative committee could both sit with and vote with the Appropriations Committee when funds for agencies under their jurisdiction were before it. This practice lasted until 1977 in the Senate.[15]

The privilege of ex officio members applied, however, only to the six legislative committees that lost power to the appropriations subcommittees created in 1922, plus the space and atomic energy committees. The other eight Senate standing committees created since then remained poor cousins. The practice made some senators more equal than others. It favored, both by accident and by design, the "pork barrel" agencies over the social agencies. There were three extra votes for public works, the Pentagon, and space extravaganzas, but not for housing, health, and mass transit. This favored the power-oriented senators over the issue-oriented senators, enhanced the power of the Senate patriarchs, reinforced the seniority system, and provided an unearned increment to senior senators for serving time.

From 1921 into the late 1960s and early 1970s, the appropriations committees remained supreme. Then their wings were clipped again by two disparate sources, First, smarting under the appropriations committees' conservative outlook on social issues, the legislative committees devised the means to get around them. A variety of back-door methods of financing were invented or extended: contract authority, borrowing authority, loans and loan guarantees, off-budget agencies and off-budget spending, and the expansion of entitlements. Second, there was the creation of the budget committees, which gained or usurped power from both the legislative and appropriations committees. But what happened to the House Appropriations Committee in 1885 and the Senate Appropriations Committee in 1899 happened to the budget committees in 1990. A major consequence of the 1990 five-year budget agreement was the power regained by the appropriations committees at the expense of the budget committees (see Chapter 10).

Initiating Appropriations Bills

In practice, the House initiates all appropriations bills. This grew out of early U.S. history, when the tax-writing House Ways and Means Committee also appropriated funds. While the Constitution states that "all Bills for raising Revenue shall originate in the House of Representatives," no such provision applies to appropriations, and indeed the requirement of House initiation of appropriations was specifically rejected by the Founding Fathers. While the House claims the exclusive right to originate all general appropriations bills, the Senate's parliamentarian emeritus lists forty-five bills for specific as opposed to general appropriations that have originated in the Senate.[16] In 1881 the House Committee on the Judiciary issued a report to the House saying the Senate had a right to initiate appropriations bills and that the power to initiate was not exclusively that of the House.[17] The Judiciary Committee then said:

> From this brief summary it will be seen that the proposition was more than once presented to the convention to vest in the House of Representatives the exclusive privilege of originating "all money bills" *eo nomine*, which was as often rejected. It would seem obvious, therefore, that the framers of the Constitution did not intend that the expression "bills for raising revenue," as employed by them, should be taken as the equivalent of that term as it was understood in the English parliamentary practice; for, if they had so intended, they would surely have used that term itself, which had already received a fixed and definite signification from long and familiar usage, instead of the one they chose to employ.[18]

A fascinating sequel occurred in 1962 in a fight some dubbed the squabble between "two stubborn old patriarchs." The warriors were eighty-three-year-old House Appropriations Chairman Clarence Cannon of Missouri, who "ruled his committee with acid tongue and iron hand,"[19] and the eighty-four-year-old Senate Chairman Carl Hayden of Arizona. While the House had historically initiated appropriations bills, the conference committee to iron out differences between the House and Senate versions by practice had been presided over by a senator and was held on the Senate side of the Capitol. Near the end of the session in 1961, when the Senate members of a conference committee had politely refused to go to the House side to meet, the House passed a $1.1 billion supplemental appropriations conference report with a series of provisions that were anathema to the Senate. The House then adjourned *sine die* (without day), which meant the Senate no longer had the option to reject the report and go back to conference. It instead had to pass the report or force the president to call a special session of the Congress.[20] The Senate was furious. During the next session, the House proposed that conference committees alternate their meetings and chairmen. The Senate responded by agreeing, provided it could initiate half the appropriations bills. The spat got uglier as time passed. Appropriations bills passed by the House and Senate remained in limbo, money to run the government was endangered, and the principals made fools of themselves. The dispute finally ran its course. Meetings were held in the Old Supreme Court Chamber, which is roughly halfway between the two houses, and the chairmanships were alternated, but the House continued to originate the bills. That condition remains, but the comity between the two bodies has since largely been restored.[21]

It is ironic that the House of Representatives is so adamant about its right to initiate appropriations bills, for which it has no clear constitutional mandate, and is so willing to allow the Senate effectively to initiate tax bills, for which it does have a clear constitutional mandate. The unprecedented Reagan administration tax reductions of 1981 and tax increases of 1982 were both initiated in the Senate. In the case of the 1982 bill, the House, in an extraordinary move, went to a conference with the Senate on the Senate bill without having passed its own bill.[22] It has been relatively common for widespread and organic changes in the tax laws to be added by rider to minor and unimportant tax bills from the House or initiated under reconciliation directions.

Members and Subcommittees

Characteristics of Members   Historically the appropriations committees are composed of very senior and very powerful members. At the beginning of the One-Hundred-Second Congress, the members of the Senate Committee averaged thirteen years of seniority, with the Democrats with fourteen and the Republicans just under twelve years of service. Five of the ten most senior Democrats in the Senate were the five senior Democrats on the committee; they averaged twenty-six years of Senate service. Senators Robert Byrd (D.-W.Va.), Quentin Burdick (D.-N.Dak.), and Daniel Inouye (D.-Hawaii) had served thirty-two, thirty, and twenty-eight years, respectively. While the two senior Republicans had served for twenty-four and twenty-two years, eight of the thirteen Republicans had served ten years or less. No freshman senator was a member.

In the House the Appropriations Committee Chairman, Jamie Whitten (D.-Miss.), was in his fiftieth year of service and was called the "Father of the House." Its fourth-ranking member, Sidney Yates (D.-Ill.), had served for forty years but only twenty-six of them consecutively. The average service of the top ten Democrats was almost thirty years. The five senior Republicans averaged twenty-six years of service, and the top ten had served twenty-one years. Of the fifty-nine committee members, only one was a freshman.

The appropriations committees receive special treatment from their respective bodies. In the House, when the party membership ratio was 56 percent Democratic and 44 percent Republican, the committee had a majority party–minority party membership ratio of 60:40, or thirty-three Democrats to twenty-two Republicans, to ensure majority party control. This oversize ratio was not carried over to the One-Hundred-Second Congress, when the committee membership of thirty-seven Democrats and twenty-two Republicans was almost the precise ratio of Democrats to Republicans in the House (62:38), because that proportion was sufficient to control legislation. The Senate committee, more bipartisan and collegial by nature, has more accurately reflected the overall party ratios in that body. Its 16:13 Democratic majority since the Democrats recaptured the Senate in 1986 has nearly duplicated the 55:45, 56:44, and 57:43 Democratic to Republican ratio in the body as a whole in the six years which followed.[23]

The Senate committee has the special privilege of being allowed to meet at any time, even when the Senate is in session, a privilege not routinely afforded other committees. Its staff has unlimited access to the Senate floor, does not abide by the floor privilege rule applied to staff members of other committees, and for years was not required (unlike other committees) to ask the Senate Rules Committee for authority for its staff and funds. What right had the Rules Committee to tell the Appropriations Committee how many staff members it could have? The Appropriations Committee's Legislative Subcommittee would have merely retaliated by cutting the Rules Committee's staff and funds. In fact, a truce or comity now exists between the two committees, and the estimates of each are honored by the other. Historically both have had small and efficient staffs. In the House, appropriations bills do not require a rule and are eligible to be called up for immediate debate after a routine waiting period following publication of the committee's report.

Characteristics of Subcommittees

The work of the House and Senate Appropriations Committees is done in thirteen subcommittees of each house. Their names are the same and their jurisdictions are identical. In the House, the chairman of each subcommittee is selected by seniority on the subcommittee. In the Senate, although the practice has varied, the selection of the chairmen of the subcommittees is based on seniority in the full committee. The House practice has led to the anomalous situation in the One-Hundred-Second Congress in which the seventh-ranking member, Louis Stokes (D.-Ohio) had no chairmanship, while the nineteenth-ranking Democrat, Vic Fazio (Calif.), was the chairman of the Legislative Subcommittee.[24] The political unpopularity that Legislative Subcommittee members must endure if they cut the money requests of their colleagues has been a more important reason than seniority for this incongruous situation.

The Political "Double Whammy"

House members generally serve on only one major standing committee (rotating membership on the Budget Committee is an exception), but senators serve on two or more. The latter situation leads to the extraordinarily powerful political positions of some senators who are either chairmen or senior members of a major legislative committee and are able to exercise jurisdiction over the funding of their legislative programs as chairmen of a Senate appropriations subcommittee. Insiders call this the political "double whammy."

In the One-Hundred-Second Congress, Senator J. Bennett Johnston (D.-La.) was chairman of both the Energy and Natural Resources Committee and the Energy and Water Development Subcommittee of Appropriations. This was of special political value to Louisiana, a major oil state that has many off-shore producing rigs and the port of New Orleans. The Energy and Natural Resources Committee has jurisdiction over oil and gas production, the outer continental shelf, and energy-related aspects of deep-water ports, while the Energy and Water Development Subcommittee funds not only these programs but, more importantly, the massive public works levee projects of the Army Corps of Engineers on the banks of the lower Mississippi and Lake Pontchartrain. South Carolina's Ernest F. Hollings was chairman of the Senate Commerce, Science, and Transportation Committee, which authorized programs funded by the Senate Appropriations Subcommittee on Commerce, Justice, State and Judiciary, which he also chaired. Republican Jake Garn (R.-Utah), was the ranking minority member of the Senate Committee on Banking, Housing, and Urban Affairs and of the HUD-Independent Agencies Subcomittee of the Appropriations Committee, which funded the housing programs. When the Republicans controlled the Senate from 1981 to 1987, he was the chairman of both.

Subcommittee Supremacy

Long before the House and Senate spawned a myriad of subcommittees in the 1970s as a means to mute seniority and to throttle the power of tyrannical chairmen, both House and Senate appropriations committees functioned by subcommittee. Committee chairmen reigned supreme, but the sheer quantity of work made subcommittee dominance essential. Long before the April 15 deadline for the first concurrent resolution on the budget—when, theoretically, congressional spending ceilings are established—the subcommittees are at work. For example, in the last week in March of a recent year, the House appropriations subcommittees scheduled no less than fifty-nine sessions to hear agency witnesses.[25]

The Commission on the Operation of the Senate (the Hughes Commission), in a study of the number of committee and subcommittee meetings in a year, reported that the Senate Appropriations Committee and its subcommittees met more times than any other committee, or 318 times during the year. Of the others, eight of the eighteen standing committees met less than 100 times, six met from 100 to 200 times, and three met from 200 to 300 times. Some 92 percent, or 293, of the Appropriations Committee meetings were held by its subcommittees. No other committee approached either mark.[26]

The Hearings

Characteristics of the Hearings   Subcommittee hearings are detailed, lengthy, and laborious. Budget proposals are gone over seriatim, line by line and paragraph by paragraph. More often than not, only the chairman and the ranking minority member are present. As almost all members of the full committee are subcommittee chairmen or ranking members, they are occupied elsewhere. As information is power and other members are absent, the chairman is free to develop a record, monopolize the proceedings, and dominate the funding. The quality of work and the knowledge and expertise that most subcommittee chairmen develop, especially in the House, are often extraordinary. Their diligence, attention to detail, and responsibility to duty are among the features of Congress that are little known and seldom acknowledged.

Generally the hearings are crowded, but not with members of the general public or press. The hearings are ex parte, and often only those interested in the money attend. When the Housing and Urban Development (HUD) secretary or the director of the National Aeronautics and Space Administration (NASA) appear, they bring with them rows and rows of minions prepared to answer questions on any minor point the chairman or members may raise. Seated behind the rows of agency partisans are layers of lawyers, legal aids, and lobbyists of the clients or the agencies, the funds of which agencies are later funneled to the clients through programs, contracts, or research grants. The witnesses testify in favor of full funding for the programs. The Senate's former Appropriations Committee staff director, who served for a quarter of a century, noted that in all those years not one witness in a thousand opposed the funding.[27]

When pressed to justify every dollar or to rebut critical General Accounting Office (GAO) reports or inspectors' general reviews, the term "the president's budget" is regularly invoked. While the president may have no interest at all in the item, if it is challenged, his name is extolled as the pope's is over morals or Webster's is over words. Sometimes the intonation of the witness even seems to capitalize the "He" or "His."

Both House and Senate subcommittees have investigative staffs to augment their regular employees. The House generally borrows experts from executive agencies, while the Senate tends to rely on those detailed from the GAO. Both are useful, for under the jurisdiction of an objective or critical chairman they can greatly serve the public interest.

For those who notice, the hearings highlight the public schizophrenia about government spending. While the National Chamber of Commerce deplores excessive spending, hundreds of local chambers petition the committee or its members to fund public works projects, government buildings, and local levees or harbors. Architects who petition their senators to cut programs and balance the budget importune them at the same time to increase funds for historical preservation and urban development. As the saying goes, "Don't cut him. Don't cut me. Cut the man behind the tree."

There is another important characteristic of the hearings and committee action—namely, both public and private reciprocity. Almost never does a member of the Fortune 500 or of a major trade association testify against a fellow company or association, even when that member's own vital interests are at stake. Thus the Pennsylvania Railroad refused to testify publicly against the $90 million dredging of the Delaware River that benefited U.S. Steel's Fairless Hills work in Pennsylvania even though it meant the shifting of steel shipments from the railroad to heavily subsidized barge traffic. McDonnell Douglas Aircraft refused to testify against the Lockheed loan even though it meant lost sales and financial difficulties for McDonnell Douglas and its DC-10, although in a rare appearance the builder of the plane's engine, General Electric, did testify. Neither Ford nor General Motors publicly opposed the Chrysler bailout, in part because of the rule of reciprocity and also because at least one of them feared it might be next in line. The reciprocity practice applies even more strongly to members of the appropriations committee.

It is an anomaly that the press largely ignores the hearings of the appropriations committees, for it is here that much power lies and many priorities are determined. The member who controls the money controls the program. While the lobbyists swarm to the meetings, the press is elsewhere. The explanation is that while the press reports the byplay of political battle, speculation on the outcome of a critical vote, and conflicts between personalities, it regularly fails to report the hard, grubby decisions on the budget. It is so intrigued by tactics that it misses the substance. This is one reason why the appropriations committees attract power-oriented members rather than issue-oriented members. The former are delighted to take home the political bacon carved out in the secret labyrinthine chambers of the Capitol without the attention of the national press. Issue-oriented members, dismayed by the lack of public attention, seek to serve on more visible committees, such as the Foreign Relations Committee. Yet the testimony and hearing record of the appropriations subcommittees are a gold mine of factual nuggets on which one diligent Washington newsman, I. F. Stone, built a monumental reputation. By reading the detailed public record that others forsook, he revealed events and predicted policies with an uncanny ability. In general, because of the obtuse nature of the press, the substance of the hearings of the appropriations committees is added to the great unread literature of the world.

The Mark

The Chairman's Mark and the Subcommittee's Mark   After several hundred—sometimes a thousand—pages of hearings are compiled, the next step is something called the subcommittee "mark" or "mark-up," which occurs when the subcommittee meets to propose, amend, add, delete, increase, or decrease budget figures. This also provides an opportunity to propose report language, which is a part of the legislative history and can have (depending on how it is written) a binding effect on the agencies. Language is often put in the report instead of being added to the bill to avoid having a member raise a point of order that the proposed language is legislation on an appropriations bill.

But even before the subcommittee meets, most of the major decisions have been made by the chairman, the ranking minority member, and their staffs in a private meeting of the parties called the "chairman's mark." This meeting is usually held in a committee room or in the chairman's personal or a Capitol hideaway office.[28] This is the most critical point in deciding what the House or Senate will do. The chairman's mark gives the chairman and the ranking member the initiative. It determines the general level of funding, which in most cases is how much "below" the president's budget the appropriations committee will cut. It provides a secret opportunity for the two key members, as a prerequisite of political office, to bury funds for their state or districts deep in the bowels of budget line items. Provisions will be added or deleted as "trading material" with the other house of Congress. A chairman who adds a weak project for his or her state or district may well delete an item dear to the heart of his or her opposite House or Senate colleague. In the conference committee meeting of House and Senate, both items are often accepted. The language in the report—which few members actually read—is determined during or even before the chairman's mark. With rare exceptions, 95 percent or more of the items and the funds are decided in this unknown, unpublicized, secret conclave. Only those issues on which the parties cannot compromise are taken to the subcommittee itself. After the meeting, the gallery sheets of an earlier written proposed report are edited and sent off to the Government Printing Office for an overnight reprint, and are in the hands of the principals in time for the subcommittee mark-up, often on the next day.

At the subcommittee mark-up, members of the subcommittee and even the chairman and ranking minority member of the full committee, who "are *ex officio* members of all subcommittees of which they are not regular members,"[29] swarm to the meeting. Members who have not attended a single hearing will be there, surrounded by staff members and armed with proxies from absent members. A high school civics class or a member of the good government league would be appalled at some of the proceedings. In the defense subcommittee mark there is almost no talk about national defense needs, the relative power of the Russians, the threat of a Saddam Hussein, how to improve procurement, vital American interests, the value of the volunteer army over the draft, or the readiness of the navy. At issue instead are whether helicopter training will be in Florida or Alabama, whether a ship will be renovated in Philadelphia or Norfolk, or whether Boeing or Lockheed, Kansas City or Burbank, will get funds for a cargo plane. The Senate subcommittees almost always "up," or increase, the House figures (from which practice the Senate got the ironic name of "upper house"). The great agencies—state, treasury, and defense—use the Senate to "appeal" House cuts. Technically, the agencies write a *reclama*, or a revision of the language and figures, to sustain the original request.

Agencies are often more interested in their perquisites than their programs. The Nixon administration imposed a housing moratorium, which by chance coincided with the energy crisis and gave the Senate Appropriations Subcommittee on HUD-Independent Agencies the opportunity to cut out the limousines for the undersecretary, the assistant secretaries, and the head of the Federal Housing Administration. The practice of driving these officials to and from work was both illegal under Title 31, Section 638a, of the U.S. Code and wasteful of fuel. Driving an assistant secretary to and from work means four trips a day rather than the two trips involved if he or she were to do his or her own driving. The frenzied lobbying on the bill by HUD's hierarchy focused on keeping the limousines while the affected officials fought against restoring funds for the housing programs.

This was reminiscent of the self-pity shown by that imperious figure, Lord Reith, the first head of the British Broadcasting Corporation, who wrote in his diary that he loathed the common people. He was also Minister of Information and Transportation under Neville Chamberlain, but was removed by Winston Churchill. After a luncheon with Lord Portal, who both succeeded him in the cabinet and gained entitlement to his limousine, Lord Reith noted in his diary:

He [Lord Portal] sailed off in the car I had, leaving me to push about in bus queues and such like. I had a great struggle with myself. Tears flooded my eyes several times.[30]

The rapaciousness with which members propose funds for their pet projects must be seen to be believed. Call it what you will—pork barreling, logrolling, or back scratching—it is both unseemly and true. One of the unwritten rules is that a senator "does not press objections to another's pet project unless that project adversely affects vital interests in his own state. To do otherwise would violate the norm of reciprocity."[31]

A similar scene takes place at the full committee mark, when all members of the committee have their day. But the unwritten rule is that as the bill moves from chairman to subcommittee to full committee marks, it becomes progressively more difficult to get amendments accepted. If one has to "take it to the floor," more often than not it is a lost cause.

How is the public interest protected at all from this carnage, when members have their nose and all four feet in the public trough? There are several answers. Fortunately, first, the amendments adopted at both the subcommittee and full committee marks seldom represent more than a minuscule part of the funds. Second, some amendments are there for "posturing" purposes. The member takes credit for getting an amendment into the bill or his or her side of the Capitol but does not fight too hard when it is thrown out in conference. Third, if members get *too* greedy, they lose the respect of their colleagues and their influence is limited. Fourth, if the Congress itself goes too far, there is the danger of a presidential veto; even the mere threat of a veto has a dampening effect. Fifth, House and Senate subcommittee chairmen know the game, and are astute negotiators and wily performers. Contentious items are often deliberately left out of a bill by one house in the knowledge that it if is not in both bills, it will most likely get "lost" in the conference. Further, subcommittee chairmen have their ceilings and goals, and the chairman's mark has left room for the political mischief and raids on the Capitol dome they know will come.

Floor Debate

After the full committee mark, the bill is reported to the House or Senate. In the House an appropriations bill is "privileged" and may be called up for immediate debate. In the Senate an appropriations bill must "lie over" on the calendar for one legislative day, which, unlike a calendar day, begins when the Senate adjourns. If it only recesses, the legislative day remains the same. The rules of the Senate are devised to prevent almost any legislative action except by unanimous consent or general agreement, and they stipulate that a new legislative day must begin before many procedures can take place (discharging a committee, for example). Thus during fights over civil rights, abortion, or school prayer a legislative day has often lasted several weeks. Further, both Houses require that the committee report be available to members before debate. The Senate requires that it be available three calendar days before consideration, although this provision can be waived by agreement between the majority and minority leaders and does not apply to, among other things, the consideration of a declaration of war.

The chairman and ranking minority subcommittee members are the floor leaders for a given bill. On the whole, they agree on strategy and tactics, stand together to oppose weakening amendments, agree on time limitations, and decide the order of debate. From the 1920s to the early 1970s, the appropriations committees wielded awesome power on the floor of the House and Senate. Except for amendments to cut funds for such highly unpopular programs as foreign aid and for some progressive social programs, the appropriations committees seldom suffered defeat. When they did, it was generally by acquiescence. They wielded power by several means. First, the committee members stood together. This provided about one-quarter of the votes in the Senate. Second, the chairmen and ranking members of the legislative committees joined them. If anyone tried to cut a public works project or add money for public housing, the chairmen circled the wagons. When Senator Paul H. Douglas (D.-Ill.) made his routine attack against pork-barrel public works appropriations bills and was routinely overwhelmingly crushed, floor manager Senator Dennis Chavez (D.-N.Mex.) said, "I don't understand why the Senator from Illinois is against this bill. There's something in it for everybody."[32] Third, the members of the Senate or House establishment, those in or who wanted to be in the "Inner Club," who practiced the "to get along, go along" principle, joined with them. Fourth, if necessary, those with special projects or programs of their own were appealed to or reminded that their political fortunes rested with the good will of the committee. Thus for a half-century, the appropriations committees were omnipotent.

Special rules apply to floor procedures when the Congress acts on appropriations bills. The first involves the two-step procedure of authorizing and appropriating previously described. Under the rules of the House and Senate, no amendment to an appropriations bill "shall be received . . . unless it be made to carry out the provisions of some existing law."[33]

The second special rule is that "the Committee on Appropriations shall not report an appropriation bill containing amendments to such bill proposing new or general legislation."[34] In addition, there can be no limitation not provided by law or any restriction depending on a contingency.[35] The Senate, for example, ruled that an amendment to a foreign aid bill that said the aid would be cut off if the country thereafter nationalized its industry was out of order because it was a limit or restriction based on a contingency.[36]

Third, there is the rule of germaneness: No amendment "not germane or relevant to the subject matter contained in the bill [shall] be received."[37]

There are also rules against amendments advancing private claims or reappropriating unexpended balances.

These rules have several exceptions, however, Authorizing committees often appropriate funds through such back-door methods as borrowing authority, contract authority, and entitlements. Appropriation bills regularly and routinely contain legislation. Further, funds are often appropriated before the authorizing legislation has passed. Language containing restrictions, limitations, contingencies, and nongermane provisions is often found. One egregious example from recent history will make the point.

In the lame-duck December session of the Congress before Ronald Reagan was inaugurated, no fewer than 148 Senate amendments were added to the continuing appropriations resolution necessary to keep the government running after Congress had adjourned. Many of these were nongermane legislative amendments containing restrictions, limitations, and contingencies. Included were both the authority and funds for flood control projects, the creation of new offices for inspectors general, severance pay for several hundred retiring Senate employees, and even an anti-abortion provision. The rules against legislation on an appropriations bill were in shambles.[38]

How does one account for the breakdown of the procedures that for fifty years or more had made the appropriations committees omnipotent? Through a number of special provisions, these committees became exempt from the rules generally applied to others. The Senate rules provided that by direction of an appropriations committee or a standing or select committee an amendment could add funds to a money bill without previous authorization or legislation. A member could not add money without a previous authorization, but a committee could.

In addition, Senate Rule Sixteen was written and interpreted to mean that if a House-passed bill contained legislation, further legislative amendments were in order. The principle was that if the House opened the door by adding legislative language, the Senate should not be prevented from improving or perfecting it.

A third device was the rule requiring "germaneness," little known but often used. The Senate rules provide that a point of order may be made against any violation of the rules—an appropriation without an authorization, legislation on an appropriations bill, or limitations and contingencies. But if before the chair rules a senator raises the question of the germaneness of an amendment to a general appropriations bill:

> the Chair does not then rule on the question, but instead, he submits that question to the Senate for decision, to be determined without debate; if the Senate votes in the affirmative (that is, the amendment is germane) the point of order fails and the amendment is before the Senate for action.[39]

Proposed ideological amendments on abortion, busing, school prayer, or the line item veto have been a major reason why the Congress has failed to pass appropriations bills before the beginning of the new fiscal year. Here is an example of how this can happen.

It is late September in an election year. The Department of Health and Human Services' appropriations bill is before the Senate. It must be passed by October 1, or there will be no funds for that department or for the departments of Labor and Education, whose funds are in the bill as well. Senator Jesse Helms (R.-N.C.) proposes an anti-abortion amendment to the bill. This is clearly legislation on an appropriations bill and thus subject to a point of order, which is raised by the bill's manager, then Senator Lowell Weicker (R.-Conn.).

Before the chair rules, Helms poses the question of germaneness. He has told his colleagues that this is *the* abortion vote of the year. The galleries are packed with anti-abortion supporters. Every senator knows that these groups will flood the mails between then and election day with reports on how they all voted on the amendment. Without debate the chair puts the issue to the Senate with the words, "Is the amendment of the senator from North Carolina germane?" A recorded roll call is ordered after a dozen of Helm's allies support his call for the "yeas and nays." Under the circumstances a majority votes for the amendment, even though it is clearly not germane and out of order.

At this point the opponents of the amendment threaten a filibuster. In the past such a filibuster was threatened by the manager of the bill, Senator Weicker, who would rather scuttle it than pass it with the Helms right-to-life amendment attached. In the end there may be no bill, a continuing resolution to run the departments may be passed, or some compromise watering down the amendment may be reached. Such nongermane legislative amendments, often proposed by members of the president's party, create chaos and cause the gridlock that has plagued the Congress and the budget in the 1980s and 1990s.

If it were not for the special procedures outlined above, an individual senator or a committee would have to move to suspend the rules, which takes a two-thirds vote of those present and voting, in order to propose either legislation on an appropriations bill or a non germane amendment.

Further, the rules provide that a committee may propose amendments on an appropriations bill that an individual senator may not. Thus in certain instances a bare majority of a committee—as few as eight members of a fifteen-member committee—has proposed amendments on an appropriations bill that an individual could do only by moving on the Senate floor to suspend the rules and winning that motion with the votes of two-thirds of the one hundred senators present and voting.

The rules and their exceptions had two purposes. The first was to defend segregation and to defeat civil rights riders proposed by individual senators on a money bill that had to be passed to keep the government functioning. The second was to keep power in the hands of the committees, and especially the appropriations committees.

Ruling southern senators had written the Senate rules to prevent a civil rights bill from being passed. For years, under Rule Twenty-Two, it took two-thirds of the Senate to cut off a filibuster. Further, amendments to legislative bills did not have to be germane. This provided for virtually unlimited debate and unlimited amendments to legislative bills, and made the Senate the graveyard for civil rights bills. As William S. White wrote approvingly in *Citadel*, "The Senate might be described without too much violence to fact as the South's unending revenge upon the North for Gettysburg."[40]

The dominant southerners could prevent civil rights language or a civil rights bill from being attached to a money bill by using Rule Sixteen, which provided for no legislation, no contingencies, and no limitations on a money bill. And amendments had to be germane.

But there were times when money was needed for unauthorized projects, when there was no other vehicle but a money bill to pass urgent legislation, and when the Congress could avoid a presidential veto of controversial legislation by adding it to a money bill the president had to sign. How could this be done? The answer again was Rule Sixteen. Make exceptions for the committee. Avoid points of order by using the rule of germaneness. These devices, which in fact were used regularly and routinely, allowed the Senate Appropriations Committee, with the backing of fifty-one members, to put legislation on an appropriations bill without let or hindrance. There was one set of rules against civil rights bills or civil rights riders, and another set for everything else. The duplicity and mendacity were clear when, under Rule Sixteen, the restrictions on individual senators did not apply to the committee itself.

On the issue of germaneness, a majority of senators (51) was needed to preserve an amendment clearly in violation of the rules. How were these votes obtained? The Appropriations Committee was packed with members from the deep South; year after year, six of its eight or seven of its nine most senior Democrats were from this region. Unlike their recent southern Democratic successors, who are national Democrats, most were "Dixiecrats" rather than Democrats. Further, they chaired not only appropriations subcommittees but the Senate armed services, agriculture, labor, and government operations committees as well. Fellow southerners not on the Appropriations Committee chaired the finance, foreign relations, and judiciary committees. With this chokehold on both legislation and money, they traded southern support for western wheat, sugar beets, minerals, wool, water, and public works projects for western support for southern tobacco, cotton, military installations, and public works, and most importantly, for opposition to civil rights legislation and any change in the filibuster rules that would aid such legislation. They were also aided by conservative, trans-Mississippi Republicans who, like the senators from the small western states, had heavy fiscal needs and few minority constituents. When attacked, the Senate Appropriations Committee could produce fifty-five or sixty votes on almost any issue. In most cases this was done within the general limits of the president's budget. What the appropriations committees did during their powerful days was to reorder priorities. Defense, public works, space, water projects, waterways, and commodity subsidies were funded at the expense of the social programs.

Since the passage of the civil rights acts of the mid-1960s, the death or defeat of the Dixiecrat hierarchy, the decline of the seniority system, the fall of the autocratic chairmen, and the rise of subcommittee government in general, the procedures used when an appropriations bill is on the floor have changed. The special rules devised to prevent civil rights legislation but to allow the appropriations committees to attach legislation to an appropriations bill boomeranged. These rules have since been used to add legislation on the most controversial social issues. As a result, budgets for foreign aid, the Department of Health and Human Services, and the Department of Justice have been filibustered, delayed, and killed by a minority after a majority decided that controversial legislative matters were either not legislation on an appropriations bill, although they clearly were, or were germane to an appropriations bill, although they clearly were not. The House and Senate seem unable to find a norm somewhere between the not-so-benevolent dictatorship of the "Senate Bourbons" and the breakdown and anarchy so characteristic of recent days.[41] Devices born in another era and for other purposes still haunt the Congress.

The Conference Committee

After an appropriations bill is passed in the Senate, it goes to a conference committee formed by members of both houses of the Congress. The proceedings of what is called the "third house of Congress" are little known but of great importance, for it is here that a compromise on differing figures and language in each bill is struck.

Historically, on an appropriations bill, unlike a budget resolution, the House routinely wins the battle. It wins because, first of all, its members are better informed on the substance of the bill than are their Senate colleagues. Most House members serve on only one major committee, and thus concentrate their time and energy on becoming experts on the subject of their jurisdiction. Senators, on the other hand, serve on at least two major committees and usually on one or two additional minor committees. Their time and authority are thus diffused.

The House also wins the battle because its members are better prepared. Not only are they more expert, but they meet and plan their strategy before the conference with the Senate. They agree ahead of time on their position and stick with it. Senators, meantime, seldom meet before the conference takes place. They almost never have an agreed, detailed position on differences.

Further, because there are fewer senators—100 as opposed to 435

House members—the legislative demands on senators are greater and they drift in and out of conference committee sessions, and leave the bargaining and details to their staffs. It is this uneven political battle that the House routinely wins, for no Senate staff person, however knowledgeable, can bargain on equal terms with a thoroughly informed elected official with a public mandate who has systematically planned his or her tactics and strategy and who operates from a position of strength because of a prearranged united stand with his or her colleagues.

Finally, the House wins because of a sense of inferiority that leads to the stubborn intransigence of its members that supplements their superior knowledge and organization. While both Houses are equal in the eyes of the Constitution, House members smart under the unequal relationship that exists in fact. Because there are fewer senators, they get more public and press attention for less work—and often less knowledge and intelligence. A diligent House member may serve for twenty years and be unknown in the country. But even a junior senator is quoted in *The New York Times* or *The Washington Post*, may appear on "Meet the Press" or "Face the Nation," and receives radio and television attention that a House member can obtain only as one of a handful of leaders. The House members redress their grievances in part by winning the major battles in the House-Senate conference committee sessions on appropriations and other bills. The result is that the more diligent oversight, the more detailed review, and the larger budget cuts imposed by the House on the president's or agencies' requests win the day.

Continuing Resolutions, Supplementals, and Reappropriations

In addition to the regular appropriations bills, there are at least three and perhaps four additional types of appropriations to which the preceding principles and procedures apply. The first is the continuing resolution, which, as defined by the Budget Reform Act, provides "budget authority for specific ongoing activities in cases where the regular fiscal year appropriations bills for such activities have not been enacted by the beginning of the fiscal year."[42] The start of the fiscal year was moved from July 1 to October 1 to give the Congress an extra three months to finish all appropriations bills and to reconcile the total amounts with the congressional budget resolutions. However, the intensity of the conflicts over divisive social issues and the sheer volume of work under the 1974 Budget Act have made the additional three months inadequate, and the problem remains unsolved. Under a continuing resolution, spending at specific rates is authorized. Sometimes the rate is based on the previous year's amount. Often, it is based on the amount recommended by the president or the amount passed by one house of the Congress or the other, whichever is lower or higher. The particular continuing resolution sets the level of spending, and very different rates may be set for different departments, agencies, or programs covered by the bill.

The failure of the Congress to pass its regular appropriations bills and the need to function by continuing resolution have occasioned criticism in editorials and by public interest groups and members of the House and Senate. Senator Thomas F. Eagleton (D.-Mo.) complained at the end of the Ninety-Seventh Congress about the "slipshod, slapdash manner in which the Congress now handles the Appropriations process."[43] Not one of the thirteen appropriations bills had been signed by the president by the start of the new fiscal year. No more than six were passed and signed when the Congress adjourned *sine die* in late December. As Eagleton commented:

> This hectic, frantic, helter-skelter way of doing the nation's business is unacceptable. To rush through, on a last-minute basis, the [continuing resolution] which funds 78 percent of appropriated monies makes a mockery of the Senate tradition as "the world's greatest deliberate parliamentary body." This year's continuous resolution stands as a monument to nondeliberation.[44]

The continuing resolution not only funds much of the government but has become the vehicle for both the notorious Christmas tree tax bill and the Christmas tree appropriations bill. As Nancy Drabble, the director of Public Citizens' Congress Watch, wrote in *The New York Times*:

> Congress never goes home for the holidays without bestowing special treats on its favorites. Although this lame-duck session fudged or fumbled most of its major bills, it passed lots of trivial ones. Not every bill . . . passed both houses but together [the] trinkets provide a glimpse of the merriment pork-barrelers and political action committees had at the public's expense in the tumultuous days before Christmas.[45]

Cited were amendments to the continuing resolution to continue funding of Tennessee's Clinch river Breeder Reactor; the "sugar beet sweetener" amendment to allow highly sugared cereals to be included in the Department of Agriculture's nutrition program for undernourished pregnant mothers, children, and infants; a congressional pay raise; and the repeal of limits on senator's outside income.

In addition to the fact that foreign aid, the Health and Human Services bill, and the Justice Department appropriations bills have been held up because of objections to military aid being given to dictators, abortion and busing riders, and attempts to deny jurisdiction to the Supreme Court on sensitive social issues, there are at least three other reasons why the regular appropriations bills are not passed and why more and more government funding is by continuing resolution.

First is the sheer amount of fiscal and budget work forced on the Congress. The highly contentious budget, tax, and debt proposals have put more issues on the legislative plate than the Congress can consume, even in its extended fiscal year.

The second is a matter of internal politics. Since 1974 and especially since 1980, the appropriations committees have lost much of their power to the budget committees although the appropriations committees took back power in 1990 (see Chapter 10). Through both the budget resolutions and the reconciliation bills, the budget committees and the House and Senate as a whole are making decisions and setting priorities that in the past the appropriations committees made piecemeal. Smarting under this state of events, the appropriations committees have delayed their regular bills. This forces members to come to them hat in hand at the end of the congressional session to bargain for what specific items will be included in the continuing resolution, which is in fact an omnibus appropriations bill. The delay is a means of restoring the committees' power vis-a-vis the budget committees, and gives the appropriations committees the arenas of both the House and Senate floors and the conference committee, where the two houses work out their compromises, to bargain and to restore their powers as brokers with their colleagues.

Third, in several years, particularly in 1985, the president and the White House staff importuned the Republican Senate to delay House-passed appropriations bills to the end of the year. Like the members of the House Appropriations Committee, the president believed he would be in a stronger bargaining position at the end of the year than if he dealt with appropriations bills one by one. By both castigating the Congress and threatening to veto the continuing resolution, the White House could exchange approval of higher appropriations levels for some domestic programs favored by the Congress for some increases in the defense budget. Notwithstanding the finger pointing and the blame laying, *mea culpas* were appropriate from both the president and the Congress.

The second type of bill is the supplemental appropriations bill. Agencies come to the Congress for additional funds after their original appropriations bills are passed. A supplemental bill may appropriate budget authority for numerous agencies and programs. At times funds are deliberately left out of the original appropriations bill, such as money for a civil service pay raise that was clearly anticipated but was not authorized by the date the first bill passed the Congress. Another form is an unanticipated supplemental. Some committee and staff members are extraordinarily hard-nosed and demand that such a request be a genuine emergency. Others are less rigorous in their demands. Unforeseen events, additional actions by the Congress itself, and situations where the law requires payment of a pension or contract may all require or be used to justify a supplemental appropriation. Supplements now include "deficiencies," situations where agencies have exhausted their funds before the end of the fiscal year. This was once done by a separate bill.

The third kind of bill is the reappropriations bill. Funds are authorized as one-year, multiple-years, or no-year appropriations (no-year money remains available until expended). The Congress often reappropriates unused (technically unobligated) funds from one-year and multiple-year appropriations. No-year money does not lapse unless the program for which it was intended has ended.[46]

In the past, some of these forms of appropriations were handled by additional subcommittees, such as a deficiency subcommittee. The regular subcommittee chairmen, who believed they knew the programs of the agencies over which they had jurisdiction better than a special subcommittee dealing with a program on an ad hoc basis, objected. Now the subcommittee having original jurisdiction deals with funds for its agencies in supplemental or continuing appropriations resolutions, and the special deficiency or supplemental subcommittees have been abandoned.

Ideology, the constraints of time, the 1974 Budget Act, and the internal struggle for power have radically changed the appropriations procedures from a once staid and steady process that was both timely and predictable to a struggle in which street smarts are more important than an adherence to the traditional and ritualistic rules.

THE TAX-WRITING COMMITTEES: THE HOUSE WAYS AND MEANS AND THE SENATE FINANCE COMMITTEES

Power and Jurisdiction

The tax-writing committees have more power over the budget than do the budget committees. Some sense of this power in the Congress in general and over the budget in particular can be gained by examining the committees' jurisdictions as provided for in the rules of the House and Senate. Rule Twenty-five of the Senate provides for a "Committee on Finance" to which committee shall be referred all proposed legislation, messages, petitions, memorials, and other matters relating to the following subjects:

1. Bonded debt of the United States, except as provided in the Congressional Budget Act of 1974.
2. Customs, collection districts, and ports of entry and delivery.
3. Deposits of public moneys.
4. General revenue sharing.
5. Health programs under the Social Security Act and health programs financed by a special tax or trust fund.
6. National social security.
7. Reciprocal trade agreements.
8. Revenue measures generally, except as provided in the Congressional Budget Act of 1974.
9. Revenue measures relating to the insular possessions.
10. Tariff and import quotas, and matters relating thereto.
11. Transportation of dutiable goods.[47]

The Finance Committee also has jurisdiction over the nominations of the secretary of the treasury, the head of the Internal Revenue Service (IRS), tax and customs court judges, members of the International Trade Commission, the commissioner of Social Security, and numerous undersecretaries and assistant secretaries of the treasury. The Ways and Means Committee, except for the advice-and-consent responsibility, has substantially the same jurisdiction and authority, although it also has the power to initiate revenue measures. Article I, Section 7, of the Constitution states that

> All bills for raising revenue shall originate in the House of Representatives; but the Senate may propose or concur with Amendments as on other bills.

This authority balances the Finance Committee's authority for advice-and-consent and makes the Ways and Means Committee the most powerful and formidable committee in all of the Congress. As so often happens its power is reflected in its hearing rooms in the Longworth House Office Building, which are the largest and most ornate committee rooms on Capitol Hill.

How formidable the jurisdiction of the tax-writing committees is can be seen in an examination of the major elements of the president's proposed budget. In fiscal year 1992, for example, estimated revenues were $1,165.1 billion. The ways and means and finance committees had jurisdiction over it all.[48]

1. *Taxes* (100 percent)

Individual income taxes	$529.5 billion
Corporate income taxes	101.9 billion
Social insurance taxes and contributions	429.4 billion
Excise taxes	47.8 billion
Other	56.5 billion
Total	$1,165.1 billion

Spending was estimated at $1,445.9 billion. The ways and means and finance committees had jurisdiction over at least $793.3 billion, or 54.9 percent, of that amount.[49]

2. *Spending* (54.9 percent)

Medicare	$113.7 billion
Medicaid	59.8 billion
Social Security	288.6 billion
Unemployment compensation	27.2 billion
Interest	304.0 billion
Total	$793.3 billion

This means that authority over 75 percent of the budget—all of the tax side and over half of the spending side—is in the hands of the tax-writing committees.

But the committees' jurisdiction exceeds even these numbers. The Department of the Treasury estimated tax expenditures for individuals and corporations in fiscal year 1992 at $480.2 billion. These amounts are outside the budget but the result of tax committee actions. There are about 130 tax expenditures that, if they are financed by spending instead of tax expenditures, would be under the jurisdiction of the legislative committees and would be a part of the budget. As tax incentives have gained popularity as a means of promoting social, political, and economic ends, the tax committees have gained power at the expense of other committees.

The tax-writing committees also have jurisdiction over both the deficit and the debt. For fiscal year 1992, the latter was estimated at $4.0 trillion and was expanding at a rate of more than $348 billion a year.

The tax-writing committees are now the most formidable in the Congress. While the budget and appropriations committees may share the spotlight, the lion's share of the political power, especially over the key aspects of the budget, now lies with the ways and means and finance Committees.

Notwithstanding their legislative jurisdiction over taxes, the debt, Medicare, Medicaid, unemployment compensation, tariffs, and trade, the 1990 five-year budget agreement limited their right to legislate lower taxes or increases in entitlement (direct) spending without a concurrent legislative increase in taxes or reduction in entitlement spending. Failure to abide by these pay-as-you-go rules and ceilings is subject to points of order on the floor of the House or Senate and/or sequestration by the president.

The Politics and Power of the Tax-Writing Committees

In addition to their immense power, the House Ways and Means Committee and the Senate Finance Committee are characterized by their similar histories, generally conservative members, and probusiness bias. Both panels began as temporary ad hoc or select committees. A Ways and Means Committee was established even before there was a Treasury Department:

> Congress had appointed a committee of three on April 29 [1789] to prepare and report an estimate on supplies and revenues. On July 24, a 10-man Committee on Ways and Means was appointed, but it disbanded several weeks after the establishment of the Treasury Department.[50]

The committee was revived in 1794, abandoned after one session, and revived again in 1795:

> Although it was not until 1802 that Ways and Means was formally included in the House Rules as a standing committee, it had existed and functioned in that capacity ever since December 1795.[51]

The Senate Finance Committee had something of the same metamorphosis, but it did not become a standing committee until 1816. One reason for this was that in the beginning there was little need for such formal committees. The Senate had twenty members, only a few more than regularly serve on the Finance Committee today. Very few bills were introduced. Senate rules required that a senator seek the permission of a majority of senators, after giving a one-day notice of the request, to introduce a bill. In the Senate during the first session of the First Congress, only four bills were introduced.[52]

From their birth until the Civil War, the House Ways and Means Committee and the Senate Finance Committee acted not only as the tax-writing committees but as appropriations and banking committees as well. Their power over appropriations was not omnipotent and was shared from time to time with the legislative committees. The increase in responsibilities brought about by the Civil War led to the break-up of the two committees' jurisdiction. In March 1865, the House divided the Ways and Means Committee into three committees. Ways and Means retained its jurisdiction over taxes and tariffs but gave up jurisdiction over discretionary spending to an Appropriations Committee and over banks and credit to a new Committee on Banking and Bank Currency. A similar change occurred in the Senate in 1867.

As noted, the formal insistence by the House today that it initiate both tax and spending bills dates from this early history. The Constitution provides only that the House initiate tax bills, but the fact that the House initiated both types of bills because of the jurisdiction over appropriations held by the Ways and Means Committee until 1865 has led in modern times to several heated controversies between the two houses of the Congress, which the House of Representatives has now won (see above, "Initiating Appropriations Bills").[53]

Because of their modern jurisdiction over both taxes and many entitlement and tax expenditures, the tax-writing committees today exercise power as formidable as in the days before their jurisdictions were split. If anything, they are relatively more powerful because of the rise of entitlements and tax expenditures.

Several features of the modern House Ways and Means Committee explain its enormous power. First, it is the key House committee. Regardless of the ratio of Democrats to Republicans, it has traditionally had a disproportionate number of the majority party members to ensure party control. For example, in the Ninety-Ninth Congress, when Democrats held 253 seats and the Republicans held 182—a 58:42 ratio—Democrats held 23 of 36 Ways and Means Committee seats, or almost two-thirds of the total.[54]

When Democrats are in power there are certain unspoken rules to be followed in choosing Democrats as members. First, they have to have considerable seniority. Second, they have to be members in good standing with the House establishment. The committee is dominated by southern or border-state Democrats from safe constituencies and by big-city or big-state regular Democrats. Third, after 1926, and until very recent times, a member had to be in favor of the oil depletion allowance, or at least not active or energetic in efforts to seek its repeal. Describing the discourtesies heaped on him as an opponent of the oil depletion allowance by members of the Senate Finance Committee, Paul H. Douglas wrote in his autobiography that:

> On the House side, Charles Vanik, of Ohio, led a similar crusade against the 27½ percent depletion allowance, and he met with similar discourtesy. Indeed, when he took the floor Speaker Rayburn (D.-Texas) habitually showed his irritation by wheeling his chair around to face the flag, rather than look at Vanik. Everyone caught the point, although this intrepid young Congressman continued to brave the open contempt of Rayburn.[55]

Finally, until the South switched from the predominance of growing cotton to the manufacture of textiles—from low-tariff to protectionist politics—one also had to be a free or freer trader to become a member. While there were and are obvious exceptions to these rules, they are the major criteria for membership. The Democratic members of the Ways and Means Committee are thus a microcosm of the political, regional, and economic interests which dominate the party on tax and business matters.

In addition, for sixty-four years, from 1911 through 1974, the Democrats on the House Ways and Means Committee were also the Democratic Committee on Committees. This awesome political power made sure that both new members of the House and those seeking more important committee positions after several reelections learned to "go along to get along," did not offend the big-city/big-state southern Democratic establishment, and were careful not to attack oil, cotton, tobacco, or public works too strenuously. In 1974 the Committee on Committees function was transferred to the Democratic Steering and Policy Committee, which is more representative of the Democrats in the House than the Ways and Means Committee Democrats. Over time this has transformed the Democratic members from big-city, machine-oriented, and southern and southwest conservative gas and oil supporters to more progressive and liberal minded members.

Republican Ways and Means Committee members tend to represent the more conservative members of their party. The Ways and Means Committee was not and is not now the Republican Committee on Committees, and hence historically it has not had as much power when Republicans control it. But its members tend to be senior, power-oriented, conservative Republicans. Since Republicans are on the whole more disciplined than Democrats and tend to fight their intraparty battles behind closed doors rather than in the open, Republican Ways and Means Committee members need less clout than their Democratic opposites to carry the day with their party in the House.

On the Senate side, the Finance Committee is today just as powerful as the House Ways and Means Committee and is probably the strongest and most powerful committee in the Senate.

As pointed out proudly in the *History of the Committee on Finance*, all of the Senate's five outstanding senators, chosen by a special Senate Committee chaired by Senator John F. Kennedy in 1959, served on the Committee on Finance. They were Daniel Webster, Henry Clay, and John C. Calhoun of the nineteenth century and Robert M. LaFollette and Robert A. Taft of the twentieth. Nelson W. Aldrich of Rhode Island, whom Randall B. Ripley called "probably the single most powerful senator in the history of the body,"[56] served on the Finance Committee for thirty years, from 1881 to 1911, and was its chairman from 1898 to 1911. Names of the committee's powerful and famous members are legion. Three presidents (Martin Van Buren, John Tyler, and Lyndon B. Johnson) and eight vice-presidents served on the committee (including such recent vice-presidents as Walter Mondale, Lyndon Johnson, and Alben Barkley). Nine of its members also served as secretaries of the treasury, eleven served as secretaries of state (including Webster, Clay, Calhoun, John Sherman, and Cordell Hull), eighteen served in other cabinet positions, and three were speakers of the House of Representatives before coming to the Senate.[57]

While there are exceptions to every generalization, the Finance Committee was and still is first and foremost a safe harbor for senators from the small states. Since 1949 there has always been a member from Delaware, and from 1951 to 1961 there were two. A small state with limited resources, Delaware is for corporations what Nevada is for gambling and Florida is for the elderly. Hundreds of corporations are chartered there with no specific relationship to the state except for having their name, along with a dozen or so others, inscribed on an office door. It is the corporate haven of the country and is well represented on the Finance Committee, with its jurisdiction over corporation taxes and finances.

Especially on the Republican side, the committee has been inundated with senators from the small states of Vermont, Nevada, Kansas, Rhode Island, Utah, New Hampshire, Idaho, Arizona, Wyoming, New Mexico, Oregon, and Kentucky as well as Delaware. While an occasional big-state senator is appointed, the small-state predominance was illuminated by the appointment of Daniel P. Moynihan of New York in 1977—he was the first New York senator to serve on the Finance Committee in a century.

There are a variety of reasons for the small-state and western-state dominance. In particular, the election of a senator in those states costs a great deal less money than an election in New York, Massachusetts, Ohio, Illinois, or California. Relatively small amounts of money can be spent by groups with major interests before the Finance Committee to help elect senators who are persuaded by their cause. The protection of the mining industry from imports of foreign raw materials has been a major reason why western senators have sought membership.

Well into modern times, the Democratic Finance Committee members had three characteristics. First, members from states below the Mason-Dixon line were almost always in the majority. Second, they were overwhelmingly, like their small-state Republican colleagues, defenders of the special tax provisions for gas and oil—percentage depletion, the intangible drilling and development cost provision, the dry-hole write-off, and the "golden handshake" regulations which allowed American oil corporations to treat royalty payments abroad, especially in the Middle East, as payment of or credit against taxes instead of a deduction of costs.

The major oil-producing states—such as Texas, Oklahoma, and Louisiana—are not only routinely represented on the Finance Committee but often dominate the committee's work. This was true of Senator Kerr of Oklahoma, Senator Long of Louisiana, and Senator Bentsen of Texas, the latter two chairmen under Democratic Senate majorities.

Ordinarily, at least one of the two Louisiana senators is a member. Why that is so can be understood by examining the economic interests of that state and the legislative jurisdiction of the Finance Committee. Louisiana is not only an oil-producing state, it is a major producer of sugar cane and has one of the nation's biggest ports. New Orleans' wharves are crowded with both ocean-going vessels and Mississippi River barges which have carried goods to the warehouses that line the docks. Further, as a result of Huey Long's Populism, Louisiana has one of the most advanced and generous welfare systems in the country.

The Finance Committee has jurisdiction over oil and energy taxes, over imports of sugar, sugar subsidies, and the taxes assessed against sugar refineries within the United States, over trade and tariffs generally, over user taxes for barges, and over welfare payments and Medicare and Medicaid, all of which are important to the state. It is not only an obvious but a required choice of committees for at least one of Louisiana's senators. Similar economic or political interests compel others to seek membership.

BUDGET REFORMS

Both Presidents Reagan and Bush have called for a number of budget reforms that they claim would solve or help to solve the budget problem. Among them are proposals (1) to establish a two-year budget cycle, (2) to combine the two-step authorization and appropriations procedures, so that, for example, the Armed Services Committee would both authorize a new weapon and appropriate the money for it, (3) to change the congressional budget resolution from a concurrent resolution affecting only the Congress to a joint resolution requiring the president's signature or a two-thirds vote in each house to override its veto, (4) to give the president a line-item veto for money bills, and (5) to ratify a constitutional amendment to require a balance budget. The last issue is discussed in Chapter 5, but it should be noted here that neither President Ronald Reagan nor George Bush ever submitted a balanced budget in the more than a decade they were calling for one.

The transformation of the budget resolution and the line-item veto are both highly partisan issues pitting a Republican president and his congressional supporters against a Democratic Congress. But the calls for a two-year budget cycle and a combination of the authorizing and appropriating committees have more widespread support, except where support is needed most, namely in the Congress.

The Two-Year Budget Cycle

The argument for a two-year budget cycle has certain attractions. By appropriating funds in the first year, the Congress could spend more time exercising genuine oversight procedures in the second. It would provide more time for better planning and performance by the agencies, and reduce the time spent without knowing what funds will be available and beginning a new budget cycle before the old one has been completed.

There are several arguments against the two-year cycle, however. There is no guarantee that the Congress would in fact pass the two-year budget before the new fiscal year begins. Before 1974, when the budget was proposed in January and the new fiscal year began six months later on July 1, the Congress usually finished its work by that date. Seldom was there a need to pass continuing resolutions, or to shut down or to threaten to shut down the government, as happened routinely from 1981 to 1991. With the passage of the Budget Act in 1974 and its Gramm-Rudman-Hollings amendments in 1985, so many budget issues, budget processes, and deadlines were heaped on the congressional calendar that the Congress was choking itself to death on the enormous increase in its workload. There are those who believe that if the cycle is extended to two years, difficult issues will not only be postponed until the end of the first year but until the end of second year. Perhaps a better proposal would be to return to the old system and again start the fiscal year on July 1. The Congress needs a deadline to hold its feet to the fire, and it is more apt to meet a six-month than a two-year schedule.

There is a second institutional problem with the proposal. The appropriations committees, with their existing power, have objected, because they are unwilling to forgo the control over spending that a one-year process provides. They also argue that budget decisions are now made in the executive branch from eight to twenty months before the new fiscal year begins, and twenty to thirty-two months before it ends. They see no purpose in extending the cycle another twelve months. If that happened, they argue, in the second year the Congress would not have more time for oversight but instead would be flooded with new and supplemental requests from almost all agencies, as the conditions under which the original budget was passed would have drastically changed for program after program.

There is presently an experiment for a two-year defense budget. The armed services committees have authorized funds for two years in many areas, but the appropriations committees have not followed suit and appropriated for two fiscal years. With the end of the Cold War, the decline in the number of troops in Europe, and the cost of Desert Storm, a two-year budget cycle for defense proved impossible to manage because of the rapid changes in events.

Combined Authorizing and Appropriating Functions

It is argued that to have one committee to authorize and a second to appropriate is a waste of time and a duplication of effort both for the Congress and the executive. Secretaries of departments complain about having to repeat their testimony before both House and Senate and legislative and appropriating committees. A secretary of defense may appear not only before the armed services committees, but the foreign relations, foreign affairs, energy, government operations, budget, and joint economic committees as well. At least one appearance for each might be eliminated if the authorizing and appropriations functions were combined.

Another supporting argument is that for much of the history of the United States, particularly until 1921, many of the legislative committees, and most of the important ones, also appropriated funds, which left jurisdiction over some of the less important agencies to the appropriations committees. In addition, the failure of the authorizing committees to complete their work on time has been a regular complaint of those seeking to speed up the process and finish the budget before the beginning of the new fiscal year.

Some of the above arguments are double-edged, however. It was the alleged failure of the legislative committees to appropriate properly that led to the creation of two strong appropriations committees after 1921. This was considered a major reform and was accomplished only after much struggle with the powerful heads of the legislative committees.

There is also one very strong argument against combining the two budget functions. The authorizing committees are routinely packed with supporters of the programs they fund, especially because of congressional district or state interest. The agriculture, interior, public works, armed services, and commerce committees are among those that are notorious in this respect. Historically they have authorized far more programs and far greater amounts than either the president or the appropriations committees have been willing to fund or that the country could possibly afford. At times about as many public works projects have been authorized but not funded as are actually receiving funds. Many believe that combining the functions would result in a bigger spending splurge.

Finally, some argue that both steps are needed. The authorizers become experts on the programs, and the appropriators make the choices between competing priorities. Both are necessary, but neither is indispensable. To combine them would short-change one or both of these important procedures.

The Joint Budget Resolution

Substituting a joint for a concurrent budget resolution is an institutional issue. The Congress is not about to delegate yet another power over the purse or a constitutional prerogative to the president, for that would make it possible for the president to prevail with a veto and the support of only one-third plus one of either the House or Senate. Sometimes, with thirty-four votes in the Senate to sustain his veto and only a handful in the House, as on the Chinese Tiananmen Square resolution, the president has prevailed with the support of only about 10 percent of the entire Congress.

For the first forty years of the American government, the veto was used only when the president believed a bill was unconstitutional. It was not until Andrew Jackson that the veto was used against bills the president opposed on policy grounds. Because the money power clearly resides in the Congress, because since the time of Magna Carta control of funds has been the safeguard of legislatures against the excesses of the executive, and because it was not until 1921 that there was even such a document as a presidential budget, on institutional grounds alone the Congress will oppose a president's claim to the right to veto a congressional budget designed to instruct its own committees and members on the priorities it determines by majority vote to be in the best interest of the country. The president continues to have the right to veto when the result of the congressional plan comes to his desk in the form of authorizing legislation or appropriations bills. In the view of the Congress, a proper respect for the division of powers would make a veto of its internal budget document and the prerogative it represents unthinkable and untenable.

The Line-Item Veto

The same institutional arguments apply to the proposal to give the president a line-item veto of budget items. The president has the constitutional authority to veto an entire bill, but the right to pick and choose certain items would return the money power to the executive. Both the Glorious Revolution in England and the American Revolution were fought in large part against the unlimited sovereignty of the executive and for parliamentary and congressional jurisdiction over the purse.

There are also practical reasons for the Congress's objection to the line-item veto. First, members believe the president would use it as a judicious form of blackmail: "Senator," he would say, "I have the Public Works Appropriations bill with three projects in your state on my desk. I was just calling to find out how you feel about my Supreme Court nominee. I certainly need your help on this."

Most members also believe that with the line-item veto the president could kill certain projects without killing the entire bill and thus still retain the money for numerous programs he had proposed in the states of his political supporters. This in fact is the most powerful congressional argument against the proposal.

But there is another and more important fact, which few of the proposal's advocates or opponents understand, that makes the line-item veto of dubious merit. In reality, there are very few items to veto, even in a public works, military construction, or foreign aid bill. Congress and the president function under a treaty of comity. The secretary of defense, for example, testifies that if the defense department gets the $10.6 billion asked for shipbuilding and conversion, the following ships will be constructed. However, unlike bills in state legislatures, which detail every bridge, road, or building to be constructed, no such detail is given in defense or foreign aid or public works appropriations bills. Instead the line item will give only a single figure for Navy shipbuilding or aircraft procurement Air Force. In a recent bill, the item for the latter read, "Aircraft procurement, Air Force, $14 billion." There was no mention of the Stealth or B-2 bombers, or the F-16 or A-10 fighters. Scarcely a single weapons system, public works project, or foreign aid recipient is mentioned in either the president's budget or an appropriations bill. Instead the details are found (1) in the testimony of the agency, and (2) in the committee report that accompanies the bill. Neither the president nor the agency nor the Congress wants it any other way. If the details are written into the bill, then any funding change desired by an agency in any project would require new legislation. But under the existing system of more general appropriations, shifts can be made in what funds are spent for what project merely with the informal approval of the congressional committee. If an agency abides by this understanding, it has little trouble with the Congress over needed funding changes. If, however, it attempts to trick the Congress, fails to keep its word, or conceals altered spending, it will find an inflexible Congress that will retaliate at the next request for funds.

In fact, in those relatively rare instances when the Congress actually writes details into an appropriations bill on how Navy procurement money for ships and/or aircraft is to be spent or foreign aid funds are to be distributed, the Congress is charged by vociferous executive branch officials or their political supporters in the press with attempting to micromanage the Navy or trying to act as 535 secretaries of state. The State Department, for example, strongly and routinely objects to the Congress designating in the foreign aid appropriations bill which countries shall receive what amounts. Instead the department pleads for and usually gets a nondesignated lump sum for distribution to foreign nations.

The Prognosis for Budget Reforms

At the very best a two-year budget, combining the authorizing and appropriations committees, a joint instead of a concurrent budget resolution, or a line-item veto might have a marginal, or minor positive effect on the budget. More likely these proposals would have some of the negative effects detailed above; and some might in fact change the very nature of the system of checks and balances and the division and sharing of powers provided in the Constitution. There is very little prospect for their passage.

NOTES

1. *The New York Times*, 10 February, 1982, p. Al. Reprinted by permission.
2. There are those who argue it could be changed by two amendments, by first repealing the provision of Article V and then amending Article I, but this is an exercise in imagination, not reality.
3. 369 U.S. 186.
4. 377 U.S. 533.
5. For an exception see Lawrence D. Longley and Walter J. Oleszek, *Bicameral Politics: Conference Committees in Congress* (New Haven: Yale University Press, 1989).
6. John T. McEvoy in *The Congressional Budget Process After Five Years*, ed. Rudolph G. Penner (Washington, D.C.: American Enterprise Institute for Public Policy Research, 1981), p. 78.
7. Ibid.
8. Roger H. Davidson and Walter J. Oleszek, *Congress and Its Members* (Washington, D.C.: CQ Press, 1990), p. 196. Chapter 12 of their book contains a very clear presentation of congressional committees and their evolution.
9. Woodrow Wilson, *Congressional Government* (New York: Meridian Books, Inc., 1960), p. 69.
10. Senate Committee on Appropriations, 90th Cong., 1st sess., S. Document 21 (Washington, D.C.: U.S. Government Printing Office, 1967), pp. 1–5.
11. Ibid., p. 1.
12. Ibid., p. 4. Rule Thirty was adopted on 19 December 1850.
13. Ibid., p. 8.
14. Ibid., p. 13. Clause 1 of Rule Sixteen of the Standing Rules of the Senate.
15. Howard E. Shuman, "Canonizing Pork," *The New York Times*, 19 November 1976, p. A27. Copyright 1976 by *The New York Times* Company. Reprinted by permission.
16. Floyd M. Riddick, *Senate Procedure, Precedents and Practice* (Washington, D.C.: U.S. Government Printing Office, 1981), p. 122 n. 4.
17. *Congressional Record*, 46th Cong. 2d sess., 11 March 1880, p. 1483; *Congressional Record*, 46th Cong. 3rd sess., 2 February 1881, p. 1146.
18. Riddick, *Senate Procedure*, pp. 122–123.
19. Stephen Horn, *Unused Power* (Washington, D.C.: The Brookings Institution, 1970), p. 167.
20. Under Article I, Section 5, "Neither House, during the Session of Congress, shall, without the Consent of the other, adjourn for more than three days . . . ." Both the House and the Senate had passed the *sine die* concurrent resolution, so the House adjourned and left the Senate with no choice. Under Article II,

Section 3, the president can "on extraordinary Occasions, convene both Houses, or either of them . . . ."

21. For a precise and delightful exposition of the 1962 conflict, see Horn, *Unused Power,* pp. 165–173.
22. "House Bypasses Constitution on Tax Boost," *Los Angeles Times,* 29 July 1982, part I, p. 1. Copyright 1982, *Los Angeles Times.* Reprinted by permission.
23. Figures are from *Congressional Directory, 101st Congress* (Washington, D.C.: U.S. Government Printing Office, 1989), pp. 318–331, 334–336, 366–368, and House and Senate Appropriations Committees, January 1991.
24. *Congressional Directory, 101st Congress,* p. 367.
25. *Congressional Record* (daily ed.), 25 March 1982, p. D336.
26. *United States Senate Legislative Activity Sourcebook,* prepared for the Commission on the Operation of the Senate (Washington, D.C.: U.S. Government Printing Office, 1976), p. 13.
27. Conversation with Tom Scott, former staff director.
28. Senators are, on the basis of seniority. assigned hideaway offices or suites in the Capitol, where they can work without interruption by the stream of constituents or lobbyists who daily seek their attention.
29. Senate Committee on Appropriations, *Subcommittees and Subcommittee Assignments,* 97th Cong. (Washington, D.C.: Government Printing Office, 1981), p. 4.
30. Charles Stuart, ed., *Reith Diaries* (London: Collins, 1975), p. 299.
31. Horn, *Unused Power,* p. 91.
32. Howard E. Shuman, "Congress, the President, and Urban Policy" (paper delivered at the 1978 Meeting of the American Political Science Association, New York, 3 September 1978), p. 5.
33. *Senate Manual, Containing the Standing Rules, Orders, Laws, and Resolutions Affecting the Business of the United States Senate* (Washington, D.C.: U.S. Government Printing Office, 1979), Rule XVI, p. 14.
34. Ibid.
35. Ibid., p. 15.
36. Riddick, *Senate Procedure,* , p. 153.
37. *Senate Manual,* p. 15.
38. *Joint Resolution Making Further Continuing Appropriations for the Fiscal Year 1981, and for Other Purposes, H. J. Res. 637,* 96th Cong. 2d sess., 11 December 1980, pp. 1–73.
39. Riddick, *Senate Procedure,* p. 130.
40. William S. White, *Citadel* (New York: Harper & Brothers, 1965), p. 68.
41. For a thorough and expert discussion, see Louis Fisher, *The Authorization-Appropriation Process, Formal Rules and Informal Practices* (Washington, D.C.: Congressional Research Service, Library of Congress, 1979).
42. Senate Committee on the Budget, *Congressional Budget Reform, Public Law 93—344* (Washington, D.C.: U.S. Government Printing Office, 1976), p. 70. Under the act, the comptroller general of the United States, in cooperation with the secretary of the treasury, the director of the OMB, and the director of the Congressional Budget Office, was directed to develop and publish standard terminology and definitions. A glossary of definitions is printed as part of the Budget Reform Act.
43. *Washington Post,* 21 December 1982, p. A13.
44. Ibid.
45. *The New York Times,* 28 December 1982, p. A23. Copyright 1982 by *The New York Times* Company.
46. See Louis Fisher, *Budget Concepts and Terminology: The Appropriations Phase* (Washington, D.C.: Congressional Research Service, Library of Congress, 1974).

47. *Rules and Manual of the United States Senate, 1979* (Washington, D.C.: Government Printing Office, 1979), pp. 30–31.
48. *Budget of the United States Government Fiscal Year 1992* (Washington, D.C.: U.S. Government Printing Office, 1991), pt. 3, p. 3. A very small amount of revenues is in the form of user fees or admission funds, which, because they are called fees rather than taxes, remain under the jurisdiction of other legislative committees. Some of these are earmarked and do not go into the general fund. However, the tax committees exercise jurisdiction over all taxes.
49. Ibid., pt. 4, pp. 9–11, 13.
50. Louis Fisher, *Presidential Spending Power.* Copyright © 1975 by Princeton University Press, p. 12.
51. Ibid., p. 13.
52. U.S. Senate, *History of the Committee on Finance,* pp. 14–15.
53. Horn, *Unused Power,* pp. 165–173.
54. *Congressional Directory, 99th Congress* (Washington, D.C.: U.S. Government Printing Office 1985), p. 353.
55. Paul H. Douglas, *In the Fullness of Time* (New York: Harcourt-Brace-Jovanovich, 1971), pp. 452–453.
56. Randall B. Ripley, *Power in the Senate* (New York: St. Martin's, 1969) p. 27.
57. U.S. Senate, *History of the Committee on Finance,* pp. 11–13.

4

Politics and Taxes

INTRODUCTION

Revenues are as important to the budget as expenditures. Historically there has been as much political controversy over taxes as over spending.

For more than one hundred years, from 1789 until 1893, except during periods of panic and war, the budget was in balance every year. This was the result of two major factors: (1) the federal government was proportionately much smaller than it is today; and (2) tariffs and customs duties supplied a surfeit of revenues.

The income tax was unknown until the Civil War. It then became dormant until 1894, when President Cleveland convinced the Congress to lower tariffs and substitute a modest tax on incomes to recoup the revenues. This brought a heated political debate and an adverse Supreme Court decision characterized more by the fierceness of the rhetoric than the logic of the arguments. The Sixteenth Amendment to the Constitution, which gave the Congress the power to lay and collect taxes on incomes from whatever source, without apportionment among the states and without regard to any census or enumeration, was ratified in 1913. It was passed in time to provide about two-thirds of the revenues raised during World War I.

The income tax was a latent force until World War II, but from then until recent times the progressive personal income tax and the corporate income tax together provided more than 70 percent of federal revenues. Several things have happened to federal taxes in recent years. The proportion of personal and corporate income taxes has declined and now provides only slightly more than half the revenues. Payroll taxes now make up more than one-third of the total amount of federal taxes collected. As a result, the federal tax system as a whole can no longer be characterized as progressive, meaning a system that in its totality is based on the ability to pay. The system is also characterized by tax expenditures, which some call loopholes. Before the monumental Tax Reform Act of 1986, the loss of revenues from tax expenditures was equal to almost half the revenues collected. The act repealed or reduced some of the corporate tax expenditures and many of the deductions for individuals. Individual and corporate tax rates were lowered substantially in order to provide a "revenue-neutral" bill during its first five years.

In 1981 the Congress reduced federal taxes by $750 billion over the succeeding five years. The cuts were geared toward reducing the taxes of corporations and higher income groups, and guaranteed massive budget deficits into the 1990s. The cuts were passed by Republicans and Democrats alike. The major justification for the action was that it would increase savings and investments and hence stimulate employment and production. The increase in revenues, according to the secretary of the Treasury, would "wipe out the red ink" and lead to a balanced budget. But much of the savings was borrowed by the Treasury to finance the burgeoning debt, and this crowded out funds for investment and for housing, autos, and other consumer purchases. In eight years the deficit almost tripled.

The tax revenue hemorrhage was so great that in spite of President Reagan's repeated threats to veto any tax bill presented to him, the Congress passed and he signed four substantial and one minor tax increase bills in 1982–1984. One of these, the Tax Equity and Fiscal Responsibility Act of 1982, was initiated by the Republican Senate at the expense of Article I, Section 7, of the Constitution, which grants the power to initiate taxes to the House of Representatives. In 1985–1988 there were additional small tax increases every year, usually as part of the annual reconciliation bill.

TAXES AND CONTROVERSY

The tax side of the budget is equal to its spending side in its political and economic importance. It was Supreme Court Justice Oliver Wendell Holmes who said that "taxes are what we pay for a civilized society."[1] His equally famous brother, Judge Learned Hand, who sat on the lower Circuit Court of Appeals, pointed out that no one is required to pay more taxes than the law states:

> there is nothing sinister in arranging one's affairs as to keep taxes as low as possible. Everybody does so, rich or poor; and all do right. Nobody owes any

public duty to pay more than the law demands; taxes are enforced exactions, not voluntary contributions. To demand more in the name of morals is mere cant.[2]

Mississippi Senator Pat Harrison, who served on the formidable tax-writing Senate Finance Committee from 1923 to 1941 and was its chairman for almost ten years during six Congresses, put it succinctly:

There's nothing that says a man has to take a toll bridge across a river when there's a free bridge nearby.[3]

Taxes have been the subject of comment, controversy, and politics since the country was founded. The Constitution provides in Article I, Section 8, that "the Congress shall have power to lay and collect taxes, duties, imposts and excises, to pay the debts and provide for the common defense and general welfare of the United States." This provision heads the list of powers delegated to the Congress, and represents an extraordinarily broad and sweeping grant of fiscal authority. It covers almost any form of taxation one can conceive. As constitutional scholars have emphasized:

The possession of adequate sources of revenue and broad authority to use public funds for public purposes are essential conditions for carrying on an effective government. Consequently the first rule for judicial review of tax statutes is that a heavy burden of proof lies on anyone who would challenge any congressional exercise of fiscal power.[4]

However, "the power to tax is a potent economic weapon, and the framers sought to make sure it could not be used to the advantage of some states at the expense of others."[5] For this reason they added specific constitutional limits on this broad grant. One was the phrase added to Article I, Section 8: "all Duties, Imposts and Excises shall be uniform throughout the United States." Another limit (Article I, Section 9) adopted to protect the agricultural states, was that "no tax or duty shall be laid on articles exported from any State." This same article also provided that "no capitation, or other direct tax shall be laid, unless in proportion to the Census or Enumeration herein before directed to be taken." While the problem of defining what a direct tax is would haunt the politics and economics of the late nineteenth century in the various income tax cases, this provision was the direct result of the politics of slavery. As Justice William Paterson, who was present at the Constitutional Convention, as a delegate from New Jersey, pointed out in *Hylton v. United States* (1796):

The provision was made in favor of the Southern States. They possessed a large number of slaves; they had extensive tracts of territory, thinly settled and not very productive. A majority of states had but few slaves, and several of them a limited territory, well settled, and in a high state of cultivation. The Southern States, if no provision had been introduced in the Constitution, would have been wholly at the mercy of other States.[6]

As "the power to tax involves the power to destroy," as Chief Justice Marshall wrote in *McCulloch v. Maryland* (1819), the South was protecting both slavery and its land from the taxing power of the central government.

There were three types of early taxes. The first tax was a tariff:

> Before any Treasury Department had been organized, before even the President had been inaugurated, Congress began debating a customs measure. By July 4, 1789, a tariff bill had passed both houses and been approved by the President. The United States had its first national tax.[7]

That tax brought in 99.5 percent of the new federal government's revenues during its first two years of existence and provided a surplus of almost $150,000.

Until the Civil War, customs revenues provided the preponderance of receipts, and even into the 1890s they provided more than half of the government's revenues. For more than a century, from 1789 until 1894 (except for periods of war and panics), customs receipts were the main reason that deciding what to do about surpluses rather than hand-wringing over deficits characterized the political arguments about the budget and dominated U.S. fiscal policy. In those 104 years, there were seventy-seven surpluses and only twenty-seven deficits. At least twelve of the latter were the direct result of increased spending for the military during the War of 1812, the War with Mexico, and the Civil War. So successful were customs as a source of revenue that in 1837 the government was entirely free of debt, and for the 28 years from 1866 through 1893 there was a surplus every year.[8]

"Internal excises," or taxes on "sin," were the second form of early taxes. Under Alexander Hamilton's advocacy and astute political hand, the federal government both assumed the state debts and paid off the country's domestic and foreign war debt. There were heavy burdens consisting of $11.7 million in foreign debt, $40.4 million in domestic debt, and $25 million in assumed state debts, for a total of $77 million.[9] Additional forms of revenue were solely needed. Hamilton proposed a series of taxes on luxuries and indulgences. Opposition arose immediately. It was argued that "several of the items to be subjected to these federal excises, whiskey in particular, were not luxuries at all but the poor man's necessities."[10] The attempts to enforce the whisky excises in 1794 fomented the Whiskey Rebellion in western Pennsylvania. Finally, "urged by Hamilton, Washington sent a strong force against the rebels. They were overawed, and the revolt ended."[11] It was ironic that those who had fought a war against taxation without representation were put down by their new government when they objected to heavy taxation on the products of their industry.

Western Pennsylvania was not alone in objecting to the taxes on whiskey and sin. As Albert Bolles points out in his *Financial History of the United States*:

> Grog was declared to be a necessary article of drink in the Southern States and consequently this mode of taxation was odious, unequal, unpopular, and

oppressive. Jackson of Georgia complained during the debate over taxation in the Second Congress, "I plainly perceive that the time will come when a shirt shall not be washed without an excise."[12]

These congressional arguments of the 1790s were echoed in the 1980s by the chairman of the House Ways and Means Committee, Dan Rostenkowski (D.-Ill.), who denounced the excise tax increase on tobacco and alcohol contemplated by the Reagan administration as "a most regressive consumer tax."[13] To many politicians the rich man's indulgences remained of the poor man's necessities. But eighteenth-century taxes on "sin" and "indulgences" were echoed in tax increases at the end of the twentieth century. The Omnibus Budget and Reconciliation Act of 1990 raised $14.7 billion in sin taxes on beer, wine, and hard liquor, and another $1.5 billion in taxes on luxuries and indulgences (private planes, yachts, expensive cars, furs, and jewelry); this totaled more than the entire government revenues in 1942—$14.6 billion.

By 1798 direct taxes were enacted on houses and slaves as well as an ad valorem tax on land. A stamp tax on legal documents was also passed. The house tax was a progressive tax with a levy of one-fifth of 1 percent on houses worth $100 to $500, rising to a full 1 percent on houses valued at $30,000 or more.[14] "The total $2,000,000 levy was distributed among the states in proportion to population as required by the Constitution,"[15] but collection was slow, and direct taxes did not become an important source of revenues because of the complexity of the machinery needed to assess and collect them. Many of these early taxes are now generally the province of state and local governments and compose a substantial source of their revenues.

Sumptuary taxes were heavily satirized in the pamphlets of the time. Critics proposed with tongue in cheek that if taxes on sin were universalized, they might save the day. It was suggested that if perjury, drunkenness, blasphemy, slander, and infidelity were taxed, vast revenues would be raised. One critic considered perjury to be the most important and stable source of revenues. It was proposed that drunkenness could be taxed at sixpence. Taxing swearing would be a universal source of revenue, but the writer feared that military men would object to it.

> Conjugal infidelity, as the world goes at present, would furnish the public with a large sum even at a very moderate tax, for it is now made an essential part of the polite gentlemen's character, and he that has prevailed on the greatest number proportionally rises in reputation.[16]

But like direct taxes, sumptuary or excise taxes were not an important element in the early tax history of the country. Customs and tariffs were the real nineteenth-century moneymakers.

From the beginning, revenues from customs and tariffs, like those from luxuries and indulgences, were also the subject of hotly contested political debate. On the one hand were those who supported the tariff for its money-raising ability. They cry went up, "A tariff for revenue only." But others wanted to impose duties to protect American mines and manufacturing from foreign competition, thus making the so-called infant industries argument for protection. As Frank Taussig, America's foremost historian of the tariff, pointed out, "Of the arguments in favor of protection, none has been more frequently or more sincerely urged than that which is expressed in the phrase 'protection to young industries.' "[17] Obviously the two purposes are contradictory. The degree to which a tariff prevents imports is the degree to which it reduces revenues.

It was Congressman James Madison, one of the Founding Fathers and later president, who proposed the first customs bill before the House of Representatives in April of 1789. It had three main provisions. Specific duties would be levied against a handful of items: liquor, molasses, wine, tea, pepper, sugar, cocoa, and coffee. A 5 percent ad valorem tax would be levied against the rest. In addition, a duty would be levied on the tonnage of ships, with American vessels treated more favorably. The political and regional flavor of the argument is seen in this quote from Shultz and Caine:

> Debate in the House showed that its members had in mind other functions for a customs duty than the bare raising of revenue. The rum makers of New England, the owners of iron mines in Pennsylvania and New Jersey, the makers of boots and shoes, of woolen and cotton cloth, of candles—each newborn industry that had struck root in American soil—now demanded protection from foreign competition. Some of the duties proposed were sheerly prohibitory, and would have produced no revenue whatsoever. Against the protective demands of the northern and central states rose the protests of the planters and settlers of the South and West, who had much to lose and nothing to gain from a protective tariff.[18]

Special interest groups are thus not a new phenomenon in government.

While the "infant industry" argument was first raised in 1789, it was not until 1808, after the passage of Jefferson's Embargo Act, "that the most decided attempt was made to apply protection to young industries in the United States."[19] The Embargo Act was retaliation against British impressment of American seamen in the war between France and Great Britain. Often called the war between the elephant (France) and the whale (England), the English Orders in Council declared a blockade from the River Elbe to the French port of Brest and in 1807 extended it to all French ports. American ships carried much of the trade between the United States and both France and England. "About 1,600 American vessels and $60,000,000 worth of property were captured by French, English, and other privateers."[20] The self-imposed Embargo Act prevented American ships from leaving American ports for ports of any foreign power. They were limited to the coastal trade.

The American embargo had unintended results, as U.S. exports fell from $108.3 million in 1807 to $22.4 million in 1808 and brought disaster to the shipping and shipbuilding industries and associated industries as well as an extraordinarily high rate of unemployment among seamen. "This law acted like an overloaded gun, which shoots backwards as well as forward."[21] The results focused attention on the economic and political vulnerability of the new American nation. As Taussig pointed out, "During the twenty years which followed the war of 1812 the protective controversy was one of the most important features in the political life of the nation; and the young industries argument was the great rallying-cry of the protectionists."[22]

The fight between those who advocated the tariff for revenue purposes and those who pushed it for protection spilled over into the jurisdictional political rights of the Congress itself. The formal system of committees known in the Congress today did not exist in the earliest years, but by 1816 a number of more or less permanent or standing committees had been established. A battle soon brewed in the Senate between its (temporary) Select Committee on Manufacturers, which was protectionist, and the Committee on Finance and An Uniform National Currency, which favored tariffs not for protection but for revenues. Even though the Finance Committee had jurisdiction over taxes and tariffs.

> The sections of the 1815 President's message dealing with tariffs had been referred to a Select Committee on Manufacturers. This Committee became the standing [permanent] Committee on Commerce and Manufacturing in December 1816; its membership in the second session of the 14th Congress was limited to Senators from Rhode Island, New Hampshire, New York, and Pennsylvania. Given its composition, it was naturally sympathetic to raising tariffs to protect American industry.[23]

In 1816, these two committees divided jurisdiction over four tariff measures, but for ten years, no significant tariff bills were referred to the Finance Committee:

> A distinction was apparently made between tariff measures for revenue purposes only (such as the duty on salt), which were referred to the Finance Committee, and tariff measures on manufactured goods for the purpose of protection, which were referred to the other Committee.[24]

The highly protective tariff act of 1824 and the 1828 "Tariff of Abominations" were in part the result of this political infighting. It was not until 1834 that the Finance Committee regained permanent jurisdiction over tariffs from the Committee on Commerce and Manufacturers. The protectionists, with a few exceptions, continued to win tariff battles until the passage of the infamous Smoot-Hawley Tariff Act of 1930 and the advent of the reciprocal tariffs of Cordell Hull and Franklin Roosevelt.

Thus the dominant sources of government revenues from 1789 to the end of the nineteenth century—customs and tariffs—were the subject of the most heated partisan and regional politics. The tariff not only separated

Whigs from Federalists and Democrats from Republicans, but North from South, industry from agriculture, protectionists from free traders, presidents from the Congress, House from Senate, and committees on taxes from committees with jurisdiction over commerce and manufacturing. During the first third of the twentieth century, after the tariff declined as a major source of revenues, the battles continued. While the financial and economic historians have written extensively on the politics of tariffs and taxes, the revenue side of the budget has too often been ignored by students of the politics and procedures of the budget. Yet historically tariffs and taxes have composed more than half of the budget and have engaged the president, the Congress, interest groups, and the public in some of the most heated and vitriolic political arguments in the course of the nation's life.

ORIGINS OF PERSONAL AND CORPORATE INCOME TAXES

Unlike customs and excise taxes, which date from the eighteenth century, personal and corporate income taxes in the United States had their origins with the Civil War, "when the federal government sought revenue from every conceivable source."[25] During the war, taxes were levied on business in three ways—license taxes, gross receipts taxes, and taxes on banks (on stocks, deposits, capital, and bank note circulation). During the same period, the first federal personal income tax was levied to answer the same desperate need for revenues. By 1865 it amounted to 5 percent on incomes between $600 and $5,000, and 10 percent on incomes greater than that.[26] By fiscal year 1866, income and profit taxes raised $73 million.[27] The corporate business taxes were abolished by 1870, and the personal income tax was ended in 1872. They had raised more than $350 million.[28]

When Grover Cleveland and the Democrats lowered tariffs in 1894, they levied the second federal income tax to pick up the revenue slack. That tax carried out the campaign pledges of the Democratic party under the banner of Cleveland for president and Adlai Stevenson of Illinois for vice-president in 1892, and the law was considered a major political victory both for the progressive forces in the country and for the South and West against the Northeast. Incomes below $4,000 were exempt, and the tax was a modest 2 percent on incomes above that amount. Virtually all income was included—income from real estate, stocks and bonds, state and local government bonds, wages, salaries, and professional services.

The forces of wealth and privilege to which the tax was applied were outraged—$4,000 was a considerable income in 1894—not so much over the 2 percent tax as over the fear that it would be increased in the future. In two decisions of 1895, the Supreme Court held in *Pollock v. The Farmers' Loan and*

Trust Company[29] that the tax was direct and that, as it was not apportioned among the states by population it was unconstitutional. The case was characterized by the intense tactics of the opponents of the tax, the heightened level of rhetoric, and the lack of objectivity among the members of the Supreme Court.

Two significant cases preceded *Pollock*. The first was *Hylton* (1796), in which a carriage tax was held to be an excise tax, the importance of which lay not in the decision itself but in its dictum that direct taxes were limited to being those on land and slaves (capitation). In the second case, a lawyer named Springer objected to the Civil War income tax on two grounds: first, that it was a direct tax because it could not be passed on, and second, this being true, that it was thus unconstitutional because it was not in proportion to population. In *Springer v. U.S.* (1881), the Supreme Court turned the dictum of *Hylton* into decision, held unanimously that the income tax was an excise tax and need not be apportioned, and upheld the law.[30] The constitutionality of the income tax thus seemed to be settled.

Several features illustrate the heated political atmosphere of the *Pollock* case. The Supreme Court was so eager to take the case that it ignored the general rule that taxes can be contested only after they are paid and agreed to hear the case on appeal from a suit to enjoin a bank from paying the tax. In the first decision, there was a four-to-four tie on the main issue. Instead of letting the appeals court decision stand, as would ordinarily happen, the Supreme Court heard the case again. The missing member, Justice Howell Edmunds Jackson, who had been ill and who would die shortly after the decision in the second case, was urged to retire. That maneuver failed, and Justice Jackson voted to uphold the tax. But another member, believed to be Justice George Shiras, Jr., changed his vote, and the Court held five to four that the tax on incomes from stocks and bonds was direct and thus could only be levied by apportionment to the states on the basis of population. Even though the Court held that taxing income from wages, salaries, and professional services was constitutional as an excise tax, the entire case was thrown out on grounds that if one part was unconstitutional, the entire statute fell.

The rhetoric of the arguments and decision matched the intensity of the infighting and jockeying for position. The Court was told that this was the most important case it had ever heard or would hear. Counsel was sought from the best legal talent in the country, and Joseph H. Choate urged the Court, more than three decades before the Russian Revolution, to step in and stop "this Communistic march." In his majority opinion, Chief Justice Fuller referred to the decisions in *Hylton* and *Springer* as "a century of error."[31]

Justice Field wrote that "the present assault on capital is but the beginning. It will be but a stepping stone to others . . . till our political contests will become a war of the poor against the rich; a war constantly growing in intensity and bitterness." He believed that a decision upholding the tax would "mark the hour when the sure decadence of our government would commence."

On the other side, Justice Henry Billings Brown, known as a moderate member of the Court, wrote in a somewhat immoderate statement that "the decision involves nothing less than a surrender of the taxing power to the moneyed class. . . . Even the spectre of socialism is conjured up to frighten Congress from laying taxes upon the people in proportion to their ability to pay them. . . ." He hoped that the case would "not prove the first step towards the submergence of the liberties of the people in a sordid despotism of wealth."[32]

In *Pollock*, the Supreme Court overreached itself. There was such a popular clamor against the decision that in 1909, the Congress passed a 1 percent tax on the net income of corporations, thinly disguised as an excise, which the Court upheld in 1911. In 1909, the Congress, with the support of President Taft, also proposed the Sixteenth Amendment, which gave the Congress the "power to lay and collect taxes on incomes, from whatever source derived, without apportionment among the several States, and without regard to any census or enumeration." It was ratified in 1913.

As constitutional expert C. Herman Pritchett commented in referring to the 1895 *Pollock* decision:

> This surrender of the Court to entrenched wealth, in the same year that it refused to apply the Sherman Act against the sugar trust and upheld the conviction of Eugene V. Debs for violating an injunction during the Pullman strike, revealed only too clearly the judiciary's alignment on the side of capital, and earned the Court a popular reputation as a tool of special privilege which was not dispelled for forty years.[33]

Thus taxes were immersed not only on congressional, but in Supreme Court politics. In the case of *Pollock v. Farmers' Loan and Trust Co.* (1895), the Supreme Court failed to read the election returns.

Justice Brown has written in his dissent in *Pollock* that "my fear is that in some moment of national peril this decision will rise up to frustrate its [Congress's] will and paralyze its arm" and feared that "the decision of the Court in this great case is fraught with immeasurable danger to the future of the country. . . ." The Sixteenth Amendment prevented the disaster Justice Brown foresaw. While the income tax provided less than one-tenth of the federal revenues during the first two years of its existence, it was passed in time to provide almost two-thirds of total federal tax receipts in fiscal year 1918 during World War I. By this time, customs receipts—the historic backbone of federal revenues—were less than 5 percent of the total. The enactment of the Sixteenth Amendment was a watershed in American tax and budget history.

TAXES AND THE MODERN BUDGET

After the major role they played in World War I, the personal and corporate income taxes were a latent force until World War II. From the early 1920s until 1942, they accounted for less than half of the total net revenues. In 1934, for example, they raised only 28 percent of the total. This was due in part to the fact that for twenty years government revenues were small and did not exceed the World War I totals in any single year. It was not until fiscal year 1941 that the $7.9 billion of total receipts collected by the federal government exceeded the $6.8 billion total of two decades earlier.[34] But during World War II, an even greater proportion of the revenues was collected from the personal and corporate income taxes. In fiscal year 1945, for example, $35.2 billion, or almost 75 percent of the $47.7 billion total, was raised from them.[35]

Meanwhile, new types of taxes were emerging. During the 1930s, while revenues were relatively low, employment taxes in the form of Social Security, unemployment, and retirement taxes were initiated. While employment taxes were started during the Great Depression and income taxes were enlarged during World War II, it was after 1946 that major and dramatic changes in both the source and the totals of federal revenues took place.

As a result, the conflicts and controversies over taxes continue. Politicians and the public argue endlessly about them. Taxes and politics are almost synonymous terms. To raise the revenues necessary to pay for the services demanded by the people is the foremost purpose of taxation. Yet there have been intense arguments during more than three decades of deficits about how to achieve this fundamental and generally benign goal. Controversy has been rife over whether taxes should be used to achieve social purposes (if so, which ones?) and over how to use them to reward some social activities and punish others. Some have advocated special tax features to stimulate particular business or economic actions or to help regulate the economy in general. The issues of who should pay taxes; who should impose them, who should collect them, and the methods used to do both; whether they are progressive, regressive, or neutral; whether fees should be charged for those who use public services; whether receipts should be earmarked; and whether, in the words of Joseph A. Pechman, they "distribute the cost of government fairly by income classes (vertical equity) and among people of approximately the same economic circumstances (horizontal equity),"[36] are all subjects of controversy and dispute.

In the four decades from 1950 to 1990 there were significant changes in the tax structure. While the personal income tax rose from 39.9 to more than 45 percent of federal revenues, the corporate income tax declined from 26.5 to 9.4 percent of the total, or to one-third of its previous level. This was a massive reduction. Meanwhile there was an explosion in payroll taxes, from 11 to 36.4 percent. Excise taxes declined from 19.1 to 3.5 percent, and other taxes grew from 3.4 to 5.1 percent of the annual total. Table 4–1 documents these significant changes.

The decline of the corporate income tax, accompanied by a tripling of payroll taxes, has obviously affected the incidence of federal taxes, or the politics of who pays for the civilization that Justice Holmes said taxes buy. While there are honest differences of opinion as to who pays the corporate tax—is it shifted forward to consumers or backward to suppliers, or does it reflect a reduction in the dividends of stockholders?—there is little doubt that its decline, accompanied by the vast increase in both the proportion of the total represented by and the dollar amounts of payroll taxes, has greatly reduced the progressive nature of the federal tax system. Many believe that the overall federal tax burden is now at best proportional.

In fact, according to the Social Security Administration, 25 percent of U.S. households now pay more in Social Security taxes than in income taxes. Among female-headed households, the comparable figure is 37 percent, and among black households, it is 41 percent. These figures reflect only the half of the Social Security tax paid by employees. While the other half is paid by employers, it is generally assumed that employees pay both halves because employers either are able to shift the incidence or consider their share a part of the total wage package and subtract it from wages or benefits they would otherwise pay. If one assumes that employees pay both halves, then about 50 percent of all U.S. households pay more in Social Security taxes than they do in income taxes.[37]

Because the Social Security tax is a flat tax that is paid only on income up to a certain ceiling each year, it is a far greater burden on those with low or moderate incomes than it is on the well-to-do. This adds to the disproportionate tax burden borne by the vast middle class of American citizens. Unlike the poor, they have substantial income on which they pay income and

TABLE 4–1   The Sources of Federal Government Tax Revenues in Selected Fiscal Years

Federal Tax	(Percent of Total Revenues)				
	1950	**1960**	**1970**	**1980**	**1990**
Individual income tax	39.9	44.0	46.9	47.2	45.6
Corporation income tax	26.5	23.2	17.0	12.5	9.4
Payroll taxes	11.0	15.9	23.0	30.5	36.4
Excise taxes	19.1	12.6	8.1	4.7	3.5
Other	3.4	4.2	4.9	5.1	5.1

Source: 1950–1980: *Historical Tables, Budget of the United States Government, FY 1989* (Washington, D.C.: U.S. Government Printing Office, 1988), pp. 26–27.
1990: Executive Office of the President, Office of Management and Budget, *Mid-Session Review of the Budget,* 16 July 1990, p. D-5.

employment taxes. Unlike the rich, as their income is largely from wages and salaries, they have few methods by which to shelter their income to avoid taxation. Further, especially during inflation, they suffer from "bracket creep." Wage and salary increases, which do not keep pace with inflation, can move incomes into higher tax brackets. Middle-income citizens thus can pay more taxes on less real income.

While federal taxes have become less progressive, state and local taxes appear to be less regressive, as Table 4–2 indicates. This table shows a steady decline in property taxes as a proportion of the total. Generally considered to be among the most regressive taxes, their share has fallen from 64 percent of the total in 1927 to 46 percent in 1940, 32 percent in 1960, and 18 percent in the 1987–1988 fiscal year. Meanwhile, combined state and local personal and corporate income taxes have grown from 2 to 15 percent of the total. On the whole, they are considered to be somewhat progressive. In the last half-century, the contribution made by the federal government to state and local government revenues jumped from 1.5 to 16 percent, although it has declined from 21 percent during the Reagan presidency. In general these revenues are raised from more progressive federal than regressive state taxes. State reliance on the regressive sales tax (22 percent) has more than offset this progressive contribution of the federal government to state reve- nues. The totality of the changes at the state level means that the sources are less regressive than they once were.

Further, changes since the late 1960s have turned many assumptions about the American tax structure on their heads. Joseph Pechman, perhaps the most astute of all American tax scholars, was correct in 1970 when he wrote in the introduction to his classic book, *Federal Tax Policy*, that the most distinctive feature of the U.S. tax system is that it places great weight on the individual and corporate income taxes."[38] This is no longer true. One would have to substitute payroll (employment, disability, medical, and retirement) taxes for the corporate income tax, and that shift, plus the personal and corporate income tax changes brought about by the Economic Recovery Act of 1981, have made the federal tax system considerably less progressive. The 1990 deficit reduction tax increases added a heavy dose of regressive taxes by way of cigarette, alcohol, and gasoline taxes to the total mix.

It is now difficult to say with any authority that the federal tax system is, on the whole, progressive. The state and local system is less regressive than in the past. The tax structure is now a very different and a very mixed bag.

Other political assumptions have been overtaken as well. It can prob- ably no longer be said that taxation as proposed by recent presidents and disposed of by contemporary Congresses support Pechman's tax policy goals of vertical and horizontal equity,[39] although the Tax Reform Act of 1986 took a modest bow toward greater horizontal equity by providing that those with equal incomes should pay substantially equal taxes. The assumption that "there is a consensus in favor of at least *some* progression in the overall tax burden" is now a hotly contested political issue.[40]

TABLE 4–2 Major State and Local Revenues in Selected Fiscal Years from 1927 to 1988 (Billions of Dollars and Percentage of Total)[1]

Fiscal Year	Total	Property Taxes	Sales and Gross Receipt Taxes	Individual Income Taxes	Corporate Net Income Taxes	Revenue from Federal Government	Others[2]
1927	$7.3	$4.7 (64%)	$0.470 (6.4%)	$0.070 (1%)	$0.092 (1 + %)	$0.116 (1.5%)	$1.793 (25%)
1940	$9.6	$4.4 (46%)	$1.98 (20%)	$0.224 (2%)	$0.156 (1.5%)	$0.945 (%)	$1.872 (20%)
1960	50.5	$16.4 (32%)	$11.85 (24%)	$2.46 (5%)	$1.18 (2.3%)	$6.9 (13%)	$11.6 (23%)
1980–1981[3]	423.4	$75.0 (18%)	$86.0 (20%)	$46.4 (11%)	$14.1 (3.3%)	$90.3 (21%)	$111.6 (25%)
1987–1988[3]	$727.1	$132.2 (18%)	$156.3 (22%)	$88.3 (12%)	$23.7 (3%)	$117.6 (16%)	$209.0 (29%)

Source: Economic Report of the President (Washington, D.C.: Government Printing Office, 1990, p. 391, Table C-83; 1930 data unavailable.

1. Some percentages do not total 100 because of rounding.
2. Includes licenses and other taxes and charges plus miscellaneous revenues.
3. Data for fiscal year ending June 30.

These principles were challenged by virtually every specific tax proposal recommended by President Reagan in the Economic Recovery Act of 1981, voted on by the House and Senate, or proposed as an official alternative by the Democrats in the House. The House Democrats attempted to outbid the president for the support of a variety of specific corporate or commodity interest groups. The old-fashioned sense of horizontal and vertical tax equity was replaced by "supply-side economics" and by the view of White House counselor Edwin Meese III, who in a meeting with the press, proclaimed that "the progressive income tax is immoral."[41] The passage of the 1981 and 1982 tax bills has resulted in a radical departure from the goals, if not always the achievements, of what was avowed public tax policy for the previous half-century.

Finally, during the same period there have been two fundamental changes with respect to national, state, and local taxes. First is the increase in the total amount of taxes raised by governments at all levels. In fiscal year 1929 only $11.2 billion was raised by the federal, state, and local governments. That amount rose to $143 billion in fiscal year 1960 and to $1,776.5 billion in 1989. By fiscal year 1993 it is estimated that federal revenues alone will be $1.35 trillion.

The second change is the shift in the ratio of federal taxes to state and local taxes. In fiscal year 1929, revenues raised at the state and local level amounted to $7.3 billion, or 65 percent, of the $11.2 billion total. By fiscal year 1950, those ratios were precisely reversed. The federal government raised 65 percent, or almost $40 billion, of the $60.4 billion total. In the two decades between fiscal years 1960 and 1980, the ratios shifted back somewhat toward state and local governments. In fiscal year 1980, the federal government raised only 55 percent, or $517 billion, of the $940 billion total, while the states raised $423 billion, or 45 percent. In fiscal year 1989, the percentages remained almost the same. Because the collection of state and local data lags behind the collection of federal data, no more recent comparisons can be made. Table 4–3 gives the details.

TAX EXPENDITURES

Along with these changes in overall tax policy has come the widespread use of tax expenditures both to influence social and economic policies and to give large tax breaks to selected individuals and industries. Tax expenditures have both a good and bad meaning. The Congressional Budget Office (CBO) defines them as "revenue losses that result from provisions of the federal tax code that give special or selective tax relief to certain groups of taxpayers. Like federal spending and loan programs, tax expenditures serve to channel resources from some sectors of the economy to others."[42] To many they are little more than loopholes, "truckholes," and aberrations in

TABLE 4–3   Federal, State, and Local Government Receipts in Selected Fiscal Years

Year	Federal Receipts		State and Local Government Receipts		Total (Billions of Dollars)
	Dollars (Billions)	Percent of Total	Dollars (Billions)	Percent of Total	
1929	$ 3.9	35	$ 7.3	65	$ 11.2
1940	6.4	40	9.6	60	16.0
1950	39.5	65	20.9	35	60.4
1960	92.5	65	50.5	35	143.0
1970	192.8	60	130.8	40	323.6
1980	517.0	55	423.4	45	940.4
1989	990.7	56	785.8	44	1,776.5

Source: Economic Report of the President (Washington, D.C.: U.S. Government Printing Office, 1991), pp. 375, 383.

the tax system. To others they are incentives for economic growth, savings, and investments.

Tax expenditures are the measure of the funds that would be collected under the existing tax system if there were no special provisions, exceptions, exclusions, deductions, credits, or deferrals for certain taxpayers. Two taxpayers with identical incomes and exactly the same family size can pay very different amounts of federal tax. This depends in part on the source of the income and in part on how it is spent or saved.

No one has illustrated the problem more graphically than Philip Stern in the introduction to his book, *The Great Treasury Raid*:

> For a raid of its magnitude, the time (high noon) and setting (the United States Treasury, a stone's throw from the White House) showed a breathtaking boldness of design and planning. From out of nowhere, it seemed, they appeared—old people and young, rich and poor, an oil millionaire here, a factory worker there, a real estate tycoon, a working mother, several well-known movie stars, some corporation presidents, even the chairman of a powerful Congressional committee. It was a mixed lot, all right, that converged on the Treasury Building that high noon. Into the building they strolled, gloriously nonchalant. No one stopped them; not a guard looked up to question them. Quickly and quietly they found their way to the vaults; opened them noiselessly with the special passkeys each had brought with him. Like clock-work, with split-second timing, each went to his appointed spot, picked up a bag and walked out as calmly as he had entered. At the exits the guard sat motionless. At precisely 12:04 it was all over. Each of the "visitors" had vanished into thin air. So had forty billion dollars from the United States Treasury.[43]

Before the 1986 Tax Reform Act was passed the Treasury Department and Congressional Joint Committee on Taxation predicted that Stern's estimate of $40 billion would increase to more than $400 billion by the last half of the 1980s.[44] Tax expenditures were roughly equal in size to half the estimated receipts of the federal tax system. After the 1986 Act the figure dropped to 35 percent. Some tax expenditures are looked upon by most people as good and politically untouchable; others are considered bad and politically untouchable. In the former category are homeowners' tax preferences, which Allen Manvel referred to as "among the most costly—and, probably, also most politically invulnerable—of the preferences built into the federal individual tax system."[45] The fiscal year 1991 cost estimate for these preferences was $46.6 billion for the deduction of mortgage interest paid on owner-occupied homes and $12.4 billion for the deduction of property taxes on owner-occupied homes—a total of $59 billion.[46]

Among the tax expenditures receiving the most public pummeling that are also backed by the politically powerful are those involving the depletion allowance for oil and gas. The fiscal year 1991 estimated tax expenditure cost for both individuals and corporations was $565 million.[47]

As Stern said, while tax preferences went to "an oil millionaire here," a "real estate tycoon," and "several well-known movie stars," some also went to factory workers and working mothers. As the CBO points out:

> The identification of a provision of the tax code as a tax expenditure does not imply a judgment about the merits of the provision. Tax expenditures are simply one of the ways in which the federal government seeks to allocate resources or influence behavior in the private sector. Just as with federal spending or loan programs, evaluation of the provision depends on the purposes being served and the cost and effectiveness of the provision compared to other ways of promoting the same objective.[48]

Table 4–4 gives the total tax expenditure estimates for both corporations and individuals for fiscal years 1988–1992.

TABLE 4–4 Sum of Tax Expenditure Items by Type of Taxpayer in Fiscal Years 1988–1992 (Billions of Dollars)

Fiscal Year	Corporations	Individuals	Total[1]
1988	$62.0	$259.1	$321.1
1989	58.2	257.0	315.2
1990	61.3	274.4	335.7
1991	63.4	292.2	355.6
1992	66.6	311.2	377.8

Source: House Committee on the Budget, *Concurrent Resolution on the Budget, Fiscal Year 1988*, H. Con. Res. 95, 100th Cong. 1st sess., Report No. 100-41 (Washington, D.C.: U.S. Government Printing Office, 1987), p. 130.

1. These totals represent merely the mathematical sum of the estimated fiscal year effect of each of the tax expenditure items. See note 44.

NO SYSTEMATIC REVIEW

There are problems with tax expenditures that do not apply to regularly appropriated expenditures in the spending budget. First, appropriated funds are reviewed in a way which tax expenditures are not. Article I of the Constitution provides that "no money shall be drawn from the Treasury but in consequence of an appropriation made by law." Funds that are regularly appropriated are first reviewed by the agency involved. While to some extent this is an in-house (even a "sweetheart") examination, there are nonetheless competing priorities for limited funds within each federal department. Almost any program thus receives some critical examination even by the agency that administers the program and wants the funds. Second, the Office of Management and Budget (OMB) sits in judgment over the departments and agencies. While the quality of its reviews varies, on the whole the OMB is the nay sayer and examines the agency budgets with a critical eye. Third, the president and his budget director are limited in the totality of spending they can recommend to some figure related to the anticipated revenues. This fact puts further restraints on those parts of the budget that are subject to political control. President Bush's fiscal year 1992 budget deficit, which was estimated at $348 billion, illustrates the political price an administration pays for offending this principle. Fourth, when the budget goes to the Congress, it runs an additional gauntlet. The House Appropriations Committee reviews the president's proposals. Routinely this committee, its subcommittees, and the House as a whole reduce the president's recommendations. Fifth, the Senate Appropriations Committee, while more generous than the House, routinely appropriates less money than the president recommends. While the Senate often acts as an appeal board for House cuts of agency funds, it generally stays within or below the president's proposals. Finally, the funds go to a conference committee composed of both House and Senate members, where the disparate figures are compromised.

While spending via Appropriations Committee procedure leaves much to be desired, it is superior to a tax expenditure. The latter goes out regularly and automatically. There is no annual review, and many permanent features of the tax code prevail without oversight from decade to decade. There is neither control over the individual amounts nor an overall limit or cap on the total. It is not systematically reviewed by the agency, the OMB, or the president.

Tax expenditures go to those who meet the provisions spelled out in the tax code. This leads to the continuation of a tax preference whose purpose may have long since been fulfilled or when there are several better ways to achieve the purpose—by direct expenditure, by loans or loan guarantees, by action of a public body, or by discontinuing the preference and allowing the funds to remain in the private sector where their use might well be directed by competitive markets and their efficiency maximized. Finally, like many other expenditures, tax expenditures were out of control by the 1990s. There had been a tenfold growth in the amounts since 1960.

EXPENDITURE VERSUS ENTITLEMENT

The term *tax expenditure* is a misnomer. It might better be called a *tax entitlement*, like that form of spending that has recently received so much opprobrium and abuse and whose reform has been called for by presidents, present and former treasury secretaries, and chairmen of both the House and Senate budget committees.

Tax expenditures and spending entitlements are a common breed. They are like the animals in Noah's Ark that marched aboard side by side. Both are automatic and paid out by law and formula. Neither is regularly reviewed. Both are uncontrollable without a change in the law. Once legislated, they create powerful interest groups that are dependent on their benefits, deeply entrenched, and difficult if not impossible to oppose. Tax expenditures and spending entitlements are entered on opposite sides of the budget ledger. While they may not be of the same gender, they are of the same species.

There is a political schizophrenia between those who favor tax expenditures but oppose spending expenditures and those who defend spending expenditures but oppose tax expenditures. The reason for this division is relatively simple if unstated. It is partisan and political. Tax entitlements, in spite of Philip Stern's citation of the working mother and the factory worker as recipients, generally benefit those with higher incomes. The poor, who pay no income taxes, only casually or by serendipity receive any tax expenditures.

Low- or middle-income taxpayers get only the benefit of their marginal income tax rate for a contribution to a church or favorite charity. A $100 contribution to the Salvation Army from a married taxpayer with two children and a modest $25,000 income in the 15 percent bracket would reduce the family tax liability by $15, *provided* they filled out the long form and took the deduction. Two-thirds of taxpayers in this tax bracket, however, file the short form. Historically, they received *no* benefit, a situation only modestly changed by the Economic Recovery Act of 1981, which allowed for some deductions for short-form filers (now repealed). By contrast, the high-income taxpayer in the 33 percent bracket gets a $33 tax break for the same $100 contribution.

Tax expenditures therefore not only take the form of entitlements, but their value rises with income. They are a form of welfare for the well-to-do.

The opulent receive their federal largess by way of tax expenditure entitlements. The poor, the near-poor, and the enormous middle and lower-middle class get relatively few or no tax expenditure entitlements.

The point is that one person's loophole is another person's incentive, and that one person's expenditure entitlement may be looked upon as an object of reform while another's tax entitlement may be both advocated and extolled. These are highly charged political issues with partisan overtones. Neither spending entitlements nor tax expenditures were written in heaven or canonized in Rome. They are the consequences of the cut and thrust of contentious political debate, the power of resourceful and financially strong interest groups, and the collective effect of diffused public opinion as registered at the ballot box every two or four years.

TAXES TO PROMOTE ECONOMIC GROWTH AND STABILITY

Modern governments use taxes not only to raise revenues and to advance social goals, but to promote economic growth and stability. Political economists disagree over whether tax cuts or spending increases are the better way to stimulate the economy. There are arguments on both sides. Other factors being equal, a $10 billion increase in spending will have a greater effect, or multiplier, than a $10 billion tax cut. But the spending increase may take a very long time to go into effect, may provide for programs where the unemployment or depressed conditions are not, or may be spent for inefficient purposes. While tax cuts may not pack the same economic stimulus, once they are passed they can be put into effect almost immediately by changing the withholding provisions. Tax cuts, since they go to people, not areas, are also less discriminatory among geographical regions.

Through the Economic Recovery Act of 1981, the Reagan administration passed a massive tax program that contained numerous radical departures from previous tax bills. The Congressional Joint Committee on Taxation gave these general reasons for its support of the act:

> The Congress concluded that a program of significant multi-year tax reductions was needed to ensure economic growth in the years ahead. This tax reduction program should help upgrade the nation's industrial base, stimulate productivity and innovation throughout the economy, lower personal tax burdens, and restrain the growth of the Federal government.[49]

Table 4–5 summarizes the estimated revenue effects of the Economic Recovery Act of 1981 for fiscal years 1981–1986.[50]

TABLE 4–5   Summary of Estimated Revenue Effects of the Economic Recovery Act of 1981 for Fiscal Years 1981–1986 (Millions of Dollars)

Provision	1981	1982	1983	1984	1985	1986
Title I: Individual income tax provisions	$ −39	$− 26,947	$− 71,112	$− 114,700	$− 148,254	$− 196,162
Title II: Business incentive provisions	− 1,563	− 10,727	− 18,746	− 28,436	− 39,448	− 54,665
Title III: Savings provisions		− 247	− 1,797	− 4,207	− 5,629	− 8,485
Title IV: Estate and gift tax provisions		− 204	− 2,114	− 3,218	− 4,248	− 5,568
Title V: Tax straddles	37	623	327	273	249	229
Title VI: Energy provisions		− 1,320	− 1,742	− 2,242	− 2,837	− 3,619
Title VII: Administrative provisions		1,182	2,048	1,856	718	592
Title VIII: Miscellaneous provisions		− 16	404	711	247	− 64
Total revenue effect	− 1,565	− 37,656	− 92,732	− 149,963	− 199,202	− 267,742

Source: Joint Committee on Taxation, *General Explanation of the Economic Recovery Tax Act of 1981* (Washington, D.C.: U.S. Government Printing Office, 1981).

The act was characterized by several significant features. First was the unprecedented amount of revenues involved—almost $750 billion through fiscal year 1986. This major shift of resources from the public to the private sector did not, however, restrain the growth of the federal government, as its political sponsors advocated. This was largely the result of increases in defense expenditures, in interest payments to finance the deficit, and in entitlements, especially Social Security and Medicare, as well as the savings and loan scandals.

The second significant feature was the general regressive nature of the tax cuts. Edwin Meese's statements that "the progressive income tax is immoral" and that "I don't think we should penalize someone because he's successful"[51] were made manifest by the major components of the act, which reduced the progressive nature of the federal income tax in various ways, including the following:

1. The top rate was reduced from 70 to 50 percent. Only those persons filing joint returns with taxable income of $60,000 or more benefited at all, and the full reduction from 70 to 50 percent affected only those filing joint returns who had $215,400 or more in taxable income. Clearly this feature reduced the progressivity of the tax structure.
2. Individual income tax liability was reduced in four stages by across-the-board cuts totaling 23 percent. When fully in effect, this provided a $5,500 tax cut for those in the $50,000 taxable income bracket filing a joint return, but only a

TABLE 4–6   Tax Rate Schedules Under Prior Law and Under the Act for 1982–1984 (Joint Returns)

Taxable Income Bracket	Percent Under Prior Law	Percent Under the Act		
		1982	1983	1984
0 to $3,400	0	0	0	0
$3,400 to $5,500	14	12	11	11
$5,500 to $7,600	16	14	13	12
$7,600 to $11,900	18	16	15	14
$11,900 to $16,000	21	19	17	16
$16,000 to $20,200	24	22	19	18
$20,200 to $24,600	28	25	23	22
$24,600 to $29,900	32	29	26	25
$29,900 to $35,200	37	33	30	28
$35,200 to $45,800	43	39	35	33
$45,800 to $60,000	49	44	40	38
$60,000 to $85,600	54	49	44	42
$85,600 to $109,400	59	50	48	45
$109,400 to $162,400	64	50	50	49
$162,400 to $215,400	68	50	50	50
$215,400 and over	70	50	50	50

Source: Joint Committee on Taxation, *General Explanation of the Economic Recovery Tax Act of 1981* (Washington, D.C.: U.S. Government Printing Office, 1981).

$750 cut for those in the $15,000 bracket filing a joint return. Across-the-board cuts of equal percentage amounts are by nature regressive, for they give much larger dollar amounts to those in higher income brackets. Table 4–6 gives the tax bracket changes.[52]

3.   The act reduced the maximum tax on net capital gains in the high tax brackets from 28 to 20 percent. As almost no low-income taxpayers and few middle-income taxpayers have any capital gains, this reduced the progressivity of the federal personal income tax.

4.   Americans who live and work abroad for one year or more may exclude up to (and pay no tax on) $75,000 of foreign-earned income annually. This benefits American citizens living and working abroad who are in the upper 1 percent or less of income groups. The revenue loss is more than half a billion dollars a year when fully in effect. The provision was added as a result of a vast lobbying effort by American oil companies, the Bechtel Corporation, International Harvester, Caterpillar Tractor, Brown and Root, and other champions of free enterprise and self-reliance who prevailed on the American government and the American taxpayers to subsidize their employees abroad.

5.   In addition, some $8.5 billion annually (with the act in full effect) was provided as incentives for taxpayers to save money, to reinvest in public utility dividends, or to invest in employee stock option plans. Saving is a function of income. Low-income persons not only do *not* save but are "dis-savers" and in debt. The higher one's income, the higher are one's actual dollar savings and the proportion of one's income that is saved. This provision in general sharply reduced the progressive features of the federal income tax.

6. Estate and gift tax provisions were made more generous. Under previous law, $175,000 was exempt from estate or gift taxes. The Economic Recovery Act of 1981 raised this amount to $600,000. The revenue loss attributable to this and other estate and gift tax provisions is estimated at $5.6 billion annually by the fifth year, almost all of which would go to those in the high tax brackets.

7. Businesses benefited from a general reduction in the number of years over which a business asset could be depreciated or written off. In what were called the "10-5-3 provisions," the bill provided that automobiles, trucks, and short-lived property could be written off in three years; that most business machinery and equipment could be written off in five years; and that public utility property and other assets that in the past had been depreciated over between eighteen and twenty-five years could be written off in ten. Finally, new real property could be depreciated in fifteen years. These provisions accounted for about 20 percent of the revenue loss in the bill and, next to the personal income tax reductions, were its principal feature.

8. Special provisions were provided for the oil industry, with particular reference to more generous treatment under the Crude Oil Windfall Profits Tax. The cumulative revenue losses through the first five years amounted to $11.8 billion. These provisions were supported by both President Reagan and the House Democrats leadership in the battle to woo oil state members to support their particular version of the bill. While one may argue about the ultimate benefits of the depreciation and oil tax provisions, their immediate and direct benefit went to those in relatively high tax brackets, which reduced the progressive features of the federal tax system.

These reductions in business taxes, combined with the scheduled rise in Social Security contributions imposed in 1982 to 1985, further accelerated the decline in the proportion of collected taxes paid by corporations and increase in the proportion collected as payroll and employment taxes. As Hobart Rowen wrote in *The Washington Post*:

> In plain English, the Reagan revolution in corporate taxation—aided and abetted by the Democrats last year—changed the tax burden from a combined tap on wage and corporate income to taxes that rest mostly on wage income and consumption.[53]

A third issue is why this unprecedented reduction in individual and business taxes had almost no immediate stimulating effect on the economy. Some claimed a year after passage that the program had not yet fully begun. But the business incentive, savings, oil energy, and estate and gift tax provisions had immediately effective dates of application. Personal income tax cuts amounting to $27 billion—larger than any in the tax history of the country—were in place during the following fiscal year. Nonetheless, the first- and second-year economic effects were neither positive nor neutral, but negative.

Unemployment rose to its highest level since the Great Depression, to between 10 to 10.8 percent from September 1982 through June 1983. There was a recession in 1981–1982, using the formal definition of the National Bureau of Economic Research that two quarters of negative growth in the GNP constitutes a recession. The housing industry produced only about half its potential 2 million units per year. Business failures continued at a high rate. The automobile industry and associated businesses remained depressed. Additional savings did not translate into massive infusions of new investment in plants and equipment in the economy.

What went wrong? The answers do not lie with the tax cuts alone. In the first fiscal year almost $38 billion in tax cut stimulus was offset by a $38 billion reduction in federal government spending. Because of what the economists call the "multiplier effect," the nature of the spending reductions more than offset the stimulus of the tax cuts. Here is why.

The $38 billion reduction in spending occurred in programs largely affecting those of low and moderate income. The cuts were made in Comprehensive Employment and Training Administration (CETA) jobs, food stamps, welfare payments, aid to primary and secondary education, retiree cost-of-living increases, aid to state and local governments, dairy price supports, and other federal government functions.

There are several characteristics of these programs and of those who receive the funds. First, there was little delay in spending the money. On the administrative side and in the education programs the money was quickly used to pay wages and salaries. Second, most of the direct recipients of the funds were low-income persons deeply in debt, who spent what they received. Third, as low-income people pay very little or no federal income taxes, the funds had a bigger immediate stimulus than equivalent amounts paid to those of higher income.

On the other hand, the $38 billion in tax cuts generally went to those in high-income tax brackets, who have a much higher savings rate than low-income persons. In effect, what the Reagan administration did was to cut $38 billion from programs that put money (or the equivalent) into the pockets of the poor and that had a very high first-round multiplier or stimulus effect because the recipients spent almost every dollar they received. It transferred that money into tax cuts that went into the pockets of very high-income persons and groups where the stimulus or multiplier effect was smaller because much of the money was saved rather than spent.

Further, an additional first-round effect or stimulus results from direct federal spending that is not found with tax cuts. By cutting spending and transferring the funds to tax cuts, this one-time stimulus was lost. As Joseph Pechman pointed out in *Federal Tax Policy:*

> If expenditures and taxes are increased simultaneously by the same amount, the effects of these two actions will not cancel one another because, dollar for dollar, expenditures have a more potent effect on the economy than do tax changes.[54]

The same holds true if expenditures and taxes are cut simultaneously.

Because of the differences between those who received funds from the Reagan tax cuts and those who lost funds from the Reagan spending programs, on the one hand, and the fact that there is an extra first-round multiplier effect or stimulus with spending that is not obtained with tax cuts, on the other, the tax cut stimulus was heavily offset. If, for example, the multiplier effect for tax cuts was two and the multiplier loss from the spending reductions was three, a tax cut stimulus of some $76 billion ($38 billion times two) was offset by $104 billion ($38 billion times three) in spending reductions. Instead of stimulating the economy, the totality of the tax and spending programs had a major negative economic effect.

The Reagan tax program was successful in its goals of reducing the progressive features of the federal income tax and in allowing the successful to keep a larger proportion of their income. However, at least in its first- and second-year effects, it failed to promote economic growth, stability, and efficiency.

The tax program had one further negative economic effect. The size of the tax cuts, combined with the increases in military spending, ensured a historic deficit and made it impossible for the Reagan administration to carry out its promise of a balanced budget in fiscal year 1984 or earlier. The budget deficit of $91.5 billion proposed for fiscal year 1983 in President Reagan's original budget document (the estimate ultimately ballooned to $208 billion) almost precisely equaled the estimated $92.7 billion to be lost in revenue in fiscal year 1983 as a result of the tax program. At a time of rampant inflation and high interest rates, the goal of a balanced budget was thus sacrificed for tax cuts and huge deficits. Virtually no combination of spending cuts and tax increases could remedy the situation. As economist Michael Evans noted after the Congress passed the first budget resolution for fiscal year 1983:

> While the House and Senate have agreed to hold the deficit to the "modest" level of $100 billion or so next year, only the truly naive can believe this projection. Congress has refused to fill in the details of alleged spending cuts and tax increases, leaving financial markets to suspect that a $180 billion deficit figure is far more realistic.[55]

Concerned about the huge deficit and the negative reaction of the financial markets to President Reagan's budget, Senate Republican leaders, over the initial opposition of the president, introduced a modest tax increase in 1982. It was a somewhat daring political act in an election year. Senator Robert Dole (R.-Kan.), chairman of the Senate Finance Committee, successfully steered the Tax Equity and Fiscal Responsibility Act of 1982 through the Senate and Conference Committee. The Senate *Report* said it had four principal objectives: to raise revenues as part of an effort to narrow the unacceptably large budget deficit, to ensure that all individuals and businesses pay a fair share of the tax burden, to reduce the distortions in economic behavior that result from the present tax system, and to increase the extent to which those responsible for specific Federal Government spending pay the costs of that spending.[56]

The act was passed under unprecedented procedures for a major tax bill, especially in view of the requirement of Article I, Section 7, of the Constitution that "all Bills raising Revenues shall originate in the House of Representatives; but the Senate may propose or concur with Amendments as on other Bills." The Senate initiated the major provisions of the bill by adding them to a minor House bill, H.R. 4961. The House Ways and Means Committee did not initiate or act on any of the major provisions but contented itself with going to conference with the Senate on the Senate bill. A summary of the major revenue provisions are given in Table 4–7. Because of the later repeal of the 10 percent withholding provisions on dividends and interest under massive political pressure from savings and loan and bank industries, the revenue gains were reduced by a total of $12 billion in fiscal year 1983, 1984, and 1985.

As a result of this modest congressional effort to reduce the deficit, interest rates dropped somewhat but remained relatively high. Funds necessary to stimulate housing, consumer buying, or loans for farmers and businesses were stifled by a growing and insatiable demand by the federal Treasury for borrowed funds to finance the deficit. The totality of the

TABLE 4–7   Summary of Estimated Revenue Effect of the Tax Equity and Fiscal Responsibility Act of 1982. Provisions as Reported by Senate Finance Committee, Fiscal Years 1982–1987 (Fiscal years, Millions of Dollars)

Provision	1982	1983	1984	1985	1986	1987
Individual income tax provisions	$	$ 240	$ 2,984	$ 3,261	$ 3,548	$ 3,856
Business tax provisions	175	5,927	12,755	18,162	30,559	42,262
Compliance provisions[1]		6,698	7,056	8,646	10,115	11,112
Pension provisions		211	588	673	762	848
Life insurance and annuities	489	1,487	1,510	2,183	2,935	3,167
Employment tax provisions		1,814	3,104	3,869	4,012	3,862
Excise tax provisions		2,509	3,847	4,734	4,873	4,929
Miscellaneous provisions	−1	−38	−37	−34	−32	−30
Total, tax provisions	663	18,848	31,870	41,494	56,772	70,006
Revenue gain resulting from additional IRS enforcement personnel		2,100	2,400	2,400	1,300	600
Grand total, all provisions	663	20,948	34,207	43,894	58,702	70,606

Source: Senate Committee on Finance, 97–2, *Report on Tax Equity and Fiscal Responsibility Act of 1982* (Washington, D.C.: U.S. Government Printing Office, 1982), p. 101.
1. Includes $4.3 b., $3.6 b., and $4.1 b. in fiscal years 1983, 1984, and 1985 for withholding on dividends and interest later repealed.

situation, both factually and psychologically, reduced the stimulus that might otherwise have been expected from the initial tax cuts. It was not until the early months of 1983 that the economy began to recover from the recession that had begun in the summer of 1981.

In addition to the massive tax cut under the Economic Recovery Act of 1981 and the modest tax increase under the Tax Equity and Fiscal Responsibility Act of 1982, four additional revenue-raising or tax-increase bills enacted in 1982, 1983, and 1984: the Highway Revenue Act of 1982, the Social Security Amendments in 1983, the Railroad Retirement Revenue Act of 1983, and the Deficit Reduction Act of 1984. The estimated additional tax receipts for these four acts for 1985–1989 are given in Table 4–8. They amounted to more than $58 billion in fiscal year 1989.

TABLE 4–8   Effect of Major Enacted Legislation on Receipts (Billions of Dollars)

Legislation	1985	1986	1987	1988	1989
Highway Revenue Act of 1982					
Individual income taxes	$−1.2	$−1.3	$−1.3	$−1.3	$−1.3
Corporation income taxes	−0.2	−0.2	−0.2	−0.2	−0.2
Excise taxes	5.7	6.0	6.2	6.3	6.5
Total Highway Revenue Act of 1982	4.2	4.5	4.7	4.8	5.0
Social Security Amendments of 1983					
Individual income taxes	2.7	3.2	3.4	2.6	2.8
Social insurance taxes and contributions	6.0	4.8	5.7	17.3	22.0
Miscellaneous receipts	0.1	0.1	0.1	0.1	0.1
Total, Social Security amendments of 1983	8.7	8.0	9.2	20.0	24.9
Railroad Retirement Revenue Act of 1983					
Individual income taxes	0.3	0.3	0.3	0.3	0.3
Social insurance taxes and contributions	0.4	0.8	0.8	0.8	0.8
Total, Railroad Retirement Revenue Act of 1983	0.7	1.1	1.1	1.1	1.1
Deficit Reduction Act of 1984					
Individual income taxes	5.6	8.0	10.2	13.1	16.0
Corporation income taxes	3.3	5.8	8.1	9.7	10.6
Social insurance taxes and contributions	1	1	1	1	1
Excise taxes	0.4	2.0	3.1	1.7	0.6
Estate and gift taxes	1	0.3	0.4	0.4	1
Miscellaneous receipts	1	1	1	1	1
Total, Deficit Reduction Act of 1984	9.3	16.0	21.8	24.9	27.2

Source: Budget of the United States Government: Fiscal Year 1987 (Washington, D.C.: U.S. Government Printing Office, 1986), pp. 4–5, 6.
1. $50 million or less

THE TAX REFORM ACT OF 1986

Background and History

The Tax Reform Act of 1986 was a modern political miracle. Of all the domestic issues on the reformers' agenda in the post–World War II era, tax reform was the most difficult to effect. The issue epitomized the ability of entrenched special interest groups to prevail over the diffused power of ordinary citizens and the average taxpayer. Voting rights, civil rights, consumer legislation, federal aid to education, environmental protection, Medicare, and disability coverage under Social Security were all reforms that had been enacted into law. Even gerrymandered legislative districts were reformed after the Supreme Court took jurisdiction once it became monumentally clear that the political beneficiaries of gerrymandered political districts were incapable of self-reform and would never vote themselves out of office. But reform of the tax system remained the perennial lost cause.

While the legislative gestation period for most reforms was seven years from the time a bill was introduced until the day it was signed into law by the president, tax reform took almost four decades.

Tax reform became important only after World War II. From the time the Sixteenth Amendment was ratified in 1913 until 1946, tax rates and the fairness of their application were not a major political issue. During the Great Depression of the 1930s, unemployment was so high and incomes so low that those with sufficient income to be subjected to federal income taxes considered themselves among the fortunate few. And tax rates in that decade as well as during the 1920s were a fraction of those enacted in the 1940s. When the notorious 27½ percent oil and gas depletion allowance was passed in 1925, it encountered little political opposition as tax rates were so low and its benefits seemed relatively benign.

Tax rates were high in both world wars, but patriotic fervor and support of the wars muffled controversy. Beardsley Ruml's plan for withholding taxes from wages and salaries at their source, which was enacted during World War II, made paying taxes relatively painless compared with paying them in a lump sum at the end of the year.

When the high tax rates of World War II persisted after the war, a massive erosion of the tax code took place. Powerful economic interests received or retained exceptions to the high marginal rates. This was particularly true for minerals, oil and gas, banks, savings institutions, insurance, real estate, and firms doing business abroad. On the grounds that they stimulated investment and created jobs, special provisions for investment and capital were written into the law. A variety of groups that were unable to convince the Congress to appropriate funds for their particular social purposes were successful in gaining special provisions in the tax code that reduced the rates or forgave the taxes they would otherwise pay. Some groups and individuals with relatively high incomes and considerable political clout successfully pressed for a variety of deductions from income before taxes were assessed. These deductions became relatively more valuable as income rose.

All of this led to a smarting sense of injustice among those not highly favored, and had serious consequences for the tax system. First, there was an erosion of horizontal equity. Two individuals or two families with relatively equal incomes were paying very different amounts in taxes, depending on the source of their income and how it was spent. Second, there was a great erosion in the progressive nature, or vertical equity, of the tax system. In some cases those with high incomes were paying a smaller proportion of their income in taxes than those with low incomes, although it was generally believed that those with higher incomes should pay a somewhat higher proportion of their income in taxes than the other way around. Third, the tax code, because of the various exclusions, deductions, credits, deferrals, exceptions, and special rules, became inordinately complicated for those who filled out the long forms. Fourth, there was a tremendous increase in state and local taxes (see Tables 4–2 and 4–3), which were often confused with an increase in the federal taxes. Many taxpayers did not distinguish between the routine reduction of federal tax rates and the regular increase in state and local taxes, and often blamed the latter on the federal system. Fifth, the growth of regressive Social Security and other federal employment taxes increased the demand for reform. Finally, the inflation of the 1970s created havoc with the tax system. Because during inflation prices take the elevator while wages and incomes take the stairs, individuals who did get belated raises were thrown into higher tax brackets and paid more taxes on less real income. This "bracket creep" led to a movement for both tax reduction and tax reform.

The intellectual effort for reform had two main sources, first the treasury officials and working tax experts themselves, and second the tax economists at the great universities. The latter were divided into two groups. One saw the system as basically unjust and unfair, whereas the other saw it as anticompetitive. Capital was drawn off into inefficient tax havens instead of being invested in endeavors that were more efficient but provided smaller after-tax returns. A school of economists at the University of Chicago were the major proponents of the latter view, although arguments from each group were routinely advocated by the other.

The first major legislative effort for tax reform began when the Korean War tax bill was before the Senate in 1950. Under the tutelage of Randolph Paul, a former general counsel at the Treasury Department and tax lawyer who epitomized the first school of reformers, and Joseph Pechman, a former expert at the Bureau of Tax Research at the Treasury, teacher at MIT, and Brookings Institution fellow who represented the academic reformers, Senators Hubert H. Humphrey (D.-Minn.) and Paul H. Douglas (D.-Ill.) proposed a series of reform amendments to the bill. In nars the two tax experts provided the ammunition that the two senators fired on the Senate floor.

They were prevented by the Senate establishment from getting roll-call votes on most of their amendments by the failure of one-fifth of a quorum to support their request. The difficulty of getting tax reform is highlighted by the fact that on one key amendment they mustered only eighteen votes, and on an amendment to reduce the oil depletion allowance from 27½ to 15 percent they got only nine.

In 1955, under Douglas's chairmanship, the Congressional Joint Economic Committee held a historic set of hearings on tax reform. Norman Ture of the Chicago school was the subcommittee staff director. Congressman Wilbur Mills (D.-Ark.) who left in midstream to become chairman of the House Ways and Means Committee, chaired the subcommittee hearings in their early stages. As head of the Ways and Means Committee Mills abandoned tax reform after suffering defeat on the first major tax bill he brought to the House floor. Academics Pechman, Stanley Surrey, and Richard Musgrave, among a host of others, appeared as witnesses and provided a massive intellectual underpinning for tax reform through both their testimony and academic articles. Randolph Paul, the father of the movement, then in private tax practice and author of the classic *Taxation in the United States*, testified against the narrow interests of his clients and for the broad interests of the public. He collapsed and died of a heart attack while presenting his testimony.

From those early beginnings in 1950 and 1955 tax reform lost ground, and tax loopholes and tax expenditures grew both in number and in value. By 1986 the revenue lost through tax expenditures was equal to half the revenues collected by the federal government.

Year by year new provisions were added to the tax code, new economic and social goals were promoted by tax expenditures, and the "Christmas tree" tax bill to which these ornaments were added became an annual event.

The Economic Recovery Act of 1981 was the ultimate blow to a fair tax system. The top tax rate was reduced by 20 points and almost 30 percent. The capital gains provision was cut from 28 to 20 percent for high-bracket individuals. These provisions vastly reduced the progressivity of the tax system and were compounded by the stiff rise in Social Security taxes. Instead of closing tax loopholes to offset the revenue losses, additional tax incentives were passed. Income from savings was taxed at a lower rate than income from wages and salaries. As savings is a function of income—the higher the income, the higher the savings rate—this benefited upper-income groups. Both corporate tax rates and depreciation rates were cut in dramatic fashion. This reduced corporate income taxes from about one-third of federal tax revenues in the early post–World War II period to about 10 percent of the total after 1981.

By 1984 there was a universal feeling that the tax code was in shambles and that reform was necessary. Taxpayers thought the system was both unfair and too complicated. Those who believed in competition and free enterprise saw the loopholes in the tax code as undermining efficiency and competitiveness. Progressives agreed with both groups. There was also considerable support among some business groups, especially from retailers, wholesalers, and high-tech industries, who actually paid the statutory rates while many of their business brethren paid little or no taxes at all. The stage was therefore set for tax reform, although few believed that its widespread general support could overcome the specific organized groups determined to keep their particular deduction, credit, or loophole.

The Fair Tax, the FAST Tax, and Treasury I

In a little-noticed effort in the spring of 1982, two progressive Democrats, Senator Bill Bradley of New Jersey and Representative Richard A. Gephardt of Missouri, introduced in the Senate and House their Fair Tax Bill, respectively. It was a modification of the intellectual reformers' assertion that if the major loopholes and tax expenditures were eliminated, tax rates could be cut in half yet still raise the same amount of revenue. The bill proposed that a wide range of both business and individual deductions be eliminated in return for a system of individual tax rates in which the top rate would be 28 percent (in lieu of 50 percent) and the 46 percent corporate rate would be reduced to 30 percent.

In his State of the Union Address at the end of January 1984, President Reagan embraced tax reform as the cornerstone of his domestic election-year program. He announced he had directed the Treasury to bring forth a study and proposal on how to make the tax system both more simple and more just. Three months later two Republicans, Representative Jack Kemp of New York and Senator Robert W. Kasten, Jr., of Wisconsin, proposed their own tax reform plan called FAST (Fair and Simple Tax). It was both an attempt to capitalize on the favorable tax reform climate and a Republican answer to the Democratic Bradley-Gephardt proposal. Its key provision was a reduction of the top tax rates to 25 percent for both individuals and corporations, which was to be paid for by the elimination of many tax expenditures.

Curiously, while the Republican platform of 1984 supported tax reform and the Kemp-Kasten version of the flat tax, Democratic presidential nominee Walter F. Mondale rejected tax reform as a major campaign issue, although for three decades it had been a cornerstone of the program of the progressive wing of his party. Republican fears of a Democratic preemptive strike on tax reform vanished, and it became a nonissue during most of the campaign. Meanwhile, Mondale's call for a tax increase was pounced on by the president, to the overwhelming delight of his backers.

However, in October an obscure Washington group called Citizens for Tax Justice (CTJ), headed by Robert McIntyre, issued a bombshell report. It found that 128 large American corporations had paid no taxes in at least one year between 1981 and 1983, even though they had earned $57 billion in corporate profits. In a later study, CTJ reported that 40 major companies with earnings of $59 billion paid no federal income taxes in the three-year period from 1982 to 1985. To add insult to injury, they had received more than $2 billion in refunds, although their average net tax rate was minus 3.5 percent. Among the 128 were such firms as General Electric, General Dynamics, Boeing, W. R. Grace & Co., Dow Chemical, Grumman, and Lockheed. Senator David Pryor (D.-Ark.) said that the report had the effect of "touching a spark to kindling."

At the end of the year, after President Reagan's landslide victory, the Treasury unveiled its proposal to lower rates and close loopholes. Called Treasury I, it was an extraordinarily far-reaching plan. It proposed to raise corporate taxes by $120 billion and to offset individual taxes by the same amount. It proposed three individual tax rates of 35, 25, and 15 percent.

Some thought the plan was politically flawed, and it was not sent to the Congress. Instead interest groups adversely affected by its provisions were given six months to comment on and lobby against its provisions. It is not uncommon for an administration to send a measure to the Congress hoping for half or three-quarters of a loaf. But to open a package for public bargaining before it was made final was to ensure a hefty erosion in its substance and to give its opponents months to organize. Treasury I was doomed when unveiled. This was only the first of numerous occasions when tax reform appeared dead.

The President Proposes

In May of 1985 President Reagan received Treasury II, a considerable watered-down version of Treasury I but nevertheless a proposal containing substantial tax reform. The president sent it to the Congress and then toured the country extolling its virtues. It received strong bipartisan support from House Ways and Means Committee Chairman Dan Rostenkowski (D.-Ill.), who made a moving, nationally televised speech welcoming the president's initiative. However, when the Congress returned from its summer recess, it found that the budget deficit had considerably more political pizazz than tax reform and passed the notorious Gramm-Rudman-Hollings measure instead.

In December the tax reform bill was rescued again. House republicans balked at considering the bill on the House floor. Democrats said they would sit on their hands and let it die unless the president could muster fifty Republican votes for the measure. This he did in a persuasive Capitol Hill appearance, and the bill came up for debate and vote. The good offices of Treasury Secretary James A. Baker III and his deputy Richard Darman were critical to this success.

In an unusual parliamentary proceeding on such a major measure, the House voted 256 to 171 to reject the Republican substitute for the House

Ways and Means Committee bill, but no one from the Republican side rose to call for a roll-call vote on final passage of the bill. "Someone was asleep at the switch," a Republican leader commented, and this far-reaching bill passed on an unrecorded voice vote.

The bill became an endangered species once again in March 1986, when it came before the Senate Finance Committee. Republican Chairman Robert Packwood of Oregon proposed a version of tax reform in the Senate that kept many business tax benefits, including protection for his state's timber industry, coupled with an increase in excise taxes to defray some of the tax rate cuts. Sensing business as usual, his Senate Finance Committee colleagues spent a month proposing to restore loophole after loophole on grounds that they were merely following the chairman's leadership. Facing defeat and disaster, Packwood pulled the bill off the table and sent it back to the drawing board.

In three weeks Packwood returned to his committee with a new radical proposal for tax reform. It repealed the investment tax credit, provided for a stiff minimum corporate tax and a general corporate rate of 33 percent, reduced individual rates to 15 and 27 percent, raised the personal exemptions and standard deductions so that those below the poverty line would pay no federal income taxes, and neutralized the capital gains rate. His conversion to reform was attributed to self-reflection, political reality, Senator Bradley, and Packwood's chief of staff William Diefenderfer.

The proposal was referred to as Packwood's Inchon Landing. The *New Republic*, which had called him Senator "Hackwood," now showered praises on his name. He was referred to as both a "born-again" tax reformer and as a modern Lazarus rising from the dead.

The spirit of reform caught on, and on May 7, in an amazing moment of magic, his committee voted 20 to 0 for the package. On June 24 the Senate passed the bill, which escaped major Senate amendment, by an overwhelming 97 to 3 vote.

The bill was not without its flaws. The oil and gas industry once again escaped relatively unscathed, in part because of its then depressed condition. Several dozen special transition rules were added protecting specific industries and companies from the immediate consequences of the new provisions. But unless one is willing to make the perfect the enemy of the good, it must be said that both the Senate and the House tax reform bills, with their differing but not antithetical provisions, were modern political miracles. The margin of the Senate passage and the joy and enthusiasm by which it was enacted ensured the rout of the remaining special interest groups and the ultimate enactment of the bill into law.

After a month of conflict and compromise in the conference committee between the House and the Senate, the final version was passed by a vote of 292 to 136 in the House and 74 to 23 in the Senate. The President signed the Tax Reform Act of 1986 into law on October 22. Table 4–9 sets forth its major provisions.

TABLE 4–9   Major Provisions of the Tax Reform Act of 1986

Provision	Previous Law	New Law When in Full Effect
Individual tax rates	15 rate brackets from 11 to 50% (indexed)	2 brackets: 15% and 28%; 33% hidden rate for very high-income taxpayers
Personal exemption	$1,080	1988: $1,950 1989: $2,000 (indexed)
Standard deductions	Single $2,480 Joint $3,670 Head of household $2,480	$3,000 $5,000 (indexed) $4,400
Personal deductions Mortgage interest Personal interest State and local taxes Charitable contributions Interest on home equity loans	 Deductible Deductible Deductible Deductible Deductible	Deductible Phase out by 1991 Deductible except for sales taxes Deductible only for itemizers Limited to original purchase price plus improvements, and for education and a few other specific purposes
Medical expenses	Amounts above 5% of adjusted gross income	Amounts above 7.5% of adjusted gross income
Two-earner deduction	Yes	No
Entertainment expenses and business meals	Deductible	80% deductible
Other (e.g., professional dues)	Deductible	Above 2% of Adjusted Gross Income
Earned income credit	11% of $550 maximum	14% of $800 maximum (indexed)
Income averaging	Yes	No
Individual Retirement Accounts (IRAs)	$2,000 interest tax deferred	Same as previous law for those not covered by company plans with income limits of $40,000 married and $25,000 single; interest tax deferred
Section 401(k) plans	Up to $30,000 tax deferred	Limited to $7,000 tax deferred; other restrictions.
Minimum tax	20% rate	21% for individuals; 20% for corporations; expanded coverage
Corporate tax rates	Graduated up to 46%	Graduated up to 34%
Dividend exclusion	$100 single; $200 married	Repealed
Investment tax credit	6 to 10%	Repealed
Capital gains	60% excluded; top rate 20%	No exclusions; taxed as regular income
Depreciation	Fast write-offs (from 3 to 19 years) under Accelerated Cost Recovery System	Slower write-offs (from 3 to 31.5 years)

Source: House of Representatives, *Conference Report, Tax Reform Act of 1986, to Accompany H.R. 3838,* 99th Cong., 2d sess., Report No. 99–841.

Was It Tax Reform?

Several basic questions should be asked about the act. Did it in fact reform the tax system? First, did it provide for more vertical equity, that is, greater progressivity in the federal income tax system? The answer is yes, even though the rate structure was both reduced and compressed from fifteen brackets with tax rates at 11 to 50 percent to two brackets at 15 and 28 percent. Most high-income individuals had not paid the high statutory rate because of loopholes and tax expenditures. The lower rates would bring in about as much income as before. Strengthening the minimum tax also helped vertical equity, as did removing the distinction between capital gains and ordinary income. Further, the increase in the personal exemptions and standard deductions removed millions of low-income taxpayers from the tax rolls. It should be noted, however, that many of them continued to pay very heavy Social Security taxes.

Second, did the act provide for more horizontal equity? The answer is yes. Two taxpayers in similar family circumstances and with roughly equal incomes were now more apt than before to pay essentially equal amounts in taxes.

Third, did it improve fairness between and among corporations? The answer is yes. Corporate loopholes were closed, rates lowered, and the minimum corporate tax strengthened. However, the question of who pays corporate taxes remains. Are they shifted forward to consumers, or backward to suppliers and raw material providers, or do they come out of profits and/or investments? Whatever the real incidence is, the corporate income tax became fairer between and among corporations.

One statistical measure of these three points is the dramatic reduction in the estimates for tax expenditures brought about by the 1986 Tax Reform Act. Table 4–10 gives the estimates made by the Congressional Joint Committee on Taxation and included in the Budget Committee Reports in 1986 and 1987.

Finally, did the act simplify the tax code? Because individual taxpayers calculate their taxes with tax tables, the reduction in the number of tax brackets does not simplify the paperwork. Moreover, the bill was almost a thousand pages long, and the new provisions plus the new regulations that

TABLE 4–10 Comparison of Estimated Tax Expenditures Under the Tax Reform Act of 1986 and Under the Tax Laws as of December 1985

Fiscal Year	Under Tax Laws as of December 1985	Under Tax Reform Act of 1986
1988	$486.2	$321.1
1989	529.8	315.2
1990	578.3	335.7
1991	631.5	355.6

will accompany them may make the tax code as complex or more complex than before. This is offset somewhat by the smaller number of deductions that can be taken. The answer to the question is the Scottish verdict—not proven.

There will also be some winners and losers with respect to economic stimulation or social purposes. But as the actual effect of many allegedly stimulating provisions is questionable, far more may be gained in general from the lower rates than from any beneficent effect claimed for a former specific tax expenditure.

Nonetheless, the Tax Reform Act of 1986 is a monumental and unprecedented piece of legislation. Its achievements can be measured by the old saying that success has a thousand fathers but that failure is an orphan. Its parentage was claimed by a galaxy of people.

OTHER TAX INCREASES, 1987–1990

There were additional tax bills and increases in fees in 1987–1990.

The Continuing Resolution and the Omnibus Budget Reconciliation Act of 1987 raised $11.5 billion in fiscal year 1988 and additional amounts in later years. The 1988 reconciliation provisions raised taxes by $6.1 billion for fiscal year 1989. In 1990 the five-year deficit reduction bill raised taxes by $146.6 billion over the five years and about $16 billion in the first year, fiscal year 1991.

Thus, notwithstanding the Reagan-Bush pledges of no new taxes, there were no less than nine major or minor tax bills that raised substantial amounts of revenues in the years 1982–1990. (See Chapters 9 and 10 for the details of the tax bills of 1987–1990.)

THE CHRISTMAS TREE TAX BILLS

One reason that the tax code is cluttered with complex special provisions, exceptions, and amendments is what is called the Christmas tree tax bill. At the end of almost every session of the Congress, a large number of tax bills and amendments are trotted out and proposed in the Senate to be attached to some minor House-passed tax bill. They are so obviously drawn to benefit a particular interest group or individual—a wine company, a National Football League team, an airline—that they have been dubbed the "bearded, one-eyed man with a limp" amendments.

Years ago, when the Congress adjourned by July 4 or Labor Day, a catch-all House-passed tax bill to which a variety of tax loopholes, private relief, or special interest bills were attached was called the "bob-tail" bill. Now that the Congress meets the year around, this bill is called the Christmas tree bill, named both for the time of year that it comes before the Senate and the nature of the gifts and goodies it bestows.

Just before the recess for the 1980 election, for example, the Senate Finance Committee agenda included some ninety-three tax and tariff bills or amendments that committee members had set in place to be raised in the lame-duck session after the elections. Some were good, some were bad, and some were simply terrible. At the end of November, the Finance Committee reported to the Senate more than forty of the bills and amendments, which took more than twenty mimeographed legal-sized pages to describe.

At Christmas in 1982, during a similar lame-duck session, special tax provisions were added to exempt gasohol from the 5-cents-a-gallon gasoline tax; tax deductions were allowed for cruise ships (in what some dubbed the "love boat" amendment); an amendment to the gas tax increase was passed giving longer, wider, heavier trucks access to the interstate highway system; and restrictions to the outside income senators could earn were lifted. Even the Tax Reform Bill of 1986 had special provisions for oil and gas companies, and special "transition rules" for a number of firms in other industries. Under the five-year deficit reduction agreement in 1990, particular small plane manufacturers in Kansas, and beer and wine companies in Missouri and Oregon, all three states of members of the Finance Committee, benefited from Christmas tree riders. A Christmas tree tax bill has been passed or can be expected to pass in virtually every election year.

What's wrong with the Christmas tree amendments? First, they violate the spirit of the constitutional provision that revenue-raising measures start in the House. While technically the bills are "amendments" to a minor House-passed bill, they are in fact "riders" that have no germaneness to the general subject of the tax bill to which they are proposed.

Second, some of the biggest tax loopholes in history were begun this way. Before the minimum tax became law, from time to time the Treasury issued a report listing the number of persons in the country with a million dollars of income or more who paid no federal taxes. In addition to the oil depletion allowance and the capital gains provisions, an item called the "unlimited charitable deduction" was the cause of this revenue hemorrhage. Ostensibly begun to enable a Philadelphia nun whose vows of poverty and family inheritance had led to a large estate which she wanted to give to charity without a heavy tax burden, the provision in fact opened one of the largest tax loopholes in modern times and benefited the wealthiest persons in the country, very few of whom had taken the nun's vows of poverty. It provided that all charitable contributions would be exempt from federal taxation if in eight of the previous ten years 90 percent of a person's taxable income had been given away or paid in taxes. It had several "sleepers"— unintended or unanticipated results.

The 90 percent test applied only to taxable income. Amounts exempted from taxable income—such as capital gains, depletion, and income from abroad—might reduce one's taxable income to a very small percentage of the total real income. In addition, the amendment was passed when contributions to a personal foundation over which the donor retained control were a major scandal of the tax code. Further, one could concentrate income earned over a ten-year period into one or two years and meet the eight-out-of-ten-years test. This all began as just a little old Senate amendment to a House-passed tax bill on behalf of a saintly nun.

A third objection to Christmas tree tax amendments has to do with procedures. Often the amendments or bills have had no hearings in either the House or the Senate. Unlike other bills, they often have no report explaining their provisions or (especially) who will benefit from them. They are often not accompanied by an estimate of the revenue loss they will cause or a Treasury recommendation. Often the bills take the form of amendments upsetting unanimous tax court or Supreme Court decisions, as in the famous *Thor* case.[57]

Perhaps the most famous recent example of a Christmas tree tax bill that also violated the goal of horizontal equity (treating all taxpayers alike) was the $75-a-day expense account bonanza Congress gave itself. This started when the majority whip, Senator Stevens (R.-Ala.), offered the provision as an amendment to an appropriations bill. William Proxmire (D.-Wis.) raised a point of order that it was tax legislation on an appropriations bill. The chair, on the advice of the Senate parliamentarian, ruled the amendment out of order. So eager were senators to get the tax break that they overruled the chair by ten votes and then passed the amendment itself by a scant margin of fort-six to forty-four.

The Treasury, however, ruled that the provision applied only to House and Senate members who either were single or actually commuted from their home state or district from day to day. If they in fact lived in Washington, they were ineligible.

To offset this adverse ruling, Senators Robert Dole (R.-Kan.) and Russell Long (D.-La.), the chairman and ranking Democrat on the Finance Committee, respectively, offered an amendment to universalize the provision. Again it passed by a two-vote margin as an amendment to a bill providing medical and other payments to victims of black lung disease. House members were never required to vote directly on the proposal. In leading the fight against the provision, Proxmire said that it was outrageous that at a time when ordinary citizens were paying taxes through the nose, members of the House and Senate got a big tax break denied to all other citizens. "There are all kinds of things wrong with this provision," he said:

> First, a member of the House or Senate doesn't even have to incur the expense. He or she gets $75 a day or the actual expenses, whichever is higher. This is a unique provision which so far as I know is not available to any legitimate business or professional person.

Second, it's a sneaky, backdoor way for the members of the House and Senate to vote themselves a pay raise. It's worth at least $10,000 a year and probably much more.

Third, not only did Congress vote itself this largess but made it fail safe. The Internal Revenue Service cannot audit it or challenge it. While other taxpayers can be dragged into the IRS office to prove by receipt that their deductions were legitimate, members of Congress don't have to prove anything.

Fourth, deductions are based on something called a "Congressional day." But a Congressional day and a real day are two different things. A Congressional day is a day in which Congress meets within any four day period or less. In 1981, for example, the Senate met 165 days. But under the IRS calculations expenses can be deducted at $75 a day for 241 "Congressional days."

This kind of special interest legislation for itself is exactly what brings Congress into disrepute. It should be repealed not only to right an obvious wrong but to restore credibility to the Congress itself.[58]

Proxmire failed to mention that during some of the congressional days when members were in their home states or district, they could be reimbursed for their travel, motel, food, taxi, and other expenses and also qualify for the $75 tax deduction. The tax break was so controversial that it was soon repealed.

THE VALUE-ADDED TAX

The value-added tax (VAT) is a form of sales tax levied on the value added to a product at each stage of production. It is widely used in Europe, especially among the Common Market countries, and has many advocates in the United States.

Its advocates argue that it could raise a great deal of revenue very quickly. A decade ago former Secretary of the Treasury John B. Connally, one of its supporters, argued that a 2 percent VAT without any exemptions or exceptions could raise $80 billion a year, or $40 billion for each 1 percent levied.[59] It is supported by those who favor taxes on consumption as opposed to taxes on income on the grounds that spending rather than earnings should be taxed if one wishes to dampen inflation and stimulate savings and investment. Further, it is advocated as a relatively painless way of raising revenue, for most consumers do not realize it has been imposed.

Its virtues are also its shortcomings. Its opponents argue that its painless nature also makes it a secret or hidden tax. It is also opposed as a regressive tax in that it falls more heavily on those with low rather than high incomes and those who spend most of their money for food, rent, clothing, and other necessities as opposed to the well-to-do, who have high levels of income and savings. Some of its supporters argue that a series of exemptions or rebates on needed consumer goods can compensate for much of its regressive nature.

Its opponents also argue that it is an inflationary tax that adds to and pyramids costs at each level of production. Because it is hidden and, once imposed, relatively painless to increase, it is called by some a bureaucrat's tax that greatly favors those who support the expansion of government programs because the means to pay for them is easily available.

Among the Common Market or European Economic Community, a range of VAT rates apply, from zero on exempted items to low, standard, and higher rate schedules. The standard rates range from a low of 10 percent in Ireland and Luxembourg to a high of 18 percent in the Netherlands and 20 percent in Denmark.[60]

In the United States, the VAT has not been politically popular since a former chairman of the House Ways and Means Committee, Al Ullman (D.-Oreg.), lost his congressional seat after his advocacy of the tax was made a dominant issue in the reelection campaign.

The value-added tax is an issue for the future.

AMERICAN TAX HISTORY REVIEWED

No subject is more central to budget policy than taxes. No subject is more political or controversial.

Three major types of taxes have dominated American tax history. First, customs and excise taxes dominated tax policy from 1789 until 1913. Tariffs and taxes on "sin" provided the bulk of the revenues and were sufficient in most years to provide a balanced budget.

The passage of the Sixteenth Amendment in 1913 made the income tax constitutional. Since World War II individual and corporate income taxes have provided as much as 70 percent of all federal revenues. In more recent times employment taxes for retirement, health, disability, and unemployment have increased dramatically from their modest origins in the 1930s. They now provide more than one-third of the federal revenues and have replaced the corporate income tax as the second most important source of federal revenues.

The massive 1981 tax cuts plus a growing percentage of expenditures for the military, entitlements, and interest on the debt have been the major cause of the increase in the annual budget deficit. In every year since 1981 the Congress and the president have raised taxes, either by a specific bill or budget reconciliation procedures, in an attempt to recoup some of the revenue losses from the 1981 tax cut. The deficit has grown from $25 billion or less before 1975 to more than $300 billion a year since then. The huge losses brought about by the savings and loan scandal have ominous portents for future deficits.

In 1986 the Congress passed its first major tax reform bill. It did away with many tax expenditures, preferences, or loopholes in order to provide very much lower tax rates without actually losing significant amounts of revenue.

In 1990 the Congress and the president raised taxes by an estimated $146.6 billion for the period 1991–1995 (see Chapter 10), which deepened both the rift between the president and the Democrats in the Congress and between the president and the conservative wing of the Republican party. It illustrated, as few other issues could, that the budget is not a drab accounting document but the epitome of the struggle between the Congress and the president over politics and priorities.

NOTES

1. *Compania de Tobacos v. Collector*, 275 U.S. 87, 100 (1940).
2. *Commissioner v. Newman*, 159 f (sd) 848, 850–851 (1947).
3. U.S. Senate, *History of the Committee on Finance* (Washington, D.C.: U.S. Government Printing Office, 1977). Harrison was chairman from the start of the 72nd Congress on 3 December 1931 until his death on 22 June 1941 during the 77th Congress. Although he served in 6 Congresses, he served less than 10 years, because the 72nd lasted for only a year and 3 months, from December 1931 to March 1933.
4. C. Herman Pritchett, *Constitutional Law of the Federal System* (Englewood Cliffs, N.J.: Prentice Hall, Inc., 1984), p. 201.
5. Robert E. Cushman, and Robert F., Cushman, *Cases in Constitutional Law* (New York: Appleton-Century-Crofts, 1958), p. 251.
6. *Hylton v. United States*, 3 Dallas 171, 234 (1796). Paterson was also one of the two first senators fromNew Jersey.
7. William J. Shultz and M. R. Caine, *Financial Development of the United States* (New York: Prentice-Hall, 1937), pp. 104–106.
8. *Statistical Appendix to the Annual Report of the Secretary of the Treasury on the State of the Finances, Fiscal Year 1979* (Washington, D.C.: U.S. Government Printing Office, 1980), pp. 4–7.
9. Shultz and Caine, *Financial Development*, p. 97.
10. Ibid., p. 108.
11. Ibid, pp. 109–110.
12. Albert Bolles, *Financial History of the United States* (New York: August M. Kelley, 1969), p. 103. Quotes from the *Annals of Congress* 2: 1842, 1844.
13. *The Washington Post*, 8 January 1982, p. A6. © *The Washington Post*.
14. Shultz and Caine, *Financial Development*, p. 106.
15. Ibid., p. 111.
16. Ibid., p. 108n.
17. Frank W. Taussig, *The Tariff History of the United States* (New York: G. P. Putnam's Sons, 1905), p. 1.
18. Schultz and Caine, *Financial Development, p. 106.*
19. Taussig, *Tariff History*, p. 8.
20. E. L. Bogart and Donald L. Kemmerer, *Economic History of the American People* (New York: Longmans, Green, 1948) p. 196.

21. Ibid., p. 197.
22. Taussig, *Tariff History*, p. 7.
23. U. S. Senate, *History of the Committee on Finance*, pp. 21–22.
24. Ibid., p. 23.
25. William J. Shultz, *American Public Finance and Taxation* (New York: Prentice-Hall, 1931), p. 457.
26. Ibid., pp. 526–527.
27. *Statistical Appendix*, p. 6.
28. Ibid.
29. 157 U.S. 429; 158 U.S. 601.
30. 102 U.S. 586.
31. This is what historian Alfred H. Kelly called "law-office" history. It is defined as "extended essays in constitutional history usually written for the purpose of justifying the reversal of precedent by proving that the precedent itself was contrary to the original intention of the Constitution. Nineteenth-century illustrations of law-office history are Chief Justice Taney's essay in the *Dred Scott* case... and Chief Justice Fuller's essays in the Income Tax cases, designed to break down the established precedents that income taxes were not direct taxes." Pritchett, *Constitutional Law*, p. 36.
32. Loren P. Beth, *The Development of the American Constitution, 1877–1917* (New York: Harper and Row, 1971), p. 159.
33. Pritchett, *Constitutional Law*, p. 203.
34. *Statistical Appendix*, p. 8.
35. Ibid., p. 10.
36. Joseph A. Pechman, *Federal Tax Policy*, 4th ed. (Washington, D.C.: The Brookings Institution, 1983), p. 5.
37. *Social Security Bulletin*, December 1982, pp. 12–18.
38. Pechman, *Federal Tax Policy*, rev. ed. 1971, p. 1.
39. Ibid., p. 5.
40. Ibid., p. 6.
41. *The Washington Post*, 8 May 1982. © *The Washington Post*.
42. CBO, *Tax Expenditures: Current Issues and Five Year Budget Projections for Fiscal Years 1982—86* (Washington, D.C.: U.S. Government Printing Office, 1981), p. xi.
43. Philip Stern, *The Great Treasury Raid* (New York: Random House, 1964). © 1964 by Random House, Inc.
44. CBO, *Tax Expenditures*, p. 35. The CBO warns that estimating tax expenditures is a very tricky business, that using different assumptions produces very different results, and that estimates vary widely depending on other components of the tax system (ibid., p. 8).
45. Allen Manvel, "Tax Notes," *Taxation with Representation Fund* 9 (8 October 1979): 503.
46. *Budget of the United States Government: Fiscal Year 1991* (Washington, D.C.: U.S. Government Printing Office, 1990), sec. 2, IV, A–71.
47. Ibid.
48. CBO, *Tax Expenditures*, p. 2.
49. Joint Committee on Taxation, *General Explanation of the Economic Recovery Tax Act of 1981* (Washington, D.C., U.S. Government Printing Office, 1981), p. 17.
50. Ibid., p. 380.
51. *The Washington Post*, 8 January 1982. © *The Washington Post*.
52. Joint Committee on Taxation, *General Explanation*, p. 29.
53. *The Washington Post*, 18 February 1982. © *The Washington Post*.
54. Pechman, *Federal Tax Policy*, p. 11.

55. Michael K. Evans, "Flat-Rate Tax Would Crack Cycle," *Los Angeles Times*, 28 June 1982, pt. IV, p. 3. Copyright, 1982, *Los Angeles Times*. Reprinted by permission.

56. Senate Committee on Finance, 97–2, *Report on Tax Equity and Fiscal Responsibility Act of 1982* (Washington, D.C.: U.S. Government Printing Office, 1982), p. 96.

57. See Douglas, *In the Fullness of Time*, esp. pp. 423–474, for additional details about the struggle for tax reform. Stern's *Great Treasury Raid* includes numerous specific examples on how special provisions for famous individuals got into the code.

58. See *Congressional Record*, 24 October 1981, 30 October 1981, and 14 December 1981, for the debate when the $75 provisions were passed.

59. *Los Angeles Times*, 20 January 1983, pt. I, p. 7. Copyright, 1983, *Los Angeles Times*. Reprinted by permission.

60. A. R. Prest, *Value Added Taxation: The Experience of the United Kingdom* (Washington, D.C.: American Enterprise Institute for Public Policy Research, 1980), p. 49. See also Joseph A. Pechman, ed., *What Should Be Taxed: Income or Expenditure* (Washington, D.C.: The Brookings Institution, 1980).

5

Fiscal Policy: Government Responsibility for the Economy

INTRODUCTION

The year 1933 was a watershed: It was the year the American government took responsibility for the health of the economy. From 1789 until then the doctrine of laissez faire, or "hands off," had prevailed. But not all was void and darkness in the early period. Most of the great departments of the government were established. The government delivered the mail, provided for the army and navy, managed huge tracts of land, and gave millions of acres to the railroads and for public schools. In the late nineteenth century it became the umpire and regulator of monopolies, and began to protect the health and safety of the people. During both the Civil War and World War I government intervened extensively in the economy.

When Franklin Delano Roosevelt was sworn in as president in March of 1933, the United States was at the depth of the Great Depression. Roosevelt, without an overall plan or ideological program, acted in a myriad of different and experimental ways to promote recovery. Essentially the New Deal did five things: (1) it strengthened the umpire functions of government; (2) it sought to provide greater economic justice and equity for the people; (3) it attempted to rationalize production; (4) it initiated a series of programs to create jobs; and (5) it engaged in "pump priming, "or a countercyclical fiscal policy in which the government poured large funds into the economy in an effort to stimulate production, consumption, and recovery.

The Employment Act of 1946 celebrated the change in policy initiated in 1933. It called on the president to use the annual economic report to propose programs to provide maximum employment, production, and purchasing power.

For the next twenty years the effort to stabilize the economy through government fiscal and monetary policies worked very well. Prices and interest rates remained relatively low and stable, recessions were mild and short-lived, the economy grew at rates above the historical averages, and unemployment remained relatively low by American standards.

Starting in 1966, however, a period of chronic inflation ensued. It was characterized by high prices and high interest rates, and culminated in 1979–1981 with both double digit inflation (13.5% in 1980) and relatively high and chronic unemployment (7.6% in 1981). This condition is called *stagflation*. The situation was aggravated by the costs of the Vietnam War and two oil "shocks." In 1981–1982 the most severe post–World War II recession reduced inflation to the 3 to 4 percent level, but employment rose to more than 10 percent and did not decline to 6 percent for four years (6.2% in 1986).

Throughout this period the government ran chronic deficits (except in 1969, when there was an almost imperceptible surplus; see Table 5–1); after the 1982 recession, the deficit ranged from $173 to $348 billion annually. Although this chronic deficit policy was inappropriate for the period, it was strongly advocated by "supply-side" economists. It did result in sustained economic growth from 1983 to 1989, when a downturn combined with a third Middle Eastern oil "shock" again brought stagflation, which this time took the form of inflation coupled with rising unemployment and severely declining economic growth. This presented the monetary authorities with a dilemma, for they faced the Hobson's choice of expanding the money supply to fight unemployment, which would worsen inflation, or tightening the money supply to fight inflation, which could throw more people out of work.

The economic and financial community was critical of the inability of both the new and traditional economic theories to provide stable prices, strong growth, and relatively full employment. Time and again in 1966–1989 the president and the Congress missed opportunities to balance the budget or reduce the insatiable deficit. In 1990 they reached an agreement to reduce spending, raise taxes, and cut the deficit by a projected $492 billion over five years. But raising taxes and cutting spending at a such time of low or negative economic growth, high prices, and rising unemployment were inappropriate economic policies. To offset this problem, few tax increases or budget cuts were scheduled for the first year.

HOOVER AND ROOSEVELT

In the closing speech of his 1928 presidential campaign, Herbert Hoover outlined the philosophy that would guide him:

> During the war we necessarily turned to the government to solve every difficult economic problem. When the war closed...we were challenged with a peacetime choice between the American system of rugged individualism and a European philosophy of diametrically opposed doctrines—doctrines of paternalism and state socialism.
>
> The acceptance of these [European] ideas would have meant the destruction of self-government through centralization of government. It would have meant the undermining of individual initiative and enterprise through which our people have grown to unparalleled greatness.[1]

By a popular vote margin of 58.1 to 40.8 percent and an electoral college victory of 444 to 87, Hoover won the presidency over Alfred E. Smith on a platform that stressed rugged individualism and private initiative.

On October 29, 1929, a year and a week after Hoover's speech, the stock market crashed, and panic and the Great Depression began. By 1933, some 12.8 million Americans, or 24.9 percent of the labor force, were out of work.[2] Farms and businesses were foreclosed. Homes were lost, factories became idle, and the jobless were riding freight trains, going from door to door seeking work and food, and living in shacks along the river bottoms and lowlands of the great cities. These shack communities were derisively called "shantytowns" and "Hoovervilles."

True to his principles, Hoover told the Congress in 1930 that "economic depression cannot be cured by legislative action or executive pronouncement," and instead advocated "self-reliance" and government encouragement of "individual and community cooperation."[3]

He vetoed a bill to provide flood relief and another for government ownership and operation of the Muscle Shoals power plants in the Tennessee Valley; he vetoed the latter on the grounds that it was a form of "state socialism" that would negate "the ideals upon which our civilization has been based."[4] However, contrary to his reputation, Hoover did in fact take some positive actions. He established the Reconstruction Finance Corporation (RFC) and the Home Owners Loan Corporation (HOLC), which extended federal credit to both businesses and individuals facing bankruptcy and foreclosure. He signed a bill to extend credit to cities and states for aid to the poor and the unemployed. "The popular criticisms launched against President Hoover," wrote Charles and Mary Beard, "were not to the effect that he had done nothing, but that he had not done enough of the right things on a scale commensurate with the magnitude of the national catastrophe."[5]

By contrast, in his inaugural address on March 4, 1933, Franklin Delano Roosevelt, after first asserting that "the only thing we have to fear is fear itself—nameless, unreasoning, unjustified terror which paralyzes needed efforts to convert retreat into advance," rejected Hoover's warning that more centralized government action would destroy self-government and called for the use of wartime powers to meet the crisis:

> I shall ask the Congress for the one remaining instrument to meet the crisis—broad executive power to wage a war against the emergency as great as the power that would be given me if we were in fact invaded by a foreign foe.[6]

March 4, 1933, was a watershed in American history. The country would never be the same; from this date the presidency, the budget, and the government would be used as instruments to effect, regulate, and control the economy in an attempt to achieve recovery, prevent depressions, and provide for jobs, economic growth, and price stability. No longer would the government be a neutral or benign instrument whereby depressions would be "left to blow themselves out,"[7] as Hoover had described the government's attitude.

But neither state socialism nor central planning were implemented. Instead, on the whole, macroeconomic fiscal policies to stimulate or dampen the economy through taxes and spending and/or monetary policies to increase or decrease the supply of money were used in lieu of government ownership of the means of production and centralized state planning. Presidents, the Congress, and the leaders of both major political parties accepted responsibility and were held politically liable by the electorate for the success or failure of their economic policies.

THE DOMINANCE OF LAISSEZ FAIRE

Herbert Hoover's philosophy of a relatively passive government and individual self-reliance had deep roots in American history. For almost 150 years, the federal government eschewed responsibility for economic conditions. Even during panics and recessions, the government was not required to act. No citizen expected the government to act. No president took decisive action. No administration prepared plans to end a panic, a recession, or a depression.

From 1789 to 1932, the prevailing economic philosophy of the country was laissez faire, or noninterference by government in the affairs of individuals and lack of action to change economic conditions. While this principle was sometimes negated by the imposition of protective tariffs, by the antitrust and antimonopoly laws of the late nineteenth and early twentieth centuries, and by occasional wartime interventions to stimulate production or to ration goods, it was essentially followed.

Before 1819 in the United States and abroad, recessions or depressions were commercial in nature and generally due to speculation or the interruption of trade. But the industrial revolution and accompanying changes in agriculture, banking, and transportation brought a change. Economic historians Ernest L. Bogart and Donald L. Kemmerer described the new nineteenth-century economic crises or panics:

> They seem to have been due to the development of credit, as extended both by banks and in other ways, by which a rhythmic or cyclical character was introduced into modern industry. The cycle generally began with the investment of capital in enterprises that promised large returns: then followed great activity, expansion, large production, speculation, doubt, impairment of confidence, curtailment of credit, panic, stoppage of production, unemployment, liquidation, depression, recovery—and the cycle started again in its endless round.[8]

As they pointed out, "The crises of 1819, 1837, and 1857 occurred when there was no interference with trade and in periods of profound peace."[9] However, those of 1819 and 1837 were initiated, although not necessarily caused, by the action of government institutions. In 1819 the economy collapsed when the Second Bank of the United States presented a vast accumulation of private bank notes to their issuers for redemption, which the private banks were unable to redeem. In 1836, the Treasury of the United States issued its famous "specie circular," which prevented government agents from accepting anything but specie (coined money, not paper bills or IOUs), or the bills or notes of banks that paid in specie, in payment for public lands. This halted not only land speculation but land buying. When crops also failed and creditors demanded the repayment of other loans, the Panic of 1837 ensued. Thus while the principle of laissez faire did not prevent the government from taking action, often justified, that started panics, the government steadfastly refused to do anything to end them.

The panics occurred about every twenty years, in 1837, 1857, and then, interrupted by the Civil War, 1873, and 1893. In each case the presidents, regardless of party—Van Buren, Buchanan, Grant, and Cleveland; Jacksonian Democrat, Conservative Democrat, Republican, and Conservative Democrat—refused to act. They either opposed government action, as Ulysses S. Grant did in his veto of a bill to expand the currency, or acting on the analogy that a government is like a family or business, took steps to cut back and contract government activity. In the twentieth century, in the panic of 1907 and the crash of 1929 and the ensuing Great Depression, presidents Theodore Roosevelt and Herbert Hoover followed a similar course. At the depth of the Depression, Hoover continued to proclaim, "Prosperity is just around the corner," and on at least one occasion asserted that the crisis was over. Hoover, the Great Engineer, was not alone in this. The Harvard economic forecasters predicted at the depth of the Depression in 1929 that there would be revival and prosperity by the fall of 1930.[10] Forecasting was as inexact a science then as it is now. Economists practice it at their peril.

None of these presidents can be accused of playing politics by their lack of action. They failed because they acted on false principles rather than on expediency. The consequences were harmful to both them and their political parties. Martin Van Buren lost his bid for a second term. James Buchanan, a weak president at a time the country was split by the issues of slavery and impending civil war, did not run for reelection. The Republicans under Grant and Warren G. Harding lost heavily in the congressional races following the panics of 1873 and 1920–1921. In the case of Grover Cleveland and Hoover, the events surrounding panic, crash, and depression helped build political watersheds in American history. Cleveland's economic inaction, his position on gold against silver and hard against easy money policies, and his anti-union action in sending federal troops to Chicago to break the Pullman Strike in 1894 fractured his party. His actions led to a fundamental change in the character of the Democratic party, which brought the domination of progressive rather than conservative forces and ultimately the presidential nominations of William Jennings Bryan, Woodrow Wilson, and Franklin D. Roosevelt. Hoover's economic and budgetary positions not only cost him the presidency, but they cost the Republican party the domination of American politics it had exercised from Abraham Lincoln's election in 1860 until 1932. The political effects for his party were almost as dire as were the economic effects for the country. A measure of the Republican party debacle can be seen in the fact that at the beginning of the Seventy-Fifth Congress in 1937, the Democrats prevailed over the Republicans in the House by 331 to 89 and in the Senate by 76 to 16 (four seats were held by independent or third-party members). Except for four years during the Eightieth and Eighty-Third Congresses, the Democratic party controlled both the House and the Senate for forty-eight years, from 1933 through 1980, and the presidency in thirty-two of those years.

NOT ALL WAS VOID AND DARKNESS

Although 1933 was a watershed for government intervention in the economy, one must not assume that nothing had happened earlier. To borrow phrases that Louis Fisher applied to the period preceding the 1921 Budget Act, not all was void and darkness before then, nor was 1933, with respect to government intervention, "the secular counterpart of the Creation."[11]

The great departments of State, Treasury, War, Justice, and the Navy date from the earliest days of the republic, as do the Customs Service (1789) and the Bureau of the Mint (1792). Both a First (1791 to 1811) and a Second (1816 to 1836) bank of the United States were chartered and then for political reasons allowed to die. Post offices and post roads were initial government functions. The General Land Office was created in 1812. The War Department had a Bureau of Indian Affairs by 1824. A Bureau of Engraving and Printing and the Internal Revenue Service were established in 1862 during the Civil War, when vast quantities of "greenback," or "legal tenders," were printed and the first income tax was introduced. The Homestead Act was passed in the same year, as well as the Morrill Land Grant Act providing for the state universities. The Office of the Comptroller of the Currency, which still regulates national banks, dates from 1863. The Bureau of Fisheries, now the Fish and Wildlife Service, was created in 1871. The murder of President Garfield by a disappointed job seeker occasioned the establishment of the Civil Service Commission in 1883. The Immigration and Naturalization Service was formed in 1891 to process the second great wave of migration to the United States. While government was neither omnipotent nor intrusive during the first century of the country's existence, it nonetheless provided an abundance of services and performed functions that Lincoln defined as the legitimate objects of government, namely to do for the people "whatever they need to have done, but cannot do at all, or cannot so well do for themselves in their separate and individual capacities."

Near the end of the nineteenth century, government took on additional functions. The industrial revolution and the monopoly of the railroads stimulated both an urban and an agrarian radical revolt, which culminated with the establishment of the Interstate Commerce Commission in 1887 to regulate railroad shipping rates and the passage of the Sherman Antitrust Act in 1890 to help break up industrial monopolies. Sparked by the Populist and the Progressive movements, the government not only became the regulator and umpire for some economic activities, but it intervened to protect both health and safety. The Bureau of Standards dates from 1901. The Pure Food and Drug Act was passed in 1906. The Bureau of Mines was established in 1910. Other regulatory agencies or functions were provided in the first third of the twentieth century. They include the Federal Reserve Board (1913), the Federal Trade Commission and the Clayton Act (1914), and the Tariff Commission (1916).

The government also fought five declared wars from 1789 through 1918. In two of them, the Civil War and World War I, the government mobilized the overwhelming human, industrial, financial, and economic resources of the country on behalf of the effort. But even in peacetime, government activities went beyond such essential functions as providing for the army and navy and regulating health and monopolies, and actually provided subsidies or services to both special interest groups and the general public. The Bureau of Reclamation, which provided below-cost loans for water and power, was established in 1902; the Department of Commerce and Labor, a single agency, in 1903; the Forest Service in 1905; a Fine Arts Commission in 1910; the Coast Guard in 1915; and the National Park Service in 1916. The Shipping Act of 1916 provided maritime operating and shipbuilding subsidies to that industry. President Hoover, who opposed government production of electric power as a major purpose at Muscle Shoals, supported "the construction of great dams and reservoirs, where navigation, flood control, reclamation or stream regulation are of dominate importance and . . . beyond the capacity or purpose of private or local government capital to construct."[12] It was his administration that began the great Boulder (now Hoover) Dam that spans the Colorado River and produces water and electricity for millions of people in several western states.

WHAT THE NEW DEAL DID

Franklin Delano Roosevelt had no initial grandiose plan. His programs were innovative, pragmatic, and experimental without ideological overtones but he was determined that the government should act in diverse ways to relive the economic disaster. The effect, however, was to increase the size of the government, to extend the functions of the government, and to take responsibility for the state of the economy and actions to provide employment, stable prices, and vigorous growth.

The New Deal built on both past experience and existing government functions. Essentially it did the following things.

First it strengthened and enlarged the regulatory or umpire functions of government which began in the late nineteenth century. The Federal Deposit Insurance Corporation (FDIC) was set up in 1933 to insure bank deposits and to regulate banks further. The Securities and Exchange Commission (SEC) was established in 1934 to enforce the Securities and Exchange Act, which required objective disclosure of essential facts before bonds or stocks could be issued. This was a reaction against the speculative issue of stocks that had helped bring on the 1929 crash. The Federal Communications Commission (FCC) was created by the Communications Act of 1934 to regulate interstate and foreign communications by wire and radio. The Federal Savings and Loan Insurance Corporation (FSLIC), the counterpart of the FDIC, was set up under the Housing Act of 1934 to insure deposits in neighborhood thrift and home financing institutions. The Civil Aeronautics Board (CAB), which regulated air routes and fares, was created in 1938. While these agencies expanded the functions of government and no doubt helped create confidence in regulated private industries and institutions, they did little to stimulate recovery or the economy.

Second, a number of institutions designed to provide more equity and economic justice in the society were established. In 1935 collective bargaining was provided by the Wagner Act and the establishment of the National Labor Relations Board. The National Mediation Board had been set up the previous year. The Fair Labor Standards Act, which set a 40-cent minimum wage and a forty-hour week, was passed in 1938. The Railroad Retirement Act of 1935 and the Railroad Unemployment Insurance Act of 1938 were similar measures.

Third, there was the attempt to rationalize production through the limitation of output. The National Industrial Recovery Act (NIRA), generally referred to as the NRA for the National Recovery Administration that carried it out, established trade or industry codes of fair competition. Passed on June 13, 1933, the last day of the first session of a historic Congress, it went beyond the codes to provide for collective bargaining and for public works and construction projects. Henry Steele Commager described the NRA as "in some respect the most extraordinary law ever passed by an American Congress," as it "provided for the federal control of the entire industrial structure of the country through the mechanism of codes drawn up by government administrators and special industries."[13] The Agriculture Adjustment Act (AAA, or Triple A) of May 12, 1933, had a similar purpose. It attempted to raise farm prices by adjusting production through voluntary crop reduction and provided for commodity processing taxes to raise revenues for rental or benefit payments. Although both acts were struck down by the Supreme Court as unconstitutional, much of the Triple A was reenacted, while the NRA codes mercifully were abandoned.

Fourth, a number of programs were designed for the direct creation of jobs. They fell into three major categories. The first was the Public Works Administration (PWA), which along with the Tennessee Valley Authority (TVA) constructed dams, roads, and power stations, primarily in the South and the West, including the Grand Coulee Dam, the Bonneville Power Administration, and the completion of Boulder Dam. The second was the Works Project Administration (WPA), which provided some very useful and necessary work but which was heavily criticized and ridiculed for its alleged "leaf-raking" and "shovel-leaning" activities. There was a certain opprobrium attached to working for the WPA, much of it unnecessary and exaggerated, for much good work was done under its auspices. Unemployed writers provided histories of towns and communities. Murals were painted in public buildings. Abraham Lincoln's boyhood home of New Salem, Illinois, was reconstructed, and many roads and buildings in parks were built. Some of the writings and works of art have recently been highly praised, and the authors and artists, as well as much of the program, have been redeemed by the verdict of history. Third were the Civilian Conservation Corps (CCC) camps. Young men volunteered for a life of work in the woods, forests, and national parks under quasimilitary conditions. Initial construction of the Skyline Drive in the Blue Ridge Mountains of Virginia was initiated by the NIRA in June 1933, and both the PWA and CCC were involved in its construction. All these programs had many beneficial results but were obviously insufficient to solve the unprecedented unemployment problem of the 1930s.

Finally, there was a series of actions variously described as "pump priming," or countercyclical fiscal policy, whose purpose it was to pour enough money and credit into the economy to increase demand and hence spark economic recovery. Accompanying it were a number of social programs, termed the "automatic economic stabilizers," that were designated to expand in periods of depression or recession and contract in periods of prosperity and recovery.

With respect to spending, by 1940 the federal government had tripled its annual net expenditures of 1929 and doubled the 1932 level. As prices fell from 1929 to 1932 and were stable from 1932 through 1940, this was a doubling or tripling in government spending in real terms. The public debt tripled from just over $16 billion in 1930 to $48.5 billion by 1940.

During this period the supply of credit was dramatically increased through both a series of government programs making credit available, such as farm loans, an expanded RFC, the creation of the Export-Import Bank, and an accommodating monetary policy through which the Federal Reserve System purchased government bonds.

The "automatic economic stabilizers"put in place included unemployment compensation, Social Security, and payments designed to raise the level of farm prices to 90 percent of parity. Parity was defined as the ratio of prices farmers received to the prices they paid for the costs of production in 1910–1914. Government payments under all of the programs rose as either farm prices fell, unemployment increased, or the economy turned down. Combined with the reduction in revenues because of high unemployment and relatively low industrial production, these programs produced deficits that theoretically would stimulate demand and promote recovery.

From 1933 to 1940, the economic effects of these programs were substantial but not dramatic. The programs gave hope to millions of people, and helped preserve the self-respect of millions more. They saved many farmers and businessmen from bankruptcy and catastrophe. But the economy did not fully recover until 1943, during World War II. Unemployment dropped from the 24.9 percent peak in 1933 to 14.3 percent in 1937, but rose again to 19 percent during the 1937–1938 recession and still averaged 14.6 percent in 1940.[14] It took a mammoth eightfold increase in wartime spending, from $9.1 billion in 1940 to $79.4 billion in 1943, to provide relatively full employment and recovery from the Great Depression.[15]

THE EMPLOYMENT ACT OF 1946

The Employment Act of 1946 did not signify the death of laissez faire, the beginning of countercyclical fiscal policies, or the federal government's acceptance of responsibility for the health of the economy. Laissez faire was buried in 1933. The new doctrines were more than a decade old. Passage of the Employment Act was not so much the beginning of an era as the celebration of accepted precepts.

The act was a child of the Depression and the war, and was begotten by the fear of a new postwar economic disaster. Like the Budget Act of 1921, it transferred the initiative over the economy and the elements of economic affairs from the Congress to the president and the White House staff. It established as the responsibility of the federal government the use of all practicable means "to promote maximum employment, production, and purchasing power."[16] It required the president to monitor the economy and to recommend action if it faltered.

The Employment Act enthroned compensatory fiscal policy. First, during recessions and depressions, the government would actively intervene in the economy through increased spending or tax cuts to offset the fall in private demand. This would be accompanied by adoption of an expansionary monetary policy by the Federal Reserve System that would create money and credit to offset the diminished supply of savings and investment funds in private banks and businesses. Because prices fell precipitously in panics and depressions, there was little danger of inflation during such periods. Second, and alternatively, during periods of price rises and prosperity, the federal government would pursue a policy of a balanced budget and a surplus to offset the deficits brought about during the periods of decline. Monetary policy would also be tightened, the money supply would be expanded at a slower rate, and price rises and inflation would be avoided. Over the business cycle, the surpluses would offset the deficits.

The passage of the act represented some compromises. The word "maximum" was substituted for "full" employment. Planning on a large scale was rejected. Specific goals and targets for employment, production, and investment were eschewed, and no mention was made in the original act of price levels and inflation for fear that the act's administrators might use them as an excuse to undermine the employment goals.

The 1946 Act directed the president to present the *Economic Report of the President* to the Congress early in each regular session and had the effect of elevating it to the level of the State of the Union Address and the budget message. The act established the President's Council of Economic Advisers (CEA) in the Executive Office of the President. While it represented yet another transfer of authority and responsibility from the Congress to the president, the act did establish the Joint Committee on the Economic Report (now the Joint Economic Committee or JEC), which was directed to make its own findings, and to report to the Congress and the public early in the year on the *Economic Report of the President*. While the JEC has no power to initiate legislation, through its hearings, studies, and informing function it elevates both the level of public knowledge and debate over economic matters.

TWO DECADES OF SUCCESSFUL FISCAL POLICY

Countercyclical fiscal policies were generally successful from 1946 to 1966. If the polices were not perfectly executed in that period, at least the country suffered from no post–World War II depression, as had been feared. If not directly occasioned by wars, the panics of the past had followed closely after the end of wars. The Panic of 1819 followed the War of 1812 (1812–1815), and the Panic of 1873 occurred only eight years after the end of the Civil

War (1861–1865). World War I (1917–1918) was followed by the sharp recession of 1920–1921 and the Great Depression in 1929.

After an initial post–World War II surge, prices remained remarkably stable until 1966. Recessions occurred and had their economic and political consequences, but on the whole they were short-lived. The economy grew at rates comparable with if not somewhat in excess of its historical average. There was a decline in the level of poverty; a surge in prosperity, especially of the middle class; and a vast expansion in production and homebuilding in the two decades or more following World War II. In that period the Employment Act worked and worked very well indeed.

Stable Prices One of the first actions under the Employment Act was taken in 1947. At a time when the removal of wartime price controls had brought an explosion in prices and inflation, President Truman vetoed a Republican-sponsored tax cut on the grounds that in times of relatively full employment and rising prices, the country needed a budget surplus. The Congress sustained his veto that year but could not resist cutting taxes in the election year of 1948, when it overrode his veto. Essentially true to his principles and those of compensatory fiscal policy, Truman provided budget surpluses in each of three immediate post–World War II fiscal years and a fourth in 1951, a policy that both continued prosperity and stopped inflation. Truman acted on the advice of his economic counselors, Edwin Norse and Leon Keyserling.

When the Korean War broke out in the summer of 1950, Truman requested and the JEC endorsed a tax increase to offset inflationary pressures. A $3 billion increase was passed with spectacular speed, but an additional $10 billion request was cut to $5 billion and delayed until October 1951. This was equal to a 16 percent increase in taxes. Prices rose 5.8 and 5.9 percent in 1950 and 1951, respectively, but for the next sixteen years price increases, as measured by the consumer price index, remained at incredibly low levels. In five of the sixteen years from 1952 through 1967, they either rose less than 1 percent or actually fell. During twelve years, they rose by less than 2 percent. In only one of those sixteen years did prices go up by more than 3 percent. President Eisenhower followed suit and produced three budget surpluses in eight years, and prices remained stable throughout his two terms (1953–1961).

Recessions The 1947–1966 period, however, was not free of recessions. They occurred in 1949, when unemployment averaged 5.9 percent; in 1953–1954, when it averaged 5.5 percent for the latter year; and in 1957–1958, when it averaged 6.8 percent. These recessions had their political cost for both Truman and Eisenhower. The Democrats lost twenty-nine seats in the House and five in the Senate in 1950. The Republicans lost control of both the House and the Senate in 1954. In 1958 the Republicans lost forty-seven seats in the House, while the Democrats gained fifty-one, for a

285-to-153 Democratic edge. In the Senate the Democrats gained sixteen seats and increased their slim 49-to-47 majority to a 65-to-35 margin. The Republicans lost twelve seats and the Democrats gained four more with the admission of Alaska and Hawaii to the union.

In 1960 the JEC, chaired by Senator Paul H. Douglas (D.-Ill.), conducted a study of employment, prices, and growth that had a profound effect on economic policies for the next five years. Its staff director was Otto Eckstein, later (1964–1966) a member of the Council of Economic Advisers under President Johnson. Warren L. Smith, later a member of both the council and the Federal Reserve Board, was its chief monetary economist. Charles L. Schultze, director of the Bureau of the Budget under Johnson and chairman of the council under President Carter, wrote *Study Paper No. 1*. Walter W. Heller, James Tobin, Kermit Gordon, Gardner Ackley, and Arthur Okun, all of whom where later chairmen or members of the Council of Economic Advisers,[17] took part either as witnesses or advisers. Senator John F. Kennedy (D.-Mass.) was also a member of the JEC. While his attendance at the hearings was limited by his campaign for the presidency, he was so profoundly influenced by the study papers and reports that he routinely read them while traveling.

President Kennedy's Council of Economic Advisers—with Heller as chairman and Tobin, Gordon, and Ackley as members—and their immediate successors carried out the proposals of the 1960 report with substantial results. Unemployment fell from 6.7 percent in 1961 to 4.5 percent in 1965. The consumer price index (CPI) rose from 1961 through 1965 by the following minute amounts: 0.7 percent, 1.2 percent, 1.6 percent, 1.2 percent, and 1.9 percent, respectively.

Except for calendar year 1961, when the figure was 2.6 percent, the gross national product (GNP) grew in real terms at a spectacular rate—between 4 and 6 percent in each of the next four years. The period from 1961 through 1965 is a textbook example of how the economy should function in peacetime. It provided relatively high and sustained economic growth accompanied by a major reduction in unemployment and a stable price level.

The government's extraordinary economic success in the first two decades following World War II—from 1946 through 1965—has not been matched by presidents and policy makers since then.

STAGFLATION AND THE FAILURE OF FISCAL POLICY

From 1965 to 1968 the military budget in real terms grew by 30 percent.[18] The initial attitude of the Johnson administration was that the government could provide both guns *and* butter. In early 1966, however, Johnson's Council of Economic Advisers—Ackley, Eckstein, and Okun—advised otherwise and proposed a tax increase both to help pay for the Vietnam War and to dampen inflationary pressures. For a variety of reasons, which the president explained later most importantly included the political impossibility of getting it passed, the advice was not taken. As it was, the Republicans gained forty-seven seats in the House and four in the Senate in 1966. It was no idle administration fear that a tax increase in an election year would have made the outcome, from their point of view, even worse. When a surtax was proposed in early 1967, Republicans and conservative Democrats, led by House Ways and Means Committee Chairman Wilbur Mills (D.-Ark.), held it hostage to cuts in domestic programs. Almost a year and a half passed before the president and the Congress could negotiate both the surtax and domestic budget cuts.

In 1968 a budget surplus was clearly needed. Unemployment was at a low 3.6 percent. The economy grew in real terms at a strong 4.6 percent rate. But consumer prices had risen 4.7 percent, a level exceeded since World War II only during the first year and a half of the Korean War. Instead of a surplus in 1968, there was a $25.2 billion deficit, double that of any postwar year, which was clearly inappropriate and excessive for the times.

Vietnam inflation had arrived. The surtax, finally in place, provided a small surplus, $3.2 billion in a $184 billion budget in fiscal year 1969, which, while more appropriate than another major deficit, was hardly sufficient for the economic conditions that prevailed. Unemployment was still at a low 3.5 percent, but inflation had doubled since 1967, and the CPI was at a post–World War II high of 6.1 percent.

Meanwhile, the Great Society legislation proposed by President Johnson, rivaling that of Woodrow Wilson's first term and exceeded only by Franklin Roosevelt's famous first one hundred days in office, had been put in place. The combination of spending for the War on Poverty and the war in Vietnam had unprecedented social effects. Between 1964 and 1969, the number of poor people in the country, as measured by the poverty level adjusted for prices, had fallen from 39 to 26 million, or by one-third.

Many economists and political advisers believed that the end of the Vietnam War would result in a large budget surplus, or a "peace dividend." Unfortunately, it vanished like the morning mists on the beach at San Clemente. Other economists argued that due to higher growth rates, rising incomes, and inflation, additional revenues from the existing tax structure would become so large they would create a "fiscal drag" on the economy. They proposed a program of "revenue sharing" with the states and cities to prevent the "drag." Like the "peace dividend," the excess budget surpluses never arrived, and the federal government, under a Nixon administration proposal, shared with the states and localities $6 billion a year of revenues it did not have to share. Based on these optimistic assumptions, during both the Johnson and Nixon administrations there was less concern about the dangers of inflation, deficits, and spending for both guns and butter than prudent persons should have exercised.

Chronic Inflation Historically, the United States has experienced inflation only during wartime, when the classic problem of too much money chasing too few goods drove up prices. From 1948 through 1967, there were only two years, 1950 and 1951 during the Korean War, when the CPI exceeded 3 percent. In thirteen of those years, it was below 2 percent.

But the Vietnam War and the worldwide inflation caused in part by the oil embargo of the early 1970s changed the American economy from one in which prices remained relatively stable at low levels to one characterized by roaring, raging, chronic inflation. In every year from 1969 through 1981, except for 1971 and 1972, when price controls were in effect, the CPI rose by more than 5 percent, and in some years it rose at double-digit levels. It exceeded 3 percent every year until 1986, when it was 1.1 percent, and was then at 4.4 percent or higher into the 1990s.

Unemployment and Stagflation During each postwar recession, unemployment became progressively worse. Following some recessions, the unemployment rate returned to a level during relatively prosperous years only marginally lower than that at the peak of some of the earlier recessions. During the 1949 recession, unemployment averaged 5.9 percent. In the 1958 recession, it was at a new high and averaged 6.8 percent. In the 1975 recession, it averaged 8.5 percent, and in 1982 unemployment averaged 9.7 percent and reached 10.8 percent by the end of the year.

Not until 1982 did the extraordinarily high levels of unemployment bring a significant reduction in the inflation rates, a price many thought was excessive. For eleven years, from 1976 through 1986, except for 1978 and 1979, unemployment was 7 percent or more. In some of those years, especially 1976–1979 and 1983–1984, there was strong economic growth. Inflation not only persisted, but in 1979 and 1980 it was at 12 and 13 percent, respectively. Inflation, as measured by the CPI, finally declined to a 3.9 percent average for 1982; it essentially remained at this level until the exceptional year of 1986, when it was 1.1 percent. But the next year it returned to 4.5 percent, where it stayed until stagflation returned after the oil "shock" of 1990. The recession of 1982 was followed by more than seven years of sustained economic growth until 1990 to 1992 when there was another recession.

Chronic Deficits After 1969, these conditions were accompanied by budget deficits every year, some of which were staggering. In some years, particularly the recession years of 1975 and 1981–1982, a deficit of some magnitude was appropriate, although one can question whether the $53.2 billion deficit in 1975 and the $127.9 billion deficit in 1982 were not excessive even for recessions. But there were also very large deficits during periods of relatively strong economic growth and runaway inflation. Deficits totaled just over $200 billion, or an average of $50 billion a year, from 1976 through 1979, when there was strong growth in the GNP and when prices were extraordinarily high. These deficits were justified by some on grounds of the relatively high levels of unemployment, but they seemed to have had only minor effects in reducing unemployment. The same was true in the recovery years of 1983–1985, when deficits were in the $200 billion range a year. Reagan economists believed there would be an underlying structural deficit of $150 billion a year by the end of 1985, even if the economy recovered and unemployment dropped to about 6 percent, a prediction that was uncharacteristically accurate. As Reagan Office of Management and Budget (OMB) economist Lawrence Kudlow said, ". . . the bulk of the deficit was structural and therefore would remain, even if the economy recovers" (see Table 5–1).[19] But the projection did not foresee the disastrous savings and loan bailout, take into account the masking of the real deficit by the surplus in the Social Security accounts, or predict the cost of the war in the Persian Gulf, which by the early 1990s had raised the deficit to more than $300 billion.

High Interest Rates   The failures of fiscal policy, adding to stagflation and deficits, also made it impossible for monetary policy to work. Interest rates in the period responded to both rising prices and budget deficits. Until 1965–1966, short-term treasury bill rates were 3 percent or below, and long-term bond rates were only marginally higher. The prime rate—the interest rate commercial banks charge their best customers—was almost always below 5 percent, and until 1960 was usually in the 2 to 3 percent range. Until 1966, interest rates on new home mortgages were 6 percent or less.

From 1966 through 1978, interest rates rose again, but gradually. While short-term treasury securities fluctuated somewhat more widely, long-term treasury bonds, new home mortgages, and the prime rate rose from the general level of 6 percent in the late 1960s to 8 or 9 percent by 1978.

In 1979, interest rates started an unprecedented climb. By December 1980, the prime rate was over 20 percent, where it remained through the spring and summer of 1981. The rate for a new home mortgage was 15 percent or more. Long-term treasury notes sold at 13 to 14 percent, and short-term rates fluctuated from 10 to 16 percent. Consequently, the housing industry became a basket case. New housing starts, which were more than 2,000,000 units in 1978, dropped to 1,084,000 units in 1981 and to a seasonally adjusted annual rate of less than 900,000 units in the five months from September 1981 through January 1982. The domestic automobile industry faced a crisis caused not only by Japanese competition but also by the inability of consumers to borrow. Business and personal bankruptcies set new records, and neither farmers nor Main Street businesses could afford to borrow from their friendly local banker to pay for their spring plantings or to replenish their inventories.

TABLE 5–1   Federal Receipts, Outlays, Surplus or Deficit, and Debt for Selected Fiscal Years 1929–1992 (Billions of Dollars)

| Fiscal Year or Period | Total | | | Gross Federal Debt (End of Period) | | Addendum: Gross National Product |
	Receipts	Outlays	Surplus or Deficit (−)	Total	Held by the public	
1929	$ 3.9	$ 3.1	$ 0.7	$ 16.9[1]		
1933	2.0	4.6	−2.6	22.5[1]		
1939	6.3	9.1	−2.8	48.2	$ 41.4	$ 88.4
1940	6.5	9.5	−2.9	50.7	42.8	95.8
1941	8.7	13.7	−4.9	57.5	48.2	113.0
1942	14.6	35.1	−20.5	79.2	67.8	142.2
1943	24.0	78.6	−54.6	142.6	127.8	175.8
1944	43.7	91.3	−47.6	204.1	184.8	202.0
1945	45.2	92.7	−47.6	260.1	235.2	212.4
1946	39.3	55.2	−15.9	271.0	241.9	212.9
1947	38.5	34.5	4.0	257.1	224.3	223.6
1948	41.6	29.8	11.8	252.0	216.3	247.8
1949	39.4	38.8	.6	252.6	214.3	263.9
1950	39.4	42.6	−3.1	256.9	219.0	266.8
1951	51.6	45.5	6.1	255.3	214.3	315.0
1952	66.2	67.7	−1.5	259.1	214.8	342.4
1953	69.6	76.1	−6.5	266.0	218.4	365.6
1954	69.7	70.9	−1.2	270.8	224.5	369.5
1955	65.5	68.4	−3.0	274.4	226.6	386.4
1956	74.6	70.6	3.9	272.7	222.2	418.1
1957	80.0	76.6	3.4	272.3	219.3	440.5
1958	79.6	82.4	−2.8	279.7	226.3	450.2
1959	79.2	92.1	−12.8	287.5	234.7	481.5
1960	92.5	92.2	.3	290.5	236.8	506.7
1961	94.4	97.7	−3.3	292.6	238.4	518.2
1962	99.7	106.8	−7.1	302.9	248.0	557.7
1963	106.6	111.3	−4.8	310.3	254.0	587.8
1964	112.6	118.5	−5.9	316.1	256.8	629.2
1965	116.8	118.2	−1.4	322.3	260.8	672.6
1966	130.8	134.5	−3.7	328.5	263.7	739.0
1967	148.8	157.5	−8.6	340.4	266.6	794.6
1968	153.0	178.1	−25.2	368.7	289.5	849.4
1969	186.9	183.6	3.2	365.8	278.1	929.5
1970	192.8	195.6	−2.8	380.9	283.2	990.2
1971	187.1	210.2	−23.0	408.2	303.0	1,055.9
1972	207.3	230.7	−23.4	435.9	322.4	1,153.1
1973	230.8	245.7	−14.9	466.3	340.9	1,281.4
1974	263.2	269.4	−6.1	483.9	343.7	1,416.5
1975	279.1	332.3	−53.2	541.9	394.7	1,522.5
1976	298.1	371.8	−73.7	629.0	477.4	1,698.2

1956. Debt = 2/3 GNP
1992   "   "   "   "

TABLE 5–1 *(Continued)*

Fiscal Year or Period	Total			Gross Federal Debt (End of Period)		Addendum: Gross National Product
	Receipts	Outlays	Surplus or Deficit (−)	Total	Held by the public	
Transition quarter	81.2	96.0	−14.7	643.6	495.5	448.7
1977	355.6	409.2	−53.6	706.4	549.1	1,933.0
1978	399.6	458.7	−59.2	776.6	607.1	2,171.8
1979	463.3	503.5	−40.2	828.9	639.8	2,447.8
1980	517.1	590.9	−73.8	908.5	709.3	2,670.6
1981	599.3	678.2	−78.9	994.3	784.8	2,986.4
1982	617.8	745.7	−127.9	1,136.8	919.2	3,139.1
1983	600.6	808.3	−207.8	1,371.2	1,131.0	3,321.9
1984	666.5	851.8	−185.3	1,564.1	1,300.0	3,687.7
1985	734.1	946.3	−212.3	1,817.0	1,499.4	3,952.4
1986	769.1	990.3	−221.2	2,120.1	1,736.2	4,180.8
1987	854.1	1,003.8	−149.7	2,345.6	1,881.1	4,424.7
1988	909.0	1,064.1	−155.1	2,600.8	2,050.3	4,780.4
1989	990.7	1,144.1	−153.4	2,867.5	2,190.3	5,131.3
1990	1,031.3	1,251.7	−220.4	3,206.3	2,410.4	5,405.6
1991[2]	1,091.4	1,409.6	−318.1	3,617.8	2,717.6	5,615.8
1992[2]	1,165.0	1,445.9	−280.9	4,021.1	2,995.4	5,985.5

Source: Department of Commerce (Bureau of Economic Analysis), Department of the Treasury, and Office of Management and Budget, *Economic Report of the President, 1991* (Washington, D.C.: U.S. Government Printing Office, 1987), p. 375.

1. Not strictly comparable with later data.

2. Estimates. Later revised by the 1991 midyear budget review (16 July, 1991) to $282.2 b. (fy 1991) and $348.3 b. (fy 1992).

Note.—Through fiscal year 1976, the fiscal year was on a July 1–June 30 basis; beginning October 1976 (fiscal year 1977), the fiscal year is on an October 1–September 30 basis. The 3-month period from July 1, 1976, through September 30, 1976 is a separate fiscal period known as the transition quarter.

Refunds of receipts are excluded from receipts and outlays.

See "Budget of the United States Government, Fiscal Year 1992" for additional information.

The crisis was not the result of the classical cause of inflation of too much money chasing too few goods. Industry was operating at 70 percent of capacity and below, and pressures on prices were not caused by excessive demand. It was a crisis in credit and a period of stagflation in which relatively high levels of unemployment and inflation occurred at the same time.

After 1982 interest rates and bond yields declined from their double-digit levels until 1987, when they began to rise again. By 1989 most were above 8 percent, and both new home mortgage rates and the prime rate charged by banks to their most favored customers were 10 percent or more.

These rates persisted to the end of 1990, even as the economy declined. There was a new crisis in credit as the federal government, savings and loans institutions, banks, businesses, and consumers were all living far beyond their means.

DEFENDERS OF FISCAL POLICY

There are those who defend the spectacular rise in government spending, the recurring and growing budget deficits, and the growth in the public debt under both Democratic and Republican administrations after 1967. Ironically, it is not only post-Keynesian partisans who justify a burgeoning national debt on the grounds that the country owes it to itself or that it is a manageable proportion of the GNP. The same arguments were heard by the advocates of supply-side economics during the Reagan administration. What are the various arguments used by the defenders of the economic and budgetary policies followed by presidents Johnson, Nixon, Ford, Carter, Reagan and Bush?

Budget Outlays Not Out of Line   First, it was argued that budget outlays as a percentage of the GNP were not out of line. During the stagflation under six presidents, budget outlays as a percent of the GNP hovered between 18 and 25 percent. The higher percentage occurred in periods of recession, when outlays for unemployment compensation, welfare, Social Security, and food stamps rose as a result of the recession at a time when the GNP was falling, thus creating a somewhat misleading statistic. Spending as a percentage of the GNP was not that much out of line and compared favorably with some industrialized countries with larger budget outlays, larger percentages of the GNP in spending, and smaller amounts of inflation.

Deficits a Small Part of the GNP   Second, it was argued that the annual budget deficit was a relatively small proportion of the GNP. It was generally less than 2 percent until 1975, and generally between 2 and 5 percent in most years since, even when off-budget items were included.

Reduction of Debt Held by the Public   Third, there has been a spectacular reduction in the debt held by the public as a percentage of the GNP. In 1954 the debt held by the public (about 85 percent of the total) was over 60 percent of the GNP. By 1965 the percentage had fallen to less than 40 percent. In every year during the 1970s, it was below 30 percent (it was 25 percent in fiscal year 1974) and fluctuated around the 30 to 45 percent level through the 1980s but rose to 50% in the early 1990s (see Table 5–1).[20]

The factual evidence appeared to be that budget outlays, the annual deficit, and the public debt were not out of line with the GNP and that, in the case of the public debt and the ability of the country to carry it, conditions had improved somewhat. Supply-side economists would argue that these were manageable proportions. The evidence and arguments were included in the presidents' budget documents.

Family Budget Comparison   Even those who compare the national debt with the family budget could hardly fault the government. Most families assume a mortage debt for their home that is about two and one-half times their annual income, and this plus their debt for their automobile, consumer durables, and other items increases the proportion. By comparison, the total national debt is about three times the federal government's annual revenues. Before the Reagan administration the ratio was routinely below two.

Comparison with Business Debt   If one compares the government budget and debt with those of most businesses, the government fares even better. Most businesses depreciate their capital investment, machinery, and equipment over a long period. What they try to balance each year is the operating budget. Further, assets are offset by liabilities to determine the worth of the firm.

If similar accounting methods were used for federal government finance, the operating budget would usually be in balance and the assets of the government would offset its debt. Under the federal government's budget, spending for land; spending for buildings, housing, and military hardware with ten- to thirty-year lives; and investment in heavy machinery are treated as one-year outlays instead of being put below the line in a capital budget and depreciated over their lifetime. Further, the assets of the government in land, buildings, timber, strategic commodities, and other equipment and supplies are never offset against its debt or liabilities. If all this is true, what then is the problem? Why is there a crisis in both the budget and the economy?

THE PROBLEM OF CROWDING OUT

Many economists believe that the problem is not the size of the national debt, the annual deficit per se, or their relation to the GNP. Neither is it the absolute level of federal spending or the percentage these budget outlays are of the GNP. The problem, they believe, is what the financial markets call "crowding out." Through its various activities, the federal government competes with the private sector for the savings in the country.

Keynesian theory propounds that total savings should equal total investments in the economy. Thus, when there is high unemployment, stable or falling prices, great unusued industrial capacity, and idle savings, government deficits or "pump priming" can provide an outlet for or offset the idle or excess savings. Additional monetary purchasing power can be used to put idle men and women to work on idle machinery to make goods that would not otherwise be produced. There is little danger of inflation because the increase in the money supply is offset by an increase in the supply of goods and services. In such periods there is no danger of too much money chasing too few goods because of the increase in the supply of goods.

The theory, appropriate for periods of deflation, recession, or depression, has not worked since 1966 under Republican and Democratic administrations alike. There are several reasons. First, because of the need for the government to borrow to finance the deficit, plus the variety of direct loans both on and off the budget, loan guarantees, and loans of government-sponsored enterprises, the debt and deficit did not provide an outlet for "idle" savings but were in competition with the private sector for a limited pool of savings. As liberal economist Lester C. Thurow wrote:

> Additional pressures for higher long-term interest rates are created by large deficits in the Reagan budget. The problem is not that these deficits will cause inflation—that is virtually impossible given the amount of idle capacity and labor in the system—but that they are negative savings. Last year individuals saved $107 billion in the United States. If the budget deficit is $107 billion or larger, the government is absorbing all of personal savings.[21]

While referring to government loan guarantees, President Reagan's first budget director, David Stockman, told reporters at an OMB briefing that "every time you do it, you knock someone else out of the pew."[22] This statement applies equally to government borrowing to finance the debt, to provide a direct loan, or to pay off a loan guarantee.

While some supply-side economists played down the debt and deficits, President Reagan's first chairman of the Council of Economic Advisers, Murray Weidenbaum, told a Houston audience that "we cannot view substantial budget deficits with indifference—deficits do matter," and financial market analysts such as Henry Kaufman of Salomon Brothers and Albert Wojnilower of the First Boston Corporation believed that "so long as mammoth deficits are in prospect a sustained economic recovery and lower interest rates are not possible."[23]

On the debate over House Joint Resolution 265, which provided the first trillion-dollar debt ceiling, Senator William Proxmire (D.-Wis.) said:

> So the federal government . . . is in the credit markets and has to borrow that trillion dollars all over again every year. When we borrow that massive amount, we shove the home buyer, we shove the auto buyer, we shove the farmer, we shove the small businessman right out of the credit market.[24]

The problem was compounded by the Reagan administration's combination of massive tax cuts and increases in the military budget. As Weidenbaum said in a farewell interview with the Associated Press:

On balance we really haven't cut the budget. Instead the much publicized reductions in nonmilitary programs the President has won from Congress have been fully offset by the unprecedented growth in military spending sought by [President] Reagan.

When you add that to the big tax cuts, you . . . horrendous deficits.

What worries me [about the military buildup] is that these crash programs rarely increase national security. They strain resources, create bottlenecks.[25]

His views were echoed by Otto Eckstein and George Brown in testimony before the JEC:

In the current circumstance, it must be recognized that we have chosen the path of a massive increase in defense spending without asking the public to pay for it . . .

With the defense bill paid for by personal income taxes, resources are principally drawn from consumption, leaving the rate of capital formation more or less intact. If the defense budget is not paid for and the deficit is allowed to increase, interest rates are driven up by the combination of increased activity initially created by defense spending and by the monetarist policy. This substantially reduces the volume of house building and automobile sales and, to a lesser extent, also reduces the rate of business fixed capital formation. Defense spending under this—alas realistic—assumption, does crowd out investment, which, after all, was one of the principal goals of the Reagan program.[26]

As a result of the tax cuts and spending increases, the first two full-year deficits of the Reagan administration were $127.9 billion and $207.8 billion and continued at the $185 to $220 billion level for the next three years. These compounded the debt and deficits accrued by every administration in all but one year since the beginning of the Vietnam inflation of the late 1960s. As Martin Feldstein, Weidenbaum's successor as chairman of the Council of Economic Advisers, testified during his confirmation hearing, the projected budget deficits of $200 billion a year or more are too large and cause a "drastic reduction" in the potential rate of private investment.[27] Later, in testimony before the Senate Banking Committee at hearings confirming his appointment to his second term as Federal Reserve Chairman, Paul A. Volcker said that financing the deficits could take about three-fourths of all net private savings.

In the final three fiscal years of the Reagan administration, the official budget deficits were between $150 to $155 billion. Critics complained, however, the actual figures were $20 to $53 billion higher because the surpluses in the Social Security trust accounts masked the real deficits in the rest of the on-budget accounts.

In his first two full-year budgets (fiscal years 1990 and 1991) President Bush submitted projected deficits that met the Gramm-Rudman-Hollings targets of $100 and $64 billion, respectively. In the *Mid-Session Review of the*

Budget in July 1990, however, he had raised the deficit estimates to $218.5 and $231.4 billion for each of those two years (including savings and loan clean-up costs and the Social Security surpluses). This rendezvous with reality led him to abandon his "Read my lips: no new taxes" campaign pledge and call for a budget summit with the Congress. In the agreement reached two and a half months later, changes in the economy and savings and loan clean-up liabilities had added another $61.8 billion to the 1991 deficit estimate, or a total of $293.2 billion in that short period. Without counting the Social Security surplus, the figure would have been closer to $370 billion. The budget reality, as opposed to its fiction, was that Bush's estimated $64 billion deficit for 1991 had increased by $230 to $306 billion, depending on how Social Security was treated in the calculations (see Figure 10–1 for estimates).

One of the most negative consequences of the size of the budget deficit was that as the economy turned down or entered into a recession so that tax receipts dropped and spending for interest, unemployment compensation, welfare payments, food stamps, and other countercyclical measures increased, there was no room for either increases in public works spending or tax cuts to stimulate the economy. The budget deficit itself inhibited additional antirecession or compensatory fiscal policy measures. It forced a return to Herbert Hoover's view that recessions and depressions should be "left to blow themselves out."

INTELLECTUAL CHAOS

Fiscal policy, which worked so well from the end of World War II until 1966, clearly failed in the nearly three decades that followed. Both policy makers and economists were at a loss to provide the confident answers they had given for economic problems before stagflation. Economist William Nordhaus of Yale told the American Economic Association that there was "intellectual chaos" in the profession. Many economists thought it was the outsiders, not the economists, who were to blame. Nordhaus also claimed the profession had been "polluted by the nonsense often talked by people in government who want to justify what they are doing, or by others who want to promote ideas that do not have the backing of much of the profession."[28] *The Washington Post* commented that:

> President Reagan's supply siders are an obvious candidate. The supply side notion of having tax cuts to boost the economy, together with monetary controls to fight inflation, swept the political scene and influenced Reagan's economic policy. But it was never taken seriously by the economics profession.[29]

While supply-side policies seemed to have exacerbated both unemployment and the deficits after 1980, the more orthodox economists were without the confident answers they had given in previous periods. The government, through taxes, spending, deficits, and surpluses, still influenced the economy. But these were mindless, not deliberate acts, and the results were accidental, fortuitous, or serendipitous. In the fifth decade after the Employment Act was put in place, the country had not come to grips with the fundamental problem of a burgeoning deficit.

EVALUATION OF FISCAL POLICIES

How does one account for both the failures and successes of fiscal policies? Two profound modern economists, one a conservative and one a liberal but both classically trained, may provide some of the answers. It was Paul Douglas, the liberal, who wrote in his memoirs that his firefighting experiences as a youth in Maine

> made me doubt the classical theories of equilibrium as applied to economics and to human history. I had seen how fires behave. As the initial sparks spread, a blaze is created. The blaze heats the air. Since hot air is lighter than ordinary air, it rises. This creates a vacuum into which other air rushes. But this in turn brings a wind that fans the flames and heats more air, creating a further vacuum into which the colder winds rush. And so it goes on in cumulative fashion.

He stated that

> after that searing experience, I could never hold to the pendulum theory of history: that social events swing from right to left and back again with decreasing momentum until they come to rest at dead center.

What he saw instead were "impetuous" forces that once set in motion release latent forces until a cumulative process of change takes place in which the final, unpredictable result is out of proportion to the initial cause.

> It was the failure of businessmen, politicians, and orthodox economists to understand these simple concepts that made them ignore the dangers of the Great Depression of 1929 until it was almost too late.[30]

Douglas commented that fighting fire in the Maine woods led him to wonder if there were not equally unstable elements in the economic system that could lead to the cumulative breakdown of employment, demand, production, purchasing power, and price levels that in a vicious fashion would feed on and reinforce each other.

> And so I shocked my economic colleagues of the 1920s and '30s by proposing the injection at critical times of additional monetary purchasing power, through public works and unemployment benefits. When the orthodox economists broke into angry reproaches, I recalled the behavior of that Maine fire which had threatened our lives so far away and long ago.[31]

Arthur Burns, the conservative economist who served as President Eisenhower's chairman of the Council of Economic Advisers and later as chairman of the Federal Reserve Board and Ambassador to the Federal Republic of Germany, echoed Douglas's point on timing:

> The first principle is that when the economy shows signs of faltering, prompt countermoves are required. Even mild measures on the part of government can be effective in the early stages of an economic decline. On the other hand, if action is withheld until a recession has gathered momentum, strong and costly measures may prove insufficient.[32]

Paul Volcker also testified that the same principle applies when inflationary pressures mount: "Sometimes a restraining action in the short run may avoid the need for much larger actions later."

Does timing account for the success of Truman's veto of the 1947 tax cut and the equal success of the modest $3 billion tax increase designed to offset inflation at the beginning of the Korean War? Does timing account for the relative failure of the enormous "pump priming" during the 1930s? Had cumulative forces gathered so much momentum between 1929 and 1933 that even massive recovery measures proved insufficient? Was timing why the tax cuts and burgeoning deficits of the early 1980s had so little immediate effect in initiating recovery and growth? Is it possible that modern economists, with their excessive training in mathematics, have ignored "impetuous" forces and instead canonized classical mechanics through computer runs that spew out pseudoscientific answers to problems more profound and complex than their models can provide?

While it is hard to prove cause and effect, Carlyle's "dismal science" of economics has never been in greater disarray than since its recent love affair with predictions and projections based on models and mechanistic principles. As Nobel economist James Tobin of Yale commented, "On most prominent issues of political economy the profession offers counsels more divided than at any time since the 1930s."[33]

A CONSTITUTIONAL AMENDMENT
TO BALANCE THE BUDGET

Because of the repeated deficits and the failures of fiscal policy, a constitutional amendment to require a balanced budget has gained popularity in recent years. A version of it has overwhelmingly passed the Senate and received a majority vote in the House, although short of the necessary two-thirds. The legislatures of more than thirty of the required thirty-four states have sent resolutions to Congress calling for a constitutional convention to propose a balanced-budget amendment. The seriousness of the issue is highlighted by the fact that the convention method of amending the

Constitution under Article V has not been used since 1787 and the original constitutional convention. President Reagan worked for the amendment throughout his presidency.

Proponents' Arguments

The amendment's proponents argue that the budget and the economy are out of control. It took 173 years—from 1789 to 1962—before the total budget exceeded $100 billion. In the few short years since then, it has reached the $1.5 trillion level, and the real annual deficit is routinely triple the $100 billion figure. Neither self-discipline, the disciplines of the 1974 Budget Act, the Gramm-Rudman-Hollings amendments, countercyclical fiscal policy, the full employment–balance budget theory, nor the disciplines of the presidential budget or the OMB have been able to bring the budget under control.

This permissive and self-indulgent fiscal freedom, according to amendment advocates, has brought dire results and must be put right. Since the late 1960s the nation has suffered from inflation. In the 1970s the nation suffered from stagflation. Excessive borrowing to finance the debt and deficit raised interest rates and brought chaos to farmers, small businesses, homebuilders, auto workers, the consumer credit industry, banks, savings and loan associations, and the economy as a whole. The failure of fiscal policy has also made it difficult for monetary policy to work as well. Even the 1983–1989 period of sustained economic growth saw both unemployment and consumer prices remain stubbornly high.

Supporters of the amendment argue that since most states, cities, and families are required either to balance their budgets or to live within their means, surely the federal government should be required to do the same. In the long run our economy is the strongest bulwark of our defense, so that not only our economic welfare but our security itself depends on getting the buget and the economy under control. Most versions of the balanced-budget amendment provide an escape hatch whereby its provisions would not apply if an extraordinary majority in both houses of Congress voted that a national emergency existed.

Finally, it is argued that Congress should pass such an amendment and submit it to the states to prevent the chaos of another constitutional convention. This would open up a Pandora's box, create alarm and fright, result in the possible repeal of the Bill of Rights, and fasten into the Constitution specific and detailed ideological provisions that have no place in a general document and that represent only momentary passions.

The popularity of the balanced-budget amendment, although now considerably diminished, is attested to by the facts that more than a dozen versions have been introduced in the Senate and that more than fifty House members introduced some form of the proposal in the first ten days of a recent congressional session.

Opponents' Arguments

The opponents argue that imposing a rigid balanced-budget requirement year in and year out would only make the deficit and economic conditions worse. This happened during the panics of the nineteenth century, and such a requirement was tried in the first years of the Great Depression with catastrophic results. The language of the safety valves to provide exceptions is so unclear and imprecise as to be harmful and, in any case, could delay by months of argument needed action during a recession, depression, or national security emergency.

Former budget director and former chairman of the Council of Economic Advisors Charles L. Schultze, examined the magnitudes of budget cuts that would have been needed to bring a balanced budget in 1975 and 1976, in retrospect years of relatively small deficits. He argued that expenditures would have had to be cut by about $50 billion in 1975 and $100 billion in 1976 in order to get a balanced budget. The unemployment rate would have been about 12 percent, the GNP would have fallen not by 2 percent but by almost 10 or 11 percent, and we would have had the first full-fledged, major depression since the 1920s.[34] And this was with deficits of $50 to $75 billion. The consequences of cutting $300 billion or more to achieve a balanced budget today could have catastrophic consequences for unemployment, the GNP, the balance of payments and trade, and the overall economy. It would insure a depression.

It is argued that this kind of detailed provision has no place in the Constitution. Some versions use the language of macroeconomics and computers in lengthy paragraphs that would not only be incomprehensible to the Founding Fathers but represent a form of modern barbarism. Only a few reputable economists can be found who support such a proposition, many versions of which are poorly thought out and badly constructed. Mathematics should not be written into the Constitution.

Opponents argue that the federal government differs from the cities and states, which have no power to create credit and money. Refusal to allow the federal government to go into debt in times of economic or national security emergency would place the country in an economic and fiscal straitjacket. The comparison of federal with family economics is also misleading, as most families have a proportionately heavier debt structure, with borrowings to finance both house and cars, than the federal government does. Furthermore, if the government kept its books as modern businesses do, it would be in the black almost every year.

Finally, opponents argue that such an amendment is unenforceable. Former House Minority Leader John Rhodes (R.-Ariz.) commented that "it would be easy to end-run it,"[35] and the former staff director of the Senate Budget Committee argued that "a Congress so profligate as to require a constitutional amendment to limit its spending propensities will certainly be ingenious enough to figure ways to avoid it."[36] Walter Heller has said that "a meaningful amendment would not be workable, and a workable amendment would not be meaningful."[37] Among the loopholes and escape hatches are the inclusion or exclusion of Social Security, highway, and other trust funds from the budget depending on whether they helped or hurt the deficit figure; conversion of spending programs into loans, loan guarantees, or tax expenditures; placing large chunks of the budget off-budget; and going to a capital budget under which spending for land, buildings, military hardware, and public and other subsidized housing would be placed "below the line" and not counted in the expenditure or operating budget, a form of bookkeeping routinely followed by many industrial nations. Opponents point out that even the auditors and accountants have great difficulty in defining receipts and revenues, on the one hand, and spending or outlays, on the other. According to former Senator and Budget Committee Chairman Edmund S. Muskie (D.-Maine):

> A nightmare of semantics, administration, accounting, potential evasion, inherent incentives for poor management and misleading bookkeeping would be sure to accompany any of the sweeping proposals which have been advanced.[38]

Finally, it is argued that such an amendment is "an affront to responsible democratic government":

> The essence of that government is to adapt economic, social and other policies to the changing needs of the times and the changing wills of the majority. It is the job of the Constitution to protect basic human rights and define the framework of our self-governance. Taking the very stuff of democratic self-determination out of the hands of legislative bodies and freezing them into the Constitution would not only hobble our ability to govern ourselves but dilute and cheapen the fundamental law of the land.[39]

These are the pros and the cons of the controversy over a constitutional amendment to require a balanced federal budget.

COMMENT

While the arguments that the federal government lacks self-discipline and that since the mid- to late 1960s the budget has been out of control by any reasonable measure of what the appropriate levels of spending, revenues, and deficits or surpluses should have been, have great merit, a constitutional amendment to require a balanced budget every year except when two-thirds of the Congress deems otherwise seems an excessive answer to a difficult and stubborn problem. To rivet such a requirement into the Constitution is a dubious proposal.

While the existence of deficits every year since 1969 has been inappropriate and wrong, a requirement for a balanced budget year in and year out is also wrong. It is bad economic policy, which is not to say that the economic policies of the late 1960s, 1970s, 1980s, and early 1990s have been good.

Two other critical questions arise. The first focuses on timing and the need to take quick and decisive action when the facts show that an economic downturn has begun. To get a two-thirds vote of both houses of the Congress at an early and decisive stage appears to be an impossible requirement. The second critical issue is whether we should even consider an amendment that is admittedly almost impossible to write in clear, direct, and simple terms; whose enforcement is dubious; and whose public policy aim, if carried out faithfully, is of questionable merit.

NOTES

1. Henry Steele Commager, *Documents of American History* (New York: F. S. Crofts, 1946), p. 403.
2. *Supplement to Economic Indicators, Historical and Descriptive Background*, 90th Cong., 1st sess. (Washington, D.C.: U.S. Government Printing Office, 1967), p. 35.
3. *The State Papers and Other Public Writings of Herbert Hoover* (New York: Doubleday, Doran, 1934), ed. William Starr Myers, vol. 1, pp. 429–430.
4. Commager, *Documents*, p. 407.
5. Charles A. Beard and Mary R. Beard, *The Beards' Basic History of the United States* (New York: Doubleday, Doran, 1944), pp. 453–454.
6. Commager, *Documents*, p. 422.
7. Herbert Hoover, *The Memoirs of Herbert Hoover*, Vol. 3, *The Great Depression, 1929–1941* (New York: Macmillan, 1952), p. 29.
8. Ernest L. Bogart and Donald L. Kemmerer, *Economic History of the American People* (New York: Longmans, Green, 1948), p. 334.
9. Ibid.
10. Paul H. Douglas, *In the Fullness of Time: The Memoirs of Paul H. Douglas* (New York: Harcourt-Brace-Jovanovich, 1971), p. 15.
11. Louis Fisher, *Presidential Spending Power.* Copyright © 1975 by Princeton University Press, p. 1.
12. Commager, *Documents*, p. 407.
13. Ibid., p. 451.
14. *Supplement to Economic Indicators*, p. 35.
15. Ibid., pp. 35, 127.
16. P.L. 79–304.
17. *Economic Report of the President* (Washington, D.C.: U.S. Government Printing Office, 1986), p. 238.
18. Congressional Budget Office, *Reducing the Federal Deficit: Strategies and Options* (Washington, D.C.: U.S. Government Printing Office, 1982), Figure III-1, p. 24.
19. *The Washington Post*, 9 December 1982, p. D13. © *The Washington Post*.
20. "Special Analysis E," *Borrowing and Debt, the Budget of the United States Government, 1983* (Washington, D.C.: U.S. Government Printing Office, 1982), Table E-3, p. 9.

21. *Los Angeles Times*, 4 July 1982, Part V, p. 3. Copyright 1982, *Los Angeles Times*. Reprinted by permission.
22. *The Washington Post*, 3 March 1981, p. A1. © *The Washington Post*.
23. Ibid., 18 January 1982, p. A2.
24. *Congressional Record* (daily ed.), 28 September 1981, p. S.10605.
25. *Des Moines Register*, 27 August 1982, p. 14A.
26. Otto Eckstein and George Brown, "Can We Afford Increased Defense Spending?" (Paper presented to the Subcommittee on Economic Goals and Intergovernment Policy of the Joint Economic Committee, 15 December 1982).
27. *Los Angeles Times*, 23 September 1982, p. 25. Copyright, 1982, *Los Angeles Times*. Reprinted by permission.
28. *The Washington Post*, 2 January 1983, p. F1. © *The Washington Post*.
29. Ibid.
30. Douglas, *In the Fullness of Time*, pp. 14–15.
31. Ibid., p. 15.
32. Arthur F. Burns, *Prosperity Without Inflation* (New York: Fordham University Press, 1957), pp. 30–31; quoted in James L. Sundquist, *The Decline and Resurgence of Congress* (Washington, D.C.: The Brookings Institution, 1981), p. 68.
33. *The Washington Post*, 30 December 1982, p. C14. © *The Washington Post*.
34. Charles L. Schultze, "Politics and Economics of a Balanced Budget Amendment," *The Constitution and the Budget*, ed. W. S. Moore and Rudolph G. Penner (Washington, D.C.: American Enterprise Institute for Public Policy Research, 1980), pp. 123–124.
35. Quoted in Walter W. Heller, "Con," *Congressional Digest* 58 (May 1979): 159.
36. John T. McEvoy in Rudolph G. Penner, ed., *The Congressional Budget Process After Five Years* (Washington, D.C.: The American Enterprise for Public Policy Research, 1981), p. 81.
37. Heller, "Con," p. 159.
38. Ibid., p. 141.
39. Ibid., p. 159.

6

The Politics of Money and Credit

INTRODUCTION

The power to create money is a prerogative of the Congress. In 1913 this public function was delegated to the Federal Reserve System, which is often referred to as a "banker's bank."

Monetary policy or power over the money supply is not a part of the budget, but an accompanying issue of critical importance to the success of budget or fiscal policy. Monetary policy has been a hot political issue since 1789. There have been fights over it between debtors and creditors; hard and easy money and gold and silver advocates; East and West; and monetarists and the advocates of more orthodox policies. The names of Hamilton, Jackson, Bryan, McKinley, Wilson, Hoover, and Franklin Roosevelt are all associated with its controversies.

The Federal Reserve controls the money supply through the fractional reserve system. It can increase or decrease the supply of money by three basic methods: It can buy or sell government bonds; lower or raise the reserve requirements; or lower or raise the discount rate.

From its inception in 1913 the Federal Reserve has received criticism from both Democrats and Republicans and has been the whipping boy of the Congress and presidents alike. Criticism has been especially severe since

1967, with the onset of inflation, stagflation, and high interest rates. But in the absence of a more responsible fiscal policy, in an era of real budget deficits of $300 billion or more the monetary authorities have had few options other than those offered by the Federal Reserve.

In addition to the credit provided by the Federal Reserve, the government itself provides more credit to the economy than it spends through the budget. It does this through direct loans, guaranteed loans, and loans provided by government-sponsored enterprises. A little-known agency called the Federal Financing Bank (FFB) has had an enormous effect over government credit and has provided off-budget direct loans to some highly favored customers.

Since 1980 there has been a growing interest in providing a credit budget to accompany the traditional budgets. This is now done by both the president and the Congress through the presidential and congressional budgets (see Appendix B).

THE POWER TO CREATE MONEY

Under Article I, Section 8, of the Constitution, Congress has the power "to coin money and regulate the value thereof." This power over the money supply and the creation of credit was delegated to the Federal Reserve System in 1913. The "Fed," as it is called, is a semipublic, semiprivate institution that is "independent" of the president but is the "agent" of Congress.

Historically, the Federal Reserve System has been reluctant to acknowledge its congressional paternity. In its formative years, the secretary of the Treasury served as the chairman of the Federal Reserve Board of Governors, and the system almost became an arm of the White House. The Treasury secretary was removed as a member of the board and the name was changed from the Federal Reserve Board to the Board of Governors of the Federal Reserve System in 1935. The Fed's literature abounds with references to its "independence" or its status as being "independent within Government,"[1] without reference to its statutory relationship as an agent of the Congress. One of its abler former governors, now a professor of economics, wrote a strong defense of the Federal Reserve's independence from the Treasury without mentioning its role as the instrument or agent of the Congress.[2] Its prospective members are often untutored in its history and functions. Consider this excerpt from the nomination hearing of Charles Noah Shepardson to become a governor of the board, held before the Senate Banking Committee:

Senator Douglas   Do you believe that the Federal Reserve Board should be independent of the Treasury?

Senator Douglas	Do you believe that the Federal Reserve Board should be independent of the Treasury?
Mr. Shepardson	Mr. Chairman, frankly I have not had a lot of opportunity to study the functions of the Board and the System. From what I have read or heard of it, I have understood that it was to a large degree independent. I do not think I have had enough background....
Senator Douglas	Do you regard the board as the agent of Congress, or the agent of the Executive?
Mr. Shepardson	I am not sure that I can answer that.
Senator Douglas	I think you had better read the statute.
Mr. Shepardson	(after conferring with Chairman of the Board William McChesney Martin). My impression is it would be an agent of Congress.
Senator Douglas	The statute makes it perfectly clear that the Federal Reserve Board is an agent of Congress and not the agent of the Executive.
Mr. Shepardson	That is my impression.
Senator Douglas	... I urge you to read the statute very carefully and to place on your mirror before you shave in the morning the statement "The Federal Reserve is the agent of Congress and not the Executive." If you read that every morning as you shave, either before or after you say your prayers, you will be in a much better position to help administer the affairs of the Board.[3]

Fiscal policy deals with spending, taxes, and the budget deficit or surplus. Monetary policy deals with interest rates, price levels, and the supply of money and credit. Most works on the budget ignore monetary policy as irrelevant to and separate from the budget. But monetary policy has an important and often a dominant effect on the budget and its politics.

For example, the economic assumptions on which the president's budget is based are crucially dependent on monetary policy. Control over the money supply, its expansion or contraction, and the rate of its increase affects interest rates, employment and unemployment, price levels, incomes, and production, and hence both the level of spending and the size of revenues. Particular industries or groups are especially sensitive to monetary policy. Among them are homebuilders, automobile manufacturers, and farmers. The Federal Reserve's action to increase the discount rate in the spring of 1920, for example, was largely responsible for the farm depression of 1920–1921.

The best-laid plans proposed in presidents' budgets have been thwarted by a rise in unemployment compensation payments, food stamp expenditures, welfare payments, or Social Security spending occasioned by inflation, or by economic recessions sometimes caused by and always affected by the actions or inactions of the Federal Reserve. The Fed's policies also directly affect the cost of government through their effect on interest rates and hence the amount the Treasury must pay to finance or carry the national debt. "Net" interest is now the third largest item, after defense and Social Security, in the federal budget. The total interest the government pays, not counting the subtractions for interest received by the trust funds, student loans, and the like, is about $310 billion a year, an outlay exceeded by no other function including defense.

Unlike other modern industrial nations, the United States had no central government bank, like the Bank of England, that could act as both a government depository and an institution that could create and regulate the supply of money and credit until 1913. Vestiges of such an institution were found in the First (1791 to 1811) and Second (1816 to 1836) Banks of the United States and under the National Banking Act (1863). Neither the institutions nor the act adequately provided an elastic currency that could expand and contract with the needs of the economy.

As a result of a series of financial panics and depressions, particularly the depression of 1893 and the financial panic of 1907, a National Monetary Commission was created in 1908. The issues of money and credit, of gold and silver, and of debtor and creditor were at the center of political controversy, particularly in the presidential contests between Republican William McKinley and Democratic-Populist William Jennings Bryan in 1896 and 1900, and between Republican William Howard Taft and Bryan in 1908. It was Bryan's "cross of gold" speech—"You shall not press down upon the brow of labour this crown of thorns, you shall not crucify mankind upon a cross of gold"—that catapulted him to the nomination.

As a result of the report of the National Monetary Commission and compromises among the Congress, the banking community, President Wilson, and leaders of the agrarian forces, the Federal Reserve Act was passed in 1913 and the Federal Reserve System was established in 1914. Unlike the central banks of Europe, the Federal Reserve is not an arm of the executive branch or of the president. Its creation was the first major delegation by the Congress in modern times of its constitutional powers, first over the money supply, and then over the debt, the budget, and the economy. The pattern for further delegation of these enumerated congressional powers was set at the time of the formation of the Federal Reserve System. This and future delegations were preceded by a series of crises and the establishment of study commissions. Once having tasted the joy of giving up power and the luxury of criticizing those who exercised it, the Congress became addicted and continued the practice for eighty years.

The Federal Reserve essentially acts independently of both the president and the Congress, for a variety of institutional reasons. The Federal Reserve Board is composed of seven members appointed by the president, with the advice and consent of the Senate, for fourteen years. By law, no two may be from any one of the twelve Federal Reserve Districts into which the country is divided, and technically they are supposed to represent a variety of business, agricultural, and commercial interests in addition to banking. The regional and professional requirements are routinely breached, however, by designating prospective members on the basis of the regions in which they were born or went to college rather than those in which they work or reside. With respect to profession, recently there have been two conflicting trends. Through 1982 economists from the Treasury, the Federal Reserve in Washington or its regional bank staffs, the Council of Economic Advisers, and the universities dominated the nominations. Only an occasional banker or businessman was appointed. The members have been extraordinarily Federal Reserve establishment-oriented. At the confirmation hearing of Lyle E. Gramley, an able and qualified candidate who had served for seven years as an economist for the Kansas City Reserve Bank, was for many years on the staff of the Washington Board, and had been for three years a member of the Council of Economic Advisers, Senator Jake Garn (R.-Utah) made the following comment:

> One thing that concerns me in general, . . . as I have watched the last several Federal Reserve Board appointments, they all seem to come generally from the same geographical area of the country or at least from the Fed. Look at Chairman Volcker from the New York Fed; Mr. Schultze, the only exception, a Florida businessman; Governor Partee, an economist with the Federal Reserve Board; Nancy Teeters, Congressional Budget Office; Governor Wallich, the professor formerly with the New York Fed; Governor Coldwell came from the Dallas Fed; and it disturbs me in general that we are picking people from within the Fed system's geographical area that tend to be getting away from the geographical requirement of not more than one from one Fed district by picking where they were born regardless of where they have lived or worked for a long number of years.[4]

Senator Garn might have mentioned that chairman William McChesney Martin was an undersecretary of the Treasury; Chairman Arthur F. Burns was President Eisenhower's chairman of the Council of Economic Advisers; Chairman William Miller was a businessperson who had served on the Board of the Federal Reserve Bank of Boston and who had resigned from the Fed to become secretary of the treasury; Chairman Paul Volcker was not only president of the New York Federal Reserve Bank, the most powerful and the dominant of the twelve regional banks, but was also an undersecretary of the Treasury; and Anthony M. Solomon, a former undersecretary of the Treasury, had become president of the New York Federal Reserve Bank. They were referred to as "mandarins" and the board was criticized for both its lack of regional and professional balance. From 1982 until the appointment of Alan Greenspan as chairman in 1987, nonestablishment commercial bankers dominated the nominations. Greenspan, however, was a "mandarin" with wide Washington experience, including the chairmanship of President Ford's Council of Economic Advisers.

The board, when President Bush took office, was characterized by traditional past occupations. Five of the seven had been presidents, vice-presidents, or chief executive officers of banks, or directors of banks or bank holding companies; three had been employees of the Federal Reserve or directors of regional Federal Reserve banks; two others had served as assistant secretaries of the Treasury. Several had full or part-time academic experience. Only one was a full-time businessman. Agriculture was represented by a Kansas professor of economics and college dean who was an active partner in running a large farm.

The fourteen-year term, with one term ending every two years, was designed to give members a strong sense of independence so that they could resist temporary popular political pressures and provide continuity. In recent times, few members have served the full term. No member may be reappointed if he or she has served more than half of an unexpired term to which he or she was appointed. Some have criticized the Fed's recent "rolling membership," characterized its repeated resignations and appointments as a game of "musical chairs," and referred to its members as a group of "pinch hitters." By the sixth year of President Reagan's presidency he had had the opportunity to name six new members and had reappointed Chairman Volcker in 1983. When Volcker resigned and Greenspan took over in 1987, no member had served for three years and only one for more than eighteen months. When President Bush took office, the longest-serving member had been on the board for only four years and six months, and no other member had served as long as three years.

The board's rapid turnover offends against the intent to provide experience, institutional memory, and independence. The problem stems in part from the tradition of a strong chairman. In the past chairmen wielded considerable influence over appointments, and often sought relatively weak and inexperienced members to ensure this domination. At least one recent chairman was so powerful as to make life on the board unpleasant.

The chairman is designated by the president from among the members and serves for four years. However, the term is not coterminus with the president's term. In the early years, chairmen had the political power to be reappointed, if they wished. Recently they have served short terms. In the past, the specter of the loss of confidence by the banking or business community by the failure to reappoint an orthodox, sound-money, conservative chairman was generally sufficient to ensure reappointment, if desired. This is no longer true, as witnessed by President Carter's replacement of Arthur Burns with Paul Volcker, the speculation and political anguish that preceded President Reagan's 1983 reappointment of Volcker as chairman, and the replacement of Volcker in 1987 because, it was said, he was both too independent and too powerful.

As important as, if not more important than, the seven-member board is the Reserve System's Federal Open Market Committee (FOMC). It is composed of the seven members of the Board of Governors plus the presidents of five of the twelve regional Federal Reserve Banks. The president of the New York bank is a regular member and the other four rotate among the remaining eleven banks, with the Chicago president serving every other year. The chairman of the FOMC is by tradition the chairman of the Board of Governors, and the New York president is the vice-chairman.[5]

The FOMC meets in Washington every four or five weeks to determine what transactions the Federal Reserve will conduct in the securities markets to affect the supply of money and credit in the country. "In addition to its operations in the domestic government securities market, the FOMC authorizes and directs operations in foreign exchange markets for major convertible currencies."[6]

Each of the twelve Federal Reserve Banks, from whom five of the members of the FOMC are selected, has a board of nine members. In addition to New York and Chicago, they are in Boston, Philadelphia, Cleveland, Richmond, Atlanta, St. Louis, Minneapolis, Kansas City, Dallas, and San Francisco. Directors of each Reserve Bank are divided into three classes. There are three Class A directors, who represent member banks; three Class B directors, who are elected by member banks in each reserve district but may not be bankers; and three Class C directors, appointed by the Board of Governors in Washington, two of whom are designated by the Board of Governors as chairman and deputy chairman of the Reserve Bank's board. None of the last three may either be bankers or hold bank stock. The nine directors appoint and set the salary of the Reserve Bank president, subject to the veto of the Federal Reserve Board.

These details are important because of the power exercised by the Federal Reserve Board and particularly its FOMC over the economy. In fact and in practice they may have more power over the economy than either the president or the Congress.

Although the elected president may appoint members of the board, he has no constitutional or statutory power over Federal Reserve policy. The Congress, which is also elected, does have a constitutional prerogative over the money supply and monetary policy, but in practice it has delegated this power to the Federal Reserve System, or at least has allowed it to be usurped, lost, or atrophied. There are reasons for this. The Congress has 435 members of the House and 100 senators. No committee of 535 people can ordinarily act promptly to direct policy. Further, monetary policy is presented, often deliberately, in a complicated way and with a certain mystique that is aided and abetted by the banking community itself. How many college graduates or members of the Congress know, for example, the differences between and among M_1, M_2, and M_3, the common measures of the money stock that the Federal Reserve regulates?[7] In fact the Federal Reserve is independent of both the president and the Congress, and operates within limits heavily and overwhelmingly influenced if not set by the banks and banking community themselves. Thus former Senate Majority Leader Howard H. Baker, Jr. (R.–Tenn.), could say that the Congress has "ceded away to the Federal Reserve an unseemly share of the responsibility for designing the economic policy of this country."[8]

The FOMC is where the levers of power are exercised. Not one of its twelve members is elected by the people. Five are private citizens essentially appointed by bankers instead of the president, and their appointments are not confirmed by the Congress.

This is how the power to create money—a public and not a private function—has been delegated to and is exercised by the private banking system. This delegation has had profound political, economic, and budgetary effects.

The private banking system has been historically dominated by those with prudent and conservative views and who in good faith represent a particular and often narrow or limited political and economic position. There are few iconoclasts in bank board rooms. If the power to create money and credit were delegated to some other interest group, such as the National Farmers Union, the National Association of Homebuilders, or the U.S. Conference of Mayors or the National League of Cities instead of private commercial bankers, the point would be clear.

A consititutional prerogative that belongs to the Congress and the people is now exercised by an economic interest group. One need not charge conspiracy or malfeasance to understand that there is a certain economic and political bias in their views. In practice, the system is a form of economic syndicalism run by a modern version of a medieval guild.

In addition, members of the Federal Reserve spend much of their working hours in what can be called a bankers' ghetto. The Federal Reserve Act provides for a Federal Advisory Council that is composed of one member from each of the Federal Reserve Districts appointed by each bank's board of directors and that meets with the Federal Reserve Board four times a year. "It confers with the Board of Governors on economic and banking matters and makes recommendations regarding the affairs of the Federal Reserve System."[9] In addition, there are a variety of committees and conferences in which bankers routinely talk to bankers. On the whole, farmers, debtors, trade unionists, or shopkeepers need not apply.

It may be that, like modern football, the Federal Reserve should operate on a two-platoon system. Bankers tend to see and fear inflation at all times. Farmers, workers, employees, and debtors have the same fear of unemployment, tight money, and deflation. One could send in the bankers' defensive platoon in inflationary periods and substitute the offensive squad of farmers, workers, and debtors in periods of recession. This might help make sure that the right mix of money and credit for the particular prevailing economic conditions would be met.

HOW THE FED CONTROLS THE MONEY SUPPLY

The Federal Reserve affects prices, interest rates, employment, credit, and production by expanding or contracting the rate of growth of the money supply. Technically it does this in three ways: (1) buying and selling government bonds; (2) raising or lowering reserve requirements; and (3) raising or lowering the discount rate.

Buying and Selling Government Bonds The first and most important way is by buying or selling government bonds. When the Federal Reserve buys bonds through the FOMC, it adds to the reserves of its member banks, which in turn can make more loans, increase their customers' deposits, and expand the money supply. When the Federal Reserve wishes to contract the money supply, it sells bonds. The member banks then have fewer reserves, can make fewer loans, and create fewer deposits. Over time it is not really a question of whether the Federal Reserve will contract or expand the money supply but at what rate the money supply will grow. Ideally it should grow at a rate sufficient to fund the productive activity of the economy and provide relatively full employment, all the while maintaining stable prices and avoiding inflation. To be successful, an appropriate fiscal policy—taxing, spending, and the budget surplus or deficit—must also accompany the monetary policy.

Raising or Lowering Reserve Requirements The Federal Reserve System can expand or contract the money supply by raising or lowering member bank reserve requirements. Banking operates under what is known as a fractional reserve system. If the banking system operated under a 100 percent reserve requirement system, it would be required to keep $1 on reserve for every $1 it lent. If it had a 10 percent reserve requirement, the system would be required to keep only $1 on reserve for every $10 it lent. When the Federal Reserve lowers the reserve requirement, it expands the money supply. When it raises the reserve requirement, it contracts the money supply.

Formerly there was a variety of reserve requirements, depending on the location and size of a bank. Reserve requirements were higher for big banks in the central reserve cities than for banks in the reserve cities or for country banks. Central-reserve-city and reserve-city bank requirements were merged some time ago, and in the Monetary Control Act of 1980, reserve requirements were based on the size and not the location of the banks. Reserve requirements for virtually all depository institutions were set at 3 percent on the first $25 million of transactions (indexed annually, beginning in 1982) and 12 percent on transactions above $25 million. Vault cash counts as a part of the reserves. This means that for every $1 the banking system has on reserve, about $8.50 can be lent.

Raising or Lowering the Discount Rate The third method of expanding or contracting the money supply is by raising or lowering the discount rate. The discount rate is the interest rate the Federal Reserve charges its member banks for funds they borrow from the Fed. Raising the interest rate discourages member bank borrowing. This has the effect of contracting the money supply for member banks, which then either have less money to lend or lend the borrowed money at a higher price (the interest rate), which discourages borrowing by the member bank's customers.

The Federal Funds Rate   There is yet another rate that has a major effect on banks and the money supply that is *not* exercised directly by the Federal Reserve System. It is called the federal funds rate, which is the rate at which member banks borrow from each other. Some banks have excess reserves. Other banks are fully "loaned up." The interest rate at which the former lend money to the latter is the federal funds rate. It is watched very closely by the banking community as an indication of the level of interest rates and the availability of credit.

Banking Privileges   Banks and the banking system have two important economic privileges. First, there is limited entry into the business. The number of banks is limited by the charters extended to them by federal or state governments. A bank charter is in fact a limited local or regional monopoly. Unlike the grocery or restaurant business, entry is limited by the state. A bank charter confers a valuable public benefit.

Second, the banking system creates money. Before the era of public sophistication about how they functioned, banks constructed their buildings with formidable Greek pillars on the front and heavy iron vaults inside to create the impression that vast quantities of bullion resided in their coffers to stand behind their loans and the money transactions of the local Main Street businesses. The pillars and the vaults were largely illusory, as the crash of 1929 and the closing of the banks proved. Deposits and money are in fact "created" through the fractional reserve system. Only a small proportion of the total amount of money is coins or paper currency made at the mints or printed at the Bureau of Engraving and Printing. The paper money is redeemable not in gold or silver but in other printed paper money.

The origins of modern banking and the fractional reserve system go back to the goldsmiths. Owners of gold or valuable metals took them to the goldsmiths for safekeeping. The owners were issued a receipt or an IOU for the amount. The goldsmith pledged to redeem the voucher by giving back the gold. Two things happened. First, the vouchers began to circulate as money. Instead of giving gold, Merchant A gave his IOU to Merchant B in payment for goods or services. Second, the goldsmiths found out that not all of their customers came back to redeem their gold at the same time. They therefore issued more IOUs or certificates against the gold than the value of the gold they had on hand. In fact, they made loans to their customers by issuing IOUs in excess of their holdings that circulated as money and on which they charged interest.

In the United States, the Founding Fathers gave this valuable power to the Congress under Article I of the Constitution. The Congress not only delegated it to the Federal Reserve System and the private banks, but also protected the system against runs on its cash or reserves. In 1933, the Congress established the Federal Deposit Insurance Corporation (FDIC), which all Federal Reserve member banks were required to join and which most banks—state, national, and others—soon joined. The federal government now guarantees each depositor's account up to $100,000. However, the comptroller general of the United States, Charles Bowsher, testified to the Senate Banking Committee that the FDIC is in a "precarious condition," with reserves of only $13 billion, or 70 cents for each $100 of deposits of the roughly $1.9 trillion in deposits it insures. The fund is financed by a tax on banks of less than two-tenths of a percent on each $100 of deposits and ..."could be eliminated by the costs related to the failure of one or more large money-center banks."[10]

Further, in practice the bank regulatory agencies—the Federal Reserve, the FDIC, and the comptroller of the currency—bail out banks that have made unsound loans or that are on the brink of failure. These banks have been taken over or merged with stronger banks not only to protect bank customers, but to spare the shareholders and managers the full consequences of their folly.

Thus with historically low capitalization requirements, with insurance fund costs paid by charges passed on to the depositors, and with the full faith and credit of the federal government standing behind the deposits of failed banks that exceed the FDIC fund, banks themselves offer very little to support their depositors if they fail.

In addition, the Federal Reserve System has avoided congressional oversight because it has been allowed to finance itself. Instead of coming to the Congress for an annual appropriation to finance its activities, it has been allowed to use up to 10 percent of the interest it earns on its portfolio of government securities to pay its expenses. The Federal Reserve System has a total income of about $26.0 billion a year and can spend up to 10 percent, or about $2.6 billion, a year to finance its administrative operations. The remainder, or about $23.4 billion a year, is returned to the Treasury.[11] For years Federal Reserve funds were neither audited nor subjected to oversight by the appropriations committees. This enlarged its effective power and independence from the Congress beyond that anticipated in the Federal Reserve Act. Now its operating expenses are subject to a General Accounting Office (GAO) audit, but the GAO has no jurisdiction over its monetary policies. It should be noted that when the Federal Reserve expands the money supply by buying bonds, the public gets approximately one-eighth of the additional earnings and the banks seven-eighths, as the Federal Reserve returns its earnings to the Treasury. When the money supply is expanded by lowering reserve requirements, the banks retain all the additional earnings.

MONETARY POLICY

How has the Federal Reserve exercised monetary policy? Almost immediately after its inception, it was called upon to help finance World War I. About one-quarter to one-third of the cost was paid through the creation of additional demand deposits, which essentially raised prices and caused inflation. In the absence of higher taxes or larger savings, this action was needed to pay for the war. The Fed's creation in 1913 was a timely and fortuitous act.

In its early years the Federal Reserve, dominated by the Treasury and those who held orthodox economic views, made what some believe in hindsight were mistakes. In the spring of 1920, it raised the discount rate, which initiated the farm depression of 1920–1921. On the other hand, its policies from 1922 to 1929 provided an amazingly stable price level. However, after the 1929 crash and well into the early 1930s, it followed a relatively tight money policy. In 1931 the New York Federal Reserve Bank, which then dominated the system and then and now is responsible for international transactions, insisted that the British government follow a policy of economic contraction in order to qualify for loans and credit from U.S. banks.

In 1936, during the Great Depression, Franklin Roosevelt appointed the Utah banker Marriner S. Eccles as chairman, and the Federal Reserve followed a policy of supporting the Treasury and financing the deficit through the FOMC's purchase of government securities. In spite of its large increase in holdings and the creation of additional reserves in the 1930s, price levels remained stable until World War II.

From the beginning of World War II until the Federal Reserve–Treasury Accord of 1954, the Fed followed a consistent policy of buying government bonds to keep interest rates low. This was called "pegging the interest rate." While this policy had a salutory effect and whereas by comparison with the inflation and interest rates of the late 1970s, 1980s, and early 1990s, the conditions it created appear almost ideal, the policy was criticized as a potential engine of inflation. As the Federal Reserve constantly purchased treasury bonds to keep interest rates down, it was incapable of carrying out its countercyclical monetary policy responsibilities. Instead of buying or selling bonds and expanding or contracting the money supply according to the needs of the economy, it had a single, consistent policy: it bought bonds and expanded the money supply in both bad times and good. In 1954, under the leadership of Senator Paul H. Douglas of the Joint Economic Committee, the Federal Reserve and the Treasury reached an accord in which the Federal Reserve gave up its policy of pegging the interest rate. Instead, it agreed to follow a policy that allowed the interest rate to rise or fall more or less competitively to reflect conditions in the economy. During periods of excessive economic exuberance, the Fed could sell bonds that would tighten money and raise the interest rate in order to bring down prices, prevent inflation, and limit expansion.

Policies worked reasonably well from 1955 until the late 1960s, when an inappropriate fiscal policy and a rise in military spending put an excessive strain on monetary policy. Monetary policy was unable to fight inflation alone. It could only do so in conjunction with fiscal policies. When presidents and the Congress in the late 1970s and early 1980s abdicated their responsibility to raise taxes or cut spending or a combination of both to help quell unprecedented rises in the price levels, monetary policy became the only game in town. The board opted for a tight money policy that had the effect of raising interest rates and slowing down the economy. For this action it was heavily criticized but ultimately vindicated.

The criticisms came from two sources, the monetarists and the expansionists. They sang the same song but for quite different reasons. The monetarists believed that the tax-cutting fiscal policies of President Reagan should be accompanied by a low and very stable expansion of the money supply. Their essential point was that the economy can be controlled only by strictly regulating the money supply. The monetarists' leading spokesman, the Nobel Laureate Milton Friedman, blamed the Federal Reserve for an "erratic" growth in the money supply and for causing the 1981–1982 recession to exact a greater toll than necessary to bring inflation down from the double-digit levels of 1979–1981.[12] According to Friedman, "No other institution in our country has such a poor record of performance and such a high public repute."[13]

In a rebuttal to the charge that there was too much volatility in the money supply, then Chairman Paul Volcker said:

> the U.S. record compares favorably with most other major nations. The only "steadier" country in this respect is Italy. In the short run we pay too much attention to stability [of money growth]. What counts is the trend over time.[14]

Throughout the period Volcker consistently urged that the Congress and the president take the pressure off the Federal Reserve and monetary policy by tightening fiscal policy. "The budget deficits proposed by President Reagan," he argued, "are exposing financial markets to a 'major hazard today and in the future.'"[15]

There is also controversy between those who believe that the Federal Reserve should regulate the money supply and those who believe it should concentrate on providing enough money and credit to keep the interest rate low. Listen to supply-side advocate, then Congressman Jack Kemp (R.-N.Y.):

> In October, 1979, Volcker announced that henceforth the Fed would conduct its business with only one objective in mind—to control the growth in the money supply.... The Fed abandoned its concern with interest rates; it would

no longer use its powers to ensure that credit would be available or affordable. The results have been ruinous.[16]

Kemp's views were echoed by liberal economist Lester Thurow, who wrote that

> the final source of high interest rates is to be found in the Federal Reserve's conversion to monetarism. Under this doctrine the central bank is supposed to control the money supply and ignore interest rates. . . . When it does so, however, interest rates become much more erratic.[17]

Thurow differed with Kemp. Thurow believed that "additional pressures for high long-term interest rates are credited by the large deficits in the Reagan budget,"[18] which were largely due to the size of the Kemp-Roth tax cut.

The Federal Reserve Board and its chairman are in a no-win situation, especially when the president and the Congress abdicate their responsibility to cut spending or to raise taxes or both to provide an appropriate fiscal policy during periods of unprecedented deficits. They became the scapegoat of presidents and the Congress alike. As Senator William Proxmire (D.-Wis.) told Chairman Paul A. Volcker during the confirmation hearings for his second term:

> For the next four years, Paul Volcker, you will have a job that will certainly bring you more condemnation, denunciation, criticism, and, at the end, the overwhelming likelihood of failure.
>
> You are about to ride into the valley of death to your present reputation. You could become a Herbert Hoover of monetary policy. You will be the fall guy who takes a Niagara Falls of blame for an economy that will stagger along under the weight of immense debt.[19]

But by early 1987, Federal Reserve critics, especially at the White House, were singing a different tune. The Fed was following a strongly expansionist policy. Interest rates were down, inflation was below 2 percent, and there had been more than four years of economic expansion. When Volcker left he was universally praised.

But the good feelings did not last long. Almost two years to the day after Volcker's retirement and Alan Greenspan's appointment as chairman, President, Bush's Budget Director Richard G. Darman said the Fed would be to blame if a recession occurred because it had erred on the side of caution,[20] keeping the money supply tight to fight inflation instead of expanding it and lowering interest rates. But Greenspan insisted that a credible budget deficit cutting package[21] was needed to instigate the Fed's action and to bring down real interest rates.

The conflict continued with private warnings from Bush administration officials that Greenspan's reappointment as chairman would be jeopardized if the Fed continued its anti-inflation policy and a recession resulted.[22]

But in the late summer of 1990, just as the economy entered into a period of slow growth, stagnation, and recession and the Federal Reserve seemed to be ready to expand the money supply to stimulate the economy, Iraqi leader Saddam Hussein invaded Kuwait. Oil supplies and markets were endangered, the price of oil and the vast number of related commodities rose dramatically, and the economy and the Federal Reserve once again faced the dilemma of sharp price increases and declining economic growth. Stagflation, so virulent in the 1970s, thus threatened again. The economy needed to be stimulated, but to do so might bring back double-digit inflation. Thus conditions were perilous not only in the Persian Gulf but also in the U.S. economy. A deep recession accompanied by runaway inflation was as great a peril to George Bush as a Middle Eastern dictator. The Federal Reserve once again was the obvious target of both the president and the Congress, neither of which could control the Fed's policies.

After the five-year budget agreement was reached at the end of 1990, Greenspan declared it a "credible" effort to deal with the budget crisis, and the Federal Reserve relaxed its policies. This, combined with the recession, brought a drop in interest rates. But the endangered financial condition of banks limited their willingness to make new loans and offset much of the stimulus that might otherwise have occurred.

In summary, there are at least three general schools of thought about monetary policy. First there are the monetarists, who are relatively unconcerned with the budget deficits but believe in a firm, limited, strict, and steady growth in the money supply. Second, there are those, represented by Kemp, who believe the Federal Reserve should create such additional money and credit as is needed to bring down interest rates. Third, there are those who are less concerned with either the money supply or interest rates, but who believe that additional monetary puchasing power can be provided and that interest rates can be lowered and sustained only if the chronic budget deficits can be brought down and limited through fiscal policies.

These differing views are complicated by the new complexities in defining and measuring the money supply. For years the Federal Reserve has defined the money supply as the currency in circulation plus demand deposits (M_1). But the rise in inflation, the deregulation of bank and savings institutions, and the creation of new money and money market instruments have complicated the matter. Preston Martin, former vice-chairman of the Federal Reserve, said that M_1 had become "virtually meaningless in the short run."[23] The Fed now attempts to control what it calls M_2, which is broadly defined as M_1 plus bank time and savings deposits.[24] But in addition to checking accounts, savings accounts, and certificates of deposits, there are now sweep accounts, money market accounts, NOW accounts, and "super NOW" accounts. As John Berry has written, "The moorings of monetary policy are slowly going adrift.[25] Divided counsels and intellectual chaos thus not only afflict fiscal policy but monetary policy as well.

CREDIT POLICY

The Explosion of Credit

Federal credit takes three forms. The first involves direct loans made by a federal agency to an individual or institution. Examples of the nearly one hundred types of such loans are the public housing loans made by the Department of Housing and Urban Development (HUD) and the Farmers Home Administration, the price supports for farmers made through the Commodity Credit Corporation, the financing of export transactions abroad made by the Export-Import Bank, and the business and investment loans made by the Small Business Administration. Most of these programs are now "on-budget"—that is, they are a part of the unified budget—but until recently many were "off-budget" and not included. The estimate for outstanding direct loans was $177 billion for fiscal year 1994.

The second form of federal credit involves guaranteed loans, which are made by private or semipublic entities and not necessarily by the federal government, although the federal government does guarantee them. The so-called bailout programs for New York City, Lockheed Aircraft, and the Chrysler Corporation took the form of such loans in which investment houses or private banks put up the money but the federal government guaranteed their repayment. In addition to these one-time or ad hoc loan guarantees, there are almost fifty permanent loan guarantee programs carried out by the federal government. Among the largest and better known are those of the Federal Housing Administration (FHA); the Government National Mortgage Association (GNMA, or Ginnie Mae), which provides a secondary market for mortgages; and the Rural Electrification Administration (REA); as well as guaranteed loans for international security assistance; and numerous programs for students, farmers, small businesses, and others. The estimate for outstanding guaranteed loans was $741 billion for fiscal year 1994.

A third form of federally backed credit is that extended by government-sponsored enterprises (GSEs). They

> act as financial intermediaries directing capital to particular sectors of the economy. Due to their "special relationship" with the Federal Government, GSE's historically have been able to borrow in the credit market at yields carrying only slight premiums above those of Treasury securities of comparable maturity.[26]

The enterprises include the Student Loan Marketing Association (SLMA), the Federal National Mortgage Association (FNMA, or Fannie

Mae), three Farm Credit Administration agencies (the banks for cooperatives, federal intermediate credit banks, and federal land banks), and the Federal Home Loan Bank System. The estimate for GSE loans was $804 billion in fiscal year 1990. They have been rising at the rate of 9 percent a year, so that the estimate for fiscal year 1994 was more than $1.14 trillion.

While there is some overlap between guaranteed loans and GSE loans, the total outstanding federal and federally assisted credit grew from $217 billion in fiscal year 1971 to an estimated $2.05 trillion in fiscal year 1994 (see Figure 6–1.)[27]

These loans and loan guarantees have certain economic effects. In some cases, loans would otherwise not be available. This is true of many SBA loans and of the loans for New York City, Chrysler, and Lockheed. In the last three cases, the financial markets or the banks refused to lend the funds without a government guarantee. Similarly, during periods of tight money and credit stringency some exporters got credit from the Export-Import Bank that would otherwise not have been available and was available at rates much lower than those of the commercial market. In certain instances, the rates for the borrower are the government borrowing rates plus a small administrative fee. In other cases, such as the Export-Import Bank and student loan examples, the cost of borrowing for the borrower was below the

FIGURE 6–1 **Federal and Federally Assisted Credit Outstanding** (*Source: Special Analyses Budget of the United States Government: Fiscal Year 1990* [Washington, D.C.: U.S. Government Printing Office, 1989], Special Analysis F)

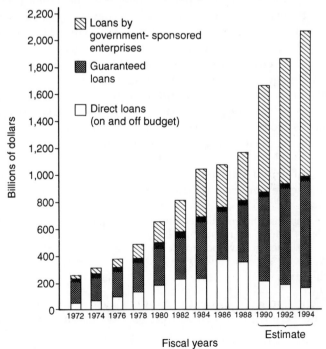

cost for the government and represented an absolute government subsidy. The GSEs, because of the line of government credit available to them, because their securities may be held by federally regulated institutions, and because they enjoy certain tax preferences, hold a preferred position in credit markets and pay an interest rate well below that which banks give their best customers and only slightly higher than the Treasury itself pays for securities.

One must distinguish between the intrinsic value of these programs and their effects on the budget and inflation. With respect to their intrinsic value, some are good and others are not so good. Few would quarrel with the FHA loan guarantee program, which has helped to provide 58 million, or 64 percent, of owner-occupied houses. The money for many programs is paid back with interest, and the programs are thus said to earn money for the federal government. This was claimed for the Lockheed and Chrysler loan guarantees, as each company paid the government a loan fee. That claim, however, did not take into account the fact that the funds loaned to Lockheed and Chrysler were not available to some more credit-worthy customers. Other programs have provided a very deep subsidy or are of questionable value. Loans and loan guarantees made by the SBA, by HUD for New Towns, and under the Economic Development Administration have been heavily criticized.

The problem of these programs with respect to the budget and the economy is a very different one—namely, "crowding out." In recent years, funds raised under federal auspices have amounted to a third or more of the total funds raised in all U.S. credit markets. The rise in and the growing cost of financing the federal debt as well as other direct borrowing, borrowing for guaranteed loans, and borrowing by government-sponsored enterprises either limit the amounts of money available to homebuilders, homebuyers, farmers, cities, and small businesses, or help drive the interest rates to levels where the money is too costly even when available. Further, a form of credit rationing occurs as those favored under the programs can either get credit and/or get it at preferential rates when others, perhaps equally or more deserving socially or economically, cannot get credit or cannot pay the interest rates.

The totality of federal participation in the credit markets, however worthy the individual programs may be, has raised interest rates, helped prolong and compound inflation, and helped create the crisis over the budget.

THE FEDERAL FINANCING BANK

The Federal Financing Bank (FFB) is a little-known agency. It was established by an act of the Congress in 1973, is housed at the Treasury Department, and is governed by a board composed of the secretary of the Treasury and five members. It was created because in 1973 at least eighteen government agencies, in addition to the Treasury, were borrowing money in the government securities market. Each agency had its own securities staff and financial experts. Each was offering its own financial instruments, some for very small amounts and some for little-known purposes and programs that were often in competition with each other. The proliferation of these agency-backed securities, according to the Congressional Budget Office, "strained the capacity of the government securities market.[28] The FFB was set up to help solve these problems. By law, it can purchase or sell any obligation that is issued, sold, or guaranteed by a federal agency. Thus instead of eighteen or more agencies competing with each other in the government securities market, the FFB borrowed for them. One staff of experts was substituted for a dozen and a half. Instead of a proliferation of small securities and with a plethora of unfamiliar provisions, a single large issue could be offered by the FFB. As a result, the FFB could borrow at a rate only slightly higher than the cost to the Treasury itself. The FFB was given authority to borrow up to $15 billion from the securities markets on its own and an additional unlimited amount from the Treasury. The results were spectacular. After seven years, it had outstanding loans of almost $110 billion and net lending of almost $25 billion a year. These were the results of procedures not originally contemplated. In 1974, when the FFB first auctioned its own bills, they traded above the rates for Treasury securities for equal or comparable instruments. Because of this the FFB abandoned the practice of borrowing for itself. From then on it decided to borrow exclusively from the Treasury at interest rates that the Treasury paid in the market. The effect of this was that while the agencies could borrow from the FFB at a lower rate than would otherwise have been the case, the total amounts were more than seven times the original $15 billion ceiling put on the FFB borrowings. In effect, the FFB and the agencies it served had an almost unlimited source of funds. As the Congressional Budget Office has said, "As a debt management tool, the FFB has been a success: federal agencies and guaranteed borrowers have saved millions of dollars in interest costs each year."[29] But some of the effects of FFB transactions on the budget and budget concepts have been equally harmful.

Both because of the explosion of FFB borrowings and because its activities were off-budget, the agencies most favored by FFB practices reaped an advantage not available to others. From 1978 to 1985, FFB outlays accounted for 96 percent of all off-budget outlays. Particularly favored were the REA, Defense Department guaranteed loans to foreign countries for the purchase of American military equipment, HUD, and the Tennessee Valley Authority.

Two kinds of FFB transactions resulted in the favoritism. The first was the FFB's purchase of guaranteed loans, particularly from local rural electric cooperatives and foreign governments. The effect was to convert a loan guarantee to an off-budget direct loan. A direct loan is a budget outlay. But because the transactions were off-budget, the agencies could "spend" the funds without having them count against their budgets. This practice was adding $15 to $20 billion a year to the national debt, but did not show up in the budget. The Gramm-Rudman-Hollings Act changed this by putting the transactions on-budget and having them counted as outlays or spending by the agencies using the FFB in this manner.

The second was the FFB's purchase of something called certificates of beneficial ownership (CBOs) from certain agencies. Because the FFB was off-budget, the sale had the same budgetary effect as if the agency had sold the asset to a private party. It was a receipt to the agency.

The Congressional Budget Office study of the FFB concluded that

> the use of the term "loan asset sales" for these transactions is, thus, a misnomer. The agencies are not selling loans; in fact, they are selling guaranteed securities that only incidentally represent a pool of loans. As such, sales of CBO are identical to agency borrowing, not asset sales.[30]

In addition, the agency replenishes its loan portfolio and can lend the additional funds, even though the old loans have not been paid off. As Rip Van Winkle said when he was on the wagon but took a drink, "We won't count this one." In fiscal year 1992 the FFB held $262 billion in outstanding loans.[31]

COMPREHENSIVE CREDIT BUDGET

In 1980, the congressional Budget Committees took some first steps to bring the credit budget under control. Starting with fiscal year 1981, the concurrent resolution on the budget included recommendations on credit levels for new direct loans, primary loan guarantees, and secondary loan guarantees. Further, these recommendations were proposed by broad functions such as national defense, commerce and housing credit, and agriculture. For example, the concurrent budget resolution for fiscal year 1984 contained a nonbinding sense of Congress resolution that the president, through administrative action, should limit the total FFB origination of direct loans guaranteed by other agencies for the year to $17.3 billion and the purchase of CBOs from federal agencies to $13.2 billion.

This was a good beginning. Since then the following steps have been or are being taken. A comprehensive federal credit budget covering direct loans, primary loan guarantees, and secondary loan guarantees broken down by function is now provided in the budget resolution (see Appendix B). Credit amounts are being treated in the same manner as authorizations for new spending. The FFB and its questionable off-budget transactions have been brought on-budget, and its outstanding loans have been reduced by $35 billion over five years. More uniform standards among agencies who lend credit have been developed. Overall credit policies are now subjected to annual review by the appropriate credit committees of the Congress in the same way that monetary policy is examined.

THE SAVINGS AND LOAN SCANDAL

The savings and loan (S&L) scandal of the 1980s will cost the taxpayers an estimated $500 billion and will adversely affect the federal budget until the year 2020.[32] The policies which led to the S&L scandal have now affected commercial banks. The estimated cost of the concomitant bail-out of failed commercial banks will cost at least another $50 billion.[33]

The S&L scandal has been called the "financial crime of the century."[34] "the biggest bank heist in history,"[35] "the greatest-ever bank robbery,"[36] and "the worst public scandal in American history," an "outrage" which makes "Teapot Dome in the Harding Administration and Credit Mobilier in the time of Ulysses S. Grant... seem minor episodes."[37]

Background

American savings and loan institutions began in Frankford, Pennsylvania (now a part of Philadelphia) in 1831 when the Oxford Provident Building Association of Philadelphia County was organized. It was modeled on the English building societies started in the 1770's.[38]

Until the middle of the twentieth century the non-commercial bank thrift institutions were basically neighborhood cooperative or mutual building societies. In the beginning neighbors pooled their savings and made equal monthly contributions which were loaned to the members without interest until each member, drawn by lot, had purchased a home. Then the mortgages were cancelled and the associations disbanded.[39]

Soon loans were made to the highest bidder, interest was charged, some members did not build but chose to receive interest (or a dividend as it was called) on their contributions. As mutual or cooperative societies, members had equal votes. There were variations of the structure, particularly in the New England mutual savings banks that had begun earlier in 1816. The characteristics of the savings and loan associations were that they limited their loans to finance residential housing only, in the neighborhood or limited area, and had a high degree of fiscal integrity. The New England mutual savings banks differed by lending for some other types of real estate and investing in government and high quality corporate bonds and some blue chip stocks.[40] The essence of both was that until the last third of the twentieth century they were small, safe, fiscally sound and performed a vital public function essentially without scandal. They epitomized the American institutions of the flag, motherhood, and apple pie.

The stock market crash of 1929 and the ensuing Great Depression brought chaos to the thrifts and the need for a central credit facility to help finance them. Thirteen percent (1,700 of 12,666) savings institutions failed and $200 million, or about one-third of the value of deposits and two and a half percent of the $8 billion in assets, was lost. This was the result of the depression, not thievery or scandal.

In 1932, under the Republican President Herbert Hoover and a Democratic Congress, the Federal Home Loan Bank Act established the Federal Home Loan Bank (FHLB) System with a three-member bank board and twelve district banks. Modeled on the Federal Reserve, it provided a reserve credit system for member savings and loan associations, savings banks, and life insurance companies. Unlike the Federal Reserve System, the FHLB had no power to create money.

In 1933 under Franklin D. Roosevelt the Home Owners Loan Act created the Home Owners Loan Corporation (HOLC) and gave the FHLB Board the power to grant federal charters for savings and loan associations. The HOLC was an insurance fund financed by the federal government. It bought delinquent mortgages, refinanced the loans at lower rates and smaller monthly payments, and saved the homes of about one million Americans. It stopped making loans in 1936, repaid the funds it received from the federal government, made a small profit for the Treasury, closed its doors, and went out of business. The reason the HOLC was so successful was that the assets of the savings and loans, which their members were temporarily unable to finance because of the Great Depression, were unusually good high grade security for the loans. Such was not the case in the 1980s and 1990s when the deregulated savings and loans were not only allowed but encouraged to invest in high risk speculative assets outside the home building industry and their business experience.

In 1934 the National Housing Act established the Federal Savings and Loan Insurance Corporation (FSLIC, pronounced Fiz-lick) to insure savings up to $5,000 for each account in each thrift institution just as the Federal Deposit Insurance Corporation (FDIC) insured deposits in commercial banks. The FSLIC was also designed to prevent the default of insured institutions.

From 1934 until the Housing Act of 1964 no important legislation affecting the savings and loan banks was passed. Between 1964 and 1980 most of the legislation improved supervision, protected the consumer, aided housing by providing secondary markets for mortgages, and prohibited discrimination in credit transactions and red-lining (that is, the refusal to make housing loans in low- and moderate-income neighborhoods).

How Things Went Wrong

The Slippery Slope   The major causes of the S&L scandal are found in the 1980s. But preceding them, especially the Garn-St. Germain Act of 1982, were a series of minor events leading to the ultimate catastrophe.

In 1964, for example, the S&Ls were allowed to use depositors' funds to establish "service corporations" to perform business operations the S&Ls were otherwise prohibited from doing. This was a small first step in violation of the basic principle that S&Ls should stick to the business they knew best and were very good at, namely issuing mortgages to build residential housing in local neighborhoods.

As a result of the failure and bail-out of the State Savings Bank of Stockton, California, the Financial Institutions Supervisory Act of 1966 was passed. For a promise of a fast pay-off for depositors in failed S&Ls, the S&Ls gave up the right to set their own interest or "dividend" rates. A fixed contractual rate was substituted for a rate based on actual earnings. Instead of waiting until the end of the year to determine their profit and dividend rate, the act provided that the S&L rate would be one half of one percent above the rate paid by commercial banks. This rate was set by the Federal Reserve under its famous Regulation Q. This was later reduced to one quarter of one percent. The difference was enough to ensure that S&Ls would get an adequate share of consumer savings. Meanwhile as inflation rose there was strong competition for new savings accounts among S&Ls and between S&Ls and other financial institutions through such non-interest rate devices as free gifts—a set of dishes, a coffee pot, or electric toaster.

In 1967 under the S&L Holding Company Act, nonfinancial commercial and industrial institutions like Ford Motor Company and Sears Roebuck were allowed to own S&Ls. At least three offenses against historic practices of the S&Ls were committed by this act. First, the commercial and industrial institutions knew very little about the S&L industry. Second, holding companies with a variety of institutional assets were tempted either into conflicts of interest with the S&Ls they owned or into ignoring the needs of their S&L financial institutions in favor of other interests that might have a more profitable bottom line or a potentially profitable but far more risky bottom line. Third, the law offended the basic principle of the local neighborhood base of the S&Ls through which they gave their neighbor's interests the highest priority, knew their borrowers well, and were restrained from unsound actions by their peers and the knowledge of their own institution that the far-ranging holding companies would find almost impossible to emulate. Later some commercial and industrial groups sought to own financial institutions as a milch cow to fund loans to the parent company for unexamined and excessively risky purposes.

Also during this period, go-go operators successfully transformed state mutual S&Ls into stock or profit-making organizations. Often this resulted in millions of dollars of equity in the assets of the neighborhood S&L to be transferred from the shareholder owners to a small group of new stockholders for the latter's personal gain. Allowed, if not promoted by the regulators, it was often a form of legal theft. In 1974 this was compounded when for the first time federal charters could be issued for stock S&Ls.

In 1973, at the urging of Federal Reserve Board Chairman Arthur F. Burns, commercial banks were allowed to issue new certificates of deposit (CDs) for four years at any rate the bank decided it could pay or needed to pay to attract savings. This caused consumers to switch funds out of the S&Ls and into commercial banks. It was called by the seven syllable Latinized word "disintermediation," a modern barbarism. The Congress almost immediately passed legislation requiring the Federal Reserve to reinstate differential ceilings on interest rates paid depositors favoring the S&Ls. In 1975 the Congress put the one-quarter of one percent differential into law. This in turn became a victim of the high inflation rates of the late 1970s when the Federal Reserve declared the differential null and void when interest rates exceeded 9 percent.

Thus by 1980 the traditional neighborhood mutual building societies had been transformed into institutions that performed many non-residential mortgage real estate and other business functions; they were owned by holding companies with conflicting and diverse interests, were no longer the subject of effective Federal Reserve controls on the rate of dividends they could pay their depositors, and were in a high-risk interest rate war with competing institutions for the savings needed for both their traditional homebuilding activities and investments in new and highly speculative ventures in order to earn enough to pay the high interest rates they owed to their depositors. It was indeed a vicious circle, an American version of the French *ronde.*

It was a trial by interest rates.[41]

> By the end of 1980, many thrifts were in deep trouble, with a severe negative mismatch between the yields on their assets and the costs of their liabilities. Most of the industry's interest-bearing assets were in long-term home mortgages with low, fixed rates of interest, while more than half of its interest-bearing liabilities were in short-term (one year or less) certificates of deposit paying high, deregulated market rates. By the first half of 1981, the industry's cost of funds, at 10.31 percent, exceeded the average return on its mortgage portfolio, which was 9.72 percent. By the second half of 1981, conditions had deteriorated further; associations paid an average rate of 11.53 percent while earning an average rate of only 10.02 percent.[42]

In turn these conditions led first to the Depository Institutions Deregulation and Monetary Control Act of 1980 and to the Garn-St. Germain Depository Institutions Act of 1982. The latter was named for Senator Jake

Garn (R.-Utah), Chairman of the Senate Banking Committee, and Ferdinand St. Germain (D.-R.I.), Chairman of the House Banking Committee. These two acts, but especially the latter, combined with the ideological deregulation activity of the Reagan Administration (centered in the Office of Management and Budget), were the major sources of the S&L scandals.

The Depository Institutions Deregulation and Monetary Control Act of 1980

This act homogenized financial institutions. The sharp distinction between the function of the S&Ls to make loans for long term residential real estate mortgages and the commercial banks' function to make short term commercial loans was eviscerated. Where before there were four types of institutions—commercial banks, S&Ls, mutual savings banks, and credit unions—with different primary functions, a few of which overlapped, now there were four types of institutions with similar functions. Now all four could provide interest bearing checking accounts to their customers. All could write residential mortgages. All could make consumer loans.

In addition to homogenized functions for all the institutions, S&Ls no longer were subject to state usury ceilings on mortgage loans. Federal S&Ls could now have branches throughout a state which had prohibited state chartered S&Ls from doing that. Limits on the geographic lending areas for S&Ls and their service corporations were done away with. But most important of all, Regulation Q—interest rate controls on federally regulated depository institutions—was phased out by 1986. And, in a last-minute move engineered by Glen Troop, and the chief lobbyist for the U.S. League of Savings Institutions, Senator Alan Cranston (D.-Calif.) offered an amendment in the Conference Committee, not a part of either the House or Senate bill, to increase the insurance on deposits for each account in an S&L or other depository institution from $40,000 to $100,000. The insured amount had quadrupled, from $25,000, in only four years. The average account when the $100,000 ceiling went into effect was only $6,000.

This law compounded rather than helped to solve the massive problems now confronting the S&L industry. "By the end of 1980, many thrifts were in deep trouble, with a severe negative mismatch between the yields on their assets [long-term home mortgages with low fixed rates of interest] and the costs of their liabilities [short term certificates of deposit paying high deregulated market rates]."[43] In 1981 and 1982 savers withdrew $31.8 billion more than they deposited, S&Ls experienced staggering losses of $8.9 billion and a $6 billion decline in net worth, and 813 savings institutions disappeared, most of them merged into other institutions. In the last six months of 1981, 85 percent of all institutions insured by the FSLIC operated at a loss.[44]

The Garn-St. Germain Depository Institutions Act of 1982

By 1982 the effects of deregulation and high interest rates had brought the S&L industry to its knees. In order to save the industry the basic answer of Garn-St. Germain was more deregulation. The birth-parents of the legislation were the U.S. League of Savings Institutions and Chairman Richard Pratt of the FHLBB Board and its General Counsel Thomas Vartanian. It was the latter who noted that its key titles were "developed by the FHLBB in close consultation with the Reagan Administration, which enthusiastically endorsed and supported their passage."[45] At its signing ceremony President Reagan claimed "I think we hit a home run."[46] Here is what the bill did:

1. It shortened the phase-out of the Regulation Q. interest rate differential between thrifts and commercial banks by two years, from 1986 to January 1984.
2. It provided for a new money market deposit account with no interest rate ceiling which could compete with money market mutual funds.
3. It gave the thrifts the right to expand into additional areas of business, particularly commercial lending that had previously been the function of commercial banks.

Thrifts were allowed to broaden their holdings of short-term assets. In particular, federal associations were given the power to:

Make commercial, corporate, business, or agricultural loans, which after January 1, 1984, could constitute up to 10 percent of an association's assets.

Increase from 20 percent to 30 percent the amount of assets that could be invested in consumer loans, and make inventory and floor-planning loans beyond existing authority.

Offer individual or corporate demand-deposit accounts....

Increase from 20 percent to 40 percent the amount of assets that could be invested in loans secured by nonresidential real estate.

Invest up to 10 percent of assets in personal property for rent or sale.

Make education loans for any educational purpose, instead of just for college or vocational training.

Invest up to 100 percent of assets in state or local government obligations.

Invest in other thrifts' time deposits and saving deposits and use the investments to help meet liquidity requirements.[47]

In addition, not only new but existing federally chartered S&Ls could choose to convert to stock S&Ls.

These changes in the way traditionally conservative, financially sound savings institutions could function made it inevitable that they would succumb to the sharp operators.

As Pizzo, Fricker, and Muolo wrote in *In$ide Job,*

> The ink wasn't dry on the Garn-St. Germain legislation deregulating the thrift industry, before high-stakes investors, swindlers, and mobsters lined up to loot S&Ls. They immediately seized the opportunity created by careless deregulation of thrifts and gambled, stole, and embezzled away billions in an orgy of greed and excess.[48]

There were insider loans and investments in junk bonds and highly speculative ventures outside the traditional residential housing areas. Outside investors were attracted by the chance to make a killing by converting mutual savings banks to stock institutions. Almost any high risk venture was attractive because any funds lost by depositors were insured by FSLIC up to $100,000 and protected by a Congressional Joint Resolution signed by the president pledging the full faith and credit of the U.S. Government behind the accounts.

All of this was an invitation to steal. The owners of the thrifts had very little equity in the institutions. Big investors were invited to deposit up to $100,000 in multiple accounts so that the FSLIC, not the institution nor the investor with a million dollars or more, would bear the burden for any losses. Depositors funds were used to buy highly speculative junk bonds and other assets. Institutions engaged in a bidding war for deposits. Unlike 1933, when the HOLC was formed to rescue the neighborhood building societies and inherited valued assets, the FSLIC and the successors to the Home Loan Bank inherited assets whose value had dropped spectacularly and were often worth only a few cents on the dollar.

The religious fervor to deregulate institutions, which by the nature of their fiduciary responsibilities had traditionally been the subject of regulation, compounded the problem. Early in his administration, President Reagan issued an executive order on deregulation. It prescribed that the director of the OMB take actions to deregulate the regulated industries. He was to do so under the guidance of the Presidential Task Force on Regulatory Relief with Vice President George Bush as its chairman. In 1985 when the S&L scandal was overwhelming the FHLB Board, its Chairman Edwin Gray attempted repeatedly to get approval by the OMB for personnel and funds to audit the scandal-ridden S&L industry. In a meeting with Budget Director David Stockman's assistant Constance Horner, where Gray made an urgent request for an increase in S&L examiners from 679 to 1,400, or an increase from one to two examiners for every four and one half of the 3,200 ailing thrifts, the reply was "You want *more* examiners??" Horner told Gray "it wasn't a matter of money but of philosophy. The administration's philosophy was one of *de*regulation. That meant *fewer* regulators, not more."[49]

Other factors also contributed to the scandal. There were massive campaign contributions by S&L and banking political action committees (PACs) to presidential and congressional candidates alike. Prestigious national accounting firms gave their seal of approval to S&Ls in dire straits after the accounting firms had failed to more than superficially examine the S&Ls' assets, liabilities, and business practices. The regional Federal Home Loan Banks were caught up in massive conflicts of interest. Board members from regional institutions that had made highly risky loans were unwilling to unleash the examiners who served under them to examine the shaky S&Ls. Indeed the S&L scandal is "...the biggest heist in history."[50]

Five hundred billion dollars, including interest on borrowed funds, may be an underestimate of the financial and budgetary costs.

NOTES

1. *The Federal Reserve System: Purposes and Functions*, 6th ed. (Washington, D.C.: Board of Governors, 1980), p. 3.
2. Sherman J. Maisel, "The Fed's Independence' Should be Maintained," *Los Angeles Times*, 5 October 1982, pt. II, p. 5. Copyright, 1982, *Los Angeles Times*. Reprinted by permission.
3. Senate Subcommittee of the Committee on Banking and Currency, *Nomination of Charles Noah Shepardson, Hearing*, 84th Cong., 1st Sess., 25 February 1955, pp. 2–3.
4. Senate Committee on Banking, Housing, and Urban Affairs, *Nomination of Lyle E. Gramley*, 2d., 15 April 1982, p. 4. Governor Teeters was a member of the staff of the Federal Reserve and the Bureau of the Budget, and assistant director and chief economist of the House Budget Committee, but was not with the Congressional Budget Office.
5. *Federal Reserve System*, p. 15.
6. Ibid.
7. See "Measures of Money Stock," in *Federal Reserve System*, p. 10.
8. *Los Angeles Times*, 29 November 1982, p. 3 Copyright, 1982, *Los Angeles Times*.
9. *Federal Reserve System*, p. 17.
10. *The Washington Post*, 12 September 1990, pp. A-1, 7.
11. *Budget of the United States Government: Fiscal Year 1992* (Washington, D.C.: Government Printing Office, 1991), part seven–29. Earnings vary depending on interest rates.
12. *Los Angeles Times*, 22 October 1982, pt. IV, p. 1.
13. Ibid.
14. *The Washington Post*, 12 February 1982, p. D-7.
15. Ibid.
16. "The Future of Monetary Policy," transcript of hearing, Joint Economic Committee, 15 June 1982.
17. *Los Angeles Times*, 4 July 1982, pt., V, p. 3.
18. Ibid.
19. Senator Proxmire's Office, 15 July 1983.
20. *The Washington Post*, 14 August 1989, p. A-7.
21. Ibid., 13 May 1990, p. H-3.
22. Ibid., 27 June 1990, p. A-19.

23. *The Washington Post,* 12 December 1982, p. H-11.
24. *Federal Reserve System,* p. 10.
25. *The Washington Post,* 12 December 1982, p. H-11.
26. *Special Analysis, Budget of the United States Government: Fiscal Year 1990* (Washington, D.C.: U.S. Government Printing Office, 1989), p. F-21. This document was discontinued in 1990.
27. Ibid., pp. F-13, 18, 23.
28. Congressional Budget Office, *The Federal Financing Bank and the Budgetary Federal Credit Activities* (Washington, D.C.: U.S. Government Printing Office, 1982), p. ix.
29. Ibid., p. 1.
30. Ibid., p. 18.
31. *Budget of the United States Government: Fiscal Year 1992* (Washington, D.C.: U.S. Government Printing Office, 1991), part four-935.
32. Martin Mayer, "The Collapse of the Savings and Loan Industry" *The Greatest-Ever Bank Robbery,* (New York: Charles Scribners Sons, 1990), p. 2.
33. John D. Dingell (D.-Mich.), Chairman of the House Energy and Commerce Committee with jurisdiction over financial legislation, in an interview with *USA Today,* June 19, 1991, 4B.
34. Stephen Pizzo, Mary Fricker, and Paul Muolo, *In$ide Job,* "The Looting of America's Savings and Loans" (New York: McGraw-Hill Publishing Company, 1989), Brian Ross and Ira Silverman, NBC News. Outside back dust jacket.
35. Ibid., p. 4.
36. *Mayer, The Greatest-Ever Bank Robbery.*
37. Ibid., p. 1.
38. *A Guide to the Federal Home Loan Bank System,* 5th ed. (Washington, D.C.: FHLB System Publication Corporation, March, 1987), p. 5.
39. Ibid.
40. Ibid., p. 6.
41. Ibid., p. 18.
42. Ibid.
43. Ibid.
44. Ibid.
45. *Mayer,* p. 95.
46. Ibid.
47. *Guide,* p. 20.
48. *In$ide Job,* p. 4.
49. Ibid.
50. Ibid., p. 4.

7 ————————————————————————

The Nixon Constitutional Crisis and the 1974 Budget Act

INTRODUCTION

The events leading up to the passage of the Congressional Budget and Impoundment Control Act of 1974 were not unlike those that led to the 1921 Budget and Accounting Act. Both were preceded by wars, economic and budget crises, and study committees and commissions. But in two major respects, conditions and goals were very different in 1974 as compared to 1921. First, the 1974 act was the product of not only a budget crisis but also a constitutional crisis. Involved were the secret and unauthorized use of funds to bomb and invade Cambodia. In addition, money appropriated by the Congress for farm and city programs was impounded by President Nixon on a grandiose and unprecedented scale.

Second, in 1974 the Congress sought to retrieve power and authority it had delegated to the president. The Congress was determined to both discipline itself and to discipline the president. Through various study commissions it provided an array of budget criticism and proposed numerous reforms.

The 1974 Budget Act brought an appreciable shift of power among various groups and committees in the Congress. This was made possible as a result of a number of political changes that occurred simultaneously. The changes included the decline of the South's hold on committees, the rise of northern liberal Democrats to positions of influence, the elections of moderately progressive Republicans, the breakdown in the seniority system, and the rise of subcommittee government.

The 1974 act was forged in the crucible of conflict and crisis, a struggle between the president and the Congress.

CONSTITUTIONAL CRISIS

Next to the Budget and Accounting Act of 1921, the Budget and Impoundment Control Act of 1974 was the most important piece of budget legislation in the history of the country and, along with the War Powers Resolution, the most profound with respect to the balance of constitutional powers between the president and the Congress in the post–World War II era.

The events leading to the 1974 act were not unlike those of 1921. The act was preceded by periods of anguish and crisis. Commissions were established to study and make recommendations. Compromises between liberals and conservatives and between progressives and economizers were reached. Adjustments over political turf and committee jurisdictions were made. But there was a fundamental difference in the events that led to the 1974 act: This time the Congress was not seeking to *delegate* power to the president but to *retrieve* powers that had been lost.

Allen Schick, in his meticulously detailed work on the subject, calls the period preceding the act "The Seven-Year Budget War: 1966–73,"[1] a war between the president and the Congress, between the House and the Senate, and among rival spending and taxing committees. The budget war had many trappings and overtones of previous periods in the continuing saga of who should wield power over the purse—the Congress, as clearly enumerated by the Founding Fathers, or the president. But there was an added dimension. The Congress was battling a new and imperial president determined to exceed even the Lockean prerogative that in times of dire emergency "the laws themselves . . . give way to executive power," so that the executive may "act according to discretion for the public good, without the prescription of law and sometimes even against it." But when the truth was revealed, few agreed with President Nixon that the emergency was as dire as he claimed, that the powers he used were justified by the imagined let alone the real emergency, or that the secrecy, illegalities, and lack of accountability to the people were compatible with the demands of the Lockean prerogative. The exercise of that privilege requires the leader who takes upon himself extraordinary or unconstitutional power in the name of saving the people of the Constitution do three things. He must ultimately share the knowledge on which his actions were based. He must seek accountability from the people in whose name he acted. Finally, he must be vindicated by their ultimate verdict as to the necessity of his deeds.

This was, however, much more than a "Seven-Year Budget War." It was part of a bigger war, a crossroads in the history of the country, and a fundamental element of what became known as Watergate or the Watergate period. The war was over power and the proper relationship of the president to the Congress, the courts, and the law. The fight over the budget was a battle in that war that included conflicts over who had power under the Constitution to raise and support armies, to provide and maintain a navy, to declare war, and to draw money from the treasury in consequence of an appropriation made by law, and over the meaning of the executive power and the president's responsibility to take care that the laws are faithfully executed. In the past the congressional delegation of power over the budget to the president was the result of the increasing complexity of economic life, a consensus of the president and the Congress and their political confederates and allies as to what needed to be done, and the culmination of experience with war and depression that led to largely neutral policy solutions. In almost every case the delegation resulted in the aggrandizement of the executive at the expense of the Congress, but this was done willingly, even joyously, and had few narrow or partisan or siege-mentality overtones.

The Budget and Impoundment Control Act of 1974 encompassed greater issues than those that had driven earlier budgeting acts. The act was signed less than a month before President Nixon resigned from the presidency, was forged around issues that made up at least one of the proposed (but not approved) Articles of Impeachment drawn up by the House Judiciary Committee, and went to the heart of the issue of whether the president, by asserting implied or inherent powers, could secretly transfer funds from authorized programs and projects to wholly unauthorized and unreported military activities, on the one hand, or arbitrarily reserve, rescind, and impound funds that the Congress had authorized and appropriated, on the other. It was not only a crisis or war over the budget. It was part of the larger crisis over the Constitution.

While previous presidents had reserved or deferred or impounded funds, no previous president had done so in such a heavy-handed way or on such "an unprecedented scale."[2] While presidents had occasionally shown streaks of stubbornness or performed small acts of an arbitrary nature, none had ever used impoundment as a deliberate policy of confrontation whose purpose was to wreak a radical change in the fabric of the Constitution. In some aspects, President Nixon was more Machiavellian than Machiavelli, his reactions were reminiscent of the exercise of prerogative powers by Charles I, and his goal was that of a "plebiscitary presidency," as Arthur Schlesinger, Jr., said, modeled not on the parliamentary system of Britain "but in France—in the France of Louis Napoleon and Charles de Gaulle."[3]

> If Nixon were to complete his campaign for presidential supremacy, he had therefore to find ways to circumvent the powers given Congress by the Con-

stitution to indicate priorities through the control of appropriations. His solution was simple and direct. It was, when laws passed by Congress conflicted with his own conception of national priorities, to refuse to spend the funds Congress had solemnly voted.[4]

One must not lose sight of the fact that President Nixon's budget and impoundment actions were only a part of a grand and more strategic goal. "The essence was power to the Presidency."[5] Unlike previous struggles over money, debt, taxes, and spending, the Congressional Budget and Impoundment Control Act of 1974 had this larger dimension.

There was yet another change in the elements that led to the act. Earlier, the Congress had willingly delegated its enumerated powers to a most receptive executive, or, as James Sundquist wrote, the Congress "tosses power over a barrier, so to speak, into alien territory—out of direct control, out of easy reach, even out of sight."[6] In 1974, however, a major dimension of the struggle was an attempt by the Congress to recapture the exercise of its enumerated powers.

But if the setting was one of great constitutional struggle, other important, even traumatic, events and causes led to the act. Public Law 93-344 is not one act, but two. As Section 1(a), immediately following the enacting clause, states:

> This Act may be cited as the "Congressional Budget and Impoundment Control Act of 1974." Title I through IX may be cited as the "Congressional Budget Act of 1974," and Title X may be cited as the "Impoundment Control Act of 1974."

The Congress passed the "Impoundment Control Act" to discipline the president. It passed the "Congressional Budget Act" to discipline itself.

It was the confluence of the need for both that ultimately brought reform. The factors overlapped. Conditions that led the president to abuse or usurp power were nurtured in part by the congressional lack of discipline. The same economic problems that led the Congress to pass the act led the president to assert prerogative power on grounds of great emergency. President Nixon saw the emergency as a crisis over the budget and the economy. The country saw the emergency, which placed society in jeopardy, as a grab for exceptional power by President Nixon in the name of a budget and economic crisis. While the constitutional crisis was the catalyst that brought the act to fruition, there were nonetheless economic, institutional, internal political, and international problems leading to its passage.

DOMESTIC ECONOMIC PROBLEMS

Foremost was the rise of inflation. The period preceding the budget crisis was characterized by remarkable price stability. In some of the years between 1958 and 1965 prices may have fallen, for they rose less than the statistical margin of error.[7] Then between 1966 and 1972 consumer prices rose 3 to 6 percent and producer prices from 2 to 4 percent. But in 1973 the consumer and producer price increases were staggering, 8.8 and 11.8 percent, respectively, and in 1974 they were 12.2 and 18.3 percent, respectively. The 1974 figures were double the annual increases during World War II.[8] In addition, the $23 to $25 billion budget deficits of Presidents Johnson (in 1968) and Nixon (in 1971–1972) were five times greater than the deliberate deficits at the depth of the Great Depression (see Table 5–1).

CONGRESSIONAL SELF-CRITICISM

Preceding the passage of the 1974 Budget Act, a wide range of both macro- and microbudget criticism had flowed from numerous congressional committees. These included specific criticisms of military procurement, highway trust fund policies, housing expenditures, foreign aid, public works, water subsidy policies, tax expenditures, government productivity, and welfare expenditures. The attacks focused on the program results as well as the procedures that had led to them, which were said to be unwieldly, inadequate, diffused, and antiquated.

At the end of 1972 the Congress, after it had tangled with President Nixon over the fiscal year 1973 budget ceiling, established a joint study committee (JSC) to deal with the overall problems of the budget and budget procedures.[9] Its hearings and reports led to Titles I through IX of the Congressional Budget and Impoundment Control Act of 1974, which were cited as the Congressional Budget Act.

There was a second track to deal with the problem of impoundments and controlling the president. These issues were handled by the traditional congressional committees, the Senate Judiciary Committee,[10] and the Government Operations Committees,[11] and the House Rules Committee.[12] The result of their activities was Title X of the act, or the Impoundment Control Act of 1974.

THE JOINT STUDY COMMITTEE

The thirty-two members of the JSC were the most senior and most powerful members of the most powerful congressional committees, with twenty-eight coming from the appropriations and tax-writing committees and four at-large members representing the Joint Economic, Banking, Government Operations Committee, and the Commerce Committee.

The substance of both the JSC's interim[13] and final reports marshaled the evidence, detailed the budget problems, made the indictments, and proposed a framework for the act itself. With respect to the budget problem, the JSC produced the following bill of particulars.

The thirty-seven deficits in the fifty-four years since 1920 illustrated the lack of budget control; presidents themselves had submitted the deficits in thirty-two of those years.[14] The recent increases in the size of the deficits added to the urgency of the problem.[15]

Institutional factors were major contributors to the problems. The plethora of committees[16] and the diffusion of responsibility made it impossible to decide among competing priorities or to view the budget on an overall basis.[17] This often led to funding competing programs when spending cuts should have been made instead.[18] The JSC noted, however, that with respect to programs over which the appropriations committees had jurisdiction, every year for twenty-five years the Congress had provided less money than requested by the president.[19]

The JSC, in defense of the charge that it was unable to shift priorities[20] and the academic charge that incrementalism ruled budget practices, showed that there had been major shifts in priorities for defense, foreign aid, economic security, agriculture, commerce, and transportation spending.[21] Aaron Wildavsky's thesis that "the largest determining factor of the size and content of this year's budget is last year's budget" was in shambles.[22]

The JSC was concerned that not only the economic estimates on which the budget was based but also the testimony on its behalf was dominated by a single source, namely the executive branch—the same party that wanted the money.

The problems of loss of control over the budget by both the Office of Management and Budget (OMB) and the appropriations committees were set forth.[23] This loss of control was attributed to "back-door" spending through borrowing and contract authority and permanent authorizations, the proliferation of grants of credit authority, and the mandatory spending more commonly referred to as "entitlements.[24] Some 75 percent of all budget outlays was now considered "relatively uncontrollable"[25] in the sense that neither the Congress nor the OMB could affect the totals through any means short of a change in the law. This problem was illustrated by the fact that in the previous five years the Congress had cut presidential appropriations requests by about $30 billion, only to find that legislative bills had been passed by the Congress and signed into law by the president that exceeded budget estimates by about $30 billion.[26]

Finally, the JCS noted that the backlog of appropriated funds exceeded the amount of new budget authority[27] (see Figure 7–1 for an updated example of the backlog), that there was no coordination between taxation and spending policies,[28] and that the requirement for the annual authorization of funds was a major cause of delay in passing the appropriations bills.[29] The JSC's recommendations for reform, which in large part formed the basis of the 1974 Budget Act, flowed naturally from this indictment.

$ Billions

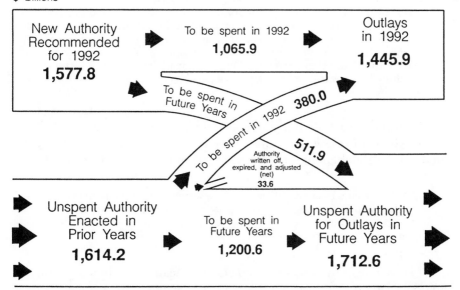

FIGURE 7–1   Relation of Budget Authority to Outlays in the 1992 Budget (*Source: Budget of the United States Government: Fiscal Year 1992* [Washington, D.C.: U.S. Government Printing Office, 1991], pt. 4, p. 206)

CHANGES IN THE CONGRESS

In the same period as the budget war was occurring, basic changes in the fabric of congressional institutions were taking place. These changes both contributed to the problems and made the solutions easier than they would have been in the immediately preceding period, when southern conservatives and their Republican allies dominated the committees and proceedings of the Congress.

The Decline of the South   There was a massive decline in the power of the southern Democrats in the Senate. This "murderers' row" of southern senators, ironically reminiscent of the New York Yankee line-up in its golden days, who were the senior members of the Appropriations Committee and chaired ten of the sixteen standing committees, were themselves mowed down by defeat, age, retirement, death, and revenge.

A sense of the progressive northern senators' frustration with the bipartisan conservative domination of the Appropriations Committee can be seen in this criticism by Senator Paul H. Douglas (D.-Ill.):

> Now I have to say something [about]...the bipartisan, unholy alliance which exists in this body...between the conservative Republicans and the conservative Democrats of the South...the members of the alliance are stronger in the Appropriations Committee, than they are on the floor of the Senate...the Appropriations Committee is one of the strongholds of the alliance; it is one of their castles; and they are saying "Put the fair maiden into this secret recess, separate her from the light of day and let murder or worse things be committed upon her.[30]

And the fiery, hair-shirt, independent senator from Oregon, Wayne Morse, who with Douglas was one of the few who was either independent enough or suicidal enough to take on the committee, put it this way:

> I shall continue to oppose the idea which seems to be developing in the Senate that when the Committee on Appropriations reports a bill God has reported to the Senate and no one ought to raise any questions as to what the Appropriations Committee proposes.[31]

The changes by defeat, retirement, and death brought new and fresh points of view and the appointment of new senior staff members, which created an atmosphere in which other changes could take place in both the geographical balance and political forces in the Senate.

The Rise of the Liberal Democrats   The decline of the South led to the rise in seniority and power of the liberal Democrats, most of them elected after 1956 and especially 1958, when the Democrats increased their control of the Senate from 49–47 to 65–35. The reelection of the Democratic class of 1958 and the influx of Democratic senators in 1964 and 1974 gave power in the Democratic caucus to liberal and progressive senators.

The Progressive Republicans   The third major change was the decline of radical Republicans and the election of more progressive Republicans. Right-wing radical Republicans Joseph R. McCarthy (Wis.), William E. Jenner (Ind.), Karl E. Mundt (S.Dak.), Herman Welker (Idaho), and John Marshall Butler (Md.) were replaced by more moderate and usually more personable senators.

House Changes

In the House, junior members were impatient with seniority, the committee system, and the power of the Bourbons or "pooh bahs" who remained. Like their counterparts in the Senate, many of the latter had retired or died, but in 1973 the impatience of new members and the need for reforms led to the establishment of the Select Committee on Committees led by Congressman Richard Bolling (D.-Mo.) by whose name it became known. While the Bolling Committee's proposals met fierce opposition in 1974, and only some were nominally accepted, the forces that helped create the committee and the unrest of much of the membership helped make possible the budget reforms of 1974.

Among the particular ways in which these changes in the institutions of both the House and the Senate affected the budget problem and the budget solution were the following.

First, impatience and frustration over the power of the Appropriations Committee in the Senate and the traditional forces in the House led a coalition of the progressive and insurgent forces in both parties to bypass the appropriations committees and to provide for social needs and funding for the Great Society programs through "back-door" spending or entitlements.

Second, as orthodox conservatives in both parties were finally rooted out of their long-established and powerful positions by resignation, defeat, or death, they were replaced both on the appropriations committees and on the legislative committees by a coalition of progressive Democrats and Republicans who changed funding priorities.

Third, because of both their frustration over and opposition to the Vietnam War, on the one hand, and their sympathy and support for the social programs (health, housing, education, environment, and aging), on the other, the Congress wrought a major change in budget priorities through its authorizing legislation and its appropriation and other funding. Military spending was decreased, and social spending was proportionately increased.

Fourth, this movement for budget reform coincided with the oil shocks, the rise of stagflation, and the riots and demonstrations over the Vietnam War. President Johnson had earlier pulled out of the 1968 campaign because of the opposition to the war within his own party.

The narrow election of Richard Nixon over Hubert Humphrey in 1968 by 43.4 to 42.7 percent of the popular vote put the Democratic Congress and the Republican president at loggerheads over the conduct of the war and intensified the conflict over spending priorities. Especially after his 1972 campaign, in which he attacked the Congress as spendthrifts, and his overwhelming electoral victory over George McGovern by a 60.7 to 37.5 percent popular vote margin, President Nixon was intent on reversing priorities to increase military spending and reduce the social programs. The Democratic Congress was equally if not more determined to wind down the war, to reduce military spending, and to use the "peace dividend" to fund its social priorities. The retirement and replacement of senior members, the creation of new subcommittees, and the election of more issue-oriented as opposed to power-oriented members made the tasks of creating new institutions and changing old ones easier.

NIXON'S CRISIS-PRODUCING ACTIONS

While these changes were taking place in the Congress, President Nixon took three actions that brought about a crisis in both the presidency and the country, and ultimately led to his resignation because of the immediate and credible threat of his impeachment by the House and his almost certain conviction by the Senate.

First, through transfer, reprogramming, and diverting funds appropriated for one purpose to another purpose, he secretly increased spending for secret bombings and the invasion of Cambodia.

Second, he deferred, rescinded, impounded, or refused to spend funds that the Congress had authorized and approved for both rural and urban domestic programs.

Third, in the name of national security and his inherent or implied powers, his agents broke the law and committed the crimes of burglary and wiretapping against his political enemies. Both he and they compounded these activities by criminal attempts to cover them up and to stonewall against appropriate legal, judicial, and legislative efforts to get at the truth.

It was all a part of a single constitutional crisis, and the budget war cannot be treated separately as a subject alien to the fundamental issues of the usurpation or abuse of the power of the presidency.

Unauthorized Spending in Cambodia

On March 17, 1969, President Nixon authorized the secret bombing of Cambodia. False records were kept to cover up this action. The bombing continued until Cambodia was invaded on April 30, 1970. The invasion provoked perhaps the greatest outcry and dissent during the entire Vietnam War, and resulted in protests throughout the country. At Kent State University in Ohio four students were killed after the National Guard was called out to enforce order. Washington, D.C., was inundated with as many as one hundred thousand students and other protestors. Police swept the streets, and many protestors were thrown in jail or incarcerated at large public holding compounds. Some of these arrests were later found to be improper and lacking in due process. Two more students were killed at Jackson State University in Mississippi.

Later, in November 1972, the Pentagon secretly obligated funds to continue the invasion and bombing of Cambodia, without the knowledge of the Congress or its appropriations committee, for several months, by which time most of the funds had been spent.

As the Congress had never explicitly authorized funds for either the bombing or the invasion of Cambodia, how were the operations financed? The secret bombings preceding the April 1970 invasion were paid for by funds authorized for Air Force operations in Vietnam. Because the records were falsified, the facts were not known until revealed by leaks in 1973, when they represented a *fait accompli*.[32]

Funds for the invasion of Cambodia were provided through the "transfer" authority under the foreign assistance program. The purpose of such authority was to provide flexibility, to enhance efficiency or economy, and to meet changing or emergency needs. No one could argue that transfer authority was provided to secretly bomb or invade Cambodia. Specifically, funds actually earmarked for Taiwan, Turkey, the Philippines, and Greece were diverted to Cambodia under the transfer authority, as were funds provided for "emergencies." There was a clear abuse of congressionally proferred discretion.

In the case of funding the continued war and bombing in Cambodia in 1972 and 1973, the Nixon administration again misused its authority. The Congress had given the Pentagon authority to transfer $750 million in funds from one purpose to another *provided* the House and Senate appropriations committees were notified *and* had explicitly given approval before the funds were used. The funds were obligated in the last two months of 1972, but the Congress was neither informed of nor asked to approve the transfer until February or March of 1973. By the time hearings were held in April 1973, the funds had been spent.

The Nixon administration used a series of arguments and devices to justify the abuses of spending after the fact. First, even though funds were never authorized for the bombings and invasion, it was argued that as the Congress had not specifically denied such use, it was appropriate. Second, when the Congress did provide language to cut off or limit funds for the Vietnam or Asian war, the language was muddied or watered down by asserted congressional intent, by executive branch interpretation, by the threat of a veto or an actual veto, by the assertion of implied or inherent powers of the president as commander in chief to protect forces in the field, or by inaccurate comparison with historical precedents. At times, the excuses and justifications had a patina of truth. At other times, the actions were an arbitrary and brazen use of power.

Arguments are often made by the champions of presidential power that by its control of the purse strings the Congress can stop a war or keep the president from engaging in military action. For several reasons, however, this power is severely limited. First, there is a backlog of a year or more of authorized funds that are available for use by the military without additional congressional approval. Second, even members of the Congress who oppose a military action are reluctant to vote to cut off funds while troops are in the field. Third, given the determination of the Nixon administration to continue the war, cutting off funds would have been ineffective in any case.

The Feed and Forage Act

In a hearing in early June 1972 on the Foreign Assistance and Related Program Appropriations by the Senate Appropriations Committee, the following exchange took place between Senator William Proxmire (D.-Wis.) and Secretary of Defense Melvin R. Laird:

Senator Proxmire: Mr. Secretary, members of this coequal branch, as you properly call it, the Congress, some Members are disappointed that the President has not been able to end the war.... But if this coequal branch which has the power of the purse should refuse to pass any Defense appropriations of any kind, what power would you and the President have after June 30, when the present appropriations expire...to pursue further military actions in Vietnam?...I am talking about no continuing resolution, none. In other words, no action by the Senate or House.

Secretary Laird: If there is not any action by the Senate at all on even a continuing resolution, then the only legislation which would permit us to operate would be the deficiency authorization legislation which was passed at the time of the Civil War which gives to the Department of Defense and to the Commander-in-Chief, the President of the United States, the authority to obligate on a deficiency basis for the subsistence of our military personnel and for other requirements needed to support those military people.

Senator Proxmire: Then could you carry on in Vietnam if the [Congress] refused to make any appropriations?

Secretary Laird: As long as the President approves we could do it to some extent under the deficiency authority and to the extent our inventories permitted.[33]

The law referred to was Section 11 of Title 14 of the United States Code, popularly referred to as the Feed and Forage Act. Its purpose was to provide feed, forage, subsistence, fuel, quarters, and the like for troops and their animals stationed at remote outposts in case the Congress failed to appropriate funds by the new fiscal year. This little-known act of March 2, 1861, was passed during the Civil War so the military would not have to let its troops or animals starve or close down infirmaries, sick bays, and hospitals if congressionally authorized funds were not forthcoming. In 1972 senators were both shocked and amazed to learn that the 1861 authorization of food for animals had been reinterpreted to include jet fuel for airplanes.

Secretary Laird further testified that "there is no limit" to the amounts that could be made available through this act and that short of positive action by the Congress, which could be blocked by a filibuster in the Senate, such funds could be spent.[34]

According to Louis Fisher, during 1960–1972 more than $1.7 billion was obligated under the Feed and Forage Act provisions. Instead of a statute invoked in periods of dire emergency for the purpose it clearly intended, it had become an "open-ended authority, invoked whenever the Department of Defense decides it is time, invoked for whatever amounts the Department thinks necessary."[35]

The abuses of power through the transfer of funds for the Cambodian bombings led to a proposed article of impeachment by the House Judiciary Committee, which asserted that Richard M. Nixon

> on and subsequent to March 17, 1969, authorized, ordered, and ratified the concealment from Congress of the facts and the submission to the Congress of false and misleading statements concerning the existence, scope and nature of American bombing operations in Cambodia in derogation of the power of Congress to declare war, to make appropriations to raise and support armies, and by such conduct warrants impeachment and trial and removal from office.[36]

The article failed in the committee by a vote of 25 to 12. The most persuasive argument against the article was that the president had asserted that he was using his powers as commander in chief to protect troops in the field. In addition, it was argued that the Congress had essentially authorized the use of funds, that the law was insufficiently clear, or that the subsequent lack of action essentially ratified what had occurred.

Nixon's Domestic Impoundments

Beginning in 1971 but particularly immediately following the 1972 election, the president took unprecedented actions to cut, rescind, or impound funds that the Congress had clearly voted for domestic programs. Having campaigned against a big-spending, "credit-card" Congress, President Nixon seemed determined to carry out a mandate provided when he got 60.7 percent of the popular vote,[37] carried all but one state (Massachusetts) and the District of Columbia, and won 520 of the 548 electoral votes.[38] But while he defeated Senator McGovern by 47 million to 29 million votes,[39] the Democrats lost only fifteen seats in the House and picked up two Senate seats. They controlled the House by forty-seven seats (239 to 192) and the Senate by a 57 to 43 margin.[40] While President Nixon had won a mandate over Senator McGovern, the Democratic Congress felt *it* had a mandate as well, justifying at least the historical compromise and comity between the executive and legislative branches.

Flushed with a highly personal electoral victory, the president acted unilaterally and imperially with respect to budget matters. His victory was achieved when he campaigned almost exclusively for himself, backed by the later infamous Committee to Re-elect the President (CREEP), while he largely abandoned his own party candidates for the Senate, the House, and governorships. This was a reversal of the path he had taken to the presidency, when as vice-president and later as candidate for the presidential nomination he campaigned from one end of the country to the other on behalf of his party and its candidates. As a result, he may have felt he owed nothing to anyone but his inner circle of White House retainers. While such a singular individualistic triumph might have led others to treat their defeated opponents with magnanimity and brought a personal sense of security, it had the opposite effect on President Nixon. His opponents were "enemies," and the mandate justified the "plebiscitary presidency."

HUD Grants

The first significant Nixon impoundment preceded his reelection and was made in 1971. In it are found the essential features of those that followed. In addition to its housing programs, the Department of Housing and Urban Development (HUD) carried out its community development functions through a series of categorical grants for such programs as open space, water and sewers, neighborhood facilities, urban renewal, neighborhood development, and model cities. It was proposed that these individual grant programs should be replaced by a community development block grant program under which funds for more general purposes and with fewer strings attached would be expended by formula.

While the specific proposals for the new community development revenue-sharing program had neither been announced nor sent to the Congress, let alone passed and in place, funds for the old programs were impounded in anticipation of the community development block grants, which were not enacted until 1974. As Louis Fisher commented succinctly, "It was familiar doctrine by the Nixon Administration; a proposal to Congress enjoyed a status superior to a public law enacted by Congress.[41]

While these actions raised the most serious legal and constitutional questions, they had their political consequences as well. The clients and constituencies of the programs were not marginally offended: Mayors, city and county managers, township supervisors, builders, developers, environmentalists, and downtown business establishments were outraged.

The Housing Moratorium

Later, on January 5, 1974, shortly after his reelection, President Nixon dropped the other shoe: HUD announced a moratorium on its housing programs, the complementary other half of its community development role. The programs put under the freeze included public housing, the Section 236 rental program, the Section 235 home-ownership program, and a variety of rental and other assistance programs. The action was not preceded by any studies or detailed justifications. It was announced abruptly and implemented arbitrarily. It coincided with the year-end increased bombing in Southeast Asia, which led Senator Proxmire to note that as the administration was going to spend several billion dollars more on bombing Asia and several billion dollars less on housing at home, the effect was to increase the housing shortage in both Asia and the United States. "This," he said, "is reorganizing priorities with a vengeance."[42]

President Nixon's actions politically offended a vast network of community groups, assisted-housing tenants, developers, homebuilders, local and county officials, charitable and eleemosynary institutions, and downtown business groups, the majority of whom to be sure were not his natural political allies, but who included a fairly large proportion of people who were. As the frozen housing and community development programs affected most urban areas, which contained about 70 percent of the population, the actions had widespread political repercussions.

Water Pollution Funds

Not content to provoke only city groups, in November of 1972 President Nixon threw down the gauntlet to another powerful, articulate, and important political constituency. This time he took on the states, the contractors, and environmental groups when he withheld Federal Water Pollution Control Act funds for waste treatment facilities. Some $18 billion over three years was provided through contract authority to the states. The method chosen to fund the program was for the Environmental Protection Agency (EPA) first to allot contract authority to the states. When the plans were approved, the state would enter into contracts for the facilities, and the Congress would liquidate the contract authority in the traditional way as the bills were presented for payments.

The withholding of funds was done in an unusual way. The president ordered EPA Administrator William Ruckleshaus to withhold 50 percent of the state-by-state allotments. Then, on the basis that no allotment had been made, $8 billion of the funding did not go forward. While the language and legislative history allowed some flexibility in the rate of payment, it would have taken a Philadelphia lawyer to argue that the allotments to the states were discretionary. It was a willful, arbitrary, authoritarian decision, particularly as the Congress had mustered more than a two-thirds vote when it overrode the president's veto only a month before he issued his withholding order. President Nixon was at it again.

Farm Program Impoundments

Next, playing the part of Scrooge, President Nixon selected the 1972 Christmas season to cut off four farm programs. It was a period when Congress was out of session. A fifth program was stopped in early January. The five programs—the Rural Environmental Assistance Program (REAP), the Water Bank Program, the Farmers Home Administration (FmHA)

Disaster Loans, the Rural Electrification Administration (REA) direct-loan program, and the Rural Water and Sewer grants—were not without their problems and shortcomings.

Some were a product of the 1930s, and had benefits and interest rates that were anachronisms of the Depression period. A case could have been made to reform features of the programs through presidential proposal and legislative action. Instead, they were stopped in their tracks.

REAP was shut down the morning after Christmas. Since the 1930s, it had provided funds for farmers to take conservation measures to stop soil erosion on hills and gullies by a fifty-fifty matching grant. Some $225 million was involved. Funds for its smaller $10 million Water Bank sister program were shut off. The next day, December 27, a moratorium was placed on applications for the FmHA disaster program. After having advised farmers to delay their applications until the end of the year, a guillotine was dropped without notice. Farmers in fifteen previously designated Minnesota counties were cut off from funding. On December 29, diverted loans for the REA electric and telephone programs were frozen. On January 10, 1973, ten days before inauguration, $120 million in planning and development grants for the FmHA's water and waste disposal programs were stopped. In each case the action was arbitrary and illegitimate, without apparent statutory, constitutional, or historical justification.

Conservatives and liberals, Republicans and Democrats alike, were outraged. Not only did liberal Democrats such as Hubert Humphrey of Minnesota object, but conservative Republicans such as Milton Young of North Dakota spoke out on the Senate floor, in committee hearings, and in public statements outside the Senate. The programs were popular not only in the areas of former Populist ferment in the Old Northwest Territories of the upper Mid West, but among farmers in the prairie states, in southwestern Oklahoma and Texas, in west coast and mountain states, in the old South, in the border states, and in New England's Vermont. Among farm groups, of whom it is said that they vote Republican when they vote their politics and Democratic when they vote their pocketbooks, there was almost universal objection. The outrage transcended political, ideological, and regional lines. President Nixon had now infuriated both liberal and conservative and both urban and rural groups. The ferocity of the public reaction was matched only by the intensity of the speeches of their congressional representatives. The Congress was furious.

President Nixon seemed determined to "stick it" to everybody—the cities, the states, the environmentalists, the housers, the farmers, and the water users. While he was dropping real bombs on the Cambodians and North Vietnamese abroad, he was dropping political bombshells at home. While suspicion and the siege mentality may have led him to impound funds in the first place, his acts of transfer and impoundment brought outcries from so many divergent groups that he was now in fact surrounded by politically hostile forces, largely of his own creation.

JUSTIFICATION AND EXCUSES

The Nixon administration defended the president's actions by a variety of arguments under three general rubrics: (1) the specific language of the authorizing or appropriations acts themselves; (2) general statutory language; and (3) appeals to the Constitution. As James P. Pfiffner noted, the administration claims and justifications provide "the only systematic defense of impoundment as a policy tool because the issue had not been a major source of friction between the president and Congress until the early 1970s.[43]

The administration asserted that under the rural programs the statutory language was discretionary and not mandatory. While it is true that a variety of conditions under existing laws—to effect savings, to enforce civil rights, to avoid spending for purposes not intended—allow discretion in spending, these limitations need not be spelled out in each and every appropriation. The Nixon administration cited no particular language in the bills themselves to justify completely cutting off the funds. Instead the language they cited was routine and discretionary, and provided no specific authority for ending the programs. The Congress replied by removing the discretionary language and substituting the words "shall" for "may" and "is authorized to" in some of them.

The administration extended its defense to more general statutory claims as well. It claimed it had a duty to fight inflation, and used the Employment Act of 1946 to justify impoundment actions under the FmHA disaster program.[44] Administration representatives invoked the budget ceiling, the debt ceiling, and the necessity to avoid tax increase as justifications. They cited the Economic Stabilization Act of 1970, under which the president was granted vast authority to control prices, wages, and other economic activities.

But none of these acts gave the president the specific power to impound these funds and to stop these programs. In fact, the Employment Act of 1946 makes no mention of "inflation" or "counteracting inflationary pressures," and its authors had specifically refused to mention inflation as a goal for fear conservatives would use that to justify the defeat of the employment goals of the act.

Finally, the impoundments were justified on constitutional grounds, which included the separation of powers, inherent and implied powers, and the precedents of other presidents. But in the past the courts had turned down such constitutional assertions of powers, as in the seizure of the steel mills by President Truman. Other cases, such as *in re Neagle*[45] and *in re Debs*,[46] were quite dissimilar and provided no specific precedent for the Nixon actions. Thomas Jefferson's deferral of funds for gunboats was not an absolute impoundment of funds, and would have been clearly appropriate under both the practices and laws of 1974, and hence provided no clear analogy.[47] Other presidents, such as Kennedy, had worked out compromises with the Congress. It is possible that the president, as commander in chief, might have more authority over military than over civilian impoundments, but the Nixon impoundments, as opposed to the transfer of funds for the Cambodian bombings, did not involve that issue.

The Nixon impoundments had no precedents in the history of the United States. As Louis Fisher wrote, they were unprecedented in their scope and severity.[48] In the past, "the issue of impoundments was of sporadic interest" and "in each case the political system made the necessary adjustments to accommodate the actions."[49] Under President Nixon, confrontation was substituted for comity and compromise. His impoundments differed from those of the past in that they were made on a massive scale against specific provisions of the law, and were intended to end programs entirely, and to further budget and national priorities that the president promoted over the opposition of the Congress.

PARALLELS IN THE ORIGINS OF THE 1921 AND 1974 BUDGET ACTS

The parallels in the events that led to the Budget and Accounting Act of 1921 and the Budget and Impoundment Control Act of 1974 are striking in their similarities and critical in their differences.

After a century in which budget surpluses were the rule rather than the exception, the twenty-six years from 1894 to 1920 saw almost twice as many deficit years (seventeen) as surplus years (nine). In 1974 the JSC complained of deficits in thirty-seven of the preceding fifty-four years and especially of their recent growth in size.

In both eras, there was concern for the rise in the general level of spending. From the end of the Civil War until 1898, budget outlays never reached $400 million a year. From then until the start of World War I, peacetime budgets grew steadily and increased from the $500 million to the $750 million level, or almost double the previous highest annual peacetime outlays. After World War II, the general level of budget outlays went up from $35 billion in fiscal year 1947 to $332 billion in fiscal year 1975, or nine to ten times.

There was a similar pattern in the concern over these budget facts in both the Congress and the country as a whole. There was considerable political churning, and each period was characterized by the appointments of a series of committees or commissions to examine the problem and seek a solution. In both eras the country perceived a budget crisis and moved to solve it.

Each budget crisis was coincidental with and brought to a head by a war that greatly expanded expenditures, increased deficits, and set off inflationary pressures.

In both periods there was a consensus between Republicans and Democrats, between liberals and conservatives, and in the country as a whole. Some have suggested that conservative Republican support for reform of congressional procedures combined with liberal Democratic support for impoundment controls to produce the 1974 Act. Richard Pious wrote that "just before the Nixon administration fell the Congress passed the Budget Reform and Impoundment Control Act, which established expenditure control provisions (to satisfy Republicans) and new provisions limiting presidential impoundments (to satisfy Democrats)."[50] But an examination of the reaction to President Nixon's impoundments, the recommendations of the JSC, and the key votes on the act and its components indicate that the Congress's effort to discipline itself and the president had strong bipartisan support. Except for President Nixon and his beleaguered White House forces, there was virtual unanimity among political groups. Except for the military, almost all domestic political forces—urban and rural, liberal and conservative, Democratic and Republican—had been the victims of the Nixon impoundments and were concerned about congressional budget impotence.

There was yet another internal congressional parallel: In both eras there was a shift in power among congressional committees. In 1921 a number of individual legislative committees that had exercised power over both the authorizing legislation and appropriations gave up power to the appropriations committees. The shift was eased by placing three ex officio members of the Senate foreign relations, armed services, argiculture, public works, post office, and District of Columbia committees on the Senate Appropriations Committee with the power to vote when the money for agencies under the jurisdictions of their committees was involved.[51] In 1974 the appropriations committees surrendered power to the new budget committees of the House and Senate. In the House, provision was made for members of the Appropriations Committee and the Ways and Means Committee to serve on the new Budget Committee, but in the Senate no such provision was made.

If there were historical parallels between the eras, there were also major historical differences. In 1921 the Congress delegated massive congressional constitutional budget powers to the president. In 1974 the purpose but not the major substance of the act was to retrieve a portion of that power from a combative president who had substituted confrontation for compromise.

A second major difference was that while both acts were the products of a budget crisis, the 1974 act was the child of a constitutional crisis as well. It is not without note that the key congressional figure of the Watergate hearings (which culminated in the exposure of criminal wrongdoing and cover-up by the Nixon administration), Democratic Senator Sam Ervin of North Carolina, was also the key figure in the Senate hearings over impoundments conducted jointly by the Judiciary Subcommittee on Separation of Powers and the Ad Hoc Subcommittee on Impoundment of Funds of the Government Operations Committee. When the Senate sought the most knowledgeable senator to run the Watergate investigation, it chose the senator with the most knowledge of the Nixon administration impoundments and the justifications and excuses given for them.

THE CONGRESSIONAL BUDGET AND IMPOUNDMENT CONTROL ACT OF 1974

The 1974 Budget Act was written by the Congress for two reasons: (1) to discipline itself by implementing the proposals of the JSC, and (2) to retrieve budget power from the president by erecting procedures to end the abuse of unauthorized spending and illegal impoundments.

The 1974 Budget Act is a political document, crafted by politicians after its provisions were examined and organized by several House, Senate, and joint committees. It has since been amended by the Gramm-Rudman-Hollings Act of 1985 and further amendments in 1987 and 1990, but to comprehend present procedures one must understand the 1974 act. There are things the act did and did not do. It did not provide a congressional budget that competes in volume and detail with the president's budget. Instead it set up a procedure for the Congress to regain control over the budget. It gave the Congress, for the first time, a method to examine the budget totals before passing on the parts. It did not call for a balanced budget, but for the appropriate level of revenues and expenditures in the light of economic and other conditions. The act established a new fiscal year that started October 1 instead of July 1.

The act did not do away with any existing institutions. Instead it erected a new superstructure on the existing framework. It established two budget committees, each with its own staff. It set up a Congressional Budget Office (CBO), with a director to provide the Congress with a source of information equal to that provided for the president by the OMB and superior to that provided for the Congress by the OMB. It also established a budget timetable, since modified: in stage 1, information is provided; in stage 2, action is taken. The critical dates provided under the original act were: (1) the presentation of the president's budget fifteen days after the Congress convenes in January; (2) action on the first congressional concurrent resolution on the budget by May 15; (3) action on the second and binding concurrent resolution on the budget by September 15; (4) action on a reconciliation bill or resolution by September 25; and (5) the beginning of a new fiscal year on October 1.

The two concurrent resolutions are not in the form of a law passed by the Congress and signed by the president. Instead, they are an agreement between the two houses of the Congress and among each house and its committees and members.

Finally, the act provided for impoundment procedures. These differ, depending on whether the president defers or rescinds funds.

The Gramm-Rudman-Hollings Act, which is explained in detail in Chapter 9, originally called for accelerating the budget timetable by a month.

WHAT HAS CONGRESS WROUGHT?

The political document that is the Congressional Budget and Impoundment Control Act of 1974 is the result of political compromise, and was neatly and masterfully fashioned by what Adam Smith approvingly called "the skill of that insidious and crafty animal vulgarly called a...politician."[52]

It followed the general outline of the proposals the JSC made in both its interim report of February 7, 1973,[53] and its final report submitted ten weeks later on April 18, 1973.[54] The recommendations were translated into bills,[55] and four additional committees and several astute and constructive politicians crafted those proposals into the final act. The benefits of public discussion, public compromise, and political procedures have seldom been as clearly demonstrated. In both its elements and its totality, the act is an organized, logical, and at times even artistic political document.

Along its legislative route from the JSC to final passage, professional politicians and journeymen legislators applied their skills. The House Rules Committee, under Congressman Richard Bolling's (D.-Mo.) leadership, modified the proposals to diminish the role of the conservative tax and spending committees to make the act not only palatable but ultimately coveted by the more representative and less conservative House as a whole.

In the Senate, three committees and four of their members crafted the major substantive provisions. Senator Lee Metcalf (D.-Mont.), with the help of Senator Edmund Muskie (D.-Maine) and a sterling staff, held hearings in the Subcommittee on Budgeting, Management and Expenditures of the Government Operations Committee. The Subcommittee made two major contributions to the act. It diminished the monopoly that the Finance and Appropriations Committee dominated Joint Study Committee members recommended for themselves on the proposed budget committees. It also proposed the Congressional Budget Office in lieu of a Joint Budget Committee staff to serve the House and Senate. Like Bolling's action in the House, this was also a move to broaden the political support for the act, as both the finance and appropriations committees were not only dominated by senior members but effectively excluded their own junior members and most of the Congress from their activities.

Senator Sam Ervin, who later became famous by chairing the Watergate Committee, was the architect of the anti-impoundment procedures through his positions as chairman of both the Subcommittee on the Separation of Powers of the Judiciary Committee and his chairmanship of the Government Operations Committee itself.

The final and critical Senate ingredients were fashioned by the hearings on S. 1541 held by the Senate Rules Committee[56] and the part played by majority whip Senator Robert Byrd (D.-W.Va.). By universalizing participation and touching virtually all the political bases, he crafted that a consensus ultimately led to the unanimous passage of the bill by a vote of 80 to 0 in the Senate on March 22, 1974. The House bill, H.R. 7130, had passed the House the previous December 5, 1973, by a 386-to-23 margin. After the Conference Committee met and worked out the differences between the bills, particularly over the impoundment provisions, the House passed the conference report on June 18 by 401 to 6, and the Senate agreed on June 21 by a 75-to-0 vote.

Seldom has an important and controversial subject affecting both relations with the president and power in the Congress received such unanimity where such fundamental issues were concerned.

MAJOR PRINCIPLES OF THE ACT

There are some things the act did do and some things it did not do. It did not provide for a congressional budget. There is no annual 660-page document called *The Congressional Budget of the United States* containing a budget message, descriptions of programs, detailed budget accounts, and summary tables to rival the president's *Budget of the United States.* No congressional press office issues a *Budget in Brief* to dazzle the public, press, and media, or a 2,000-page *Appendix* to provide the accountants, budget officers, and congressional committee staffs with back-up materials. To the degree that such alternative information is produced, it is found in a variety of CBO or budget, appropriations, taxing, and legislative committees' reports or staff documents. And even though the act does regularize some congressional information, much of it is not only diffused in source but unpredictable in timing.

What the act sought to provide was a procedure, quite independent of the president, whereby the Congress could regain control over the budget. The procedure initially set overall, nonbinding targets and ultimately overall and specific binding limitations on budget provisions. The act established a procedure to carry out the JSC's recommendation that the Congress be allowed to "examine extensively the whole budget with the purpose of passing judgment on whether the totals are satisfactory or whether the relationship of the various parts, one to another, is satisfactory.[57]

Specifically, initial tentative targets and ultimately binding ceilings were set for both budget outlays (what is to be spent in the fiscal year) and budget authority (amounts available in the present and future years). They were also set for the surplus or deficit. The recommended levels of federal revenues, the appropriate level of the public debt, and the amounts by which the statutory limits on the public debt should be increased were also established. The procedures dealt in an overall way with the totality of the budget, present and future spending, revenues, the surplus or deficit, and the level of the public debt as called for by the JSC.

The Budget Act did *not* provide for or call for either a balanced budget or a reduction in the public debt, even though the JSC used the large number of unbalanced budgets and the massive rise in the debt and deficits to illustrate the basic problem of lack of congressional control over the budget.

Instead the act provided for a procedure in the First Concurrent Budget Resolution to set forth the surplus or deficit *"which is appropriate in the light of economic conditions and all other relevant factors"* (italics added).[58] This provided for a countercyclical fiscal policy.

In addition to the overall targets and ceilings, it provided for specific targets and goals as well. The Congress designates both budget outlays (O) and new budget authority (BA) for "each major functional category in the budget. The nineteen budget functions—such as national defense, international affairs, commerce and housing credit, income security, and health—have both overlapping committee jurisdictions and somewhat general connotations. By designating targets and ceilings for broad categories, the power of the legislative and appropriations committees to determine specific budget priorities for matters under their jurisdiction, in theory at least, was not usurped by the budget committees.

The act also created a new fiscal year, to run from October 1 to September 30 rather than from July 1 to June 30. This was done to prevent the delay in appropriations bills occasioned by the two-step legislative practice that required a legislative authorization bill to precede the appropriations of funds. The JSC had noted the major increase in the number of one-year authorizations that required an annual renewal before the funds could be provided and the appropriations bill passed.[59] The JSC compilation showed that nine of thirteen bills were affected.[60] Authorizations were often delayed into the new fiscal year, but once authorized, the funding followed in a very short time. By essentially extending the period for authorizing bills until a week after Labor Day, an additional two and one-half months after the president's budget was proposed, the funding for all departments could be completed by the start of the new year.

The Budget Act did not do away with any existing institutions. Instead, it built new institutions to complement those already in place. It was an application of political principle by political practitioners who had learned early in their climb to political power that granting benefits or extending authority is feasible, while reducing, denying, or cutting off existing benefits or authority is either impossible or extraordinarily difficult. The architects of the act followed the maxim so often iterated by President Kennedy, applicable to economic and political policy alike, that "a high tide floats all the boats." While there were some shifts in congressional power arrangements, the political method used was one of addition and not subtraction.

NEW SUPERSTRUCTURE

The new superstructure created by the act consisted of the following major additions.

First, two new budget committees were created, one in the House and one in the Senate, each with its own staff. The Act originally provided for a twenty-three-member committee in the House and a fifteen-member committee in the Senate, and limited the length of membership in the House. These provisions were enacted by amending the rules of both the House and the Senate, which have since been further amended by each house to provide larger memberships and more generous tenure. In the One-Hundred-Second Congress, the House Budget Committee had thirty-five members and its Senate counterpart had twenty-three. The provision for individual staffs provided for independence from the CBO and guaranteed staff support for less senior members. It was also in keeping with the general thrust of the time, for in the 1970s the number of congressional staff members was doubled to provide more resources and expertise to the Congress.

Second, the CBO was created to give the Congress an independent source for both budget information and economic estimates. In the past, the Congress had to rely on the president's budget office, which, although a professional agency, is headed by a partisan political appointee, is biased in its estimates, is loyal to the president and his programs, and is secretive about information that might reflect adversely on either it or the president.

Even many critics of the CBO concede that the budget office is almost always more reliable than the Administration's Office of Management and Budget in estimating revenues and spending and in forecasting the rates of inflation, unemployment, and real economic growth. This is true in part

> because any Administration is a partisan advocate in the budget game; it inevitably paints a rosy economic picture as part of its campaign to sell the President's tax and spending programs.[61]

The act calls for the speaker of the House and the president *pro tempore* of the Senate to appoint the CBO director after considering recommendations from the budget committees. The director has a four-year term with the power of removal by resolution passed by either house. The term begins on January 3, or the same day the Congress convenes, so that it overlaps each presidential term by two years.

Under the act, the CBO assists the Congress and its committees in a hierarchical fashion. It is required to provide information and assistance to the budget committees. The two appropriations committees and the Ways and Means and Finance Committees are next in line, and, on request, the CBO "shall provide . . . any information which will assist it in the discharge of matters within its jurisdiction," particularly with respect to any bills providing budget authority or tax expenditures, or with respect to revenues and receipts.

In addition and on request, the CBO is required: (1) to provide to other committees and individual members information given to the budget committees; (2) "to the extent practicable," to provide additional information to other committees on budget, tax, and economic matters; and (3) "to the extent available," to provide additional information to individual members of the House or Senate.

The CBO director has the right to hire experts and consultants to augment the CBO's own staff and "is authorized to secure information, data, estimates, and statistics directly from the various departments, agencies, and establishments of the executive branch of Government and the regulatory agencies and commissions of the government." The law says all such agencies "shall furnish the Director any available material which he determines to be necessary in the performance of his duties and functions," except where it would be a violation of law. The director is authorized to work with and to get information from a variety of congressional institutions as well. The language appears to be strong enough to avoid stonewalling by any but the most recalcitrant agency.

THE NEW BUDGET PROCEDURES: TO DISCIPLINE THE CONGRESS

Title III of the act provides for a "Congressional Budget Process" for the new October 1–September 30 fiscal year. Table 7–1 on page 236 shows the original timetable.[62]

The five major events in the original timetable were: (1) the submission of the president's budget fifteen days after the Congress convenes; (2) the first concurrent resolution on the budget on May 15; (3) the second concurrent resolution on the budget on September 15; (4) the reconciliation bill or resolution of September 25; and (5) the beginning of the new fiscal year on October 1.

THE INFORMATION STAGE

The Current Services Budget   The current services budget is nothing more than the old budget and programs adjusted for inflation and the economic assumptions on which the new budget is based. It assumes no program or policy changes. The date for filing the current services budget has been changed from November 10 to the day the president's budget is released. This was done because experience showed that the economic assumptions on which the new budget was based varied so much in the more than two months between November and the fifteenth day after the Con-

TABLE 7–1 The Congressional Budget Timetable Provided in the Budget and Impoundment Control Act of 1974

On or Before	Action to Be Completed
November 10	President submits current services budget.
15 days after Congress convenes*	President submits his budget.
March 15	Committees and joint committees submit reports to Budget Committees.
April 1	CBO submits report to Budget Committees.
April 15	Budget committees report first concurrent resolution on the budget to their house.
May 15	Committees report bills and resolutions authorizing new budget authority (BA).
May 15*	Congress completes action on first concurrent resolution on the budget.
7 days after Labor Day	Congress completes actions on bills and resolutions providing new budget authority (BA) and spending authority.
September 15*	Congress completes action on second required concurrent resolution on the budget.
September 25*	Congress completes action on reconciliation bill or resolution, or both, implementing second required concurrent resolution.
October 1*	Fiscal year begins.

*Major events

gress convened in January that they were out of date when the new budget was released. It is presently presented as part of the Budget.[63]

Committee Statements of Budget Requirements   By March 15 (now six weeks after the president submits his budget), the standing committees of both the House and the Senate and the key joint committees (the Joint Economic and the Joint Taxation Committees) report their statements of budget requirements to the budget committees. These include committee budget estimates as contrasted with those of the president, the estimates for new budget authority and outlays for the year beginning the following October 1 that the committees intend to act on, and five-year projections of outlays and budget authority (or revenues in the case of the taxation committees) for programs under their jurisdiction. Because of the early deadline, these estimates are very rough and generally exaggerated.

The CBO Report   The CBO's report to the Budget Committees is of greater importance. Now due February 15, it is required under Section 202(f) of the act. The report often clashes with the president's budget estimates. The CBO's report must include "alternative levels" of spending, taxes, surpluses, and deficits based on its estimates and projections of economic factors. The purpose is to keep the president's budget estimates and economic projections honest. The CBO report not only provides an alternative but generally a more objective basis on which the budget committees can set forth the budget levels mandated under the act.

As the CBO's first director, Alice M. Rivlin, told the *Los Angeles Times:*

> We're mainstream, middle-of-the-road people. You won't find any extreme supply-side views coming out of the CBO. No one here expected that the [Reagan-backed] tax cut would increase government revenues or lead to an instant surge of investment. And I don't make any apologies for those nonexpectations.[64]

The Report of New Budget Authority The 1974 act required that legislative committees report all bills and resolutions authorizing new budget authority before the first concurrent resolution has been passed. Such bills, as well as those providing new spending authority or changes in revenues or public debt limits (but excluding entitlements), could not be considered until agreement had been reached on the First Concurrent Budget Resolution. These tough proposals were diluted in the Senate, which provided a Budget Committee "waiver" if authorizing bills were reported after May 15.

Nevertheless, with all the imperfections, the requirements for the (1) current services budget, (2) the legislative and joint committee reports, (3) the CBO report on the president's budget and its alternative budget estimates and economic forecasts, and (4) the reporting of bills providing new budget authority, armed the Congress and the budget committees with essential knowledge and information that had been unavailable in the past.

THE FIRST CONCURRENT BUDGET RESOLUTION: THE ACTION STAGE

The hearings of the budget committees and the floor debate on the First Concurrent Budget Resolution are the focal points of the Budget Act. The critical data are set forth in Section 301(a) of the act:

> On or before May 15th [now April 15th] of each year, the Congress shall complete action on the first concurrent resolution on the budget for the fiscal year beginning on October 1 of such year.

This is the cornerstone of the act. While it provides for change and modifications later, decisions taken on this first resolution establish the ground rules for the year. The procedure, unlike its executive department counterpart, is open and public, and rivets attention on budget issues as no behind-the-scenes consideration could do. To use Woodrow Wilson's phrase, the First Concurrent Budget Resolution is an "open convenant...openly arrived at."[65] It is both the culmination of one procedure—information gathering— and the beginning of another—action on the budget itself. It is the keystone which holds the fabric together, and its timing in relation to other events is critical.

Not a Law   The budget resolution does not have the status of a law. It does not change the way in which the president puts his budget together. It is a concurrent resolution that affects only the internal relations of the Congress. Congressional precedents provide that:

> Concurrent resolutions are commonly used by both Houses to take action within the scope of the power of the two bodies acting jointly.
> Concurrent resolutions do not embody legislation; otherwise under the Constitution they would have to be submitted to the President for his signature.[66]

Framework for Decision   The budget resolution is a framework within which the Congress makes its budget decisions, determines its budget priorities, and makes budget allocations. It is an agreement between the House and the Senate and between each house and its committee and members as to the actions each will take in considering those parts of the budget over which each has jurisdiction.

Multiyear Provisions   Until modified by the five-year agreement of 1990, the budget resolution provided levels not only for the new fiscal year beginning October 1, but for two years into the future. In addition, it could revise the figures for the existing year. For example, the budget resolution for fiscal year 1990 provided estimates not only for the 1990 budget but for the 1991 and 1992 budgets as well. It also could revise the figures for the fiscal year 1989 budget. It was in effect the first budget resolution for fiscal year 1990 and could be the revised budget resolution for fiscal year 1989. That could occur under Section 304 of the act, which provides that:

> At any time after the first concurrent resolution...for a fiscal year...and before the end of such fiscal year, the two Houses may adopt a concurrent resolution on the budget which revises the concurrent resolution on the budget for such fiscal year most recently agreed to.

This was important because this minor and little noticed provision, along with the reconciliation provisions, was seized upon by the Reagan administration in its first two years to enact the Reagan budget revolution (see Chapter 8). Together they had an importance beyond the language of the provisions and provided a major innovation in the budget procedures of the Congress.

Specifically, the first budget resolution provides:

1. The recommended levels of federal revenues and the amounts by which they should be changed.
2. The appropriate level of total new budget authority (BA).
3. The appropriate level of total budget outlays (O).
4. The budget amounts of appropriate deficits or surpluses in the light of economic conditions and other relevant factors.
5. The appropriate levels of the public debt as well as the amounts by which the temporary statutory limits on the debt should be increased.

In addition, the resolution states the amounts by which the levels of revenues should be increased or decreased, the appropriate reductions in outlays or increases in revenues to ensure the solvency of the Social Security trust funds, the appropriate levels of total federal credit activities, and since 1985 the revenue and outlay figures needed to meet the Gramm-Rudman-Hollings deficit reduction schedules, as amended (see Table 10–10).

The spending and loan totals are then distributed among nineteen major functional categories. The last two categories are called "allowances" and "undistributed offsetting receipts." The latter provide for both contingencies and intergovernment transfers of funds—for example, the treasury's interest payments to the Social Security trust funds.

Action on Appropriations and Authorization Bills   After the passage of the first budget resolution, action on both the appropriations bills and bills providing for new budget authority begins and under the original act was to be completed by the seventh day after Labor Day. The authorizing bills should be taken up and passed as soon as possible in order to provide the new authority the appropriations committees need to act. On appropriations bills, the House acts first. Meanwhile, the Senate is not inactive. Generally the Senate appropriations subcommittees have long since completed hearings and made tentative judgments on funding. They move to "mark-up" any House-passed bill on the first working day after House passage and are able to complete action on most bills within one or two weeks. In recent years the Senate Appropriations Committee has reported bills to the Senate even before they were passed in the House.

One reason for extending the new fiscal year to October 1 was to allow the authorizing and appropriations committees time to complete their work and to take an overall view. The legislative history of the act includes the assumption that these actions would be completed on time and that the budget committees might in fact file the second resolution even during the August recess.[67] Unfortunately, in some recent fiscal years not one appropriations bill has been passed by the Congress and signed by the president before the beginning of the new fiscal year.

THE SECOND CONCURRENT BUDGET RESOLUTION

With action on the appropriations bills and new budget authority completed by seven days after Labor Day, and with all the facts and totals in hand, the original act calls on the Congress to either ratify or adjust its action through a *binding* second budget resolution by September 15, or only fifteen days before the new fiscal year begins.

The second budget resolution, under Section 310 of the act, states that "the Committees on the Budget of each House shall report to its House a concurrent resolution on the budget which *reaffirms* or *revises* the concurrent resolution . . . most recently agreed to" (emphasis added). The provision calls for the resolution to specify the total amount by which budget and spending authority within the jurisdiction of a committee "is to be changed," and to "direct that committee to determine and recommended changes to accomplish a change of such total amount." The resolution also "directs" committees with jurisdiction over revenues and over the statutory limit on the public debt—namely, the House Ways and Means Committee and the Senate Finance Committee—to determine and recommend changes to accomplish a change in the total amounts.

Over the years the second concurrent resolution has been abandoned and the first resolution has become the binding resolution, first by practice and then by law. The Congress found it impossible to cut expenditures and/or raise taxes in the fifteen days between the passage of the second resolution and the beginning of the new fiscal year. The issues were too contentious and controversial to meet that deadline.

THE RECONCILIATION BILL OR RESOLUTION

The reconciliation procedure under the act is designed to carry out the second budget resolution. Either by a bill or by a resolution, the House and Senate direct their legislative committees to act. The original procedure was as follows.

First, the budget resolution setting forth the revised figures for both the total and the functions is passed. Second, that resolution directs committees with jurisdiction over the budget items that are to be revised to submit their recommendations to the budget committees of their respective houses. For example, Section 2(c) of S. Con. Res. 48, the fiscal 1988 budget resolution in the Senate, provided the following directions to the Senate Committee on Armed Services:

> (c) The Senate Committee on Armed Services shall report changes in laws within its jurisdiction . . . sufficient to reduce budget authority and outlays . . . as follows: $0 in budget authority and $770,000,000 in outlays in fiscal year 1988, $0 in budget authority and $2,366,000,000 in outlays in fiscal year 1989, $0 in

budget authority and $4,007,000,000 in outlays in fiscal year 1990, and $0 in budget authority and $6,031,000,000 in outlays in fiscal year 1991.

Similar instructions were given to ten additional committees.

After the House and Senate conference committee compromises the differences between the two Houses, the committees meet and make the changes as directed. The law gives the committees discretion to make the cuts in any area under their jurisdiction and hence preserve their independence and integrity. This is often more true in theory than in fact, however. When the amounts directed to be cut are large and the discretion of a committee is limited by what can be cut, the effect of the Budget Committee direction approved by the House or Senate is to cut a particular program, such as dairy price supports, subsidized housing, or retirement benefits for government military and civilian retirees.

After making the changes, the committee reports. If the House Armed Services Committee were the only committee involved, it would report a bill or a resolution directly to the House. If directions were given to several committees, the recommendations would be reported to the House Budget Committee, which packages the cuts and reports them in a single bill or resolution to the parent body. As Section 310(c) of the Budget Act states, each budget committee,

> upon receiving all such recommendations shall report to its House a reconciliation bill or reconciliation resolution, or both, carrying out all such recommendations without any substantive revision.

What is the distinction between reporting a bill or a resolution? A reconciliation bill makes changes in a law. A reconciliation resolution "is a concurrent resolution directing the Clerk of the House of Representatives or the Secretary of the Senate...to make specified changes in bills and resolutions which have not been enrolled"—that is, those that have passed the Congress but have not yet been sent to the president. This is contemplated at this stage of the budget procedures, particularly for appropriations bills.

The Budget Committee then reports to its house the reconciliation bill or resolution, or both. The provisions that change existing laws or provide new laws are sent to the president for signature. The provisions changing bills not yet enrolled are sent to the clerk of the House or to the secretary of the Senate, as the case may be, with directions to change the provisions before the bills are enrolled.

This procedure was proposed by Charles Schultze in testimony before the House Rules Committee. It is borrowed from the Budget Bureau itself, which uses similar directions from the president to the various bureaus and agencies to bring the parts of the president's budget in line with the agreed-on totals before it is sent to the Congress. It represents a unique and innovative legislative action.[68]

In its narrow sense, reconciliation is the method used to balance a personal checking account, and this connotation is indeed the sense of the Budget Act procedure with respect to bringing the parts of the budget into a proper relationship to the whole. But in its broader sense reconciliation is a method of patching up a domestic quarrel, of reaching an agreement between two bickering neighbors or warring countries. The procedure as initially contemplated under the Budget Act would not only bring the numbers into balance but provide a means to restore harmony among the jurisdictions of the Congress.

In addition, by giving members of the House and Senate the opportunity to vote on the total amounts instead of the mere details of cuts, in the consideration of both the budget resolutions and the reconciliation bills, the act provides a method of cutting the "sacred cows" not available under previous procedures.

Without specific direction from each house of the Congress as a whole to its committees, under either the budget resolutions or the reconciliation instructions, it would be virtually impossible to get the key committees with jurisdiction over health, retirement, farm subsidies, housing, public works, and other politically popular programs to cut these programs. The reconciliation method gives individual members the political argument, or excuse, of saying, "I voted to cut the budget by $8.2 billion," not a particular program, as the Senate did the first time it passed a reconciliation bill.[69] Previously the legislative committees often dictated policy to their respective houses. They were packed with strong supporters of the specific programs, the clients for whom were often political allies or contributors or represented interests in the committee members' home states or districts. The reconciliation provision of the Budget Act restores the principle that the committees should be the agents of their respective houses, rather than letting the House and Senate be agents of and dominated by their respective committees.

When the act was passed, it was thought that if action were completed by September 25 there would be sufficient time before the start of the new fiscal year on October 1 for the president to sign a reconciliation bill into law and for the House and Senate to make adjustments in their appropriations bills, to enroll them, and to send them to the White House. In practice, however, this became impossible and is another reason that reconciliation is now done on the first budget resolution.

In summary, the basic goal of the act with respect to the Congress is to provide adequate information, to set up a timetable, to enable the Congress to place limits on the fiscal action it can take, and to provide parliamentary procedures to enable the Congress to discipline itself and to regain control over the budget.

Under the Budget Act, the Congress erected a structure that it believed, if carried out, would accomplish these purposes. In its conception, compromises, and ultimate provisions, it was a masterful legislative accomplishment. How it has worked in practice is discussed in Chapters 8–10.

IMPOUNDMENT PROCEDURES: TO RETRIEVE POWER FROM THE PRESIDENT

The act also provided a means of disciplining the president through Title X, the impoundment control procedures.

Some critics question whether the enactment of impoundment controls did not grant new powers to the president. Did it delegate to the president powers to control the purse strings that the Constitution specifically gave to the Congress? The Congress was sufficiently concerned with this issue to begin Title X with a disclaimer:

> Sec. 1001. Nothing contained in this Act, or in any amendment made by this Act, shall be construed as—
> (1) asserting or conceding the constitutional powers or limitations of either the Congress or the President;
> (2) ratifying or approving any impoundment heretofore or hereafter executed or approved by the President or any other Federal officer or employee, except insofar as pursuant to statutory authorization then in effect;
> (3) affecting in any way the claims or defenses of any party to litigation concerning any impoundment; or
> (4) superseding any provision of law which requires the obligation of budget authority or the making of outlays thereunder.

The disclaimer was made because numerous issues concerning impoundment were still in the courts. On the whole, the Congress had won its impoundment conflicts with the president and had no intention of giving the president new arguments by virtue of Title X.

But the disclaimer was important and necessary because after the passage of the Anti-Deficiency Act of 1905 and its amendments in 1906 and 1950, the Congress did permit the executive branch to impound or limit spending for specific purposes and under certain conditions. The intent of the original 1905 Act was to prevent agencies from spending all their money in the first half or three-quarters of a fiscal year and then blackmailing the Congress for added funds on grounds the mail would not be delivered, the fleet would be stranded at the far corners of the earth, or the Washington Monument would be shut down at the height of the tourist season. Apportionment of funds was required or allowed by months or quarters to prevent such abuse. There were seasonal requirements for funds, and it was obviously against the public interest to continue spending when the original purpose of the appropriation had either been attained or was unobtainable. The funding by the Congress did not require either that funds be wasted when purposes had been accomplished or that good money be thrown after bad.

Also, by practice, agencies set aside reserves to make sure that funds would be available in the late months of the year. The 1950 amendments confirmed and codified a number of these practices.

Because the discretion the Congress provided the executive was abused, the impoundment control provisions of the 1974 act amended the Anti-Deficiency Act to limit presidential discretion.[70]

In 1950, the Congress gave the president power to impound funds to save money because of "changes in requirements," "greater efficiency of operations," or "other developments." What President Nixon did that was unique was to cancel entire programs, a purpose certainly not intended or sanctioned by the Congress except for the reasonable purposes that were permitted by the Anti-Deficiency Act or that had been agreed to or acquiesced to in practice. Because the Nixon administration used the "other developments" provision of the Anti-Deficiency Act to justify numerous impoundments, that provision was repealed by Title X of the 1974 act.

The Congress also provided that "reserves" may be established "solely to provide for contingencies, or to effect savings" when that was made possible by changes in requirements or greater efficiency of operations. The act further provided that "no reserves shall be established" except as "specifically" provided by "particular appropriations Acts or other laws." Further, "reserves established pursuant" to the impoundment provisions of the act "shall be reported to Congress." The Congress applied the maxim "Fool me once, shame on you; fool me twice, shame on me," and withdrew the discretion it had granted presidents from 1905 to 1974.[71]

After much confusion over the differences between slowing down of spending, the apportionment of funds, or the establishment of reserves to effect savings or to bring greater efficiency, on the one hand, and the cancellation of entire programs, on the other, the Congress finally made the distinction. It established separate categories and procedures to deal with differences between the deferral and the rescission of funds.

Deferral and Rescission

The *deferral* of funds was defined as an action or inaction that *temporarily* withholds, delays, or effectively precludes the obligation or expenditure of budget authority (including contract authority) or the establishment of reserves under the Anti-Deficiency Act for a particular fiscal year.

A *rescission* was defined as a situation in which funds in a whole or in part, will not be used at all, as when a project is cancelled.[72]

Section 1012(a) and Section 1013(a) of the act require the president to transmit a special message whenever the president determines that funds should either be deferred or rescinded. The president must specify the amounts involved; the account, department, or establishment of the government to which the budget authority is available for obligation and the specific project or function involved; in the case of a deferral, the period involved; the reasons the funds should be deferred or rescinded; the fiscal, economic, and budgetary effects of the proposed action; and the facts, circumstances, and considerations relating to or bearing upon the decision and its effect on the purposes and programs for which the money was originally provided.

In the case of a deferral, the president can defer or reserve the funds unless either house passes an "impoundment resolution" disapproving such proposed deferral. There is no time limit on when either house of the Congress can act, but as no deferral can be proposed to extend beyond the existing fiscal year, the Congress would have to act before October 1. Simply put, the president can defer the funds unless the Congress objects.

With respect to a rescission, both houses must take affirmative action before the end of forty-five calendar days of continuous session of the Congress. Days during a *sine die* adjournment or periods in excess of three days when either house is out of session do not count. The Congress takes action by means of a rescission bill. Simply put, the president cannot rescind funds unless the Congress approves. No bill, no rescission.

The act makes changes in the rules of the House and Senate to make sure that dilatory tactics cannot prevent action on either an impoundment resolution or a rescission bill. Other provisions grant authority to the comptroller general to review the president's special messages and to report to the House and Senate on the facts and effects of the proposed deferral or rescission, and, in the case of a deferral, whether it is in accordance with existing statutory authority. The purpose is to determine whether there is any justification at all for the proposed action or whether the president is rescinding funds in the name of deferral.

The comptroller general is given another important duty. If the president or any other officer orders funds to be either deferred or reserved, or has failed to report that they have been deferred or reserved by way of a special message, the comptroller general makes a report giving the facts and effects otherwise required in a special message, as he knows them (Sec. 1015).

Further, if funds are not made available for obligation, the comptroller general is "expressly empowered" to act "through attorneys of his own choosing" to bring a civil action in the U.S. District Court of the District of Columbia to require that the budget authority be made available for obligation. The act empowers the courts to enter appropriate orders to make the budget authority available and to give precedence to civil actions brought under the act. The provision that the comptroller general is "expressly empowered" to act "through attorneys of his own choosing" is a salutary provision. In numerous cases, the attorney general has failed to act on information or requests from the comptroller general, who is an agent of the Congress, against officials or agencies of the executive branch.

The impoundment control procedures are tailored to meet the specific occasions that might arise. They distinguish between a deferral and a rescission, and provide both the Congress and the comptroller general with the authority to act if a disingenuous president stonewalls or uses deliberate deception to impound funds. They are written to provide the executive branch the degree of flexibility that existed essentially from 1905 to 1971 but to give the Congress authority to act against a president who substitutes confrontation for comity.

In the summer of 1983 the Supreme Court, in a far-reaching decision, declared the legislative veto unconstitutional.[73] The specific case involved immigration proceedings, but Justice Byron White noted that the decision could affect both the War Powers Resolution and the impoundment provisions of the 1974 Budget Act.

NOTES

1. Allen Schick, *Congress and Money* (Washington, D.C.: The Urban Institute, 1980), p. 17.
2. Louis Fisher, *Presidential Spending Power.* Copyright © 1975 by Princeton University Press, 51.
3. Arthur M. Schlesinger, Jr., *The Imperial Presidency.* Copyright © 1973 by Arthur M. Schlesinger, Jr. Reprinted by permission of Houghton Mifflin Company and Andre Deutsch, Ltd., p. 254.
4. Ibid., p. 235.
5. Ibid., p. 252.
6. James L. Sundquist, *The Decline and Resurgence of Congress* (Washington, D.C.: The Brookings Institution, 1981), p. 36.
7. *Economic Report of the President, 1987* (Washington, D.C.: U.S. Government Printing Office, 1987, p. 312.
8. Ibid., p. 318.
9. P. L. 92-599.
10. Senate Committee on the Judiciary, Subcommittee on Separation of Powers, *Executive Impoundment of Appropriated Funds, Hearings,* 92nd Cong., 1st sess., March 1971.
11. Senate Ad Hoc Subcommittee on Impoundment of Funds of the Committee on the Judiciary, *Impoundment of Appropriated Funds by the President, Joint Hearings,* 93rd Cong., 1st sess., 1973.
12. House Committee on Rules, *Impoundment Reporting and Review, Hearings on H.R. 5193,* 93rd cong., 1st sess., 1973.
13. Joint Study Committee on Budget Control (JSC), *Improving Congressional Control over Budgeting Outlay and Receipt Totals, Interim Report,* 93rd Cong., 1st sess., 7 February 1973, p. 1.
14. Ibid.
15. Ibid.
16. Ibid.
17. Ibid.
18. Ibid.
19. Ibid., p. 5.

20. Ibid.
21. JSC, *Recommendations for Improving Control over Budgetary Outlay and Receipt Totals,* 93rd Cong., 1st sess., 18 April 1973, Rep. N. 93-147, Table 4, p. 37.
22. Aaron Wildavsky, *The Politics of the Budgetary Process,* 2nd ed. (Boston: Little, Brown, 1974), p. 13. "The largest determining factor of the size and content of this year's budget is last year's budget."
23. JSC, *Interim Report,* pp. 7–8.
24. Ibid., p. 8.
25. Ibid., pp. 8, 40.
26. Ibid., p. 8.
27. Ibid., p. 9.
28. Ibid., pp. 9–10.
29. Ibid., p. 10.
30. *Congressional Record,* 14 March 1961, pp. 3638, 3640.
31. Richard F. Fenno, Jr., *The Power of the Purse* (Boston: Little, Brown, 1966), p. 515.
32. For an excellent account, see Fisher, *Presidential Spending Power,* pp. 95–122; and Senate Armed Services Committee, *Bombings in Cambodia, Hearings,* 93rd Cong., 1st sess. 1973.
33. Senate Committee on Appropriations, *Foreign Assistance and Related Program Appropriations* (Washington, D.C.: U.S. Government Printing Office, 1972), pp. 837–838.
34. Ibid., pp. 842, 848.
35. Fisher, *Presidential Spending Power,* p. 239.
36. U.S. Congress, *Impeachment of Richard M. Nixon, President of the United States,* 93rd Cong., 2nd sess., 1974, H. Rep. 1305, p. 217.
37. *Statistical Abstract of the United States,* 100th ed. (Washington, D.C.: U.S. Department of Commerce, Bureau of the Census, 1979), p. 499.
38. Senate, *Rules and Manual,* p. 820.
39. *Statistical Abstract,* p. 499.
40. Ibid., p. 507.
41. Fisher, *Presidential Spending Power,* p. 192.
42. Press release, office of Senator Proxmire, 8 January 1973.
43. James P. Pfiffner, *The President, the Budget and Congress: Impoundment and the 1974 Budget Act* (Boulder, Colo.: Westview Press, 1979), p. 49; for an excellent account of the arguments, see pp, 49–76.
44. The arguments were made by OMB Director Caspar W. Weinberger in 1971 and Deputy Attorney General Joseph T. Sneed in 1973 while appearing before Senator Ervin's Judiciary Subcommittee on Separation of Powers.
45. 135 U.S. 1 (1890).
46. 158 U.S. 564 (1895).
47. Fisher, *Presidential Spending Power,* pp. 150–151. Neither Jefferson nor Congress saw any reason to spend the funds, for the emergency failed to materialize.
48. Ibid., p. 176.
49. Ibid., p. 147.
50. Richard M. Pious, *The American Presidency* (New York: Basic Books, 1979), p. 287.
51. Howard E. Shuman, "Canonizing Pork," *The New York Times,* 19 November 1976, p. A-27.
52. Adam Smith, *An Inquiry into the Nature and Causes of the Wealth of Nations* (Chicago: Encyclopedia Britannica, 1952), p. 199.
53. JSC, *Interim Report.*
54. JSC, *Recommendations for Improving Control over Budgetary Outlay and Receipt Totals.*
55. S. 1541, H.R. 7130, and others.
56. Senate Committee on Rule and Administration, *Congressional Budget Act of 1974, Report to Accompany S. 1541,* 93rd Congress, 2d sess., 1974.

57. JSC, Interim Report, p. 6.
58. Section 301(a), (3).
59. JSC, *Interim Report,* p. 10.
60. Ibid., Appendix, Table 12.
61. *Los Angeles Times,* 1 November 1982, p. 12
62. Section 300.
63. *Budget of the United States Government: Fiscal Year 1992* (Washington, D.C.: U.S. Government Printing Office, 1991), part V, pp. 15–33.
64. *Los Angeles Times,* 1 November 1982, p. 12.
65. Woodrow Wilson, "The Fourteen Points," Address to Congress, 8 January 1918; quoted in Henry Steele Commager, ed., *Documents of American History,* 3rd ed. (New York: F. S. Crofts, 1946).
66. Floyd M. Riddick, *Senate Procedure, Precedents and Practices, 97th Congress, 1st Session* (Washington, D.C.: U.S. Government Printing Office, 1981), p. 367.
67. Allen Schick, *The Congressional Budget Act of 1974: Legislative History and Analysis; Congressional Research Service Report No. 75–94S* (Washington, D.C.: Library of Congress, 1975), p. 99.
68. See Schultze's testimony in JSC, *Improving Congressional Budget Control Hearings,* 93–1 (Washington, D.C.: U.S. Government Printing Office, 1973), 18 January 1973, pp. 2–17; and House Rules Committee, *Budget Control Act of 1973 Hearing on H.R. 7130,* 93–1 (Washington, D.C.: U.S. Government Printing Office, 1973), 20 September 1973, pp. 311–336.
69. *Senate Committee on the Budget,* Second Concurrent Resolution on the Budget, Fiscal Year 1981, S. Con. Res. 119, 96th Cong., 2nd sess., Rep. 96–921, p. 18.
70. For an excellent discussion of the increasing control exercised by presidents over the rate of spending, see Pfiffner, *The President, the Budget, and Congress,* chap. 3, esp. pp. 31–44.
71. See Sections 1112 and 1003 of Title X of the 1974 Act.
72. The definitions are provided both in the act and under the act by the comptroller general in cooperation with the secretary of the treasury, the director of the OMB, and the director of the CBO. See Sections 202(a)(1) and 1011 of the act.
73. *Immigration and Naturalization Service V. Chadha, 1983.*

8

The Reagan Budget Revolution

INTRODUCTION

The election of Ronald Reagan as the fortieth president of the United States initiated a federal budget revolution. It was a revolution in many ways. It brought radical change in budget spending priorities, slashing social programs and increasing military outlays. It broke tradition by effectively initiating tax bills in the Senate. The result was the biggest tax cut in the history of the country. The combination of unprecedented tax cuts, growing entitlements, and increases in both the totals and the magnitude of military spending created budget deficits that mortgaged a balanced budget for the 1980s and 1990s, and quadrupled the national debt.

It took a device designed to bring budget figures into balance as the climactic act at the end of the new budget procedure—reconciliation—and transformed it into a budget-cutting avalanche functioning at the beginning of the congressional budget process.

It brought about a political metamorphosis by converting the 1974 Budget Act from a statute designed by the Congress to discipline itself and to retrieve power from the president into an instrument that enhanced the president's power and allowed him to discipline the Congress.

The Reagan budget revolution had its roots in politics, specifically the 1980 presidential election. Candidate Reagan campaigned against inflation, unemployment, deficits, high taxes, and debt, and promised a balanced budget as early as 1982. He won an enormous victory. He won the popular vote by 43.9 million to 35.5 million, or by 50.7 to 41.0 percent, and carried forty-four of the fifty states and the District of Columbia for a 489 to 49 electoral vote margin. His question, "Are you better off today than you were four years ago?" summed up his economic and budget attack. He claimed a mandate to cut the budget and taxes and to increase military spending.

Other issues in that election, however, may have played a part in President Reagan's victory that were as great as or greater than inflation, spending, taxes, and deficits. Among them were President Carter's lack of strong leadership, wounded credibility, as a result of the Bert Lance affair, and perceived personal weaknesses; the hostage crisis in Iran; a series of social questions that attracted one-issue ideologies; candidate Reagan's debating skill in transforming his image from a hawkish ogre into a pleasant and acceptable presidential alternative; the proliferation of Political Action Committees (PAC) and the outpouring of money for the Reagan campaign, and the sheer momentum of events at home and abroad over which no president could have more than partial control. But whether the victory at the polls was a mandate for the Reagan budget revolution is beside the point, for the president and his party chose to treat it as a budget mandate and the public perceived it as such. One top White House aide later admitted that a part of President Reagan's effectiveness in his first two years came from "a carefully created illusion":

> We were never quite as strong as we were able to give the impressions of being. We pretended we had a mandate that was very much larger than it was. A tremendous number of people voted against Jimmy Carter, not for Reaganomics. Yet, we went about the country impressing them that Reagan was carrying out a mandate.[1]

The Reagan landslide brought Republican control of the Senate and a gain of thirty-three seats in the House. The unexpected net gain of twelve Republican seats in the Senate transformed the Democratic margin of 59 to 41 seats to a 53 to 47 working Republican majority. Only one other time in the more than half-century since 1932 has such a massive shift taken place. In 1958, the Democrats captured twelve Republican seats and gained four more when Alaska and Hawaii were admitted to the union.

Seven of the 1980 Republican Senate gains were won by margins of 2 percent or less in states that candidate Reagan carried overwhelmingly. Those freshmen senators owed their wins to Reagan's coattails. Of the sixteen new Republican senators, four of whom replaced retiring Republicans, at least twelve were strong Reagan partisans, and all of them voted with the new administration on key budget and tax-cut issues. Six of the sixteen were appointed to the Senate Budget Committee, which guaranteed a clear majority for Reagan budget issues.[2] Seven were placed on the Senate Appropriations Committee, which ensured support for Reagan's budget revolution there.[3] At every critical juncture Reagan Republican majorities dominated the Senate legislative procedures.

While the Democrats retained a 242-to-193 margin in the House, the combination of an extraordinarily disciplined Republican minority and 29 to 40 or more conservative southern "boll weevils" produced a working majority for President Reagan's crucial budget and tax proposals during most of his first two years.

To the ingredients of a Reagan mandate, disciplined majorities in the House and Senate, and either public support for his program or acquiescence while the president put it into effect, another important factor was added: President Reagan and his supporters knew what they wanted to do, they had a program to do it, and they had a way to get it done. They had a purpose, a program, and a method.

Their purpose was at least fourfold. They were determined to change federal budget priorities and to shift resources from the civilian to the military sector. They proposed to shift financial burdens from the federal government to state or local governments. They were intent on shifting other activities from the government to the private sector. Finally, they were determined to shift the tax burden from the wealthy or the well-to-do to middle- and lower-income citizens.

Their program had three prongs. It was a triad comparable in the domestic sphere to the military triad in the strategic sphere. The first leg was to cut specific budget categories that funded domestic programs by a targeted $40 billion in their first full year.[4] The second leg of the domestic triad was to cut taxes. It was proposed to cut the top personal income tax bracket from 70 to 50 percent, give an annual 10 percent, across-the-board cut in the personal income tax in each of three years, and reduce corporate tax depreciation periods. This was called supply-side economics, for it was designed to stimulate savings and investment to get the economy moving. Its critics called it Reaganomics, voodoo economics, or a gimmick. The third leg of the triad was to promote a vast increase in total military spending, an estimated $1.5 trillion over the following five years.

President Reagan and the Republicans also used a new method and a new tactic to pass the program. The method to achieve spending cuts was the radical use of reconciliation, the new end-of-the-year procedure in the Budget Reform Act designed to bring the individual functional budget parts into harmony with the binding totals of the Second Congressional Concurrent Budget Resolution. The new tactic was to start both the budget cutting and the tax cutting efforts in the Senate, where the Republicans controlled the procedures and had a clear majority of disciplined votes.

THE CARTER BUDGET

Almost the last major act of the outgoing Carter administration was the submission of its lame-duck budget. On nearly the last day of his presidency,

Carter released the proposed budget for the fiscal year beginning the following October. It was a routine, regular, run-of-the-mill budget in which outlays and receipts were merely updated to account for changes in projected economic conditions. As a regular routine budget, it proposed outlays of $739.3 billion, receipts of $711.8 billion, and a deficit of $27.5 billion.[5]

That it was a perfunctory exercise in budget making was clear from the figures in the current services budget (required by the 1974 act) that accompanied it. The estimated budget authority and outlays for the upcoming fiscal year—at the same program level and without policy changes, but updated for expected changes in economic conditions, beneficiary levels, pay increases, and benefit changes[6]—were $736 billion in outlays, $705.6 billion in receipts, and a $29.7 billion deficit.[7] The difference between President Carter's proposed budget and what would have happened to spending and receipts if nothing had happened (that is, no program or policy changes, but merely an update to take account of economic changes) was $2.6 billion in an almost $740 billion budget. This was 0.3 percent, a figure smaller than the statistical margin of error by which all budget figures may be mathematically wrong.

It was not only a routine budget in its merely perfunctory increases, it was routine in that President Carter did what almost every president every year has done. The budget somewhat underestimated outlays, somewhat overestimated revenues, provided optimistic economic assumptions, and artificially narrowed the deficit. This was an annual ritual. It can be called the regular "honest-dishonest" budget. Looked at realistically, it probably had a $45 billion instead of a $25 billion deficit.

President Carter had other alternatives or budget strategies. Smarting under an overwhelming political defeat in which he was wounded by candidate Reagan's constant call for a balanced budget; charges of inefficiency, fraud, and waste; and allegations of spendthrift extravagances, he might have presented the Congress, the country, and the new president with a balanced budget. Cut here, there, and everywhere. If the new president wants a balanced budget, give it to him. Call it a "holding the feet to the fire" budget. Such a proposal, however, would have been seen as being highly political, difficult to achieve; and petty and vindictive. As the balanced budget in fiscal year 1982 promised by candidate Reagan was no doubt an unobtainable political goal, the new president would be forced to increase spending and eat political crow in his budget for his first year.

The lame-duck Carter administration did have another choice. It could have padded the outgoing budget with a surfeit of funds for every interest group, agency client, and subsidy recipient in the country. Call it a "kitchen-sink" budget. Governors, mayors, state, and local officials would rejoice. Shipbuilders, exporters, defense contractors, civil servants, law enforcement officials, postal subsidy recipients, environmentalists, farmers, regional developers, statistical users, homebuilders, transit authorities, medical researchers, secondary and higher education officers, and energy producers, among a myriad of others, would cheer. Politically, this could have put the new administration on the spot by making it cut not only from expectations but from an actual budget proposal. It would take a lot of political heat when it cut back on the political bounty and pork-barrel largess proffered by such a Carter outgoing budget offering all this and heaven, too.

President Carter did none of these things. Instead, he overcame political temptation and some proffered advice that he should seek retribution and stick it to the new administration, and sent up a routine budget.

DAVID STOCKMAN'S BLACK BOOK

Several weeks before the inauguration, David Stockman, the Republican congressman from Michigan who was designated as director of the Office of Management and Budget (OMB), was developing a budget plan. Holed up with a transition staff of a dozen or so aides at the Executive Office Building next door to the White House, he was hard at work.[8] He was looking for some $40 to $50 billion in fiscal year 1982 budget cuts. He was also examining the economic projections based on the proposed budget cuts, military increases, and tax slashes. When the OMB computers projected deficits of at least $82 to $116 billion in fiscal years 1982 to 1984, Stockman did two things. He used the figures to scare the daylights out of designated cabinet officers to win their backing for his proposed cuts. Then, to hide the deficits from the Congress and the public, he jiggered the OMB computers.[9]

The budget-cutting proposals were a Stockman, not a cabinet, exercise. During the preinaugural confirmation hearings on Capitol Hill, prospective cabinet member after prospective cabinet member was asked to provide a list of possible cuts in his or her department, as well as the areas of inefficiency, fraud, and waste he or she was going to root out as a result of President-elect Reagan's campaign charges. The designated cabinet officers failed the test, giving virtually no specific answers to the written questions about where they would make cuts submitted by that scourge of bureaucratic waste, Senator William Proxmire (D.-Wis.).[10]

On the first Wednesday in January, Stockman met for two hours with President-elect Reagan, argued that the new administration would have to shoot for at least $40 billion in budget cuts, and came away with the president's blessing for the goal.[11] Meantime, Stockman's staff was compiling proposed cuts, preparing position papers, and writing the justification for their enactment. By inaugural week, fifty to sixty papers had been prepared, and meetings with new cabinet members had been arranged.[12] In these sessions, the deck was stacked, with four or five sympathetic members of Stockman's budget working group against the new cabinet officer and his staff.

> Each meeting will involve only the relevant Cabinet member and his aides with four or five strong keepers of the central agenda. . . . . So on Monday when we go into the decision on synfuels programs, it will be [Energy Secretary James B.] Edwards defending them against six guys saying that, by God, we've got to cut these back or we're not going to have a savings program that will add up.[13]

Decisions on cuts were made by the budget working groups, after which a memo was written to the president, and, after being initialed and approved, locked up in Stockman's safe as a fait accompli not intended to be raised again.[14] Students of budget history saw that not only had the Congress delegated its authority over the purse to the president, but that the policy of the first budget director, General Dawes, which held that the budget director, acting in the name of the president, would dominate the cabinet on budget issues, was now true in spades. The only exception was the secretary of defense, who won his battle with Director Stockman. Gone was the day when a cabinet member assembled a "Book of Estimates" and sent it off to the Treasury, where it was perfunctorily packaged with other department estimates and sent up to the Congress by the Treasury secretary as a ministerial function. Notwithstanding the Budget Reform Act, it was once again the president's budget, and President Reagan took the initiative, set the goals, and changed the priorities.

At this stage, the new administration, in power less than three weeks, made a bold and risky move. Budget Director Stockman sent a 145-page "black book" listing proposed cuts with detailed numbers to the Republican barons—the House and Senate Republican leaders and the Republican committee chairmen—on Capitol Hill. He did this deliberately. Capitol Hill is a leaky sieve. The mimeograph and photocopy machines were soon at work, and copies were quickly in the hands of virtually every member of the Congress and more than two thousand members of the legislative staffs. It was also delivered to the nation's leading newspapers. As the lead paragraph of the lead story of *The Washington Post*, which played six columns across the top of page one on Sunday, February 8, said:

> President Reagan's budget architects have put together an extraordinary package of proposed budget cuts touching every level of American society and dismantling dozens of popular federal aid programs that support everything from school lunches to airports, public television and welfare.[15]

Ten columns of details were printed on inside pages, and a second front-page story noted that the Reagan crusade for reform would produce an "epic political struggle" unlike anything seen before in modern Washington.[16]

The intentional release of the details of Stockman's black book was an enormous political gamble. Everyone is for cutting the budget in general. Detailing the specifics, however, gives the special interest groups time to mobilize their forces, form alliances with other interest groups, and preserve their own program, subsidy, or tax expenditure. Time and again across-the-board or general budget-cutting proposals had floundered in the Congress on grounds they were not specific enough. When specific cuts were proposed, they failed because of opposition from powerful economic groups. Budget cutting always posed this tactical dilemma. But the Stockman release was designed to intimidate the opposition; to give the impression, if not the reality, of fairness since the ox of every group was being gored; and to capitalize on the public desire to cut government spending, to simplify existing programs, and "to get the government off the backs of the people," in the repeated phrase of the presidential campaign. Before the details could be digested, and while many of the specific programs were still in flux, President Reagan took the initiative again, and on February 18 went before a joint session of the Congress during the evening prime television time. This was the second time in two weeks he had used a prime-time talk and the "bully pulpit" of the office of the president to sell his program to the American people and, through them, to bring pressure on the Congress.[17] In his address to the Congress, he announced new overall budget figures of $695.5 billion in spending, $650.5 billion in receipts, and $45 billion deficit. This was a spending reduction based on revised economic assumptions of $41.4 billion from the Carter budget. His program envisaged a balanced budget by fiscal year 1984 and a slight ($5.8 billion) surplus in fiscal year 1985. (The actual figure was $212.5 billion.)

He pledged not to cut spending programs that would affect the "truly needy" and proposed a "social safety net" to protect them. The only obvious area to escape the knife was military spending, which would increase enormously. As time went on, various other sacred cows were found among the untouchables. President Reagan also unveiled his tax-cut program and proposed for fiscal year 1982 a $53.9 billion cut in personal income and business taxes. While the speech was couched in most general terms, it enjoyed standing ovations; prolonged cheers, most of them from the Republican side; and general success.

While the president and Budget Director Stockman leaked or released many specific proposals by way of the black book in early February or the "white paper" accompanying the speech to the Congress, the overall budget and tax figures represented moving targets. The $41.4 billion in cuts the president had proposed on February 18 were packaged in a different form when he sent his official budget revisions to the Congress on March 10. In the text of the white paper that accompanied the revisions, the president wrote:

> The budget reform plan announced on February 18 includes 83 major cuts resulting in $34.8 billion outlay savings for 1982, with greater future savings. With this message, over 200 additional reductions are proposed. An additional $13.8 billion in savings are now planned. Further, I am proposing changes in user charges and off-budget payments that will bring total fiscal savings to $55.9 billion. This compares with $49.1 billion in fiscal savings announced on February 18.

Packaging budget cuts and user charges together, combining on-budget and off-budget items, and changing both the fiscal base from which they were proposed and the economic assumptions on which they were made produced enormous confusion not only among the public, but among budget experts in both parties and on both sides of Capitol Hill. The budget-cutting barrage was so formidable it was almost impossible to digest. At times as much as $10 to $13 billion of unspecified cuts were involved, and Senate Minority Leader Robert C. Byrd (D.-W.Va.) warned that "the [Senate Budget] Committee and the Congress can't buy a pig in a poke."[18] William M. Brodhead (D.-Mich.), chairman of the Democratic Study Group in the House, complained that the administration had made a mistake "by sending Cabinet officers out to pressure for quick action before giving us even the most elementary details of its proposals."[19] Whether by accident or design, the moving and imprecise target was hard to hit.

THE RADICAL USE OF RECONCILIATION

In an attempt to strike while the iron was hot and to overcome both the opposition of special interest groups and the parochialism and power of House and Senate committees, the Reagan administration devised radical political strategy. From the boldness of its conception and the magnitude of the amounts involved, there developed a new and unique congressional institution as important in its own way as the rise of the committee system in the Congress or the decline in the autocratic power of the speaker of the house. It was called "reconciliation."

Originally designed in the 1974 Budget Act, reconciliation was the means by which the House and Senate could instruct their committees at the end of the budget procedures to come up with spending cuts or tax increases to bring into balance the spending proposals of individual committees and the overall binding targets of the second budget resolution. It was now proposed that reconciliation be used at the beginning of the budget procedures as a preemptive strike by the House and the Senate as a whole to overwhelm the individual committees and attain the Reagan budget-cutting program. It was a revolutionary method to achieve a revolutionary goal.

Reconciliation Background

During the first four years of the 1974 Budget Act, reconciliation was not used.[20] In 1979, it triggered such a "protracted dispute" when used to carry out the second budget resolution for fiscal year 1980 that the reconciliation instructions were removed from the resolution.[21] The major stumbling block was time. As Allen Schick testified before the House Task Force on Budget Process of the House Budget Committee, set up to review the act after the 1979 failure:

I have doubts however, whether reconciliation (as it is presently formulated in the Budget Act) is a viable procedure. For one thing, section 310 allows only 10 days between adoption of the second budget resolution and a reconciliation bill. This is not likely to provide sufficient time to review legislation and to make the difficult choices facing committees.[22]

The problem was that to achieve significant cuts under reconciliation, even of $4 or $5 billion, committees had to change the law with respect to the most hotly debated budget items—entitlements, contract authority, and spending for a variety of sacred cows—between September 15 and 25:

Because reconciliation would compel unwelcomed revisions in existing law, they can be expected to stir up a great deal of legislative conflict at a stage in the Congressional budget calendar when conflict can least be afforded.[23]

Schick proposed that reconciliation be used at the beginning of the budget process, as part of the first budget resolution, instead of at the end. A shift in the date would also ensure that no narrowly composed committee with its stacked membership or prejudices could bottle up the legislation beyond the beginning of the new fiscal year.

In 1980, the year before the Reagan budget revolution, Schick's advice was taken. Reconciliation was effective both for the first time and through the first budget resolution. The May 15 resolutions contained instructions to their committees to cut spending by $6.4 billion in the Senate and $5.3 billion in the House. The resolutions also called for amendments to increase revenues by $4.2 billion in the Senate and by $3.9 billion in the House. In 1980 the final result for fiscal year 1981 was a reconciliation bill whose combined spending cuts and tax increases totaled $8.2 billion.

As Representative Richard Bolling (D.-Mo.), chairman of the House Rules Committee and a major architect of the Budget Act itself, said on the House floor on May 13, 1981:

Last year as a step forward in the process, it was decided to move reconciliation up to the first resolution. It could have been argued then, and was argued, that was not what was in the intent of the law and the House when it passed the law, and through the operation of the Rules Committee and the process of the House that major change was made in the Budget Act.[24]

The fact that reconciliation was first accomplished in 1980 led Alice M. Rivlin, the director of the Congressional Budget Office (CBO), to say:

In the face of a changing economic situation, and in an election year, the fact that they completed the required [fiscal 1981] budget and did reconciliation for the first time is evidence of the strength of the process.[25]

Using the first budget resolution as a vehicle for revision and for reconciliation was not the original intent of the law but certainly was legal under Section 304 of the act, which provides at any time after the first concurrent resolution on the budget for a fiscal year has been agreed to pursuant to section 301, and before the end of such fiscal year, the two Houses may adopt a concurrent resolution on the budget which revises the concurrent resolution on the budget for such fiscal year most recently agreed to.[26]

The 1980 experience thus provided a precedent and a procedure on which the Reagan administration could build. It took perceptive and innovative legislative experts to fashion the tactics to effect the Reagan budget revolution from such a small beginning, but fashion it they did.

The Reagan Reconciliation Strategy

Among legislative veterans, "reconciliation" is now a common word, a warm friend or hated adversary, and an understood technique. On February 18, 1981, less than a month after President Reagan took the oath of office, it was almost unknown. Only a handful of people even inside the Congress understood its meaning, and even fewer saw its possibilities. The morning after the president's speech to the Congress, *The Washington Post* reported:

> Even as President Reagan was presenting his economic proposals to Congress last night, Senate Republicans were working to grease the skids for his budget cuts by packaging them in a one-shot bill that could clear its first major legislative hurdle by Easter.[27]

What was proposed was a "preemptive strike" in the Republican-controlled Senate "before the opposition can mobilize." *The Washington Post* reported that

> both Senate and House budget leaders are talking about resorting to a little-used device called "reconciliation" under which Congress can order its committees to come up with specific savings by cutting established programs.[28]

By February 23, the decisions had been made and the staff of the Senate Budget Committee had prepared a description of the reconciliation process that it distributed freely. The memorandum was welcome because all but the "insiders" were mystified by the procedure. The memorandum described the strategy, prescribed a timetable, and provided a glossary of terms such as *reconciliation, direct spending, recission,* and *deferral,* all devices to be used to achieve the spending cuts.[29]

On February 24, the first step in the timetable was taken when Senate Budget Committee Chairman Pete V. Domenici (R.-N.Mex.) and the ranking Democratic senator, Ernest F. Hollings of South Carolina, introduced Senate Concurrent Resolution 9, which revised the second budget resolution for fiscal year 1981. It called for $125.9 billion in spending (outlay) savings over three years. This total included savings of $4.8 billion in fiscal year 1981, the Reagan-proposed savings of $41.4 billion in fiscal year 1982, and $79.7 billion in savings in fiscal year 1983, most of the latter being the out-year savings from the fiscal year 1981 and 1982 cuts. The resolution was symbolic, because details were missing, but it provided a springboard for the Senate Budget Committee, to which it was referred, to begin committee action on the detailed cuts.

On March 10 the president, as promised, sent his revision of the Carter budget estimates to the Congress. The Senate Budget Committee held hearings the next day in preparation for its detailed budget cutting the following week. The total amount of the cuts in the president's estimates was unclear. The revised budget was replete with footnotes explaining that there were errors in the figures. CBO Director Rivlin, Senator Hollings, and House Budget Committee Chairman James R. Jones (D.-Okla.) complained about inaccuracies, omissions, or the lack of details. Senator Hollings later referred to it as a resolution "fashioned in a supply-side dream world made even more haunting by ghost numbers,"[30] and Congressman Thomas J. Downey (D.-N.Y.) said to Budget Director David Stockman and Treasury Secretary Donald Regan that the new numbers were based on "guesses" and "estimates." "I honestly believe a lot of assumptions you are making are hallucinogenic."[31]

Some $34.8 billion of the proposed cuts were made from the "current policy" budget, while another $13.8 billion was from the Carter recommendations, two quite different baselines. According to the CBO, the $48.6 billion total was worth only an estimated $42.9 billion. Of this amount, the president submitted specific cuts of only $34.1 billion. The remaining $8.8 billion was to come from administrative savings (fat, waste, paperwork, travel, and so on) and proposals to be submitted later. Only the military and safety net programs were exempt from the cuts, although the latter was hotly disputed and in fact cut.

On March 16, the Senate Budget Committee began its mark-up in what the *Congressional Quarterly* called "a grueling four-day work session,"[32] and on March 19 it ordered by a 20 to 0 vote that Senate Concurrent Resolution 9 be reported to the Senate. The Democrats voted with the Republicans to report the instructions to the Senate on the grounds that the president's policies deserved a chance. The president got what he wanted. While the Democrats opposed many specific reductions and offered numerous amendments and alternatives, the disciplined Republican majority won virtually every vote. While funds were added for few programs, they were more than offset by reductions in others. The resolution instructed Senate committees to cut $36.4 billion, $2.3 billion more than President Reagan's specific proposals, from budget estimates in fiscal year 1982. This was the product of a rolling Reagan juggernaut.

Reconciliation Succeeds: Senate Floor Action

In six days of debate on the Senate floor, from March 26 to April 2, the Senate stood firm on the Reagan budget proposals. More than twenty liberal Democratic amendments to restore funds were voted down, most of them by wide margins. A Daniel Moynihan (D.-N.Y.) amendment to restore $100 million for the higher education grant program was rejected by 67 to 30; Republican senators voted 53 to 0 against it. Another Moynihan amendment to add $435 million to the elementary and secondary education programs went down 65 to 33. A David Pryor (D.-Ark.) amendment to reduce military procurement by $2 billion lost by 65 to 35. A Lawton Chiles (D.-Fla.) amendment to restore $270 million in veterans' health care programs was defeated 56 to 44. Some close votes were party line. A David Boren (D.-Okla.) amendment to cut foreign aid and restore veterans' health programs lost by a 48-to-44 margin, with only two Republicans voting for it and two Democrats voting against it. Two amendments were successful when Senator Jesse Helms (R.-N.C.) added $200 million to the school lunch program (87 to 9) and paid for it by cutting $200 million from the foreign aid budget (70 to 26).

Technically, the resolution was composed of reconciliation instructions to fourteen Senate committees to cut various amounts from the budget functions over which they exercised jurisdiction. The legislative committees were instructed to submit these cuts to the Budget Committee by June 12, where the parts would be packaged into a reconciliation bill. Because of the tradition that appropriations bills start in the House, cuts made by the Senate appropriations subcommittees under the reconciliation instructions would be added to the first appropriations bill coming to the Senate from the House, either a supplemental bill or an extension of the continuing resolution. The Senate Appropriations Committee was directed, therefore, to report its cuts at a time when it would report a House-passed appropriations bill, or by June 5.

The final vote in the Senate on the reconciliations instructions was an overwhelming 80 to 10. Only one Republican, Senator Lowell Weicker of Connecticut, voted no. While the debate was emotional, the outcome was never in doubt. The new reconciliation procedure not only instructed committees to cut an unprecedented and incredible $52.8 billion in budget authority and $36.9 billion in outlays for fiscal year 1982, but also was memorable for at least four additional results.

First, it provided reconciliation instructions not only at the beginning of the year but some six weeks earlier than if they had been attached to the First Concurrent Budget Resolution.

Second, it allowed the Senate as a whole to determine priorities and by-pass its committee and subcommittee barons instead of letting the committee barons to set the agenda.

Third, the composition of the cuts was a vindication of the analysis of the budget problem as set forth by the Joint Study Committee (JSC). Of the

$36.4 billion savings required by the Senate reconciliation instructions, $23 billion came from reductions in earlier funded authorizations, or from the enormous $127 billion backlog of budget authority that had been enacted in previous years but was to be spent in fiscal year 1982.[33] This was 63 percent of the spending cuts.[34] It thus provided some control over the uncontrollables and helped meet the complaints set forth in the JSC's Interim Report that

> One of the important reasons accounting for uncontrollability of expenditures in any given year is the extent of obligational authority provided in earlier years.... The presence of large balances of funds which were committed in prior years...make(s) it increasingly difficult for either the executive or the Congress to control budgetary totals.[35]

The remaining $13.4 billion of the cuts, or 37 percent of the savings, included $12.2 billion from the direct spending jurisdiction of the authorizing committees, largely entitlements. Only $3.2 billion in instructed savings were directed at appropriations. More than 90 percent of the cuts, therefore, came from *backlog* or from *back-door* spending, which almost a decade before the JSC had identified as a major budget problem.

Fourth, as a result of choosing to make the budget cuts through the budget resolution and reconciliation, there could be no filibuster. Not only were the legislative committees prevented from bottling up legislation or cuts that were approved by the Senate but were anathema to them, but a minority on the floor could not delay, stall, or filibuster the measure. The special rules under Sections 305 and 310 of the Budget Act limited debate on the First Concurrent Budget Resolution to fifty hours, on a reconciliation bill or resolution to twenty hours, on a second budget resolution to not more than fifteen hours, and on a conference report to not more than ten hours.

One can doubt whether the fathers of the Budget Reform Act contemplated either the innovative procedures and interpretations of their work or that the new procedures would result in cuts of such size and magnitude. Many in the Senate welcomed both the procedures and the priorities of the cuts—namely, the reduction and, in a few cases the dismemberment of the domestic social programs put in place since 1932. Others, such as liberal Democratic senators Ted Kennedy, (Mass.); Howard Metzenbaum, and Donald Riegle, (D-Mich.) were dismayed with the results. The more moderate Hollings claimed the process was "brutalized,"[36] and Byrd charged that the House reconciliation bill was the result of "tyrannical majority" rule.[37]

BUDGET CUTTING IN THE HOUSE

The Democrats, with a fifty-one seat majority, controlled procedures in the House. They opposed the early budget reconciliation route taken by the Senate. Determined to take a closer look at the Reagan budget proposals, they decided to wait for the regular first budget resolution to revise the current year's budget, to set targets for the new year, and to apply reconciliation. House Speaker Thomas P. O'Neill, Jr. (D.-Mass.), warned that "legislation in haste makes waste all along the line,"[38] and the new chairman of the House Budget Committee, Congressman James Jones (D.-Okla.), wanted the House to take a much closer look at the March 10 revised Reagan budget figures than the Senate had done. To avoid charges of foot dragging, the House Democrats agreed in a caucus with House Republicans on March 10 to act on both the spending and the tax provisions by the end of July.

The House decided on the slower procedure for a variety of reasons. In addition to the fact that the specific Reagan cuts were unclear and in some cases not yet proposed, House Democrats wanted time to fashion their own alternative, to allow the committees to examine the proposals critically and in detail, and to permit the affected clients and interest groups to organize and become effective. Delay was needed to counteract the president's effective prime-time media blitzes; the vast array of corporate and conservative interest groups aligning themselves with the president's push; the White House lobbying of newspaper editors, reporters, and columnists; and group or individual meetings with key members of the Congress. They wanted time to offset the president's superior organization, his communicative skills, and his charisma.

During meetings in the first week in April, House Budget Chairman Jones presented a fiscal year 1982 alternative to the president's March 10 program. To the Reagan proposal for outlays of $695.3 billion, the Democrats would add $20 billion to push outlays to $714.55 billion. They included measures to increase tax receipts by $38.65 billion. This reduced the $45 billion Reagan deficit to $25.6 billion, a figure they thought would appeal to some of the conservative or "boll weevil" Democrats, who could then justify support of the measure on the grounds that they voted for a smaller deficit than the president proposed.

There was also a fundamental difference in the nature of the reconciliation cuts, designed to attract support from both conservatives and liberals on the legislative committees. Unlike the administrative proposal, in which more than 90 percent of the cuts coming from authorizing committees, the Jones proposal left $23.6 billion in cuts in the hands of the House Appropriations Committee in order to appeal to members who supported the traditional procedures of the House.

The Jones budget, like the president's proposal, was a hodgepodge of numbers, assumptions, baselines, and shaky premises. According to Budget Director Stockman, Jones's budget resolution was "a series of gimmicks, economic estimates, and accounting tricks."[39] But Stockman and his allies dared not attack his budget on the grounds of "political numbers." Stockman

cheerfully conceded that the administration's own budget numbers were constructed on similar shaky premises, mixing cuts from the original 1981 budget left by Jimmy Carter with new baseline projections from the Congressional Budget Office in a way that fundamentally did not add up. The Budget politics of 1981, which produced such clear and dramatic rhetoric from both sides, was, in fact, based upon a bewildering set of numbers that confused even those, like Stockman, who produced them.[40]

The politics were more important than the numbers, and this carefully politically crafted Jones budget passed his committee by a 17–13 margin, losing only one Democratic member, the conservative maverick from Texas, Phil Gramm. Meanwhile, Gramm joined with his friend and former House ally, Budget Director Stockman, to fashion an alternative to the Jones Democratic proposal. Stockman's embrace of Gramm's proposal created friction with the ranking Republican member of the House Budget Committee, Delbert L. Latta of Ohio, who, like a good soldier, had gone down the line for Reagan and Stockman's original proposal in the committee. An ultimate truce was arranged in which the final proposal, essentially the Gramm negotiated budget, was variously called the Gramm-Latta or Latta-Gramm substitute. A Stockman spokesman called it "the Reagan proposal with a few wrinkles."[41] As conservative Texan Gramm had strong ties to a group of forty-five or so Democratic representatives who called themselves the Conservative Democratic Forum (CDF); his backing was thus vital if the president's forces in the House were going to win against the Democrats with their 50-to-55 vote majority.[42]

The Gramm-Latta substitute was identical to Reagan's proposed budget with respect to the $650 billion in revenues it proposed to raise. But it cut spending by an additional $6.1 billion and the deficit to $38.9 billion in an effort to attract enough "boll weevil" votes to put it across. As pressures mounted, the Gramm-Latta forces amended their proposal further to reduce the deficit to $31 billion. This was done not by cutting spending or raising taxes, but by changing the economic assumptions.

President Reagan used the Easter recess to cajole potential Democratic votes and to play hardball with his own troops. Speaker O'Neill's inaction while he led a congressional delegation to Australia disheartened Democrats. The vote was delayed by House Democrats from the week of April 27 to May 6 and 7 in order to regroup when it appeared that Republicans would lose no more than one or two votes and that the conservative Democrats would supply the margin for a presidential victory.

First Budget Resolution Floor Action

On the first day of voting, two substitutes for the House Budget Committee proposal were overwhelmingly rejected. The first was the Black Caucus substitute sponsored by the Democratic delegate from the District of Columbia, Walter Fauntroy. It provided more spending, more taxes, and a $7.8 billion surplus, and was crushed by 365 to 69.[43] Its major features were reductions in the military budget to pay for restoration of social program cuts. A similar substitute by Budget Committee member Dave Obey (D.-Wis.) that provided a $500 million surplus was battered by 303 to 119.[44]

The crucial vote came on May 7, when the Gramm-Latta substitute was offered in place of the Democratic House Budget Committee proposal. As columnist David Broder noted, the Democratic budget was "carefully crafted." Chairman Jones, "one of the most highly respected of the House's younger leaders," had patiently constructed its provisions. "It was skillfully enough balanced to gain support from all but one of the Democrats on Jones' committee." Further, "it had the full backing of the party's House leadership and of what purported to be a powerful coalition of labor and liberal interest groups."[45] As noted, its reconciliation provisions were written to appeal to traditional House loyalties. Moreover, the Democrats went into the fray with a 241-to-190, or 51-seat margin.

When the vote came, the Gramm-Latta substitute won a smashing 253-to-176 victory. "When Reagan & Co. went to work they rolled the Democrats with surprising ease."[46] The president and the House Republican leaders provided a unanimous Republican vote. Then they pulled in sixty-three Democrats, thirty-eight more than needed to win. The House, as Helen Dewar noted, "the only citadel of government under nominal Democratic control—really marches to the tune of Republicans and conservative Democrats."[47] But more important than the shattered Democratic party in the House or Speaker O'Neill's nominal control was the fundamental change that had occurred:

> Sixty three Democrats joined a unanimous Republican minority in sanctioning what leaders in both parties called a historic reversal of course for American government, in effect a vote to dismantle or drastically cut back dozens of social welfare programs that the Democratic Party had built over the past half century.[48]

President Reagan called it an "historic moment of commitment to a government that can both serve the people and live within its means," and House Budget Chairman Jones referred to the result as "the most monumental and historic turnaround in fiscal policy that has ever occurred."[49]

The battle was not even close. As various commentators pointed out, the House Democratic budget included three-fourths of the Reagan budget cut proposals. Instead of a fight, it was really a coronation of the Reagan budget revolution.

The House Reconciliation Bill

The reconciliation provisions of the Gramm-Latta substitute for the first budget resolution instructed House committees to change existing laws or cut appropriations bills to provide $36.6 billion in budget cuts. When the Democratic written reconciliation bill came back to the House floor for action on June 26, its priorities differed somewhat from those of the Reagan administration. Another substitute, dubbed Gramm-Latta II, put together by the Republican minority-southern Democratic "boll weevil" coalition to carry out the specific Reagan priorities, was offered in its place. It provided for a $37.7 billion slash in spending. It passed by a slim 217-to-211 vote and humiliated the House Democratic majority for the second time. The incredibly disciplined House Republicans lost only 2 votes to the Democrats and picked up 29 renegades from Speaker O'Neill's alleged supporters, 26 southern Democrats, and 3 from north of the Mason-Dixon line. On the final passage of the substitute bill, the vote was 232 to 193—a margin of 39. Some 47 Democrats joined 185 Republicans, while only 5 Republicans bolted ranks and voted with 188 Democrats. Once again the Great Communicator in the White House grasped victory from the jaws of defeat and proved that he, not the Democrats or Speaker O'Neill, commanded the working majority in the House.

But Gramm-Latta II had its price. It was brought to the House floor in emasculated form, "sloppy and hastily prepared."[50] The details were not available until the morning of the vote. Congressman Tom Bevill (D-.Ala.) complained that the House was "authorizing legislation that the authorizing committees have not seen."[51] Figures were crossed out and substitute amounts penciled in. Some pages were misnumbered. Provisions were written by hand in the margins. New titles were inserted. Paragraphs and pages were deleted. To add insult to injury, one substitute amendment included the name and telephone number of Rita Seymour, a staff member of the CBO. *Congressional Quarterly* opined, "It may take weeks to figure out exactly what is in the House-passed reconciliation package known as Gramm-Latta II."[52] The procedures were so chaotic that they seemed to bear out Budget Director Stockman's earlier description of reconciliation as that "untried, unique beast."

The procedures were the result of the scramble for votes and the struggle to win. Budget Chairman Jones claimed Reagan lobbyists were "making deals like crazy in the cloakroom,"[53] and arrangements and deals were made to save funds for impacted school aid, food stamps, assistance to low income energy users, and solar electric plants. When asked directly if his vote could be bought, John B. Breaux (D.-La.) replied, "No, it can be rented,"[54] Republicans placed the cause of the chaos in part at the Democrats' door, charging that the only copy of the substitute had been purloined by an anonymous Democrat on its way to the printers.[55]

No one was happy about the procedures, including Republican Ways and Means Committee ranking member Barber B. Conable, Jr., of New York. There were cries that the proceedings had undermined the budget process and that "reconciliation had created incredible chaos."[56] Rules Committee Chairman Richard Bolling said during his committee's hearing to establish the rules for the floor debate that reconciliation was an "excessive use of Presidential power and license," and that it was "the most brutal and blunt instrument used by a President in an attempt to control the congressional process since Nixon used impoundment."[57] The year before, Bolling had been one of the architects of the innovative use of reconciliation on the first budget resolution, which saved more than $8 billion and led many from both parties to claim that the Budget Act and reconciliation were both alive and well.

When the smoke had cleared, the president, not the Democrats, had the votes. The Reagan budget revolution succeeded by combining the new reconciliation procedures, the majority rule provisions of the Budget Act, and a handful of dissident Democrats with a disciplined Republican minority to roll over the House Democratic leadership.

THE POLITICS OF THE TAX LEG OF THE PROGRAM

The president's original tax proposal contained three simple provisions that cost an enormous amount of money. As conceived, it was an uncomplicated, easy to understand, unadorned program.

Its first fundamental proposal was to cut the top personal income tax rates for unearned income from 70 to 50 percent. As the capital gains tax by law was 40 percent of the top rate, the proposal also automatically reduced the maximum capital gains tax from 28 to 20 percent. Unearned income is essentially income from dividends and interest. Its ostensible purpose was to give an incentive to those in the higher income tax brackets to invest their savings in productive activity by considerably enhancing the rewards for doing so.

The second basic element was the Kemp-Roth proposal, which candidate Reagan had strongly advocated. His chief primary opponent and later vice-presidential candidate, George Bush, labeled it "voodoo economics." It called for an across-the-board, 10 percent cut in personal income taxes for each of three years. Named for Congressman Jack Kemp (R.-N.Y.) and Senator William Roth (R.-Del.), it was dubbed "supply-side" economics. During the tax debate, it was called Kemp-Roth by Kemp and his House colleagues, but during hearings in the Senate Finance Committee and debate on the floor, Senator Roth made a special effort to call it Roth-Kemp. Later in the 1982 campaign, when Roth perceived he was in reelection trouble in Delaware in part because the Reagan economic program had not met expectations, his supporters facetiously referred to it as Kemp-Kemp. Its purpose was to reduce taxes for middle- and upper-income taxpayers substantially to provide incentives for savings and investment. It was also designed to compensate for what was called "bracket creep." As taxpayers' nominal income grew because of inflation, they were pushed into higher and higher tax brackets, even though their real incomes might have been reduced. By cutting each bracket by the same percentage, vastly more dollar amounts went to those in the higher brackets.

The third principal provision was a cut in business depreciation rates.

Originally a modest proposal, its purpose was to provide sufficient reserves for machinery, plant, and equipment so that funds would be available for the purchase of new capital equipment to replace the old. Because of the dramatic rise in prices, existing schedules often did not provide the money for replacement.

It cannot be overlooked that the largest proportion of the benefits went to well-to-do individual and corporate supporters of the Reagan administration. The program had its political as well as its economic arguments. In his March 10 message to the Congress transmitting his new budget and tax proposals, President Reagan argued that "we must cut tax rates so that once again work will be rewarded and savings encouraged" and that "budget cuts alone however will not turn this economy around." As he further claimed,

> Our package includes a proposal to reduce substantially the personal income tax rates levied on our people and to accelerate the recovery of business with capital investment. These rate reductions are essential to restoring strength and growth to the economy by reducing the existing tax barriers that discourage work, saving, and investment. Individuals are the ultimate source of all savings and investment.

President Reagan was also optimistic about the effects of his program:

> Our tax proposal will, if enacted, have an immediate impact on the economic vitality of the Nation, where even a slight improvement can produce dramatic results. For example a 2 percent increase in economic growth will add $60 billion to our gross national product in one year alone. That $60 billion adds to the state and local tax base, to the purchasing power of the American family, and to the resources available for investment.

The program President Reagan sent to the Congress had a breathtaking price tag, $53.9 billion in fiscal year 1982, the first full year it would be in effect. Both internally within the administration and externally among partisan Democrats, neutral economists, some Republican businessmen, and the president's congressional supporters, the size of the cut and the economic theory on which it was based were questioned.

Before the package went to the Congress, Budget Director Stockman had proposed what he called "Chapter II," a series of proposals to accompany his "Chapter I" black book and other budget cuts. Alarmed at the projected deficits, he proposed internally a package to save about $20 billion through a combination of military savings and the closing of tax loopholes:

> Stockman hesitated to discuss details, for the package was politically sensitive, but it included elimination of the oil-depletion allowance; an attack on tax-exempt industrial development bonds; user fees for owners of private airplanes and barges; a potential ceiling on home-mortgage deductions (which Stockman called a "mansion gap," since it would affect only the wealthy); some defense reductions and other items, ten in all.[58]

He made the proposal to help reduce the deficit, to provide a more balanced program, and to create the appearance of equity:

> It would mollify the liberal critics complaining about the cuts in social welfare because it was aimed primarily at tax expenditures (popularly known as "loopholes") benefitting oil and other business interests.[59]

Except for a willingness to consider "user fees," the president stood firm on his defense increase and tax-cut proposals. In particular he was unwilling to consider and in fact "turned down the proposal to eliminate the oil depletion allowance."[60] Stockman lost his fight to reduce the deficits through the tax bill itself and to "reduce its drain on the federal treasury and thus moderate the fiscal damage of Reaganomics."[61] Some of these provisions were initiated by Senate Republicans and passed by the Congress in 1982 (see Table 4–7).

Congressman Gramm argued on the House floor that the tax program would create wealth, not merely redistribute it; and Secretary of the Treasury Regan testified before the House Ways and Means Committee that the administration expected the reduction to spur savings and thus to "finance the red ink by freeing new money for investment."[62] Regan cited the unprecedented combination of increased employment, stable prices, and economic growth that followed the Kennedy administration's tax-cut bill in the early 1960s and its provisions for individual cuts and credits for investment.

The opponents were not so charitable. Senate Democratic Budget Committee's ranking member Ernest Hollings charged that the "administration concluded that what had worked for Treasury Secretary Mellon in the 1920s was certain to work as well in the 1980s.[63] A House budget aide said the Reagan tax and economic assumptions were "made of green cheese imported from the moon."[64] And during floor debate in the House, Majority Leader James C. Wright, Jr. (D.-Tex.), argued:

> You might call it supply side. Its real name is trickle down. It believes with George Gilder that regressive taxes help the poor, that only the rich have sense enough to invest in things that are good for America.[65]

When the package went to the Congress, it ran into three problems. The first was Kemp-Roth, or 10-10-10, which David Stockman had said "was always a Trojan horse to bring down the top rate."[66] Senator Robert Dole (R.-Kans.) chairman of the Finance Committee warned Secretary of the Treasury Regan that there weren't enough votes to pass it. Others, like Senator Robert Packwood (R.-Oreg.), gave similar warnings, and House Majority Leader Wright claimed that fifty of the sixty-three Democratic "boll weevils" who voted with the president on the budget cuts would not back Kemp-Roth. Democrats on the Ways and Means Committee agreed unanimously not to back Kemp-Roth.[67]

Second, to have a relatively clean bill and to avoid a Christmas tree tax bill, the Treasury proposed to deal with such issues as the marriage penalty, the tuition tax credit, taxation for American workers abroad, and inheritance taxes in a second tax bill. Senators balked at this on grounds they could not pass a spending and tax package without knowing what would be in a second bill. In the end, no one but the Treasury backed a second bill, and very quickly members of the Senate Finance Committee began to hang ornaments on their bill.

Third, stung by the humiliating budget defeats the president imposed on them in May and again in June, the Democrats in the House were determined to win the tax fight. It started when the Democrats proposed the more generous 10-5-3 depreciation procedures, for which the biggest and most powerful corporations in the country, organized by an astute and experienced Republican, former treasury official Charls Walker, had been lobbying. In order to win votes to assuage their wounds, the Democrats began to give away the Capitol dome:

> The White House quickly retreated—scrapped its revised and leaner [depreciation] proposal, and began matching the Democrats, billion for billion in tax concessions.[68]

As the bidding war between the two parties escalated, the tax package fell apart. The final versions, which differed very little between the House and the Senate, contained a multiple-year tax cut but limited the first year's cut to 5 percent. Included in the bill were the 10-5-3 depreciation provisions, a bail-out for the savings and loan industry, new and more generous Individual Retirement Act (IRA) provisions, child-care tax provisions, a reduction in the marriage penalty, a $75,000 exemption from income tax for Americans working and living abroad, the virtual abandonment of the inheritance tax, the indexing of future tax cuts based on the rise in the consumer price index, and generous tax concessions for both the real estate industry and the oil companies. Representative Barney Frank (D.-Mass.) exclaimed during the debate on the House floor, "I don't mind the eyes of Texas being upon us. I object to the hands of Texas being in my pockets." And William Greider wrote in *Atlantic Monthly,* "'Do you realize the greed that came to the forefront?' Stockman asked with wonder. 'The hogs were really feeding. The greed level, the level of opportunism, just got out of control.'"[69]

While the first year cost was reduced from Reagan's proposed $53.9 billion to $37.7 billion, the estimated loss of revenues through fiscal year 1985 was $750 billion. Ultimately, the Republicans outbid the Democrats and organized a massive lobbying campaign that included White House and Camp David invitations to wavering representatives. Published reports said that to ensure Democratic votes for his bill, the president promised to veto any windfall-profit tax on oil or gas, to restore the Social Security minimum payments, to keep military bases open, and to avoid reducing the peanut subsidy.[70] In his interview with Greider, David Stockman called the Republican dealers on budget issues "piranhas... They don't care, over in the White House. They want to win."[71]

The bills passed the House and the Senate on the same day, July 29. The Senate was a cakewalk for the Republicans, and the bill won 89 to 11. Critical amendments to change the personal income tax provisions from regressive to progressive cuts were beaten back easily. In the House, the key vote was on the Republican substitute, authored by Barber B. Conable, Jr. (R.-N.Y.), for the Democratic House Ways and Means Committee bill. On that vote, 48 Democrats joined 190 Republicans to pass it 238 to 195. Only one Republican deserted the president on the vote. The lead in *The Washington Post* report began:

> Humbling House Democrats for the third time in a row, President Reagan yesterday won easy approval of this three-year tax-cut bill, virtually assuring enactment of his entire economic program.[72]

President Reagan hailed the passage by contending it marked "a new renaissance in America." He said in his statement that "we have made a new beginning. We're back on the right road, and we're making progress. And if we keep working together, we can reach that new era of economic prosperity we all want."

The bill was a watershed tax bill, the likes of which had not been seen for more than fifty years, since the Republican domination of the presidency in the 1920s:

> The bills represent the abandonment by Congress of past Democratic practice, which has been to tilt tax cuts toward the poor and middle-class wage-earners. Instead Congress this time granted the larger cuts to the better-off and to business, on the Republican theory that this will stimulate savings, investment and growth, and ultimately work to benefit all.[73]

Senator Hollings called it "revenue hemorrhage legislation,"[74] that ensured massive deficits and removed any prospect for a balanced budget or the use of fiscal policy to fight inflation for many budgets to come.

Democratic criticism of the Reagan budget deficits may prove that there are great ironies in political life. During the 1930s, Democrats defended and justified massive deficits while Republicans castigated and chastized them. During the 1980s the Democrats chastized and castigated the deficits while Republicans, especially supply-side Republican proponents defended them. While distinctions can be made between deficits in depressions and deficits in periods of inflation, the overwhelming impression was that neither party was comfortable in its new political posture. Such are the contradictions of the politics of the budget.

THE MILITARY BUILD-UP

The third leg of the Reagan budget revolution triad was a gigantic shift in resources from the civilian to the military budget. In some quarters, this was little noticed. So intense was the focus on the battle over budget cuts and the tax bill that slight immediate attention was paid to the massive shift in priorities occasioned by the military build-up. Attention was intentionally focused on cuts. President Reagan's revisions of the fiscal year 1982 budget, which he sent to the Congress on March 10, 1982, included a $6.3 billion supplemental increase in the fiscal year 1981 military budget and an additional $26 billion for fiscal year 1982. The text of his message, however, mentioned neither. Throughout the initial debate, the defense spending increases were locked in the closet, seldom mentioned when the totality of the budget was discussed. It took three events for the implications of the defense spending increases to dent both the congressional and the public consciousness. The first was William Grieder's famous *Atlantic Monthly* article on David Stockman. There the totality of the Pentagon budget victories were stated in full detail. The Reagan Administration proposed a *real* increase in defense spending of 7 percent a year. Based on an estimated 8 percent inflation rate, this amounted to an initial increase of $32 billion in a $200 billion defense budget. Over five years, the total budget authority for defense would be about $1.5 trillion.[75] From fiscal year 1981 to fiscal year 1987, the president's budget reform plan indicated there would be an increase in total defense spending from 24 to 37.2 percent of the total budget outlays.[76]

The second event that focused attention on the defense increase was the release of the fiscal year 1983 budget—the first full Reagan budget. The proposed fiscal year 1983 deficit of $91.5 billion, which every student of the budget knew was a gross underestimate, shocked the president's supporters both in the Congress and around the country. As Senator John C. Danforth of Missouri, a staunch initial Republican supporter of Reaganomics who was up for election in 1982, told Secretary of the Treasury Regan in a private meeting with Republican senators, "Last year I was part of the crew sailing aboard the ship of state. This year I'm standing on the dock waving 'bon voyage.'" As Danforth gave a little wave to Secretary Regan, other Republican senators broke into laughter.[77]

The third was the resignation interview given by the mild-mannered "team player" Murray Weidenbaum, President Reagan's chairman of the Council of Economic Advisers. In an August 1982 interview with the Associated Press, Weidenbaum said that the president's insistence on a record expansion of the nation's military budget had defeated the administration efforts to control government spending and had contributed to "horrendous deficits":

> On balance, we really haven't cut the budget. Instead the much-publicized reductions in non-military programs the President has won from Congress have been fully offset by the unprecedented growth in military spending.
> When you add that to the big tax cuts, you get...horrendous deficits.[78]

The Carter and Reagan-Bush budgets for national defense in outlays (actual spending) are given in Table 8–1.

TABLE 8–1   National Defense Spending Outlays (Billions of Dollars)

Carter[1]		Reagan-Bush[2]	
Fiscal Year	**Amount**	**Fiscal Year**	**Amount**
1978	$104.5	1982	$185.3
1979	116.3	1983	209.9
1980	133.9	1984	227.4
1981	157.5	1985	252.7
		1986	273.3
		1987	281.9
		1988	290.4
		1989	303.6
		1990	299.3
		1991	297.6[3]
		1992	295.7[3]

1. *Economic Report of the President* (Washington, D.C.: U.S. Government Printing Office, 1987), pp. 332–333.
2. *Economic Report of the President* (Washington, D.C.: U.S. Government Printing Office, 1991), pp. 376–377.
3. Estimate, 1990 Budget Agreement cap.

A REVIEW OF THE REAGAN BUDGET REVOLUTION

The Reagan budget revolution achieved certain goals and failed to meet others. It clearly shifted priorities from the civilian to the military sector. It also obviously shifted many burdens from the government to the private sector. It greatly reduced the income of the state and local governments from federal sources. It made a vast reduction in the tax burden on upper-income taxpayers and on corporations. In doing so, it so reduced the revenues of the federal government that there were two results, one intended and one unintended. The intended result was to limit the growth in the civilian side of government by limiting the revenues available to be spent. The unintended obvious result was the massive deficits occasioned by the combination of tax cuts and military spending increases. This was due to the failure of the tax program to "have an immediate impact on the economic vitality of the Nation," as President Reagan had predicted in his message of March 10, 1981, or to "finance the red ink by freeing new money for investment," as Secretary Regan, the chief witness for the tax bill, argued before the House Ways and Means Committee. Instead of being available for investment, much of the savings was claimed by the Treasury to finance the burgeoning debt.

The program did bring a significant reduction in interest rates and the rate of inflation, but at the expense of the highest unemployment rates since the Great Depression accompanied by a recession in 1981–1982. The recovery that began at the end of 1982 lasted for seven years.

The deficit grew to more than $200 billion for the first full-year

Reagan budget in fiscal year 1983. But even with midterm changes in tax and spending priorities in calendar 1982, the fundamental course was set for several years to come.

The Reagan budget cuts of about $38 billion in domestic programs in the first year represented an unprecedented cut in spending. No previous modern administration had achieved as much. In view of the double-digit interest and inflation rates, a cut of that size made sense to most business and many academic economists. Countercyclical fiscal policy called for cuts in spending at the height of inflation if for no other reason than to allow an expansion of monetary policy to offset the cuts in a noninflationary way. What was contentious was where the cuts were made. In addition, the administration appeared not to know how to count. Starting with an inherited $45 billion deficit, the savings from the fiscal year 1982 budget cuts were offset by the loss of revenue from fiscal 1982 tax cuts. When the military increases were added, a deficit of $60 billion or more was ensured. This was foretold by David Stockman's OMB computer run, but it was ignored. The accompanying loss of confidence by the business community and the reduction in demand by consumers brought on the worst recession since the Depression of the 1930s. The increase in unemployment, the decline in economic growth, and the depression in sales of housing, autos, and consumer goods brought such additional declines in revenues and increases in outlays for Social Security, welfare, unemployment compensation, and other "safety net," or built-in stabilizer, programs that the deficit in fiscal year 1982 ballooned to $127.9 billion. While the rhetoric remained, the goal of a balanced budget was abandoned. No politically feasible combination of additional budget cuts, even in the military sector, or tax increases could bring that about in any foreseeable year. According to Reagan OMB economist Lawrence Kudlow, "The underlying deficit would be $150 billion a year by the end of 1988 even if the economy recovers between now and then and unemployment drops to about six percent.[79]

The Reagan budget revolution had the same goals as the Nixon budget war of a decade earlier. Both the elements and the details were much the same. Like President Reagan, President Nixon was intent on cutting social programs, housing and community development, rural electrification, the Farmers Home Administration, welfare, and unemployment training. President Nixon proposed substituting reduced block grant programs for the cities and states for existing categorical grants, as did President Reagan. President Nixon increased military spending to finance the war in Vietnam and Cambodia, while Reagan poured money into the Defense Department.

But there was a significant difference between the two programs. What President Nixon tried and largely failed to do by confrontation, impoundment, and imperial policies President Reagan achieved legally, constitutionally, by majority vote after majority vote in the Congress and with the initial support of the public. Albeit he transformed a new and little-known technical device called reconciliation into a political weapon, but he did so without offending the Constitution and with the acquiescence if not the agreement of his political opponents. In spite of Senator Hollings's charge that during President Reagan's effort, supported by his great reserves of charm and communications skill, to move his program through the Congress, "the congressional budget process was brutalized," essentially the president got his spending cuts, tax cuts, and military increases because at every critical stage he had the votes. As Lance T. LeLoup pointed out:

> Even if the Democratic alternatives to the budget resolution, reconciliation bill, and tax proposals had passed the House, Reagan would have had a victory in terms of policy. Examination of the Democratic alternatives reveals that they made slight alterations but basically endorsed the president's program.[80]

NOTES

1. *Los Angeles Times*, 9 January 1983, pt. I, p. 19.
2. *Congressional Directory, 97th Congress* (Washington, D.C.: U.S. Government Printing Office, 1981), p. 252.
3. Ibid., p. 247.
4. William Greider, "The Education of David Stockman," *Atlantic Monthly* 242 December 1981): 33.
5. *Budget of the United States: Fiscal Year 1982* (Washington, D.C.: U.S. Government Printing Office, 1981), p. M3.
6. Senate Budget Committee, *Congressional Budget Reform, P.L. 93-344*, 94th Cong. 2nd. sess. August 1976, p. 71.
7. *Budget, 1982*, sec. 7, p. 9.
8. Greider, "Stockman," p. 30.
9. Ibid., p. 32.
10. *Congressional Record* (daily ed.), 21 January 1981, pp. S.372–417; 22 January 1981, pp. S.453–548; 27 January 1981, pp. S.630–660.
11. Greider, "Stockman," p. 33.
12. Ibid.
13. Ibid.
14. Ibid.
15. *The Washington Post*, 8 February 1981, p. A1.
16. Ibid., pp. A15–16. Among the specific Stockman black book cuts in outlays from the current services budget base line were Medicaid, $1.0 billion; Disability Insurance, $600 million; Social Security student benefits, $700 million; minimum Social Security benefits, $1.0 billion; Unemployment Insurance extended benefits, $2.2 billion; Trade Adjustment Assistance, $1.0 billion; Food Stamps, $2.6 billion; Aid to Families with Dependent Children, $671 million; Health Planning, $75 million; Comprehensive Employment and Training Act, $3.7 billion; Public Health Service Hospitals, $100 million; National Endowments for the Arts and the Humanities, $85 million; Corporation for Public Broadcasting, $43 million; child nutrition (school lunch, breakfast, etc.) programs, $990 million; social/community services, health program block grant consolidation, $1.8 billion; consolidation of 57 elementary and secondary education programs, $1.3 billion; student loans and Pell Grants, $914 million; Rural Electrification Administration electric and telephone loans, $1.9 billion; Export-Import Bank, $560 million; Farmers Home Administration, $105 million; Synthetic Fuels Subsidies, $712 million; National Science Foundation, $162 million; and Urban Develop-

ment Action Grants, $64 million. Billions more in budget authority cuts were proposed, and these would have a greater effect in future years.

17. The first was on February 5.
18. *The New York Times*, 26 February 1981.
19. Ibid.
20. In 1975 the act was not in force, but Congress proceeded to follow its provisions in a dry run.
21. *Task Force on Budget Process, Hearings*, House Committee on the Budget, 96th Cong., 1st sess., 11 and 12, December 1979, p. 29.
22. Ibid., p. 30.
23. Ibid.
24. *Congressional Record* (daily ed.), 13 May 1981, p. H.2177.
25. *Congressional Quarterly*, 10 January 1981, p. 63.
26. 31 U.S.C. 1325.
27. *The Washington Post*, 19 February 1981, p. A18.
28. Ibid.
29. Who devised the strategy to use reconciliation in early 1981? When asked this question by the author, credit was taken by the counsel of the Senate Budget Committee, by the staff director of the Senate Budget Committee, for the chairman of the Senate Budget Committee by a member of his personal staff, and for Budget Director David Stockman by an aide. This was in 1981, when reconciliation and budget cutting were in vogue and the center of political attention. The universal claim carried out the old adage that success has a thousand fathers, while failure is an orphan. In an interview with CBO Director Alice M. Rivlin conducted by Tom Bigson of *USA Today* (13 December 1982, p. 11A), she commented, "Well, I do not know why Stockman should be credited with that," when asked if she was referring to him in her comment that Congress had learned that it was very important to make budget decisions early. It had been used the previous fiscal year. See p. 293.
30. *Congressional Record* (daily ed.), 4 May 1982, p. S.5320.
31. *Congressional Quarterly*, 28 February 1981, p. 377.
32. Ibid., 21 March 1981, p. 499.
33. *Budget, 1982*, 311.
34. Senate Democratic Policy Committee, *Reconciliation Briefing Book*, 23 March 1982, p. 2.
35. Joint Study Committee on Budget Control, *Improving Congressional Control over Budgeting Outlay and Receipt Totals, Interim Report*, 93rd Cong., 1st sess., 7 February 1973, p. 9.
36. *Congressional Record* (daily ed.), 14 May 1982, p. S.5320.
37. Lance T. LeLoup, "After the Blitz: Reagan and the U.S. Congressional Budget Process," *Legislative Studies Quarterly*, 3 August, 1982, p. 337.
38. *Congressional Quarterly*, 21 February 1981, p. 332.
39. Greider, "Stockman," p. 38.
40. Ibid.
41. *Congressional Quarterly*, 18 April 1981, p. 659.
42. Gramm's leadership on behalf of the Reagan forces had political implications. It cost him his Budget Committee membership in the 98th Congress, whereupon he resigned his seat and ran successfully for reelection as a Republican.
43. *Congressional Record* (daily ed.), 6 May 1981, p. H.1892, vote 32.
44. Ibid., pp. H.1911–1912, vote 33.
45. *The Washington Post*, 8 May 1981, p. A1.
46. Ibid.
47. Ibid.

48. Ibid.
49. Ibid, p. A3.
50. LeLoup, "After the Blitz," p. 337.
51. *Congressional Quarterly*, 4 July 1982, p. 1168.
52. Ibid.
53. Ibid., p. 1169.
54. Ibid.
55. Ibid., p. 1168.
56. Ibid.
57. Ibid.
58. Greider, "Stockman," p. 36.
59. Ibid.
60. Ibid.
61. Ibid., p. 46.
62. *Congressional Quarterly*, 21 February 1981, p. 335.
63. *Congressional Record* (daily ed.), 14 March 1982, p. S.5321. Andrew W. Mellon served as treasury secretary under Presidents Harding, Coolidge, and Hoover from March 4, 1921, to February 9, 1932, and was the strongest and most influential member of the cabinets. The budget ran a surplus in each of the first 10 years of the period. His term ended in economic disaster at the onset of the Great Depression. He believed strongly that tax benefits would encourage savings and investment, and that tax incentives for the top tax brackets and economic groups would stimulate production and prosperity.
64. *Congressional Quarterly*, 21 February 1981, p. 334.
65. *The Washington Post*, 30 July 1981, p. A1.
66. Greider, "Stockman," p. 47.
67. *Congressional Quarterly*, 16 May 1981, p. 841.
68. Greider, "Stockman," p. 47.
69. Ibid., p. 51.
70. *The Washington Post*, 30 July 1981.
71. Greider, "Stockman," p. 50.
72. *The Washington Post*, 30 July 1981, p. A1.
73. Ibid.
74. *Congressional Record* (daily ed.), 14 May 1982, p. S.5321.
75. Most government budgeting accounts have 2 items. One is budget authority (BA), the amount Congress appropriates, and the other is outlays (O), the amount actually spent during the fiscal year. In defense there are three categories, budget authority (BA), outlays (O), and total obligational authority (TOA), which is somewhat larger than budget authority. The Reagan administration proposed $1.5 trillion in TOA over 5 years.
76. While there was a massive increase in total defense spending, the percentage of defense spending to total budget outlays did not rise as spectacularly as proposed by Reagan. Large rises in interest costs and entitlements made the defense increases a smaller percentage of the total budget than anticipated.
77. Office of Senator Danforth. Slightly different versions appear in *The New York Times*, 11 February 1982, p. A31; and the *St. Louis Post Dispatch*, 14 February 1982.
78. *Des Moines Register*, 27 August 1982, p. 1.
79. *The Washington Post*, 9 December 1982, p. D13.
80. LeLoup, "After the Blitz," p. 336.

9

Gramm-Rudman-Hollings and the Reagan Budgets

PRELUDE TO GRAMM-RUDMAN-HOLLINGS

A little more than a decade after the landmark 1974 Budget Reform Act was signed into law, there was once again a crisis over the budget. The budget, the budget deficit, and the Budget Act procedures were in deep trouble.

Neither a president's budget nor a congressional alternative could be crafted to satisfy the needs of the country. The fiscal crisis was greater, measured by almost any objective standard, than those that preceded the passage of both the 1921 and 1974 Budget Acts.

First, there was a crisis of process. Examples abound:

- Not once since 1977 had the thirteen regular appropriations bills been placed on the president's desk by the beginning of the new fiscal year on October 1. Worse, in fiscal years 1986 and 1987, not a single one of the thirteen bills was signed into law by the new year.
- The government was functioning under a single, catchall appropriations bill called a continuing resolution (CR), passed either at the twelfth hour of the old fiscal year or well into the new fiscal year.
- Routinely the First Concurrent Budget Resolution, the cornerstone of the 1974 Act, required to be passed by May 15, was passed one to four months late.[1]
- Authorization bills, especially for defense, foreign aid, and health and human services, were seldom passed before the appropriations bills that funded them were before the House or Senate, as required by the rules of both bodies.

- The second budget resolution was abandoned after 1981 when its passage became a farce. With the full knowledge that the fiscal year 1982 deficit would exceed $90 billion (the final figure was $128 billion), the Senate merely re-passed the first resolution with its estimated $48 billion deficit on December 8. Due to be passed September 15, it underestimated the deficit by $80 billion and exceeded the timetable by eighty-four days. Senator after senator justified his or her vote for the resolution by claiming it was cast to "preserve" the congressional budget process. This was reminiscent of the view that even if Christianity dies out, the Presbyterian Church will go on.
- The reconciliation bill, designed to make the needed cuts or raise the additional taxes to bring what the Congress wrought in a particular year within the binding totals of its budget resolution, routinely was either too little or too late or not passed at all.[2]
- The details of the president's tax and spending proposals came under withering fire even before the budget was released. Presidents' budgets were considered to be dead on arrival when they got to the Congress. The Congress first formalized the process in fiscal 1987, when the House and Senate voted overwhelmingly to reject the president's budget.
- The Congress itself was in disarray. Money for more than half the government, year in and year out, was not even subjected to the scrutiny, fine-tuning, and legislative balancing that was intended in the longstanding congressional appropriations process." The Congress was doing most of its work in three large categories: a budget to set spending and taxing targets, a reconciliation package to make the program cuts necessary to keep the deficits under at least some control, and an omnibus continuing resolution to make all the requisite appropriations.[3]
- The issues of entitlements, tax expenditures, and a budget backlog as great as the fiscal year budget itself were additional problems of process, raised by the Joint Study Committee in 1974, that had not been adequately handled (see Figure 7–1.)

Not all of this was the fault of the Budget Act, for at least three other factors were involved. First, in some years the president proposed such an abundance of controversial budget matters that they were indigestible by any Congress in any twelve-month period. Second, some members of the Senate insisted on proposing highly contentious amendments to carry out the social agenda—such as abortion, school prayer and busing—to authorization or appropriations bills, notwithstanding the rule that required amendments to appropriations bills to be germane. Third, from time to time the president, the House Democrats, and the Senate Republicans deliberately delayed appropriation bills for purely tactical reasons. The House Appropriations Committee Democrats, smarting from their loss of power to the budget committees, once again became the brokers of specific fiscal programs—the pork and the boodle—when regular appropriation bills were delayed and members had to come to them to bargain to get their pet projects added to the end-of-the-year continuing resolution. The Senate Republicans, acting on behalf of the White House, quite deliberately delayed spending bills until the end of the year, because they believed with the threat of the veto they had more leverage to get their way with the Democratic House on both domestic cuts and military increases.

But there was not only a crisis in process but also a crisis of substance. Not once since the 1974 act was passed had the budget been in balance. While the act did not call for a balanced budget, it did call for the Congress to set forth "the surplus or deficit in the budget *which is appropriate in light of economic conditions and all other relevant factors*" (italics added). It may be difficult to define precisely the appropriate levels of the surplus or deficit in any given year, but it is not difficult to determine when they are wholly inappropriate. And year after year, the size of the budget deficit *was* inappropriate. Indeed in the six decades since 1930 the budget was balanced only eight times, four times under Truman, three under Eisenhower, and once in fiscal year 1969 in the budget proposed by President Johnson and inherited in its last five months by President Nixon, when there was a small $3.2 billion surplus.[4]

The annual deficit grew from the $40 billion to $80 billion range in the fiscal year 1974—1981 period of the 1974 Budget Act, to the $127 billion to $220 billion level in the 1980s, with the deficit routinely at the higher end of the scale during the crisis preceding the passage of the Gramm-Rudman-Hollings Act.[5]

The national debt almost precisely doubled from $908.5 billion to $1,817.0 billion between fiscal years 1980 and 1985, and grew another trillion dollars in the next four years. At the end of the Reagan administration, it would be three times the size of all the deficits of the previous thirty-nine presidents (see Table 5–1).[6]

The budget deficit and the burgeoning debt brought other problems, namely unprecedented deficits in the balance of payments and the balance of trade. The price of the dollar rose spectacularly, made American exports expensive abroad and foreign imports cheap at home, and brought a farm-belt depression and a major crisis in the automobile, steel, and electronic industries as well as to some regions of the country, particularly to the Middle West with its farm, farm machinery, and rust-belt industries. America became a debtor nation for the first time since World War I.

These conditions were offset by a huge decline in the rate of inflation, lower prices for consumers, a dramatic fall in interest rates, and, after the 1982 recession, a continued economic expansion for more than seven years.[7] However, the decline in inflation and the indexing of federal income taxes reduced tax receipts far below those used to justify the rosy deficit projections of the supply-side economists.

The history of the 1974 Budget Act can be divided into two periods. The first, from its inception through the first year of the Reagan presidency, was a period when the act, in terms of both procedure and policy, worked reasonably well when measured by debt and deficit, although both interest rates and the inflation rate were at times extraordinarily high. The second period, from 1982 on, was one in which neither procedures nor results, when measured by debt and deficit, were successful. Although interest rates and the inflation rate had vastly improved, they were still far higher than the historical averages.

If one had to choose a single watershed event that was at the root of the fiscal crisis and foretold the downfall of the 1974 act, it was the enactment of the president's Economic Recovery Tax Act of 1981. As passed it gave away $750 billion in revenues over five years, at the rate of $150 billion a year. This assured massive deficits and an uncontrolled budget policy for the foreseeable future. While proposed and pushed eagerly by the president, no particular partisan blame can be attached. The bill passed the Senate, 89 to 11. In the House there was a bidding match between the White House and the House Republicans, on the one hand, and Democrats on the other to see who could trade away the greatest part of the Capitol dome (see Chapter 8). David Stockman's assertion that "the greed level, the level of opportunism, just got out of control"[8] and his description of House Republicans and dealers in the White House as "piranhas"[9] are equally deserved by House Democrats.

In the first period there were few failures. Most deadlines were met. The first concurrent resolution was routinely passed on or shortly after its May 15 deadline. In the first four years even the shortly-to-be-doomed second resolution was passed before the beginning of the new fiscal year.

Beginning in 1983 and most conspicuously after 1984, on budget issues it was no longer so much House against Senate and Republicans against Democrats, but the Congress against the president. There was a potential bipartisan budget consensus in the Congress, not unlike the bipartisan consensus that had produced the Social Security revisions of 1983, that three steps were needed to deal with the budget crisis: the increase in military spending had to be slowed down; most domestic spending, including cost of living increases, had to be slowed down or frozen; and taxes had to be raised. This position was shared by most mainline economists and much of the public. But it could only succeed if there were an agreement among Republicans and Democrats, House and Senate, and the president concerning its details. If Republicans agreed to a tax increase, the Democrats would be protected against campaign charges of wanting to tax and tax and spend and spend. If the Democrats agreed to a Social Security cost of living freeze, Republicans would be protected against familiar Democratic charges that they were out to destroy Social Security. And if both agreed to a slowdown in the defense build-up, neither could be accused of harming the country's security.

Such an agreement was possible in the Congress, but there was no way the program could succeed without the president coming aboard. It would be difficult enough to vote for tax increases or a freeze on Social Security even if everyone agreed. But to vote for either only to have the president veto it would be the worst of all worlds. One would have the political liabilities of voting for it without any of the benefits of its going into effect. But the president was adamant against slowing defense spending, raising taxes, or freezing Social Security. He continued to insist that the only answers to the problem were deep cuts in that small part of the budget that remained when funding for the military, Social Security, and interest on the debt were put off-limits to the budget ax (see Table 10–3).

THE POLITICS OF THE 1985 BUDGET FIGHT

Convinced that the budget was out of control, in 1985 the Senate, led by Majority Leader Robert J. Dole (R.-Kan.) and Budget Committee Chairman Pete V. Domenici (R.-N.Mex.), made a heroic, three-pronged effort to come to grips with the crisis. First, they proposed a one-year freeze on cost of living adjustments (COLAs) on all pensions, including those for Social Security. This would save $28.3 billion, of which $22 billion was from Social Security. Second, they proposed that the military budget be held at the previous year's level with an increase for inflation, which provided a freeze in real terms.[10] Third, they proposed a small tax increase of $59 billion over three years. The first two items were proposed as part of the First Concurrent Budget Resolution, which passed the Senate May 10. The third was offered by six Republican and three Democratic senators during a House-Senate conference committee meeting on the budget resolution.

The first two survived an onslaught in the Senate only after one Republican Senator, Pete Wilson (R.-Calif.), was brought in by ambulance and cast the tying fiftieth vote from a stretcher, and after Vice-President George Bush cast the tie-breaking vote. Seventeen of the twenty-two Republicans facing reelection in 1986 voted for the Social Security freeze. It is not clear whether their vote was heroic or suicidal.

On major issues the House bill did just the opposite. It froze military spending at the fiscal year 1985 level but granted the COLA for Social Security. The Senate also proposed larger cuts in other domestic programs than did the House.

When the president indicated his opposition to the Social Security freeze, both Democrats and Republicans in the House also closed the door on them. House Minority Whip Trent Lott (R.-Miss.) said, "Domenici should forget social security. In my opinion it ain't gonna happen."[11] House Democrats were also adamant; House Speaker Thomas P. (Tip) O'Neill, Jr., of Massachusetts, not a member of the conference, suggested taxing Social Security benefits to those single and married recipients with incomes in excess of $25,000 and $32,000, respectively, as an alternative to the COLA freeze.

On June 27, during the conference committee meetings, the government announced that in May the government had spent twice as much money as it had taken in revenues and that the monthly deficit for May, including off-budget items of $1.5 billion, was $42 billion. On the same day a majority of the Senate Republicans on the conference committee offered their modest tax increase as part of the attempt to cut back the deficit.

The previous week, the president had said in his weekly radio address:

> I'll repeat it until I'm blue in the face; I will veto any tax increase the Congress sends me.[12]

And at a meeting at the White House just before he entered the hospital for an intestinal operation, he angrily broke a pencil in two and said he would not back down an inch in his opposition to any tax increase. Meanwhile there was a stalemate in the conference committee.

At the suggestion of Congressmen Jack Kemp (R.-N.Y.) and Trent Lott (R.-Miss.) to Donald Regan, chief of the White House staff, a framework was agreed to at the White House. The president and his staff agreed with House Democrats and Republicans on a budget accord. From the point of view of Senate Republicans, it was the worst of all worlds. There would be no new taxes but a compromise on Social Security and the military budget. And the "compromise" was the *higher* figure for both.

Senate Republicans were livid. After a seventy-four minute meeting with the president, Senator Dole said that the Senate "didn't sweat blood for four months to back off now,"[13] and one Senate aide remarked, "We walked the plank for the real deficit reduction, but the President and the House Democrats came out the winners."[14]

After a closed-door meeting with Senate Republicans, Dole said:

> The President says no taxes. Tip says no COLA's. They're saying they got a deal. I don't know if it's a deal. I think its surrendering to the deficit.[15]

His Senate Republican Whip, Alan K. Simpson (R.-Wyo.), said, "That's not an agreement of the 50 guys who jumped off a cliff over here,"[16] and after the closed-door session in which republican Senators vented their spleen against White House officials, Warren Rudman (R.-N.H.) said, "People feel they flew a kamikaze mission and ended up in flames and got nothing for it."[17]

Not only did the event cause a schism between the Senate Republicans and the White House but between Republicans in the House and Senate, especially between Dole and Kemp, both of whom were potential Republican presidential candidates. Dole commented acidly a few days later that Jack Kemp wanted "a business deduction for hair spray." Kemp, retorted that during a recent fire Mr. Dole's library had burned down: "Both books in it were lost, and Senator Dole had not finished coloring one of them."[18]

But more seriously, at the end of July Domenici said that "any chance for this year of getting a real, significant, reliable, credible deficit reduction package is gone."[19] He was right. The final compromise on the budget resolution projected a deficit of $171.9 billion for fiscal year 1986. When the figures were added up in October 1986, it was almost $50 billion higher—$221.2 billion. It was a significant lost opportunity.

Republican Senators, especially those from the twenty-two seats up for reelection, felt betrayed and on their own. They and their leaders' number-one political obsession was to protect their flanks against charges of failure to deal with the deficits and that they had voted to cripple Social Security. The chance to redeem themselves and to gain revenge came in October.

THE POLITICS OF THE PASSAGE OF
GRAMM-RUDMAN-HOLLINGS

Smarting under the beating they had taken at the hands of both the president and the House, Senate Republicans saw the chance to redeem themselves politically when the one-page bill to raise the debt ceiling from $1.824 trillion to $2.078 trillion arrived in the Senate from the House in September.[20]

Two freshmen Republicans, Phil Gramm of Texas, who had been a senator only ten months, and Warren Rudman of New Hampshire, who was in his first term, joined with veteran Democratic Senator Ernest F. Hollings (D.-S.C.) to propose a measure that seemed politically irresistable. Thus Gramm-Rudman-Hollings was a child of the political reforms of the 1970s. In previous decades no freshmen senators had ever expected both to sponsor and pass major or far-reaching legislation. For the first term, at least, they were supposed to be seen and not heard.

The bill proposed to reduce the annual deficit by equal cuts of $36 billion a year over five years and to bring a balanced budget by fiscal year 1991. To vote against it was to vote against motherhood, the flag, and apple pie. It had other political and parliamentary pressures going for it as well.

The debt ceiling was essential. It had to be passed in a few days or the government would run out of money. This made it both veto-proof and almost impossible to filibuster successfully. Further, members of the Senate were reluctant to vote additional authority to the Treasury to borrow more money and thus increase the public debt without taking action or at least giving the appearance of taking action—to deal with the country's number-one domestic problem. House and Senate members had returned to Washington after Labor Day with their constituents' demand that they take action on the budget crisis ringing in their ears.

Within short order the bill had forty bipartisan Senate sponsors. House Democratic leaders quickly saw that it was certain to pass when at least seventy-five of their flock made public commitments in its favor in the early days. Democratic Whip Thomas S. Foley of Washington saw it "as an excellent opening to deal with the terrible deficits and mounting debt that had continued to haunt our country's economic future."[21] President Reagan endorsed it early, either without or against the advice of his secretaries of state and defense and his national security adviser. And numerous otherwise reluctant Democrats saw it as a way to force the president to cut defense spending or raise taxes or both.

Even its sponsors and supporters had doubts about its attempt to do in a mechanical way what the president and the Congress refused to do in an intelligent way. Senator Rudman called it "a bad idea whose time had come." In a Republican conference Senator Dole is reported to have said to Senator Rudman, "Don't get up and explain it again. Some of us are for it." And Senator John H. Chafee (R.-R.I.) called it "the worst thing except for anything else."

Its opponents were even more scathing. Senator Lowell Weicker (R.-Conn.), one of only four Republicans to oppose it, called it a "legislative substitute for the guts we don't have to do what needs to be done."[22] Terms such as a pig in a poke, Draconian, Armageddon, and a sword of Damocles were applied to it. A somewhat more profound explanation came from Senator Daniel P. Moynihan (D.-N.Y.), who said:

> A majority of Democrats agreed to dismantle the domestic policies of Franklin D. Roosevelt in return for a majority of Republicans agreeing to dismantle the defense policies of Ronald Reagan.[23]

Some of the less partisan or nonpartisan experts criticized it as well. Dr. Rudolph G. Penner, the new nonpartisan head of the Congressional Budget Office warned that the bill gave an excessive amount of power to appointed officials such as himself, the head of the General Accounting Office and the director of the Office of Management and Budget who determined whether and where the automatic cuts would be made. The new Nobel Prize winner in economics, Professor Franco Modigliani, complained of its potential dire economic consequences.

After threats from the White House and the Treasury of a fiscal collapse if the debt ceiling bill were not passed quickly, an aborted attempt at a filibuster, and several unsuccessful and one successful major efforts to amend it, the Gramm-Rudman-Hollings amendment passed the Senate by a vote of 75 to 24. The only successful amendment to it—technically an amendment in the second degree—was one by Senator Carl Levin (D.-Mich.) requiring that the automatic cuts be made uniformly and according to the priorities found in the line items of congressional appropriations bills. He argued that this removed the president's discretion as to where the cuts would be made, gave him no blank check, and required him to carry out an essentially ministerial function.

The party breakdown on the vote on the Gramm-Rudman-Hollings amendment was 48 Republicans and 27 Democrats for and 4 Republicans and 20 Democrats opposed. By a vote of 51 to 37 the debt ceiling bill, as amended by the addition of Gramm-Rudman-Hollings, was sent to the House.

The House Democrats had been caught off guard when the Gramm-Rudman-Hollings amendment was proposed in the Senate. They were ill-prepared, badly divided, and had no clear plan of action. Momentum was so great in favor of it that it was not a case of whether it would pass but merely when. Republicans had scored politically, pulled off a clever political coup, put the monkey on the Democrats' back, and recaptured the political initiative.

When the bill got to the House, the Democrats had regrouped somewhat. By a party-line vote of 249 to 180, in which there were only two Democratic defections, the Democrats sent their own bill to conference with the Republican Senate. It is generally impossible to beat something with nothing and the Democratic bill provided bargaining material by which some of the Senate features could be mellowed.

The House Democratic bill did three main things. First, it outbid the Republicans and proposed to speed up the deficit reduction program and achieve a balanced budget by 1990 instead of 1991. The yearly reductions in the budget deficit were set at slightly more than $50 billion a year instead of the $36 billion proposed in the Republican five-year plan. Second, it provided a stronger first-year program than that of the Republicans. The Senate version provided only a mild reduction in fiscal year 1986 so that tough votes would not have to be taken before the 1986 election. This led Speaker O'Neill to refer to it as the "Republican Incumbents Protection Act of 1985." Third, it protected nine programs for poor and low-income families by putting the funds outside the budget-cutting mechanism.

The bill was in conference between the House and the Senate for more than a month. Meanwhile the president and the Treasury threatened to shut down the government if the debt ceiling measure with the Gramm-Rudman-Hollings amendment was not passed soon. But the Treasury blinked before the House Democrats did. It borrowed off-budget funds through the Federal Financing Bank, and to pay the bills it spent Social Security receipts instead of putting them in the trust fund, a questionable if not illegal act. In the meantime the House initiated and the Congress passed a month's extension of the debt ceiling to give them time to negotiate.

Finally, after dire warnings of disaster from the Pentagon, whose spokesman said the bill would "send a message of comfort to the Soviets"; from the mayors of the country, who said it would devastate the cities; and from farm groups, educators, and the panoply of pleaders who inhabit Washington, the bill finally passed the Congress on December 12 and was signed by the president on December 13. The vote was 271 to 154 in the House and 61 to 31 in the Senate.

MAJOR FEATURES OF GRAMM-RUDMAN-HOLLINGS

The Gramm-Rudman-Hollings Act is formally known as the Balanced Budget and Emergency Deficit Control Act of 1985. It was an amendment not only to House Joint Resolution 372 increasing the statutory limits on the public debt but also to the Congressional Budget and Impoundment Control Act of 1974. Among its major provisions were: (1) a schedule of maximum deficits for fiscal years 1986–1991; (2) a new deficit-cutting procedure if the Congress and the president failed to meet the mandated yearly deficit goals in which the terms *snapshot, trigger,* and *sequester* were prominent; (3) a new timetable for budget action; and (4) amendments to the rules of the House and Senate to help carry out the provisions of the act.[24]

Mandatory Schedule

The measure mandated a specific budget-deficit schedule for six fiscal years beginning on October 1, 1985, for fiscal year 1986. With the exception of the first year the president was required to propose and the Congress to approve a budget whose maximum deficit was reduced by $36 billion a year until the budget came into balance in fiscal year 1991. A recession would postpone the six-year schedule. A war could negate it. The following is the deficit schedule provided for the critical years:

FISCAL YEAR	DEFICIT SCHEDULE
1986	$171.9 billion
1987	$144.0 billion
1988	$108.0 billion
1989	$72.0 billion
1990	$36.0 billion
1991	$0 billion

While the figures in the schedule are referred to as the maximum deficit, in fact the deficit may be as much as $10 billion over the scheduled deficits, except in fiscal year 1991, before the emergency deficit-cutting procedures went into effect.

Emergency Deficit-Cutting Procedure:
The Snapshot and Trigger

If the Congress exceeded the deficit schedule by so much as one penny over the $10 billion cushion, an emergency deficit-cutting procedure was triggered. It worked like this. On August 15 preceding the new fiscal year that starts in October, the directors of the CBO and the OMB jointly provided a "snapshot", or an estimate of the prospective new fiscal year deficit based on actions of the Congress to that date. If they disagreed on the estimate, they split the difference and took the average of the two. If the "snapshot" indicated the deficit would exceed that scheduled by more than $10 billion, a procedure called "sequestering," was "triggered."

The Comptroller General's Report and the Sequestration Order

Under the original provisions of the act, the directors of the OMB and the CBO provide their joint estimate to the comptroller general of the United States, who heads the GAO. The GAO was established by the Budget and Accounting Act of 1921 to act as the watchdog for the Congress, overseeing how the agencies of the government carry out their fiscal responsibilities (see Chapter 2). The OMB and CBO also calculate the spending reductions necessary to bring the deficit for the year down to the deficit provided in the schedule. They provide their calculations to the comptroller general on August 20.

While taking "due regard" of the findings and calculations of the directors of the OMB and the CBO, the comptroller general reports his estimate of the deficit and the required spending reductions in specific budget programs, projects, and activities (PPAs) to the president on August 25. While the comptroller general has some limited discretion as to the amounts to be cut in the PPAs or other accounts, the president has virtually no discretion and on September 1 issues a "sequestration order," based on the comptroller general's report. The president's action is ministerial. If, as happened, this provision is declared unconstitutional, the act provides for a back-up procedure whereby the report of the directors of the CBO and OMB is made to the Congress instead of to the comptroller general and the president. At the beginning of the new fiscal year on October 1, the president's sequestration order takes effect. On October 5 the OMB and the CBO issue a revised report that reflects what if any congressional action has been taken since August 25 to get down to the deficit schedule. Thus the Congress has more than a month to put its house in order. On October 10 the comptroller general sends a revised order to the president and on October 15 the final order is effective. The timetable for the snapshot, trigger, and sequestration order, as provided by the Gramm-Rudman-Hollings Act for a full fiscal year, before the Supreme Court decision, is given in the Table 9–1.

These additional features should be emphasized:

- Under the sequestering procedures, defense and nondefense accounts are equally subject to reduction.
- Accounts to be reduced are specified by law, leaving little discretion as to where reductions may be made.
- Except for administrative or operating expenses, more than forty-five programs are entirely exempt from reduction.
- The first-year sequester was limited to a total of $11.7 billion, regardless of the deficit.

TABLE 9-1   The Original Gramm-Rudman-Hollings Timetable for the Snapshot, Trigger, and Sequestration Order

Date	Action to Be Completed
August 15	The OMB and the CBO take the snapshot of the deficit.
August 20	The OMB and the CBO report to the GAO.
August 25	The GAO issues its report to the president, based on the findings of the OMB and the CBO.
September 1	The presidential order is issued, based on the GAO report.
October 1	The order takes effect.
October 5	The OMB and the CBO issues a revised report to reflect final congressional action.
October 10	The GAO issues a revised report to the president.
October 15	The final order, based on the revised report, is effective.
November 15	The GAO compliance report is issued.

Source: Increasing the Statutory Limit on the Public Debt, House of Representatives, 96th Cong., 1st sess., Rep. 99-433, p. 77.

The New Budget Timetable

The act also provided for a new budget timetable (Table 9–2). Its essential feature, starting in January 1987, was that it required both the president's budget and the First Concurrent Budget Resolution to be submitted or passed a month earlier than under the 1974 act. Further, it required that the president submit a budget in early January that met the mandated deficit-reduction schedule of the act.

HOW THE ACT WORKED IN FISCAL YEAR 1986

Because the Gramm-Rudman-Hollings Act did not become law until December 13, 1985—well into the fiscal year—the law limited the amount that could be sequestered or cut in fiscal year 1986 to $11.7 billion. Other special features applied particularly to defense. The president was given the option, for fiscal year 1986 only, to exclude military personnel accounts from the mandatory reduction and to protect the Strategic Defense Initiative (SDI) from the cuts *provided* that equal amounts were cut from other military accounts.

There was a special timetable for the first year. The snapshot of the deficit for fiscal year 1986 was taken by the CBO and the OMB on January 10. Their joint estimate—the average of the two—was that the fiscal year 1986 deficit would be $220.5 billion, $48.6 billion more than the $171.9 billion the deficit schedule required. The law in effect provided for a $37.2 billion cushion for the first year.

TABLE 9–2 Timetable for Routine Budget Action Under Gramm-Rudman-Hollings, January 1987

On or Before	Action to Be Completed
1st Monday after January 3*	Presidential budget.
February 15	The CBO submits its report to the Budget Committees.
February 25	Committees submit views and estimates to House and Senate.
April 1	Budget Committees report concurrent resolution on the budget.
April 15*	The Congress completes action on the concurrent resolution.
May 15	Annual appropriations bills may be considered in the House.
June 10	House Appropriations Committee reports the last annual appropriations bill.
June 15*	The Congress completes action on reconciliation legislation.
June 30*	House completes action on annual appropriations bills.
October 1*	Fiscal year begins.

Source: Congressional Budget Act of 1974, as amended, Title III: Congressional Budget Process, Section 300.
*Major events

On January 15 the CBO and the OMB made their report to the comptroller general, proposing both the amounts and the PPAs, or accounts where the funds would be sequestered. On January 21, the comptroller general issued his own revised report to the president, and on March 1 the order took effect.

The first step in the calculation was to determine the amount of the reduction in the COLAs for government retirement programs. This came to almost $1 billion and was applied equally to defense and nondefense programs. There were additional nondefense reductions in other automatic spending increases, and special rules that applied to student loans and some health and welfare items. These amounted to about $45 million and were credited against the cuts needed to be made in the nondefense sequester. Finally, the uniform percentage needed to be applied to the remaining accounts in defense and nondefense areas so that each would provide half the $11.7 billion total was determined. This required a 4.9 percent reduction in defense and a 4.3 percent reduction in nondefense accounts. Table 9–3 summarizes the details.

The president's order was carried out, and $11.7 billion was cut or sequestered for fiscal year 1986. One should note that it took a $24 billion cut in budget authority (BA) to provide the $11.7 billion cut in outlays (O) or actual spending.

TABLE 9–3   Fiscal Year 1986 Sequester Under the Gramm-Rudman-Hollings Act
(Millions of Dollars)

	Defense Outlays	Nondefense Outlays	Total Outlays
Reductions in retirement COLAs (automatic spending increases)	$ 497[1]	$ 497	$ 994
Reductions in other automatic spending increases[2]	—	45	45
Reductions through application of special rule to certain programs	—	397	397
Uniform percentage reductions in other programs	5,353[3]	4,911	10,264
Total reductions	5,850	5,850	11,700

1. All the COLAs are found in the nondefense portion of the budget. One-half is applied against the defense reduction because about half goes to retired military or Department of Defense employees.
2. Guaranteed student loans, foster care and adoption assistance, Medicare, veterans medical care, community health, migrant health, and Indian health.
3. If all the military personnel accounts had been included, the percentage reduction to achieve savings of $5.85 billion would have been about 3.1 rather than 4.9 percent.

Before the end of the year, however, the Supreme Court declared the sequestering procedures to be unconstitutional. To preserve the cuts, the Congress packaged them into a bill that was then passed in both the House and Senate and signed by the president.

BLUE SMOKE AND MIRRORS:
THE FISCAL YEAR 1987 EXPERIENCE

The president, as required, submitted a fiscal year 1987 budget that estimated the deficit at $143.6 billion, or $400 million below the mandatory goal of $144 billion. He proposed no tax increase, although he did ask the Congress for an increase in fees for several federal services, proposed a 6.2 percent increase in the military budget, and asked the Congress to end more than two dozen programs or agencies, including the Interstate Commerce Commission and the Small Business Administration. He also proposed to sell the Bonneville and other public power facilities and the naval oil reserves at Teapot Dome and Elk Hills.

However, almost before the budget documents arrived on Capitol Hill in February, a court panel of three federal district judges in Washington declared part of the Gramm-Rudman-Hollings Act unconstitutional. This was the result of a court case filed within hours of the act becoming law by Congressman Mike Synar (D.-Okla.) and eleven of his colleagues. The court panel said that the comptroller general was an agent of the Congress and the legislative branch and not an officer of the executive branch. This was true because he could be removed by a joint resolution of the Congress, which, like a bill, must be passed by the House and Senate and signed by the president or, if vetoed by the president, overridden by a two-thirds vote of both houses. Thus, unlike an executive officer, the comptroller general can be removed by the Congress.

This raised separation of powers issues, because under the Constitution "the executive power shall be vested in a President of the United States," and the president, not the Congress," shall take care that the laws be faithfully executed." As the comptroller general was executing the laws when he made his report to the president on where and by how much funds must be sequestered, that part of the law was unconstitutional as a legislative branch agent cannot carry out executive functions.

In July the Supreme Court upheld the lower court decision by a 7 to 2 vote. Writing for the Court, retiring Chief Justice Burger said:

> By placing responsibility for execution [of the law] in the hands of an officer who is subject to removal only by itself, Congress in effect has retained control over the executive function. The Constitution does not admit such intrusion.[25]

The Congress had anticipated that the triggering mechanism for sequestering funds might be constitutional, and provided in the law itself for the act to be challenged and quickly reviewed by the Supreme Court. In addition it passed a back-up provision to replace the comptroller general's report and the president's order to sequester. This provision is relatively simple, but its consequences for members of the Congress and the president are profound. These are the key provisions.

Instead of issuing their report to the comptroller general, the directors of the CBO and the OMB issue a joint report on August 20 to a Temporary Joint Committee of the Congress that is made up of the members of the House and Senate Budget Committee.

Within five calendar days the Joint Committee reports to the House and the Senate a joint resolution that sets forth the content of the directors' report, that is to say, the total amount and the particular PPAs that must be cut to reach the mandatory deficit schedule. Each House then has five working days to vote on the final passage of the resolution before it is sent to the president. Time is strictly limited. A motion to postpone the consideration in the House is not in order. The motion to proceed to consideration of the joint resolution in the Senate is not debatable. Debate in each house is limited to five hours. No amendments to the joint resolution are in order to either house.

To put it simply, under the rules—if faithfully carried out—the Congress would have to vote up or down on the amounts and the details of the sequester to reach the mandatory deficit level of $144 billion.

The implications for the Congress in the fall of 1986, when it might be required to act on the CBO and OMB report, were significant. The Congress was in recess on August 20 and was not due back until September 8. Obviously the Congress did not want to vote just before an election on billions of dollars of additional budget cuts affecting virtually every powerful special interest group in the country.

The president and the White House were equally unhappy with the prospect. The CBO and OMB directors' report, with its equal cuts in defense and nondefense provisions, was anathema to the president. Several things might happen.

The Congress was in a no-win situation. If members voted for cuts only a few weeks before election, members offended both constituents and contributors. If the Congress defeated the joint resolution, members would be accused of ducking the issue through spineless and gutless inactivity in the face of a budget crisis.

Suppose the Congress acted courageously and voted the cuts by recorded votes. What would the president do? Would he sign the joint resolution or veto it? If he signed it, he would not only offend particular groups shortly before the election, when his party's control of the Senate was on the line, but, from his point of view, he would do great damage to his vaunted military build-up. If, on the other hand, he vetoed it, any credibility he had on budget matters would be severely tested.

But as has been pointed out elsewhere, any group of executive and legislative branch officials so profligate as to build deficits that require sequestering would certainly be ingenious enough to avoid voting against them. And that is precisely what they did. They avoided a vote altogether. Here, in part, is how.

The key was the August snapshot of the deficit by the CBO and OMB. The predictions of the OMB were on the whole much rosier than those of the CBO. The OMB assumed quarterly real growth in the gross national product (GNP) for fiscal year 1987 of 4.2 percent, and a year-to-year GNP growth of 3.7 percent. Comparable estimates by the CBO were 3.5 and 3.2 percent, respectively. On this basis the OMB assumed a budget deficit of $156.2 billion as against the higher $170.6 billion figure of the CBO. This low OMB estimate went into the split-the-difference figure required to be reported on August 15, which was set arithmetically at $163.4 billion.[26] This procedure reminds one of Franklin D. Roosevelt's admonition to two speech writers who had given him diametrically opposed views. He sent them back to work with the words, "Weave them together."

The amount to be cut to reach the Gramm-Rudman-Hollings $144 billion deficit schedule was now only $19.4 billion.

OMB Director James C. Miller III testified before the Joint Budget Committee on September 10, after the Congress returned from its summer recess, that he thought that the Congress and the White House could find the $19.4 billion to avoid Draconian across-the-board cuts.[27] First, he found an $11 billion windfall from the revenue effects of the Tax Reform Act.

While the act was supposed to be revenue-neutral over the first five years, in the first year there would be an excess offset by deficits in other years, which would reduce the expected deficit to $152.4 billion. Finally, through passage of the reconciliation bill, he advised the committee that it could reach the magic $144 billion. And of course there was the $10 billion "fudge factor," so that even if the estimates were too rosy, the goal might still be achieved. If all this could be done, there need be no vote at all, nor any presidential signature or veto on a belt-tightening, across-the-board cut in either military or civilian programs.

By selling some government assets, postponing increases in pay or allowances due in fiscal year 1987 until the 1988 fiscal year, underestimating agriculture payments, and using other forms of creative accounting, an escape worthy of Houdini himself was made from the consequences of the Gramm-Rudman-Hollings provisions.

Thus, through legerdemain and blue smoke and mirrors, the Congress and the president met the $144 billion mandatory goal for fiscal year 1987. But within three short months, according to the CBO, the estimated deficit had grown by $30 billion to $174.5 billion.

While this was done once, it might not be done again. At fiscal year's end, the outgoing chairman of the Senate Budget Committee, Pete Domenici, said that the Congress and the President would have to cut spending by $60 to $75 billion in the coming 1988 fiscal year to meet the new $108 billion mandatory deficit figure.

THE FISCAL YEAR 1988 EXPERIENCE

On January 5, 1987, President Reagan proposed a fiscal year 1988 budget below the $108 billion mandatory deficit. For the first time spending was estimated at more than $1 trillion. Some new revenues were proposed, although they were not called taxes. Reagan proposed defense outlays of $297.6 billion, or $15.4 billion more than the previous year's $282.2 billion level. This equaled a 3 percent increase plus inflation. He also proposed to raise $3 billion through the sale of federal loans to private investors and once again to sell off such government assets as the Bonneville Power Administration and the Navy Petroleum Reserves, which had previously been rejected. Altogether he was proposing about $50 billion in domestic cuts, sales of assets and federal credit securities, and revenue-raising devices.[28] He thus technically met the mandatory schedule of the Gramm-Rudman-Hollings deficit reductions.

The proposal was fatally flawed, however, as some of his proposed cuts were nonstarters (he proposed, for example, to end all federal funding for vocational education, a highly popular program), some savings were grossly exaggerated, and the economic estimates on which both revenues and spending figures were based glowed with more than their usual rosy hue. There was no chance that the Congress, with its newly elected Democratic Senate, would accept the president's agenda on both domestic and military priorities.

Within a month the CBO estimated the deficit in the president's proposed fiscal year 1988 budget at $26 to $32 billion higher than the president's estimate.

When asked by the Senate Budget Committee to comment on the economic consequences of reaching the $108 billion target, conservative economist Martin Feldstein, who had been President Reagan's chairman of the Council of Economic Advisers, said:

> It's a reasonable target provided you're not going to hit it.... If I thought it would actually be met, I would worry, but the likelihood of that is so small.... When you finally arrive at the $108 billion number, it would actually look like $130 to $140 billion and I would be comfortable with that.[29]

Newly elected Democratic Senator Wyche Fowler, Jr., of Georgia said in response to the numbers game that

> Gramm-Rudman is like the cross-eyed archer. He doesn't hit anything, but he scares the hell out of everyone.[30]

Within days the chairmen of the House and Senate Budget Committees proposed a more realistic goal of $130 to $135 billion for fiscal year 1988. But when the president pointed with pride to his budget and demanded that the $108 billion deficit goal not be abandoned by the Congress, the budget committees copied the president's example and adopted his economic assumptions so that their budget, like his, would meet the Gramm-Rudman-Hollings deficit target. Their budget, like his, also had $26 billion to $32 billion of phoney savings brought about by blue smoke and mirrors. When the president, his budget director, and the House Republican leadership complained the plan did not meet the $108 billion G-R-H deficit goal, the Democrats matched the president's budget chicanery. They did two things.

First, they brought up the president's budget for a vote on the House floor, where it went down to defeat, 394 to 27. Second, they substituted the president's optimistic economic assumptions for the more credible CBO estimates in their budget resolution. This reduced the recommended deficit by an additional $24.9 billion and produced a deficit figure of $107.6 billion, almost precisely the $107.8 billion found in the president's proposed budget. Not surprisingly, both figures were below the $108 billion G-R-H goal. For the third year in a row the president and the Congress conspired to meet the G-R-H goal by legerdemain. Both thus became equal competitiors for the title of "artful dodger."

"THE G-R-H FIX": SON OF GRAMM-RUDMAN-HOLLINGS

By September, when the bill to increase the debt ceiling was before the Congress, it was clear that no rosy scenario, asset sales, moving of paydays from one fiscal year to another, or other accounting devices could bring the deficit even close to the $108 billion target. To bail out both itself and the president, the Congress passed the Emergency Deficit Control Reaffirmation Act of 1987, which, as it had done with Gramm-Rudman-Hollings, was added as a rider to the debt ceiling measure and sent to the president on September 23, the day the old debt ceiling provision expired. Some thought the Congress had reaffirmed its original folly. This is what the new measure did.

1. It revised the targets (see Table 9–4). The $108 billion target for fiscal year 1988 was changed back to the fiscal year 1987 figure of $144 billion.
2. Instead of a further $36 billion cut in the deficit for fiscal year 1989, it provided for only an $8 billion reduction, to $136 billion. With the $10 billion cushion, a deficit of $146 billion (instead of the original $72 billion) would satisfy the new law. The result was a two-year period when no deficit reduction was required.
3. It restored the original G-R-H annual $36 billion reduction in the deficit target for fiscal years 1990 through 1993, when a balanced budget was required. The *Congressional Quarterly* called the action a "significant step back from the promises of the original [G-R-H] law."
4. It increased the debt ceiling from $2.1 to $2.8 trillion, or by $700 billion, which was sufficient to provide borrowing authority to the Treasury until May 1989. This allowed both the president and the Congress to avoid passing a new debt ceiling law just before the 1988 election.
5. It toughened the G-R-H procedures to disallow counting sales of government assets or receipts from loans in the G-R-H deficit calculation. It also required a

TABLE 9–4   The 1985 and 1987 Gramm-Rudman-Hollings Deficit Schedules (Billions of Dollars)

Fiscal Year	1985 G-R-H Targets[1]	1987 Revised G-R-H Targets[2]	Cushion
1986	$171.9	—	$37.2
1987	144	—	10
1988	108	$144	10
1989	72	136	10
1990	36	100	10
1991	0	64	10
1992	—	28	10
1993	—	0	0

1. Balanced Budget and Emergency Deficit Control Act of 1985 (Gramm-Rudman-Hollings; Public Law 99-177).
2. Balanced Budget and Emergency Deficit Reaffirmation Act of 1987 (Public Law 100-119).

three-fifths rather than a simple majority vote in the Senate to waive a G-R-H rule or procedure.

6. For 1988 only, it postponed the date when a sequestration would go into effect until November 20. This would give the Congress and the president time to provide additional deficit cuts to meet the new $144 billion target.
7. It modified the original G-R-H sequestration procedures (see Table 9–1) to take into account the Supreme Court decision effectively excluding the Congress and the GAO from the mandatory procedures (see Table 9–5).

THE 1987 BUDGET SUMMIT AGREEMENT

Even with the $36 billion increase made to readjust the deficit target to the previous year's $144 billion, and the postponement of the effective date of a sequester to November 20, the president and the Congress could not agree on a budget by the beginning of the new fiscal year on October 1, 1987. In fact, the Congress had not sent a single appropriations bill to the president for his signature. The combination of the Democratic fury over the president's veto of the military authorization bill and his Republican lieutenants' skirmishing in the Senate on appropriations bills prevented final action.

The conflict between the president and the Congress over their divided and shared powers as fashioned by the Founding Fathers and riveted into the Constitution provoked gridlock in the absence of consensus. No amount of additional process could prevent such an impasse when there was disagreement on major political and economic priorities.

The logjam continued well into October, when a fortuitous act gave each side a chance to save face. A disaster became the instrument, or an excuse, to forge an agreement. On October 19, almost three weeks into the

TABLE 9–5   Modified Gramm-Rudman-Hollings Timetable for the Snapshot, Trigger, and Sequestration Order Beginning in Fiscal Year 1988

Date	Action to Be Completed
August 15	The OMB snapshot of the deficit is taken. The president notifies the Congress whether he will include or exclude military personnel from the sequester action. If he excludes them, the funds must be made up from the remaining military accounts.
August 20	The CBO provides the OMB with its advisory estimate of the deficit.
August 25	The OMB sends its sequester report to the president.
August 25	The president issues the order.
October 1	The order takes effect.
October 10	The CBO issues its advisory report on the congressional action.
October 15	The final presidential–OMB report is effective immediately.

new fiscal year, the stock market crashed. The failure of the president and the Congress to tackle the deficit was given by most pundits as the cause. Serious negotiations began.

Meanwhile the formal actions required under the revised sequester provisions were put into effect. The snapshot was taken, the trigger was pulled, and the presidential sequester order was proclaimed. It detailed the military and civilian PPAs that would be cut as of November 20.

Hard bargaining and contentious debate resumed over the size of the military budget; which taxes and fees would be raised; which farm, credit, Medicare, and civilian programs would be cut; and the amount of overall reductions in spending and the deficit. The details of the thirteen appropriations bills still in limbo were reexamined. Finally, under threat of the beginning of the actual sequester, an agreement was reached on November 20, the very moment when the single thread holding the sequester's sword of Damocles was cut.

It was a two-year pact that was packaged into a budget resolution that did two things. First, it set the ceilings for military and civilian discretionary spending for fiscal years 1988 and 1989. Second, it directed the taxing and spending committees, through the reconciliation provisions, to change the laws to effect the dollar amounts of the deficit cuts. The general provisions of the pact are set forth in Table 9–6.

THE APPROPRIATIONS AND RECONCILIATION BILLS

For more than a month following the agreement, the Congress and the administration negotiated the details. These were combined into two massive bills, an omnibus appropriations bill containing the provisions of all thirteen regular appropriations bills, and a single reconciliation bill containing the changes in the existing laws, which together would provide the $33.4 billion in deficit reductions for the 1988 fiscal year. Some of the reconciliation provisions would affect fiscal year 1989 and future years as well. In addition to the deficit cuts needed to reach the military and nonmilitary

TABLE 9–6   Selected Ceilings and Deficit Targets of the 1987 Budget Pact (Billions of Dollars)

Fiscal Year	Defense Ceiling		Nondefense Ceiling		Deficit Reduction
	Budget Authority	Outlays	Budget Authority	Outlays	
1988	$292	$285.4	$162.9	$176.8	$33.4
1989	299.5	294	166.2	185.3	42.7

discretionary spending goals, the reconciliation bill contained $9.1 billion in tax increases, and $2.1 billion and $1.0 billion in legislative cuts in the Medicare and farm subsidy entitlement programs, respectively.

The reconciliation bill passed by a vote of 237 to 181 in the House and 61 to 28 in the Senate. The omnibus appropriations bill squeaked through by a vote of 209 to 208 in the House and 59 to 30 in the Senate. The House Republicans continued their policy, initiated in the first year of the Budget Act, of voting overwhelmingly against any budget pact or resolution in order to keep their fingerprints off the legislation.

These two bills were signed by President Reagan on December 22. Although the reconciliation bill was sent to the White House first, he signed the appropriations bill first, because in some respects the reconciliation bill was tougher and contained more cuts. If it were the second to be signed, its provisions would take precedence over those of the first bill. Such are the arcane tactics of the budget fight.

The reconciliation bill also provided that the sequestration order would be nullified when the bill became law. So while the sequester was in effect for more than a month, it did not result in any permanent budget cuts.

THE FISCAL YEAR 1989 "CONSENSUS" BUDGET

Under the new timetable of the Gramm-Rudman-Hollings Reaffirmation Act of 1987, the fiscal year 1989 budget was due on the first Monday after January 3, 1988, or January 4. This deadline was missed. Instead of a budget, the Congress got a two-page letter from Budget Director James C. Miller III, which, in the spirit of the November 20 budget summit agreement, was neither hostile nor contentious. It explained that submission was delayed until mid-February because the final terms of the fiscal year 1988 budget were not signed by the president until December 22. The fault belongs to "everybody," said Carol Cox of the Committee for a Responsible Federal Budget. House Budget Committee Chairman William H. Gray (D.-Pa.), also in a conciliatory mood, said he understood.[31]

On January 5, White House press secretary Marlin Fitzwater announced that the president had approved a "no surprise" budget that would give "assurance" to the financial market. The message, he said, was twofold: "We can make an agreement with the Congress and meet it and that we've got the deficit on a downward trend."[32]

The State of the Union Address

But when President Reagan gave his State of the Union Address from the podium of the House of Representatives on January 25, 1988, he was not so conciliatory. He blamed the Congress for missed deadlines, continuing resolutions, and the omnibus reconciliation and appropriations bills. He was referring specifically to the two mammoth bills he had signed on December 22. In a dramatic gesture before the Congress and the prime-time television viewers, he lifted up the two bills and their attached conference reports, and said:

> And then, along came these behemoths. This is the conference report—1,053 page report weighing 14 pounds. And this, a reconciliation bill, six months late, that was 1,186 pages long, weighing 15 pounds. And the long-term continuing resolution, this one was two months late, and it's 1,057 pages long, weighing 14 pounds. Not to mention the 1,053-page conference report weighing 14 pounds. Now that was a total of 43 pounds of paper and ink. You had three hours, yes, three hours to consider each, and it took 300 people at my Office of Management and Budget just to read the bill so the government wouldn't shut down.

Then the president made a pledge: "Congress shouldn't send another one of these. No! And, if you do, I will not sign it."[33]

What the public did not know was that when he slammed down the documents "to drive home a point," as one aide put it, "he smashed the middle finger of his right hand....He may have been beaming on the outside...but on the inside, his finger was killing him."

Later, in a speech before the Alfalfa Club, the president said:

> I want you to know I'm very angry with Congress. I've had a colon operation. I've had a prostate operation. And now I picked up the damn budget during my State of the Union and have to have a hernia operation.[34]

The president's points were effective and attest to his reputation as the "Great Communicator." But he took more dramatic license than usual in his State of the Union presentation. For example:

- In 1981, he had made no complaint about the Omnibus Reconciliation Bill, the bill by which he humiliated the Democrats and put into law the major domestic provisions of his budget revolution, and yet it was as large as or larger than the 1987 bill. Called Gramm-Latta II and fathered by his Budget Director David Stockman and then Congressman Phil Gramm, it changed the laws to cut $37.7 billion in domestic spending and was backed by 188, or all but 2, Republicans who voted in the House.
- The reconcilation bill was two and a half, not six months late. It was 2,047 pages long, not 1,186, and weighed eight, not fifteen, pounds. What the president received from the Congress was comparable in both size and weight to the budget documents he had sent to them the previous January 5.
- The total of forty-three pounds was roughly three times the actual weight of the documents, including not only the two pieces of legislation but the conference reports as well.
- He did not mention his veto of the Defense Authorization Act, the deliberate hold-up of the appropriations bills in the Senate by his own party stalwarts, and

the stalemate caused in part by his repeated threat to veto provisions that the Congress sought but that he disapproved. This was presidential initiation of delay.

- The reference that three-hundred people at his OMB were needed just to read the bill was gratuitous. The president requested most of the changes, and the Congress had to draft or amend the specific accounts to satisfy the demands of the president and his OMB director. These in turn had to be reviewed by the OMB experts in each area. In fact most of the provisions had been originally drafted by the OMB staff working either alone or with congressional legislative experts.
- The final debates on the floors of the House and Senate may have taken only three hours, but the Congress spent thousands of hours on the two omnibus bills. Lengthy hearings were held in both houses on the provisions of each of the thirteen appropriations bills. The Ways and Means and Finance Committees spent days on the reconciliation provisions. Conference committee sessions involving a third to a half the members of each body were held. The budget committees held extensive hearings on the overall figures and packaged the work of the tax and legislative committees into the reconciliation bills of both houses.

In again requesting the authority for a presidential line-item veto, the president used some dramatic examples from the omnibus appropriations bill of items "tucked away behind a little comma here and there" to illustrate his case:

> For example, there's millions for items such as cranberry research, blueberry research, the study of crawfish, and the commercialization of wildflowers. And that's not to mention the $5 million so that people from developing nations could come here to watch Congress at work. I won't even touch that one.
> So tonight, I offer you this challenge. In 30 days, I will send back to you those items, as rescissions, which if I had the authority to line them out, I would do so.
> Review this multibillion-dollar package.

Under the Budget Act a rescission is a spending item that Congress has appropriated but the president asks the Congress to cancel by a majority vote in each house.

The president sent the Congress a list of the items he wanted to cut on March 11, two weeks after the promised date, but it was $1.5 billion of examples rather than the "multibillion-dollar package" of formal rescissions. Half the dollar amount of the list was $728 million to wipe out the Small Business Administration, a request that he had made repeatedly but that the Congress had refused to carry out, but only $188.3 million of examples from the $295 billion in defense outlays was given. Cranberries, blueberries, and crawfish were not on his list. They were not line items in the budget subject to either a rescission or a proposed line-item veto. Some of the examples in the list had been obtained by his speech writers from a local Washington public relations firm rather than from the professional budget experts. Like most of the public, public relations experts were unaware that the budget contains very few line items giving specific details about projects or weapons systems.[35]

Budget Submission

The budget President Reagan submitted on February 18, 1988, for the 1989 fiscal year, proposed outlays of $1,094.2 trillion and receipts of $964.7 billion. The estimated deficit was $129.5 billion, which was $6.5 billion below the revised Gramm-Rudman-Hollings target of $136 billion.

The budget had several characteristics. Because it carried out the general outlines of the two-year 1987 budget agreement, for the first time in many years it was not dead on arrival in the Congress. Once again it was based on optimistic economic assumptions, another rosy scenario.

Ways and Means Committee Chairman Dan Rostenkowski (D.-Ill.) labeled its acceptance "the year of the big wink." A House Budget Committee official, speaking of the lack of protest of its exaggerated provisions, said, "The Administration comes up with a bullish forecast, and all you can do is accept it." Congressman William D. Gradison, Jr. (R.-Ohio), said, "There is no incentive to say the Emperor has no clothes."[36]

The CBO estimated the end of the year deficit at $170 billion rather than $136 billion or less. The rosiness of the scenario can be measured by a comparison of the key economic assumptions for the fiscal year 1989 budget with the actual figures shown in Table 9–7.

The willingness to accept the optimistic figures was the result of at least two events. The first was the two-year budget agreement of 1987. The two combatants were worn out by the fighting. "We avoided a war. At least we agreed to an outcome by peaceful means," said Budget Director Miller.[37] In addition, 1988 was an election year, and neither side wanted to renew the internecine strife of 1987 or to remain in session up to or through election day.

For the first time in years the congressional budget resolution was passed early in the year. It passed the House on March 23 and the Senate on

TABLE 9–7 The Fiscal Year 1989 Budget: Assumed versus Actual Figures

Economic Indicator	Assumption	Actual
Real GNP growth	4.4%	2.9%
Consumer price index[1]	3.9%	4.6%
Unemployment	5.5%	5.4%
91-day treasury bills	5.2%	8.12%

1. December to December.
Sources: Budget of the United States Government: Fiscal Year 1989; Economic Report of the President, 1990.

April 14; the compromise conference report between the two was passed on June 6. The latter, however, had squeaked through the House on May 30 by a 201-181 vote because, once again, most Republicans voted against it. The delay was occasioned by the differences between the House and Senate conferees.

The president and the Congress avoided the fratricidal combat of the previous years as the president signed the last six of the thirteen appropriation bills on October 1, the day the new fiscal year began. When the fiscal year ended, the official deficit was $152 billion, $22.5 billion more than the president had estimated. The "official" deficit was not a true measure of the deficit, however. The amount of additional money the Treasury had to borrow to make up the difference between the total amounts the government spent and received, or the increase in the government debt in the period, was $265.4 billion, or $113.4 billion more than the "official" deficit. This amount was hidden by rosy scenarios, off-budget items, and other fiscal deceptions by the presidential-congressional budget procedures.

NOTES

1. Senate Committee on the Budget, *Gramm-Rudman-Hollings and the Congressional Budget Process: An Explanation* (Washington, D.C.: U.S. Government Printing Office, 1986), p. 15.
2. Ibid.
3. *The Washington Post,* 22 December, 1982, p. A6.
4. *Economic Report of the President, 1991* (Washington, D.C.: U.S. Government Printing Office, 1987), p. 375.
5. Ibid.
6. Ibid.
7. Ibid., sp. 363, 376, 297.
8. William Greider, 'The Education of David Stockman," *Atlantic Monthly* 242 (December 1981): p. 51.
9. Ibid., p. 50.
10. U.S. Senate, S. Con. Res. 32, 10 May 1985.
11. *The Washington Post,* 27 June 1985, p. A18.
12. Ibid., 22 June 1985.
13. Ibid., 11 July 1985, p. A1.
14. Ibid., p. A6.
15. *The New York Times,* 13 July 1985, p. A1.
16. Ibid.
17. *The Washington Post,* 12 July 1985, p. A1.
18. *The New York Times,* 22 July 1985, p. A10.
19. *The Washington Post,* 30 July, 1985, p. A1.
20. H. J. Res. 32, Calendar 327, 99th Cong., 1st sess., 9 September 1985.
21. *The Washington Post,* 4 October 1985, p. A9.
22. Ibid., 5 October 1985, p. A9.
23. Ibid., 22 October 1985, p. A18.
24. See Senate Budget Committee, *G-R-H: An Explanation.*

25. *Bowsher v. Synar et al.*, Supreme Court of the United States, 7 July 1986. Chief Justice Burger was wrong when he said the comptroller general was subject to removal only by the Congress. He failed to distinguish between a concurrent resolution, which requires action only by the House and Senate, and a joint resolution, which is passed by the Congress and signed or vetoed by the president. The Budget Act of 1920 was vetoed by President Woodrow Wilson because it provided that the comptroller general could be removed by a concurrent resolution and thus only by the Congress. The Budget Act of 1921 was signed by President Harding when it provided for removal by a joint resolution, which required the president to sign the resolution or veto it, in which case he could be overridden by a two-thirds vote. The removal issue was not the key point. While the comptroller general is appointed by the president and confirmed by the Senate, he has always been considered the agent of the Congress, even though from time to time he exercises executive functions. The General Accounting Office that the comptroller general heads is a part of the legislative branch (see Chapter 2, "Origins of the 1921 Act").

26. The figures are from the *Report of the Comptroller General of the United States to the Chairman, Committee on Government Operations, House of Representatives, Budget Reductions for Fiscal Year 1987: Review of Initial OMB/CBO Report Under the Deficit Control Act* (Washington, D.C., Government Accounting Office, September 1986).

27. *The Washington Post*, 11 September 1985, p. A8.

28. *Budget of the United States Government: Fiscal Year 1988* (Washington, D.C.: U.S. Government Printing Office, 1987).

29. Senate Committee on the Budget, *Transcript of Hearings*, 19 February, 1987.

30. Ibid.

31. *Washington Post*, 5 January 1988, p. A5.

32. Ibid., 6 January 1988, p. A6.

33. Ibid., 26 January 1988, p. A10.

34. Ibid., 2 February 1988, p. D2.

35. Ibid., 11 March 1988, p. A4.

36. *The New York Times*, 19 February 1989, pp. A1, D19.

37. Ibid., p. D19.

10

President Bush, the Congress, and the Five-Year Budget Agreement

THE CAMPAIGN AND THE BUDGET

In the presidential campaign of 1988, candidate George Bush repeatedly promised, "I will not raise taxes,"[1] and emphasized it with the phrase—"read my lips"—which left no doubt about his pledge.

He proposed to solve the budget deficit problem through a "flexible freeze," which he defined in the first presidential debate in general terms as budget growth at the rate of inflation, which permits the president "to sort out the priorities,...we can get it [the deficit] down without going and socking the American taxpayer again."[2] In the second debate, after reasserting his "no new taxes" pledge with the promise "I won't do that," he proposed something much better" than new taxes:

> And it's going to take discipline of the executive branch. It's going to take discipline of the congressional branch, and that is what I call a flexible freeze that allows growth, about 4 percent or the rate of inflation, but does not permit the Congress just to add on spending.[3]

He also called for a cut in the capital gains tax rate to...increase jobs, increase risk-taking, [and] increase revenues to the federal government,"[4] as well as additional tax incentives for the oil and gas industry. He also called for budget reform, including the line-item veto and a constitutional amendment for a balanced budget, a stronger defense, and no cuts in Social Security.

THE 1990 BUSH BUDGET: REAGAN REVISED

When George Bush became president, in stark contrast with Ronald Reagan, there was no Bush budget revolution. With respect to the budget, he did not "hit the ground running." There was no obvious purpose, program, method, or specific tactics to rival the policy revolution of the early Reagan budget initiatives. When asked to make a judgment about a hostess's dessert, Winston Churchill allegedly said, "This pudding has no theme." The Bush budget likewise had no obvious or clearly stated theme.

On January 20, 1989, George Bush inherited a national debt of almost $3 trillion, an economy that was just beginning to falter after more than six years of sustained growth; an inflation rate, as measured by the consumer price index (CPI), of 4.4 percent, a treasury bill rate of over 8 percent, a prime interest rate of 10.5 percent, and a savings and loan scandal whose costs were estimated to reach a catastrophic $500 billion or more. He also inherited the Reagan fiscal year 1990 proposed budget with an estimated deficit of $100 billion (the Gramm-Rudman-Hollings target) that turned out to be $218.5 billion, or almost $120 billion more. The key economic estimates—real growth in the gross national product (GNP), the (CPI), and the treasury bill and bond rate—on which the budget was based were glowingly optimistic. The final Reagan budget also proposed almost $13 billion in new taxes ($8.5 billion) and user fees ($4.4 billion).

On February 9, 1989, President Bush sent a revised fiscal year 1990 budget to the Congress. Unlike President Reagan's revised Carter budget, President Bush did not propose massive cuts in domestic programs ($40 billion in the first year), a major increase in the military budget, or a huge cut in taxes. Instead the Bush budget only marginally changed the newly proposed Reagan budget for fiscal year 1990. It was a status quo budget purported to carry out the general themes and pledges of his campaign.

President Bush proposed to meet the Gramm-Rudman-Hollings budget deficit-cutting schedule of $100 billion without a tax increase. But he kept President Reagan's "rosy scenario" in every area except the interest rate projections. Because estimates for both outlays and revenues were increased by $4.5 billion and $6.3 billion, respectively, his overall deficit projection of $94.8 billion was $3.8 billion below that of his predecessor.

He proposed defense spending of $300.3 billion, which was the fiscal year 1989 outlay figure plus inflation. He called this a "constant dollar freeze." He proposed increases in spending for education ($768 million), child care ($331 million), the drug problem ($1.3 billion), the environment

($710 million), housing and the homeless ($676 million), Medicaid ($1.1 billion in proposed Reagan cuts restored), and enterprise zones ($150 million) for his "kinder and gentler" programs. Most of these he announced in his speech to a joint session of the Congress.

Without equal fanfare he applied his "flexible freeze" to $136 billion of the previous year's nondefense discretionary spending. In their totality these programs would be kept at the fiscal year 1989 level, without increases for inflation, which meant a cut in real terms. But some could go up and others could come down provided the overall ceiling was not breached, which is what he said the term "flexible freeze" implied. But he was silent on which would be cut and which would go up.

The Democrats in the Congress were furious. The president took the credit for the increases for his "kinder and gentler" programs, but neither called for new money or specified which old programs should be cut to pay for them. "Mr. Bush chose to give us only the good news," House Budget Committee Chairman Leon E. Panetta (D.-Calif.) complained. "He has left it for Congress to give the American people the bad news."[5]

The president did propose specific cuts in Medicare ($5 billion), a one-year freeze on the cost-of-living adjustments (COLAs) for federal retirees and a permanent reduction in future COLAs of 1 percent below the annual cost-of-living increase, and a cut in health insurance benefits for federal employees ($318 million).

His revised budget also proposed a series of tax breaks for investors through a capital gains tax cut from 33 to 15 percent for independent oil and gas drillers and for high technology companies.

President Bush also proposed what he called "budget process reforms," which included a constitutional amendment for a balanced budget, a line-item veto, and a two-year budget cycle. He also proposed that the congressional budget resolution setting the goals for spending, revenues, deficit, debt, and credit for the year be transformed from a concurrent resolution affecting only the Congress to a joint resolution requiring his signature. This would change the numbers needed to pass and sustain it from the simple majority required for a concurrent resolution to a two-thirds vote required to override a president's veto. He also requested an up-or-down vote on presidential rescission requests rather than the existing system whereby a rescission proposal dies if there is no affirmative congressional action.

Finally, he proposed that negotiations be held between the administration and congressional leaders to reduce the budget deficit, and appointed Budget Director Richard G. Darman and Treasury Secretary Nicholas F. Brady as his agents.

The budget revisions were greeted with mixed reviews, more critical than supportive. The overall proposal was referred to as Darman's "Stealth" Budget,[6] a comparison of the invisible Stealth bomber to Darman's "invisible," or nonspecified, budget cuts. It drew criticisms as a "minimalist" budget that was nothing but sound and fury. Sharp-tongued Senator Ernest F. Hollings (D.-S.C.), who would shortly repudiate his Gramm-Rudman-Hollings Act paternity, accused Darman of a deficit reduction plan based on "fabrication." "You're more jack-be-nimble than David Stockman," he said.[7] There were further complaints that President Bush had abandoned the work of the bipartisan National Economic Commission established in 1988 to reach a consensus on how and where to reduce the budget deficit.

THE ROSE GARDEN AGREEMENT

Negotiations between the president's agents and congressional budget leaders, in spite of the friction and frustrations among the members (one meeting was described as "90 minutes listening to Darman tell them he's really a nice guy"[8]), resulted in a budget pact on April 14 that acted as an impetus for the Congress to proceed with its work on the congressional budget resolution.

The negotiators agreed on $27 billion of deficit reduction measures, about half each in spending cuts and revenue increases. But the details were often lacking or questionable, or were gimmicks when they were specified. The U.S. Postal Service which had been running at a surplus, was put off-budget so that its estimated $1.8 billion deficit in the new fiscal year would not increase the deficit figure. A variety of government assets were to be sold. Such asset sales increase revenues in the year of the sale but often reduce revenues in future years. Some $5.3 billion in proposed tax increases were unspecified. In spite of the president's campaign pledge against sending "an army of IRS agents into everybody's kitchen,"[9] the pact called for an increase in tax revenues through tougher enforcement.

Both sides accepted the fiction that a $27 billion deficit reduction would reduce the overall fiscal year 1990 deficit below $100 billion ($99.4 billion was the agreement estimate), when in fact cuts of $55 to $65 billion were needed to reach the $100 billion level. They were $28 to $38 billion short.

Both sides accepted the fiction that a $27 billion deficit reduction would reduce the overall fiscal year 1990 deficit below $100 billion ($99.4 billion was the agreement estimate), when in fact cuts of $55 to $65 billion were needed to reach the $100 billion level. They were $28 to $38 billion short.

Both sides also had a vested interest in accepting the rosy estimates. If the Congress, for example, substituted its own Congressional Budget Office (CBO) estimates, which had routinely been more realistic than those of the Office of Management and Budget (OMB), the onus would be on the Congress to cut spending and/or raise taxes to reach the goal. But if both sides accepted the fiction at the beginning of the new fiscal year that their efforts had brought the official, on-budget deficit figure down to $100 billion, no hated sequester would have to take place, even if the figures at the end of the year were more than $50 billion higher.

The Washington Post editorialized that the agreement "greatly understates the savings necessary to reach next year's deficit target, then fails to achieve even those and covers up the failure with duplicitous accounting."[10]

The agreement also abandoned the principles of the "flexible freeze," whose purpose was to keep the increase in domestic discretionary spending at no greater than the increase in inflation, which means it would be a freeze in real terms. The agreement allowed for a 10 percent increase in nonmilitary programs, subject to annual appropriations, or an increase from $142.8 billion to $157.5 billion. The administration agreed to this in order to get a smaller congressional cut in military spending. In terms of reducing the deficit, however, this was the worst of both worlds. Instead of cutting both military and nonmilitary expenses, both would go up.

President Bush celebrated the agreement with a Rose Garden ceremony attended by his negotiators and the bipartisan congressional establishment. The best that could be said for the agreement was that it might lessen conflict and confrontation and improve relations between the two branches for the remainder of the fiscal year. But the chairman of the Senate Finance Committee, the usually mild-mannered Lloyd Bentsen (D.-Tex.), refused to attend. An aide said that the senator felt the plan was based on wildly optimistic projections of economic conditions and highly marginal real deficit reductions. House Ways and Means Chairman Dan Rostenkowski (D.-Ill.) was conveniently "out of town."

On May 18 the Congress completed its work on its $1.17 trillion budget resolution for fiscal year 1990. The terms were substantially those worked out in the Rose Garden agreement and represented the earliest date in a decade that the Congress had completed work on the broad outlines of the congressional budget. But that document merely set the binding ceilings for the spending, tax, debt, deficit, and credit decisions the Congress had to make to put the budget in place by the beginning of the new fiscal year on October 1. The real work—which programs to cut, which taxes to raise—was yet to come.

THE BUDGET GAME

Numerous procedural and substantive obstacles still lay in the path of passing a meaningful fiscal 1990 budget that met the test of the Gramm-Rudman-Hollings deficit goals. A key obstacle was the loophole that once the president and the Congress had agreed at the beginning of the year that the new deficit goal of $100 billion had been met, they were home free. This provision encourages legerdemain and is an invitation to "cook the books" instead of taking tough spending or taxing action. The devices are legion.

What started out as a potential cooperative effort ended up in an end-of-the-year political brawl. The first spanner in the works was the president's insistence that a cut in the capital gains tax rate must be included in the final budget package. Its presence was so contentious that it almost scuttled the agreement. The Republicans and some of their allies, who included Democrats from timber-producing regions, were unwilling to support a final budget package without it. Most Democrats were determined that it not be included.

A Senate fight over the antidrug laws delayed the thirteen annual appropriations bills when the Republicans held their consideration hostage to the drug bill. Considerable finger-pointing took place. The Republicans claimed the legislative dam could be broken if only the Democrats in the Senate would allow a vote on the capital gains bills. The Democrats charged that the Republicans were unreasonable in their delay of the appropriations bills and their insistence on a capital gains act. In the last week of September Budget Director Darman dropped his front-room "good guy" approach and substituted his back-room "bad guy" approach. He threatened that if the House did not include a capital gains provision, there would not be sufficient Republican votes to pass the budget bill, and the president would have to invoke the hated across-the-board cuts called "sequestration." He charged the Democrats in the Congress with a "kamikaze approach to national politics."[11] Two days before the fiscal year was to begin, the president got his capital gains bill through the House when 68 mostly southern Democrats joined with all but one Republican to pass it, by a 239 to 190 margin. In the Senate there was a different story. There the majority Democrats used the filibuster to defeat the provision. While a majority of senators favored the bill, the president's supporters could not muster the 60 votes needed to stop the filibuster and bring it to a vote. Finally, on October 13, only three days before the sequester provisions would be initiated, the Senate approved a $14.1 billion budget reconciliation bill and sent it to a conference committee to work out the differences between the House and Senate versions. There was no way to complete work on the final bill by October 16, and the across-the-board cuts went into effect.

THE SEQUESTRATION

The president's order initiating the sequestration called for cuts of $16.2 billion, the amount now needed, after appropriation and other cuts, to meet the Gramm-Rudman-Hollings deficit target. When the targets were revised in 1987, that version of the law provided for a $10 billion cushion. If, after the appropriations and reconciliation bills were passed, the budget deficit was within $10 billion of the goal, no sequestration was necessary. In this case the administration estimate was that the deficit would be $126.2 billion. As the $10 billion cushion effectively raised the target from $100 to $110 billion, a sequestration of only $16.2 billion was now needed to meet it.

The sequester law provides that equal dollar amounts be cut from both military and domestic spending. As Social Security and some other entitlements are exempt, the mathematics called for a 5.3 percent cut from the nondefense programs and a 4.3 percent cut from the military to produce $8.1 billion from each.

This was the third sequestration since the Gramm-Rudman-Hollings provisions were passed in 1985. There was a congressionally mandated sequestration of $11.7 billion during the first fiscal year (1986) of the Budget Act, which was carried out. The second sequestration, which was rescinded, was in fiscal year 1988.

President Bush said he was prepared to make the fiscal year 1990 sequestration permanent, that is, to let it run for a full year rather than sign a congressional budget reconciliation bill with different priorities even if it did provide the needed total deficit cuts. He followed this tactic for several political reasons.

First, for technical reasons the military would take a smaller cut than the domestic programs, which the Democrats favored. This was because about $5 billion of the $8 billion defense cut had taken place under the provisions of previous laws limiting the amounts from the backlogs of military funds that could be spent in the new fiscal year. Second, threatening to keep the sequester in place would give him greater leverage in bargaining with the Congress. If he held firm and was prepared to veto a budget reconciliation bill, his power to influence its contents was vastly increased. Third, a spending cut of $16.2 billion was only 1.35 percent of a total spending budget of $1.2 trillion. Spread over twelve months and divided between the military and civilian agencies, this would mean only a $675 million cut per month from each. Fourth, unlike a budget reconciliation bill, which he would have to sign and thus share in the praise or blame, the responsibility for the automatic cuts under sequestration defied accountability.

In a final compromise passed in the last week of November, almost eight weeks after the beginning of the new fiscal year, the president and the Congress agreed to accept a $14.7 billion deficit reduction bill and to leave the sequestration in effect through the first week in February. The sequestration provided about $4.6 billion in the total cuts. Darman's office projected that these actions would reduce the fiscal year 1990 budget deficit to $103 billion. Seven months later, on July 16, 1990, Darman estimated that in fact the budget deficit would be $161.3 billion, almost $60 billion higher than the estimate of cuts that had satisfied him and the Gramm-Rudman-Hollings target the previous November.

Also, in November 1989, just before the final agreement was reached, the Congress, at the president's request, raised the federal debt ceiling for the 1990 fiscal year to $3.12 trillion. It had tripled in eight years.

THE FISCAL YEAR 1991 BUSH BUDGET

The fiscal year 1991 budget, released on January 29, 1990, was unique in several ways.

First, instead of seven volumes of 3,000–4,000 pages, which cost $94.50 and which reporters, bureaucrats, and politicians carried away in shopping bags, a single, modified 1,600-page document costing only $38 was substituted. Its weight was cut in half, from 11.9 to 6 pounds. But like most bargain-basement items, it had serious deficiencies and omitted many important, useful subjects and details.[12]

Second, the Budget Message of the President, often 15 to 20 pages long, was reduced to a single page. Added for the first time was a 15-page introduction by Budget Director Darman. Departing from tradition, it was an extraordinarily informal essay whose references and subject matter included the Cookie Monster, Hidden PACMEN, and a journey through Wonderland Budgeting. In its serious conclusion, Darman claimed that the budget

> meets the Gramm-Rudman-Hollings deficit targets with specific and defensible deficit-reduction measures—and without gimmicks. It seeks to preserve a meaningful consolidated budget, while tightening the budget process. If implemented, it would reach balance in 1993 (as required by law), and would thereafter begin the process of reducing Federal debt.[13]

In other respects, however, the budget document was not unique. Its submission was late, as most budgets in the previous decade had been. It missed the newly required deadline of the first Monday after January 3 (January 8) by three weeks (January 29). The administration argued that the late delivery of the fiscal year 1990 appropriations and reconciliation bills was the reason for the delay.

This budget also gave new life to the "rosy scenario," for once again its economic estimates were optimistic (see Table 10–1). As Alan Fram of the Associated Press wrote, "If there were a truth-in-packaging law for federal spending," the forthcoming budget might have to carry this label": "This plan is optimistic at best and is likely to bear only a partial resemblance to reality.[14]

There were phantom revenues and phantom cuts. Previously overwhelmingly rejected budget proposals were included to improve the figures. The CBO projected that the deficit at the end of fiscal year 1990—the

TABLE 10–1   The Fiscal Year 1991 Budget Economic Projections

Economic Indicator	OMB	CBO
GNP (real growth)	3.3%	2.5%
Unemployment	5.3%	5.5%
CPI	4.0%	4.4%
GNP deflator	4.1%	4.0%
Interest rates		
3-month treasury bills	5.4%	7.2%
10-year treasury bonds	6.8%	7.7%
Budget deficit	$100.5 billion	$138.0 billion

starting line—would be $138 billion rather than $100 billion, and that $74 billion rather than $36 billion in deficit cuts would be needed to reach the $64 billion Gramm-Rudman-Hollings target. Once again, the OMB had "rounded up the usual suspects."

The chairman of the House Budget Committee said the budget was "not a serious effort."[15] Representative Marty Russo (D.-Ill.), a member of both the House Budget Committee and the Ways and Means Committee, declared that the budget process "stinks and lies,"[16] and Haynes Johnson called it "the annual budget charade."[17] Darman replied with the "you're another" argument. He said that he had a list of more than one-hundred budget gimmicks that the Congress had invented, and asserted that "there isn't a trace of dishonesty in this presentation."[18]

THE BUDGET DOCUMENT

The budget called for outlays of $1.233 trillion and revenues of $1.17 trillion, which would result in a deficit of $63.1 billion. Table 10–2 compares the outlays for fiscal years 1990 and 1991.

As the Bush budget was based on an inflation rate of 4 percent, any increase in a budget item of less than 4 percent was a cut in the program in real terms. The big winners were foreign aid, science and space, education, health, Social Security, and justice. The big losers were energy, commerce and housing, and community development. Marginal losers included defense, agriculture, transportation, and Medicare. An item with a reduction in net interest would be a winner, not a loser.

Some of these proposed changes were more apparent than real. The president would have to combine a gallant fight plus good fortune for his international affairs request to get its fiscal year 1990 appropriations, let alone a 24.7 percent increase. Medicare, an entitlement program, was unlikely to see a cut in real terms through administrative changes. The "decline" in net interest was based on an economic estimate of a three-month treasury bill rate of 5.4 percent and a ten-year treasury note rate of 6.8

TABLE 10–2   Outlays for Fiscal Years 1990 and 1991 (Billions of Dollars)

Item	1990 Estimate	1991 Estimate	Difference	Percent
Defense	$ 296.3	$ 303.3	$ 7.0	2.4
International affairs	14.6	18.2	3.6	24.7
Science and space	14.1	16.6	2.5	17.7
Energy	3.2	3.0	− 0.2	− 6.25
Natural resources and environment	17.5	18.2	0.7	4.0
Agriculture	14.6	14.9	0.3	2.1
Commerce and housing	22.7	17.2	− 5.5	− 24.2
Transportation	29.3	29.8	0.5	1.7
Community development	8.8	7.8	1.0	− 11.4
Education, jobs, and social services	37.7	41.0	3.3	8.8
Health	57.9	63.7	5.8	10.0
Medicare	96.6	98.6	2.0	2.1
Income security	146.6	153.7	7.1	4.8
Social security	248.5	264.8	16.3	6.6
Veterans	28.9	30.3	1.4	4.8
Justice	10.5	12.6	2.1	20.0
General government	10.6	11.3	0.7	6.6
Net interest	175.6	173.0	− 2.6	1.5
Allowances	—	− 1.1	− 1.1	
Offsetting receipts	36.5	43.6	7.1	19.5
Total outlays	$1,197.2	$1,233.3	$36.1	3.0

percent, when in fact three-month treasury bills were yielding 8.12 percent and ten-year treasury notes were at 8.5 percent in calendar 1989. With the end of the Cold War, the defense figure was due for a bigger cut, especially for the Strategic Defense Initiative, or "Star Wars," and some of the big weapons systems.

There were two fundamental problems with finding places to cut the budget. The first was that 75 percent or more of the budget was made up of "relatively uncontrollable outlays." These include benefits or entitlements mandated by law and not subject to cuts by either the OMB or the Appropriations Committees, such as Social Security, Medicare, veterans benefits, farm price supports, unemployment compensation, and other payments made if a person meets certain qualifications; interest on the debt, which is backed by the full faith and credit of the government; and outlays from prior-year contracts and obligations. The only way most of these might be cut is by changing the law. Less than 25 percent of the budget is subject to cuts by the OMB or the Congress without changing the law or breaking a contract, and the latter often includes penalties that are greater than the savings.

Another way to look at the obstacles to cutting the budget is to examine how the money is spent, as Table 10–3 shows.

TABLE 10–3   Where the Money Goes

Category	Percent
Defense	24
Social Security and railroad retirement	26
Net interest[1]	14
Medicare, Medicaid, and veterans disability	12
Federal retirement, military and civilian	6
Farm subsidies (by law)	3
Sub-total	85
All others, including foreign aid, highways, Secret Service, judiciary, law enforcement, post office, parks, education, energy, housing, civilian, research, etc.	15
Total	100

1. This figure is misleading. In fiscal year 1991, for example, the budget estimated interest on the public debt at $261 billion, or 21.3% of proposed outlays. The net interest figure was estimated at $173.7 billion, or 14.2%, because the Treasury subtracted an estimated $69 billion in payments to the trust funds (counting the funds as receipts, even though the money belongs to the recipients of Social Security and other trust funds) and $17.9 billion in "other interest" it received. This also reduced the total spending figures by the offset. In the end all of these figures were significantly higher than the estimates, but net interest clearly minimizes the costs of financing the debt and is a conspicuous example of "Miss Rosy Scenario" budgeting (see the Preface).

Both the administration and key congressional leaders had called for budget negotiations in the form of a budget summit to work out their differences. In March, House Ways and Means Committee Chairman Dan Rostenkowski proposed a five-year, $511.6 billion total deficit reduction program of spending cuts and tax increases that would reduce the deficit by $55 billion in the first year (fiscal year 1991).[19] In spite of the fact that it included $151 billion in tax increases and a freeze on Social Security and other COLAs, the Bush administration gave a "surprisingly warm welcome"[20] to the Rostenkowski proposal. White House press secretary Marlin Fitzwater said, "Basically we think there is some room to talk here,"[21] and Budget Director Darman praised the plan: "Conceptually, it's exactly on the right track."[22] But Senate Budget Committee Chairman Jim Sasser (D.-Tenn.) dismissed the Rostenkowski plan as going nowhere.[23]

Budget talks did get under way, but each side was reluctant to put either taxes or entitlement goals on the table. There was very little movement, although both parties agreed that $45 to $55 billion was about the right goal for first-year budget cuts. The House Budget Committee, backed by its leaders, voted 21 to 14 in straight party-line fashion for a budget resolution that would cut defense and increase domestic spending in ways that were anathema to the administration. At the same time the committee turned down the Bush budget by a 22 to 13 vote in which they picked up only one Republican supporter.[24]

THE MID-YEAR BUDGET REVIEW

Massive Revision

By mid-year reality had caught up with fiction. On July 16, in the *Mid-Session Review of the Budget* required by the Legislative Reorganization Act of 1970, Budget Director Darman released the administration's revised estimates of receipts, outlays, and the deficit, as well as the revised economic assumptions on which they were based. It was a political bombshell and a turning point in budget negotiations.

On the basis of the decline in the economy and the massive increase in funds needed for the savings and loan bail-out, the president and his budget director presented some honest figures. They committed truth:

1. The fiscal year 1991 deficit, before any proposed cuts, would be $168 billion, not $100 billion.
2. If the savings and loan bail-out were included, it would be $231 billion.
3. If the social security trust fund surplus was not used to mask the deficit, it would be $280 to $300 billion.
4. The fiscal 1990 budget was also revised. Instead of the $100 billion estimate of the preceding January, it would be $161.3 billion.[25]

FIGURE 10–1. The Burgeoning Deficit (in Billions of Dollars).
(*Source:* From Michael Drew, *The Washington Post* [17 July 1990]. © 1990 The Washington Post. Reprinted with permission.)

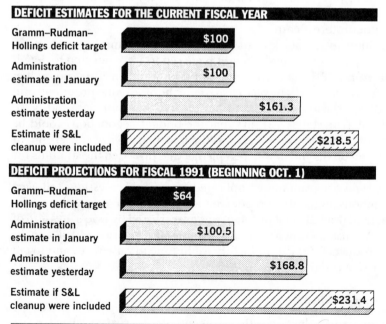

NOTE: The costs of the S&L cleanup are off–budget and exempt from Gramm–Rudman–Hollings deficit targets.

Bush Abandons "No New Taxes" Pledge

But there was a second bombshell. President Bush abandoned his "read my lips," "no new taxes" campaign pledge and agreed that he would accept some "tax revenue increases" in a budget agreement. This created a frenzy among his supporters, especially those up for reelection who had been campaigning on a "no new taxes" platform. More than half the House Republicans repudiated the shift and vowed they would not support a tax increase. Before that House Republican Whip Newt Gingrich (R.-Ga.) claimed that the president had not reversed his stand: "He very explicitly didn't say 'Raise taxes.' He said 'Seek new revenues.'" This argument was reminiscent of the words "revenue enhancements" by which the Reagan administration had tried to explain the eight tax increases during its tenure. (See Chapters 4 and 9.) Later in the year the National Council of Teachers of English gave President Bush its 1990 Doublespeak Award for official statements that are "grossly deceptive, evasive, euphemistic, confusing or self-contradictory." Third place went to Congressman Gingrich.[26]

Basis for Revision

What accounted for the difference between the estimates on which the January 29 budget was based and those in the *Mid-Session Review*? The factors included: (1) administrative actions involving laws or regulations ($2.2 billion); (2) economics ($24.2 billion); and (3) technical reestimates ($49.3 billion). The largest technical reestimate was a $9.2 billion increase in the baseline net interest cost.[27]

In addition to the stark news about the burgeoning budget deficit, some forty-six pages of the eighty-eight page report were devoted to detailing the catastrophic effects of the sequester that would ensure if no budget agreement were reached. It was clearly the hope of the president and Budget Director Darman that the Congress and the country would be so shocked by the true state of affairs that the budget negotiations could be moved forward in a decisive way. It was the mid-year review and President Bush's reneging on his "no new taxes" pledge that provided the stimulus for a meaningful budget accord.

The budget program was complicated by regional recessions followed by more ominous signs of a broader national economic downturn as the summer turned into fall. The problem was exacerbated by Iraq's invasion of Kuwait on August 2, which dramatically raised the price of oil and its secondary products. Was this in fact the right time to raise taxes and to cut government spending?

Agreement Reached

After two and a half months of negotiations, partisan charges and countercharges, and threats to close down the government, an agreement was reached at the last minute of the last hour.

The threats to close the government, even after a three-day experiment over the Columbus Day weekend, were never credible. While they may have acted as a prod to get things moving, there was no way the president could bring the troops home from the Persian Gulf, stop the Social Security checks, close down the Post Office, furlough the air traffic controllers and prison guards, or shut down the Washington Monument for more than a weekend. All this did was to infuriate the public, further lower the morale of civil servants, and continue the internecine warfare between the president and the Congress.

On one side of the bargaining table were the president and his principal negotiators, Budget Director Darman, Treasury Secretary Brady, and White House Chief of Staff John H. Sununu. They huddled with the Democratic and Republican congressional leaders in a variety of closed meetings in such arcane places as the officers club at Andrews Air Force Base just outside the Washington beltway, in the president's personal quarters in the White House, and in the secret labyrinthine hideaways in the Capitol.

A bipartisan agreement was reached, and the understanding was that Republicans in both the House and the Senate must provide the affirmative votes of a majority of their party before the Democrats would provide a majority of their members to pass the accord.

But the agreement was made behind closed doors by a handful of people without the participation or assent of either key committee chairmen in both houses or the rank-and-file members of the Congress. A further critical problem was that all 435 House and 33 Senate seats were to be contested in the November 6 election only a month away.

When the members of the Congress were given the details of the original agreement, they balked. Both its general outlines as well as its more detailed aspects are presented below.

THE ORIGINAL BUDGET AGREEMENT

The deal made deficit cuts in four major areas, for a total reduction of $500 billion over five fiscal years, 1991–1995 (see Table 10–4).

TABLE 10–4   Original 1990 Deficit-Cutting Agreement (Billions of Dollars)

Item	Amounts	Percent
Discretionary spending (military, international, and domestic)	$182.4	36.5
Entitlements (Social Security, Medicare, veterans, farm subsidies, and government pensions)	119.0	24.0
Interest	64.8	13.0
Taxes and user fees	133.8	26.5
Total	500.0	100.0

There are two important points about this agreement:

1. The reductions were heavily back-end loaded. Only 23 percent would come in the first two years, and 77 percent were to come in the last three years. The first-year impact of $40 billion was only $4 billion more than the $36 billion in cuts proposed in the original Bush budget (see Table 10–5). This was done deliberately to stifle the objections to a major tax increase or spending cuts in a year of a declining economy.

2. These were *not* cuts over five years from the $1.3 trillion in proposed spending for fiscal year 1991. Under the agreement there would not be a $900 billion spending budget in fiscal year 1995. The cuts were from what is called the "current services base-line estimates," which are defined as last year's budget adjusted for factors such as economic growth and inflation. These were not cuts from the existing spending figures but cuts from the projections of what spending would be if the existing programs plus an increase for inflation were carried forward.

The agreement also extended the statutory limit on the public debt for five years, thus avoiding the annual debate over raising the debt ceiling, which was often the occasion for obstruction and delay in passing a budget by the beginning of the new fiscal year. Further, it made numerous "process" changes, most of which appeared to have the effect of strengthening the enforcement of budget agreements.

The initial agreement's $133.8 billion in increases in tax and user fees are given in Table 10–6.

A Credible Agreement

Most independent observers and those who strongly favored a credible budget agreement believed that this agreement was far more meaningful than the "blue smoke and mirrors" agreements from the past. The fact that it was more realistic may have aroused the vehement opposition it engen-

TABLE 10–5   Proposed Deficit Reduction, 1991–1995 (Billions of Dollars)

Item	1991	1992	1993	1994	1995	1991–1995
Discretionary						
Domestic	—	—	—	$ 53.2	$ 62.0	$182.4
International	—	—	—			
Defense	$ 9.8	$22.6	$34.8	28.8	33.3	119.0
Mandatory	12.1	20.9	23.9			
Tax and receipt						
measures	16.2	26.7	27.0	32.1	31.8	133.8
Interest	2.0	6.5	12.2	18.4	25.7	64.8
Total deficit						
reduction	40.1	76.7	97.9	132.5	152.8	500.0

Source: Memorandum, Budget Summit Agreement.

TABLE 10–6 Original Budget Summit Revenue Provisions for Fiscal Years 1991–1995 (Billions of Dollars)

Item	Effective	1991	1992	1993	1994	1995	1991–1995
A. Budget outlays							
State and local Social Security offset							
a. Social Security package (target)	—	$ − 0.5	$ − 0.3	$ − 0.4	$ − 0.4	$ − 0.4	$ − 2.0
b. Medicare package (target)	—	− 0.5	− 0.4	− 0.4	− 0.4	− 0.4	− 2.0
B. Revenue-losing provisions							
1. Enterprise zones (target)	1/1/91	—	− 0.1	− 0.2	− 0.3	− 0.4	− 1.0
2. Energy incentives (target)	1/1/91	− 0.4	− 0.6	− 0.9	− 1.0	− 1.1	− 4.0
3. Extend certain expiring provisions through 12/31/91							
a. R&E credit[1]	—	− 0.6	− 0.4	− 0.1	− 0.1	[2]	− 1.2
b. Low-income housing credit	—	− 0.2	− 0.3	− 0.4	− 0.4	− 0.4	− 1.7
4. Additional growth incentives for certain small businesses							
a. Minimum basis	10/1/91	0.2	− 0.1	− 0.2	− 0.3	− 0.3	− 0.7
b. Research and development credit of 30% (1 year)	1/1/91	− 0.1	− 0.2	− 0.1	[2]	[2]	− 0.4
c. Deduction for stock purchases (25%)[3]	1/1/91	− 0.4	− 1.0	− 1.4	− 1.9	− 2.6	− 7.3
d. Indexing of common stock[4]	1/1/92	[2]	[2]	− 0.1	− 0.1	− 0.2	− 0.4
e. 2-year expansion of expensing	1/1/91	− 2.8	− 3.4	0.7	− 2.1	1.5	− 1.9
f. Additional expensing for scientific equipment	1/1/91	− 0.5	− 0.6	0.1	− 0.4	0.3	− 0.3
g. Reduce corporate phaseout rate from 5% to 2½%	1/1/91	− 0.1	− 0.1	− 0.1	− 0.1	− 0.1	− 0.5
h. Additional growth incentives subject to mutual agreement target	—	[2]	− 0.1	− 0.1	− 0.2	− 0.2	− 0.6
5. Increase EITC[5] (target)	1/1/91	− 0.1	− 1.1	− 1.2	− 1.3	− 1.3	− 5.0
Subtotals, revenue-losing provisions		− 5.0	− 8.0	− 4.0	− 3.2	− 4.8	− 25.0
C. Revenue-raising provisions							
1. Energy taxes							
a. Motor fuels tax (5 cents; 10 cents after 7/1/91)	12/1/90	5.4	10.1	9.8	9.9	9.9	45.0
b. 2-cent petroleum tax, without home heating oil[6]	1/1/91	1.4	2.4	2.5	2.7	2.9	11.8

(continued)

TABLE 10–6 (continued)

Item	Effective	1991	1992	1993	1994	1995	1991–1995
2. Increase tobacco taxes by 4 cents per pack in 1991 and by 4 cents per pack in 1993	1/1/91	0.6	0.8	1.5	1.5	1.5	5.9
3. Beer, wine, and distilled spirits taxes	1/1/91	1.5	2.1	2.1	2.1	2.2	10.0
4. 10% luxury excise tax[7]	1/1/91	0.2	0.3	0.4	0.5	0.5	1.9
5. Ozone-depleting chemical excise tax	1/1/91	0.1	0.1	0.1	0.1	0.1	0.5
6. Loss deductions and salvage values for insurance companies	1/1/90	0.3	0.2	0.2	0.2	0.2	1.1
7. Adopt foreign compliance provisions including certain provisions from H.R. 4308 and S. 2410	3/20/90	8	8	0.1	0.1	0.1	0.3
8. Amortize insurance policy deferred acquisition expenses (DAC)	9/30/90	1.5	1.7	1.7	1.6	1.5	
9. Leaking underground storage tank (LUST) trust fund (5 years)	10/1/90	0.1	0.1	0.1	0.1	0.1	0.6
10. Increase Airport Trust Fund aviation excise taxes (5 years)[9,10]	1/1/91	1.3	2.3	2.5	2.7	3.0	11.8
11. Increase harbor maintenance tax[9,11]	1/1/91	0.3	0.3	0.4	0.4	0.4	1.8
12. IRS enforcement initiatives (target)[11]	—	3.0	1.8	1.8	1.5	1.2	9.4
13. Retiree health with reversion excise increase (target)	1/1/91	0.5	0.2	0.2	0.1	0.1	1.0
14. State and local III[12] (target)	1/1/92	—	0.7	1.4	1.6	1.6	5.2
15. Corporate interest deduction partial disallowance (target)	1/1/91	1.4	0.7	0.6	0.4	0.6	3.9
16. Certain corporate and partnership provisions (target)	—	0.2	0.3	0.4	0.5	0.6	2.0
17. Limitation on itemized deductions[13] (target)	1/1/91	0.5	4.1	4.0	4.5	4.9	18.0
18. Increase III wage cap to $73,000 (target)	1/1/91	0.9	2.8	2.9	3.1	3.3	13.0
19. State and local Social Security (OASDI)[14]	—	2.0	2.2	2.4	2.5	2.7	11.7
20. Payroll tax deposit stabilization	—	1.0	2.2	3.2	—	—	—
Subtotals, revenue-raising provisions		22.2	35.4	31.8	36.1	37.4	162.9
Deficit reduction		−16.2	−26.7	−27.0	−32.1	−31.8	−133.8

Notes: Details may not add to totals due to rounding. Interaction between or among items has not been taken into account for the purpose of this table.

1. Base limitation is retained at current level of 50%.

2. Loss of less than $50 million.

3. For small business equity deduction, preference included in minimum tax, recapture deduction as ordinary income, and 25% on annual deduction per taxpayer of $50,000.

4. For stock of small business corporations purchased after date of Summit agreement, allow indexing of basis for inflation occurring after 12/31/90, sold after 12/31/91, and held for at least one year.

5. Amount does not correspond to that used in the accompanying distributional analysis.

6. Each State to receive Highway account apportionments and allocations equal to at least 95% of its contribution attributable to increased revenue.

7. Tax applies to specific newly-manufactured items with retail prices above the following thresholds: automobiles—$30,000; private boats and yachts—$100,000; jewelry—$5,000; and furs—$5,000. Tax is 10% of purchase price in excess of thresholds.

8. Gain of less than $50 million.

9. Estimate is net of income tax offset.

10. This estimate is presented relative to the CBO baseline which assumes extension of the Airport and Airway Trust Fund (AATF) taxes with the trigger in effect. The estimate reflects the effects both of removing the trigger and of increasing the rates of certain of the AATF taxes as proposed in the President's budget. Increased revenue to be dedicated to deficit reduction.

11. Estimate to be provided by the Congressional Budget Office (CBO).

12. Rate—0.8% in 1992, 1.35% in 1993, 1.45% in 1994 and thereafter.

13. Disallow itemized deductions in an amount equal to 3% of AGI in excess of $100,000 for single returns, $100,000 for joint returns, and $100,000 for head of household returns. Proposal does not apply to medical expenses or investment interest. Disallowance under the proposal cannot exceed 80% of otherwise deductible itemized deductions subject to the proposal.

14. See related outlay offset in Section A.

dered, for this time the tax increases and spending cuts would most likely be effective.

Rudolph Penner, the former head of the CBO, said, "It's much more real than any agreement we've had for many years." Carol Cox, the head of the Committee for a Responsible Federal Budget and a Budget Committee aide to former Senate Budget Committee ranking member Henry Bellmon (R.-Okla.) said that "for the most part these are real spending cuts and real tax increases."[28] One particular bright spot for the bipartisan agreement was the support of Federal Reserve Board Chairman Alan Greenspan, who said it would produce "a credible, enforceable reduction in the budget deficit."[29] His blessing was critical for support from the Federal Reserve to lower interest rates and to reassure the financial markets.

Discontents

There were criticisms of the agreement, however. Not only were rank-and-file members of the Congress unhappy with the closed door, backroom, elitist procedures by which it had been reached, but they had other reasons, good and bad, for their discontent.

Defense was a big winner. First, the $9.8 billion cut in defense for the first year was *less* than the Congress had agreed to in its work on the budget resolution, the authorization bill, and Appropriations Committee actions. Second, the estimated $2 billion monthly cost of the Persian Gulf deployment was exempt from future budget defense ceilings.

Other big winners were Texas, with the savings and loan bail-out costs remaining off-budget plus new incentives for drilling for oil and gas; corporations in general, whose taxes were not raised; and Social Security beneficiaries. The bill contained no increase in taxes on Social Security benefits, did not raise the retirement age, and did not delay or cut the annual COLAs. Another class of big winners were individuals and couples with yearly incomes over $100,000 and especially those with incomes over $200,000.

Losers included in particular those with incomes below $10,000 between $20,000 and $50,000 (see Table 10–7). Farmers and Medicare recipients took relatively big cuts in their benefits or were taxed at higher rates. A 2 percent tax on heating oil was a heavy burden for colder regions of the country, especially New England and the upper Middle West. The unemployed were required to wait an additional two weeks before drawing benefits. New taxes on gasoline, diesel, and aviation fuel would impinge on farmers, truckers, commuters, and airlines. There were heavy "sin" taxes on smokers and beer and wine drinkers. Conservative Republicans were angry with both the tax increases and with the failure to include the president's cherished capital gains tax reduction in the deal.

TABLE 10–7   Percentage Tax Change by Income in
Original Budget Agreement

Income	Percent Tax Increase
$0–$10,000	7.6
$10,000–$20,000	1.9
$20,000–$30,000	3.3
$30,000–$40,000	2.9
$40,000–$50,000	2.9
$50,000–$75,000	1.8
$75,000–$100,000	2.1
$100,000–$200,000	1.9
$200,000 and over	1.7
Average	2.4

Source: Congressional Joint Committee on Revenue Taxation

Lobbyists

The discontent was intensified by heavy interest group lobbying. Much of the public who demanded action to cut the budget in general were opposed to any specific action that affected them. This represented the endemic political schizophrenia that causes individuals and groups to demand cuts in wasteful or inefficient government spending while petitioning their representatives to support a local public works project, military base, or personal benefit.

The lobbyists, who included advocates for airline manufacturers, life insurance companies, doctors and hospitals, the oil and gas industry, ethanol manufacturers, insurance companies, and industries affected by the proposed luxury surtaxes, among myriads of others, had followed the negotiators to the Andrews Air Force Base bar and golf course. They camped outside the ways and means and finance committees hearing rooms. They swarmed over the Capitol, buttonholing members. All had a constitutional First Amendment right "to petition the government for a redress of grievances."

Fairness and Incentives

But apart from the lobbyists interested in specific details, there were two larger and more contentious issues. First was the issue of fairness. Members of the Congress and the public objected to various provisions of the accord: (1) the large increase in Medicare premiums and deductibles, (2) the 14 cent increase in the gasoline tax, and (3) the two cent increase in the heating oil tax, all three of which were regressive taxes; and (4) the burden imposed on low and middle income taxpayers as opposed to the wealthy. Many of these objections cut across party lines.

Second was the argument about incentives and taxes. This was mostly a Republican issue. There was not only opposition to many of the items making up the $133 billion in new taxes and user fees, but to both the absence of a cut in the capital gains tax and the administration negotiators' abandonment of indexing capital gains, that is, of taking inflation into account so that the tax would be paid only on the real as opposed to the inflated gains.

Such opposition came from many quarters. There was an open rebellion from the House Republican Whip Newt Gingrich, who boycotted the negotiations. National Republican Congressional Campaign Committee Co-Chairman Ed Rollins said he hoped that "my vulnerable candidates would be let off the hook" by the White House. House members who had been recruited to run for Senate seats in Illinois, Colorado, Michigan, New Hampshire, Rhode Island, and Iowa, among others, publicly opposed the agreement. So did many of their incumbent Senate Democratic opponents. Virginia's Democratic Governor L. Douglas Wilder, the country's first black governor, castigated Democratic National Chairman Ron Brown, the first black chairman of either party, for supporting the agreement. To placate the discontent of key House committee chairmen, Speaker Thomas S. Foley argued that the committees could change the details, if not the total amounts, in reconciliation procedures to write the change in the laws needed to carry out the pact.

The Vote

By the time the House vote came on the overall provisions of the agreement and the reconciliation instructions to its committees, there was open rebellion against it. The deal went down in flames. It was defeated 254 to 179, or by 75 votes along the following party lines:

PARTY	FOR	AGAINST	PERCENT FOR
Republican	71	105	40%
Democratic	108	149	42%
Total	179	254	

When the Republicans failed to provide a majority of their members, the Democrats jumped ship as well.

As success has a thousand fathers, failure is an orphan. Much of the blame was laid at the feet of the White House negotiators: Darman, Sununu, and, to a much smaller degree, Brady. Former Majority Leader and President *pro tempore* of the Senate Robert C. Byrd (D.-W.Va.) complained that he had never been treated with such disrespect as he had been by Sununu at the Andrews Air Force Base negotiations. The "good cop–bad cop" routine of the "raging bulls," Sununu and Darman, backfired. "They antagonized so many Republicans it was awful," complained Republican Congressman Bud Schuster of Pennsylvania. When Ways and Means Committee Chairman Rostenkowski referred to unnamed "unelected officials" who were ruining the budget process, members from both sides of the aisle stood, clapped, and cheered.[30]

After the defeat of the budget agreement at 1:17 A.M. on October 6, 1990, the Congress completed work on a continuing resolution to keep the government running for another seven days. This would give them time to try to renegotiate a deal that could command a majority vote. The continuing resolution had originally passed the House by a 300 to 113 margin. However, the president blamed the Congress for the disaster. He announced he would not sign the resolution and instead put into effect the preparations to shut down the government. He said he would "not be a party" to efforts by the Congress to "once again put off meeting this responsibility for a few more day." Senate Majority Leader Mitchell (D.-Me.) called the veto "counterproductive" and said, "I think it's an unnecessary and unwise action. It will not advance the president's position during the negotiating process and will cause unneeded pain and anguish to thousands of American families."[31] Speaker Foley called the veto "gratuitous and unnecessary."[32] The House failed to override the president's veto by a vote of 260 to 138, 6 votes short of the two-thirds needed. The Republicans who had voted 105 to 71 against the budget agreement, now voted 129 to 25, with 22 abstentions, to uphold the president and shut down the government.[33] As this happened over the three-day Columbus Day weekend, its effects were limited although very disappointing to several thousand tourists who had journeyed to Washington only to find most of the major attractions closed. Many of them visited the congressional galleries to watch the Congress perform in unusual weekend sessions as a substitute for a visit to the Washington Zoo, which was closed by the president's edict.

NEGOTIATIONS RESUMED

By late Monday night of the Columbus Day weekend both Republican and Democratic budget negotiators agreed to resume negotiations. The Congress passed both a new five-year, $500 billion deficit reduction budget resolution as well as a new continuing resolution that would keep the government going until October 19. The president said he would sign the continuing resolution and called off the three-day government shutdown. Budget negotiations were resumed, and the congressional committees began work in earnest on the reconciliation bill to write into law the specific tax increases and spending cuts needed to carry out the revised budget resolution.

Almost immediately President Bush committed a political gaffe: He charged up the hill and then down again. He said at a press conference on the day the government reopened that he might agree to higher income tax rates on the wealthy for a cut in the capital gains rate. "If it can be worked in proper balance between the capital gains rate and income tax changes, fine," he said. Senate Republicans who met with him later in the day vehemently opposed raising income tax rates. By the end of the day he announced that rate increases and capital gains tax cuts were "off the table."[34]

President Bush was first criticized for favoring the rich with his stand on capital gains, and now he was confusing his backers by casting that position in doubt. When asked to clarify his views during a campaign trip in Florida he said, "Let Congress clear it up." After a reporter shouted while he was jogging "Are you ready to throw in the towel on capital gains?" he pointed to his backside and yelled, "Read my hips."[35] The next day he seemed to flip-flop again. He said he favored a top tax rate of 31 percent and a cut in capital gains to 15 percent, but that there was no chance of the Democrats accepting it and that it was a "waste of time" to try. This further confused both his supporters and opponents. It led Congressman Larry Smith (D.-Fla.) to say, "Our president has now taken more positions on taxes than Nadia Comaneci."[36]

Simultaneously the pollsters reported that President Bush and the Republicans had lost ground because they were seen as favoring the rich. The president's approval rating dropped to 55 percent, 21 points below its mid-August level.[37]

NEGOTIATING TACTICS

After President Bush's mixed signals, essentially four negotiating stances emerged, two in the Congress and two at the White House.

In the House the tactics were partisan. The Democratic majority in both the Ways and Means Committee and on the floor were determined to push their budget and their agenda, which included reducing the proposed gasoline taxes, postponing indexing for a year, cutting back the Medicare increases, limiting full capital gains treatment to those making less than $100,000 a year and excluding sales of securities and collectibles from its provisions, raising the top income tax rate from 28 to 33 percent plus a 10 percent surtax on those with annual incomes over $1 million, and reducing taxes on the poor by expanding the earned income tax credit.

The Democratic plan was clearly aimed at taxing the wealthy and bestowing the benefits on the middle and lower income groups. It was able to succeed for several reasons. First, as a group the House Republicans refused to take part in the negotiations. They were nonplayers. The Democrats merely had to create a bill that would appeal to their own supporters. Second, the House Republicans had argued for months that no new taxes were needed and that a $500 billion deficit reduction over five years could be fashioned by cutting spending alone. When put to the test, however, they were unable to provide an alternative budget limited to spending cuts. This reduced their credibility. It was charged that they, as a permanent minority in the House, rejoiced in negative opposition but had forfeited the right to govern. It is a strongly held political truism that you cannot defeat something with nothing. Third, the rules of the House that prevent filibusters and limit both the number and substance of amendments made it possible for the majority to rule. The Democrats passed their bill by a 227 to 203 vote. The Democratic tax alternative, proposed as an amendment to the original bill, passed by an even larger 238 to 192 margin.[38]

In the Senate, both in the Finance Committee and on the floor, budget procedures were more collegial. Senate leaders and the administration negotiators devised a bill that neither raised income tax rates nor reduced capital gains provisions, although it did further limit the deductions that those with incomes over $100,000 could take. But with few restrictions on debate or that amendments that could be offered, provisions with majority support might succeed during floor consideration of the bill.

The administration also held two positions. On the campaign trail the president was roasting the Democrats for the failure to reach an agreement. This attack lacked credibility, however, after Congressman Gingrich and the House Republicans led the charge against the first agreement. Back at the White House Chief of Staff Sununu supported negotiations with the Democrats to highlight the president as a problem solver. What the party needed, Sununu told Congressman Guy Vander Jagt, (R.-Mich.) head of the National Republican Congressional Committee, who proposed a stand-pat position by the president and an offensive attack to lay the blame on the "tax-and-spend" Democrats for a budget failure, was a "success for the president" and a deal that would be good for the economy.[39] The president was ambivalent, and his party suffered from the divided counsels.

By the October 19 deadline the House and Senate had passed their two divergent tax proposals and were meeting in a conference committee to iron out the differences. As a result, after another round of finger-pointing and attempts at putting the blame on the other side, the Congress passed and the president signed a second continuing resolution to keep the government open from October 20 through 24. The General Accounting Office reported that it had cost $1.6 million to close down the government over the Columbus Day holiday.

The conference committee agreed on the tax provisions just a few hours before the new deadline, but not enough Democrats in the House would support the deal to pass it without significant Republican support. Congressman David Obey (D.-Wis.) said the Democratic leaders should tell "the authoritarians from the White House staff if they want Democratic votes to screw middle-income people they're going to have a very tough time."[40] The negotiators returned to the table. The Democrats dropped their proposed "millionaire's tax" and settled for an increase in the top rate from 28 to 31 percent, instead of 33 percent, and dropped the proposed surtax. The capital gains tax was capped at 28 percent, but the increase in the deductions wealthy people could take, which the Republicans had pressed for, was also dropped. A new continuing resolution was passed to keep the government running, and the package was sent tò the House and Senate for debate and a vote.

Meanwhile a new controversy broke out among Republicans. Ed Rollins, the co-chairman of the National Republican Congressional Campaign Committee advised Republican congressional candidates to oppose the president on the budget agreement tax increases and the spending cuts for Medicare. "Do not hesitate to oppose either the president or proposals being advanced in Congress," he wrote.[41] The president was "furious," and called for Rollins's resignation. Press secretary Marlin Fitzwater said it was "the understatement of the decade" to call Rollins's statements "unhelpful."[42]

THE REVISED AGREEMENT

As Table 10–8 shows, the overall provisions of the revised budget agreement differed only marginally from the original agreement voted down in the early morning hours of October 6.

The major $20.1 billion change in entitlements between the first and second agreements was a reduction in the cuts for Medicare benefits and farmers. This was offset by a $12 billion increase fashioned by: (1) raising the taxes imposed on the wealthy: (2) increasing the income subject to the Medicare payroll tax from $51,300 to $125,000; and (3) reducing the overall deficit-cutting package by $8.1 billion.

The final agreement also changed the share of taxes paid by various income groups not only from what it had been under the original agreement but from what it was under the existing tax laws. While most income groups ended up paying about the same percentage as before, there was a significant decline for those making between $10,000 and $20,000 a year, and a significant increase for those making $200,000 or more (see Table 10–9).

TABLE 10–8 Comparison of the Original and Revised Budget Deficit Agreements (Billions of Dollars)

Item	Original	Revised	Change
Discretionary cuts	$182.4	$182.4	$ 0
Entitlement cuts	119.0	98.9	− 20.1
Interest savings	64.8	64.0	− 0.8
Revenue increases	133.8	146.6	12.8
Totals	500.0	491.9	8.1

TABLE 10–9   Change in Tax Liabilities by Income Groups from 1990 Tax Law

Income	Old Tax Burden	New Tax Burden	Average Change	Percent Change
Less than $10,000	1.6%	1.6%	$ −72	−2.0%
$10,000–$20,000	7.6%	7.2%	−118	−3.2%
$20,000–$30,000	11.9%	11.8%	90	1.8%
$30,000–$40,000	13.4%	13.4%	144	2.0%
$40,000–$50,000	10.2%	10.2%	200	2.0%
$50,000–$75,000	20.0%	19.9%	229	1.5%
$75,000–$100,000	7.7%	7.7%	463	2.1%
$100,000–$200,000	12.1%	12.1%	839	2.3%
$200,000 and up	15.4%	16.1%	8,598	6.3%
Average for all taxpayers			$ 215	2.1%

Source: Joint Committee on Taxation

When the House vote came at dawn on October 27, the House Republicans once again deserted their president. On the 228 to 200 vote by which the Conference Report of the Omnibus Budget Reconciliation Act of 1990 passed the House, only 47 of 173 Republicans (27%) supported him, while 181 of 255 Democrats (71%) backed the agreement. Late that afternoon the Senate voted 54 to 45 to pass the bill; 35 Democrats and 19 Republicans voted for the measure, and 20 Democrats and 25 Republicans opposed it.

After the bill passed, the president went on the campaign trail and argued that the devil made him do it. To get his spending cuts, he argued, he had had to accept the Democratic tax increases. Ultimately the Democrats were the relative winners on the nature of both the tax increases and the spending cuts, although the president had wielded great influence throughout the negotiations by brandishing the veto threat. When the House Republicans abandoned the process, the president had to make his compromises with congressional Democrats to secure enough votes to pass any kind of deficit-cutting package. With their refusal to support the president, the views of conservative Republicans in the House became irrelevant.

Flawed Procedures

It is an oxymoron to call the procedures by which the agreement was reached a "budget process." It was indeed more like a barroom brawl. Except for the release of the mid-year budget review, not a single target date was met. The president released his budget three weeks late. The Congress missed its deadline for both reporting and passing the concurrent resolution on the budget by months, albeit because the president and Congress agreed to negotiate the figures. The deadlines for both the appropriations and authorization bills were missed. The reconciliation bill was not passed in

September or even by October 15. The new fiscal year was almost a month old before a budget was in place. Further, for at least the first six months and actually until the agreements were reached in October, both the Congress and the president were dealing with phantom figures. Finally, the Gramm-Rudman-Hollings targets were a sham (see Table 10-10). In the six years between 1985 and 1991, they were changed and extended three times. Further, they never represented the actual annual government deficit because: (1) funds paid out because of the savings and loan debacle were off-budget and not counted; (2) the net interest figure ignored double-entry bookkeeping and grossly understated the total amount of interest paid; and (3) the real deficit was masked by the surplus in the Social Security and other trust funds as well as other manipulative budget methods that obscured the figures.

THE BUDGET ENFORCEMENT ACT OF 1990

Effective Repeal of the Gramm-Rudman-Hollings Act

In an attempt to make certain that the budget agreement was enforced over the five-year period, the Congress passed Title XIII of the Omnibus Budget Reconciliation Act of 1990. It is an important and little noticed part of the massive budget agreement over which the Congress and the president struggled for most of that year.

Title XIII is called the Budget Enforcement Act of 1990. It radically revised budget procedures and amended both the 1974 act and the Gramm-Rudman-Hollings Act as amended. Among the most important provisions, it: (1) drastically revised the overall budget deficit targets (see Table 10–10); (2) changed budget concepts and excluded numerous categories of spending from the spending ceilings; (3) provided new enforcement mechanisms that appeared to strengthen procedures; (4) shifted power in critical target and enforcement matters from the Congress to the president; (5) shifted power from the budget committees to the appropriations and tax-writing committees; (6) changed the budget timetable; and (7) reformed the way in which credit and credit agencies are treated in the budget. Overall it contained the most comprehensive and complicated changes in budget procedures since the 1974 act.

In the past the Congress often did its job. It had reduced the president's budget requests virtually every year for a quarter of a century. While it cut that part of the budget over which it had control, it found that forces outside its ability to control overwhelmed what it had done. An increase in interest rates, a rise in unemployment, a savings and loan scandal, or a war in the Persian Gulf could increase the annual deficit far beyond any ability to remedy it by legislative acts. Yet the Congress was held accountable for events over which it had little or no control.

The new procedures spelled out in fairly precise terms those areas that the Congress and the president could control, and held them responsible for doing so. Thus, it effectively repealed the Gramm-Rudman-Hollings Act without appearing to do so. The act essentially became a dead letter.

With respect to sequestration, the Budget Enforcement Act provided for three sequesters where formerly there was only one, and substituted the scalpel for the meat ax when they were invoked.

The Overall Targets

In the past the budget targets were rigid but were met either through contrivances, loopholes, gimmicks, and other dodges and artifices, or were amended when no resort to expedients could possibly be justified.

The new overall budget targets are as flexible as the old ones were rigid. The president was *required* to adjust the deficit targets for 1992 and 1993 to reflect updated economic and technical assumptions and changes in budgetary concepts and definitions, and may change them for similar reasons in 1994 and 1995. The surplus in the Social Security trust funds is excluded from budget deficit calculations, which was a major reason for the massive increase in the overall targets. Among the economic assumptions that the president could use to adjust the targets is the inflation rate. He can also adjust the targets for changes in the discretionary spending limits (see page 327). Not counted in the discretionary spending ceilings were the Egyptian and Polish debt forgiveness programs, increases in contributions to the International Monetary Fund, emergency appropriations including

TABLE 10–10 The Moving Budget Deficit Targets for Fiscal Years 1986–1995 (Billions of Dollars)

Fiscal Year	1985 G-R-H Act	1987 G-R-H Amendments	1990 Budget Agreement	Annual Deficit
1986	$171.9			$221.3
1987	144			$9$149.7
1988	108	$144		$9$155.1
1989	72	136		$9$152.1
1990	36	100		$9$218.5 est.
1991	0	64	327*	
1992		28	317*	
1993		0	236*	
1994			102*	
1995			83*	

*Subject to change by presidential reestimate. On January 7, 1991, 10 weeks after the budget agreement was passed, the administration added $50 billion to the 1991 target. This figure excluded the costs for the war in the Persian Gulf and included the Social Security trust fund surplus. The 1991 and 1992 figures were revised again by the Mid-year Budget Review in July, 1991.

funds for the Persian Gulf Desert Shield and Desert Sword operations, Internal Revenue tax compliance funding, the savings and loan bail-out, and, for fiscal years 1993 and 1994, changes in the estimates of credit subsidy costs. While no cushion was provided for fiscal years 1992 and 1993, there was a $15 billion cushion for fiscal year 1994 and 1995; that is, the overall target could be exceeded by $15 billion without provoking an across-the-board sequestration. These 1991–1995 overall targets are flexible and can be changed by presidential fiat.

The Specific Discretionary Spending Limits

In addition to the overall targets for fiscal years 1991–1995, there are also specific spending limits (also called ceilings or caps) for discretionary spending. For the first three fiscal years (1991–1993) there were specific limits in both budget authority (BA) and outlays (O) for discretionary spending for defense, international, and domestic categories. For the final two years, the categories were combined, and the spending limits applied only to the total for all three (see Table 10–11). The act *required* the OMB to adjust the caps on the discretionary spending categories when the president releases the budget for: (1) changes in concepts and definitions; (2) changes in inflation; and (3) in fiscal year 1993 and 1994, changes in estimates due to credit reform.

"Pay-as-You-Go" Provisions

In addition to the overall spending targets and the discretionary spending ceilings, there are also "pay-as-you-go" provisions that apply to increases in "direct" spending and decreases in revenues brought about by

TABLE 10–11   Discretionary Spending Limits for Fiscal Years 1991–1995 (Billions of Dollars)

Item	FY 1991	FY 1992	FY 1993	FY 1994	FY 1995
Defense					
Budget authority	$288.918	$291.643	$291.785	—	—
Outlays	297.660	295.744	292.686	—	—
International					
Budget authority	20.100	20.500	21.400	—	—
Outlays	18.600	19.100	19.600	—	—
Domestic					
Budget authority	182.700	191.300	198.300	—	—
Outlays	198.100	210.100	221.700	—	—
All categories					
Budget authority	—	—	—	$510.800	$517.700
Outlays	—	—	—	534.800	540.800

Source: Memorandum, Budget Summit Agreement.

legislative action. If the Congress legislates an increase in veterans benefits, for example, that would breach the totals allowed for programs not under the jurisdiction of the appropriations committees, it would have to provide for offsetting cuts elsewhere in that category of spending. If the tax-writing committees adopt a series of new tax cuts, they would have to provide for a comparable increase in revenues through alternative taxes. This was done to prevent the legislative committees from passing additional entitlement or other legislative programs that would breach the overall five-year deficit-cutting agreement. While these direct spending and revenue targets and ceilings can be adjusted for inflation, recessions, emergencies, and certain other specified items over which the Congress and the president have limited, indirect, or no control, legislative action by the legislative or tax-writing committees that breaches the five-year deficit agreement is not tolerated.

Enforcement is provided for each of the three categories, that is, for the overall targets, discretionary spending, and pay-as-you-go offsets. First, there is a form of sequestration for each of the three categories. Second, sequestration can take place either at the end of the year or, in the case of discretionary spending excesses, during the year.

Sequestration

Overall Targets   The sequestration provisions of the Gramm-Rudman-Hollings Act are continued for purposes of meeting the overall budget targets. The difference, of course, is that the president has the authority to adjust the targets for economic or technical reasons. If, after the adjustments, the targets are exceeded, the sequester takes place. Half the funds must come from the military and half from civilian accounts, as in the past. As noted, the margin of error, or cushion, is $15 billion for the last two years. There is no cushion for fiscal years 1992 and 1993. As these targets are extraordinarily flexible, it is unlikely that a sequester will take place in these overall budget targets. For this purpose, sequestration is a paper tiger.

Discretionary Ceilings   Enforcement of the spending limits for discretionary spending is brought about by a special sequestration procedure. This sequester applies only to the categories—defense, international, or domestic—or combined categories beginning in fiscal year 1994 (see Table 10–11). Exceeding the limits can be prevented through points of order when legislation exceeding the limits is before the House or Senate. A sequester can also be prevented through offsetting legislative cuts in spending in the category. If the ceiling is breached notwithstanding points of order or offsetting legislation, a sequester takes place.

Pay-as-You-Go Provisions   If Congress fails to provide an offsetting cut in direct spending or an increase in revenues for new spending or tax cut legislation, a sequester, called a "minisequester," is also required.

The Timing of the Sequester

The three sequesters listed above can occur at the end of the year, specifically fifteen days after the Congress adjourns. A sequester for a breach of the discretionary targets can also take place during the year. The authority to invoke any sequester lies with the president and the OMB. The CBO's role in the procedure is "advisory." The timetable for sequestration reports and orders is given in Table 10–12.

All three end-of-the-year sequesters must take place on the same day. If excesses in the discretionary and/or pay-as-you-go categories are responsible for the excess in the overall deficit target, and if sequestration in those two categories is sufficient to meet the overall target, no general across-the-board sequester, divided equally between military and nonmilitary programs, takes place.

Sequestration of discretionary spending funds can take place during the year in the following circumstances. If during the first half of the *calendar* year, that is from January 3 to June 30, appropriations are passed that exceed the spending limits, fifteen days later sequestration takes place in funds in that category which would otherwise be spent in that fiscal year. If during the third quarter of the *calendar* year, that is from July 1 to September 30, appropriations are passed that exceed the spending limits, sequestration takes place in the appropriate category during the next *fiscal* year, which begins on October 1.

Other Provisions

Numerous other changes were made either to enforce the budget agreement or to provide for changes in the timetable and schedules.

The deadline for the submission of the budget by the president was changed again. In 1985 it was changed from fifteen days after the Congress convenes to the first Monday after the January 3 date a new Congress convenes. In practice this deadline was seldom met. The budget was usually

TABLE 10–12   Timetable for Sequestration Reports and Orders

Date	Action to Be Completed
5 days before the president's budget submission	CBO sequestration preview report
The president's budget submission	OMB sequestration preview report
August 15	CBO sequestration update report
August 20	OMB sequestration update report
10 days after end of session	CBO final sequestration report
15 days after end of session	OMB final sequestration report; presidential order
30 days later	GAO compliance report

submitted about the first week in February. The new law provides a deadline of the first Monday in February but urges the president to submit it on the first Monday after January 3.

The Social Security trust funds remain off-budget, but the revenues are not counted for deficit calculation purposes. The surplus in the funds will no longer mask the budget deficit, as the critics of the former unified budget, which counted all revenues in deficit calculations, alleged. This action appeals to those who believe that trust funds should be segregated and not counted. It is opposed by many economists who believe the budget should reflect all the revenue and spending actions of the government.

A procedure called a "firewall" is erected to protect Social Security financing, insure the solvency of the program, and prohibit the Treasury and others from using its proceeds or borrowing the funds for general purposes.

Title XIII also reforms the way credit activities are treated in the budget to insure that the costs they incur and the subsidies they provide are properly monitored.

An assessment of the soundness of government-sponsored enterprises (GSEs), which are private entities but have the backing of the full faith and credit of the U.S. government, is required by the act. The agencies include those providing for farm credit, mortgages, and student loans.

The Senate procedure called the "Byrd Rule" after former Majority Leader Robert C. Byrd, which was designed to prevent "extraneous matters," less formally referred to as "riders" or "pork," from being added to reconcilation bills, was also incorporated into the 1990 Budget Enforcement Act.

Provisions also rescinded the fiscal year 1991 sequestration orders issued by the president in the fall of 1990 during the budget fight, authorized back pay for those who had been furloughed during that period, and tightened the Antideficiency Act procedures that are effective during funding gaps.[43]

THE BUDGET ENFORCEMENT ACT IN PRACTICE: WILL IT WORK?

Does the new framework make sense? How will the act work in practice? Can the enforcement provisions be carried out? How does the act affect the relationship between the Congress and the president, among the committees, between the OMB and the CBO, between insiders and outsiders in the budget process, among interest groups and their lobbyists, and between off-budget and on-budget programs? Does it promote the basic principles of the 1974 act and make it possible for the Congress to look at the budget from an overall standpoint, to shift and change priorities as conditions vary, to deal with the problem of entitlements and backlogs, and to coordinate overall tax and spending goals? Will it reduce the deficit? Is it better than what is replaced?

Origins

Throughout the Reagan and Bush administrations, the president repeatedly called for budget reform. But this call was almost always followed by specific proposals for a constitutional amendment to balance the budget, a line-item veto, a two-year budget, a congressional budget resolution in the form of a joint resolution that the president could veto or sustain with the support of one-third plus one member of only one house, and combined legislative and appropriations committees. On the whole these proposals were either fig leaves to cover up the administration's own part in the budget debacle or demands that the Congress delegate even more of its power over the purse strings to the president. If the president had been given every one of the requests, the budget mess and the unprecedented deficit would have been no closer to solution.

In 1990 in his repeated calls for a budget summit and a budget agreement, President Bush combined the proposals with a condition that any final agreement must include budget "process reform." Budget experts saw this as a repeat of the usual calls, as window dressing by the executive branch, a shibboleth to cross the fords of budget insecurity, and as part of the continued effort to put the political monkey on the back of the Congress. It was disdained by serious advocates of budget deficit reduction.

What a surprise it was indeed when the $492 billion, five-year deficit reduction legislation of 1990 included Title XIII of the Budget Enforcement Act. Essentially unreported by the press, unknown to the rank-and-file members of the Congress, and unnoticed even by many budget committee negotiators, it contained massive budget "process reforms," and none of them offered the usual litany of presidential budget reform demands.

This was the direct result of the struggle between the appropriations committees and the budget committees, on the one hand, and the president and the Congress on the other. Its general origins go back to the division of power in the Constitution and the struggle for power within the Congress from the day the first Congress met, with its sixty-five authorized House members and twenty-six Senators. Its major specific origins are at least twofold.

First, in 1974 the appropriations committees lost power to the new budget committees. In the Senate, Appropriations Committee Chairman John L. McClellan (D.-Ark.) was on his deathbed and unable to fight for territorial rights. In the House the junior members, with the support of the House Rules Committee Chairman Richard Bolling (R.-Mo.), successfully rebelled against centralizing budget procedures in the hands of the powerful senior members on the appropriations and ways and means committees.

Second, in 1990 Senator Robert C. Byrd, chairman of the Appropriations Committee, former majority leader of the Senate, its president *pro tempore,* and its most knowledgable expert on the rules, was determined to regain lost authority for his committee. His experience with the fiscal year 1990 (calendar year 1989) budget agreement stimulated his actions. The House and Senate appropriations committees carried out their part of the agreement and limited total discretionary spending to the agreed-upon figures. When, however, other committees failed to implement the deal, under the reconciliation and sequestration procedures many of the accounts that the Appropriations Committee had cut were cut again. They thus had taken a double hit. This was a perennial problem with the Gramm-Rudman-Hollings Act: The efficient congressional committees and executive branch agencies were penalized, while the spending culprits received probation or were pardoned. Determined to rectify this injustice while others worked on the big ticket substantive items of the fiscal year 1991-1995 deal, Senator Byrd joined with Budget Director Darman to fashion the enforcement mechanisms that transferred power back to the Appropriations Committee and away from the Congress and the CBO to the White House and the OMB. Senator Byrd also successfully negotiated for an increase in the five-year discretionary funds over which his committee had jurisdiction. This was done behind the scenes and received public attention only after the budget deal was consummated. Whatever its consequences, it owes its paternity to the perseverance, industry, determination, and seething outrage of Senator Byrd.

Significant Results

Overall, the framework of the agreement makes sense and is an improvement on the old provisions. While it has a mechanism to deal with deliberate increases in entitlements, it is rigid with respect to changing priorities. Some of the other important results of the agreement, including specific shifts of substance, power, and influence that occurred, are outlined below.

Complexity   As Lawrence J. Haas commented, "the few White House officials, lawmakers and aides who developed the new budget rules took a budget process that was generally viewed as too complicated and made it even more so."[44] Its most likely effect will be to shift attention from the macro to the micro budget activities, from an outsiders' game to an insiders' game, and thus to blur both action and responsibility further so that it will be difficult to determine accountability. As the new overall annual budget targets are largely meaningless, can be changed and shifted for both economic and technical reasons, and can be enlarged by presidential fiat to avoid an overall sequestration, it is unlikely that much can or will be done to reduce them. Unlike the 1985 amendments to the act, an ultimate balanced budget is no longer even a goal.

Deliberate Delegation of Power to the President   Unlike the 1974 act, which was designed to retrieve power from the president yet actually increased the president's power at the expense of the Congress through unintended and unanticipated consequences, especially by the reconciliation provisions, the 1990 act deliberately transferred power from the Congress to the president.

The president, through the OMB, determines the five-year budget deficit target goals on an annual basis. The president is also the scorekeeper, umpire, and judge as to whether the discretionary and direct spending goals and the pay-as-you-go provisions have been met. Will a president who vetoed a military authorization bill because it failed to provide all the funds he asked for actually invoke a sequester on military funds if they exceed the new discretionary limits, or will he wink at the excesses? Will not a president who has proposed significant cuts in discretionary domestic spending programs find, as the power to make the judgment is invested solely in his hands, that in fact the programs do exceed the domestic limits and call for a sequester? Will not a president who is determined to reduce the tax on capital gains find that such a provision will increase revenues, even though a large body of professional tax economists estimate it will lose money? And would a George McGovern or Walter Mondale presidency, for example, do the opposite and wink at domestic spending excesses while finding that military spending, with its backlog and bow wave of unspent appropriated funds, obviously has breached the limits? The act actually appears to canonize presidential economic estimates that in the past have been grossly exaggerated.

Subjective Outlay (O) Targets   The temptations will be great, especially in the area of discretionary spending. The budget authority (BA) that the Congress appropriates is precise and objective. But the outlay (O) figures, or what will actually be spent in any fiscal year, are subjective derivatives of budget authority. Only slightly more than half of the budget authority passed in any fiscal year is spent in that fiscal year (see Figure 7–1). The proportions vary from 95 percent or more of funds for personnel and payroll to less than 10 percent for a new weapons system or housing project during the first year.

The authority of the president and the OMB to keep the score transfers powers to them at the expense of the Congress, its appropriations, legislative, and tax writing committees, and its CBO.

Congressional Scorekeeping Warnings and Admonitions   The Congress did not blindly delegate scorekeeping powers to the president and OMB, but rather because of the constraints imposed by the Supreme Court's decision in *Bowsher v. Synar.*[45] The Congress wrote into the law requirements for consultation between the OMB and the Congress to establish scorekeeping guidelines.[46] Because "the Office of Management and Budget has not always shown complete objectivity in its estimates," the Congress also included the following warnings in the act:

> The conferees considered procedures under which Congress would enact into law Congressional Budget Office cost estimates as part of any spending legislation. Should the Office of Management and Budget abuse its scorekeeping power, the conferees believe that the Congress should adopt such procedures at the time.[47]

On December 4, 1990, the House Democratic Caucus approved a rule giving the CBO and the Joint Committee on Internal Revenue Taxation the power to make the tax and entitlement spending estimates. Every tax or entitlement bill would include a provision that, for the purpose of this legislation, the CBO or Joint Committee scoring figures would be used. On December 21 President Bush sent a letter to Speaker Foley in which he said, "I will veto any bill that contains language such as that specified in the rule," because, he argued, the rule would undercut the credibility of the budget agreement.[48]

Impoundment Powers: Nixon Revisited? The Congress also appears to have given the president the power to impound funds without its specific approval, a power it had effectively retrieved from President Nixon. The president can sign an appropriations, direct spending, or tax bill, and still, in effect, reduce or veto or impound funds that he estimates will exceed the spending or pay-as-you-go provisions. It is not a usurpation of power but a delegation by the Congress to the president in areas that historically the Congress has fiercely guarded.

Five Years of Rigid Priorities? One of the major arguments in support of the 1974 Budget Act was that the Congress needed greater ability to shift budget priorities. The 1990 act diminishes such action. The caps on discretionary spending for the first three years mean that funds cut from the military budget, for example, cannot be used to increase domestic spending above the domestic ceiling. Domestic programs, as Lawrence J. Haas of the *National Journal* put it, "will compete for funds in 1991–93 only against each other. It won't be between guns and butter but instead different kinds of butter."[49] This may increase the internecine warfare between the competing factions and lobbyists of otherwise kindred groups by pitting guns against guns and butter against butter. Throughout the budget the Congress limits its discretionary power to shift priorities among categories but can do so within categories through offsetting legislation.

Shifting Costs   Another possible consequence is that the costs of new programs, which would breach the ceilings and cannot be paid for either by tax increases or alternative spending cuts, will be shifted to the states, localities, or private businesses. This is not a new phenomenon. It was a consequence of the Reagan budget revolution and the cuts in many domestic federal programs. It can be argued that the more effective the enforcement mechanism, the greater the temptation to shift these costs.

Limited Budget Committees: Ministerial Action   Finally, what will the budget committees do, at least for the first three years of the 1990 act? The president determines the budget deficit target, which is a moving, shifting, flexible goal. The ceilings for discretionary programs are set by law for five years. Revenue losses caused by changes that the tax committees make in the tax laws are required to be offset by them through revenue increases. Legislative authorizing committees, not the budget committees, have jurisdiction over the detailed content of domestic, international, and military programs. Except for occasional points of order against proposed violations of the agreement, the function of the budget committees may become ministerial, limited largely to producing a perfunctory annual budget resolution whose essential terms have previously been established.

A BUDGET DIAGNOSIS

After months of struggle and considerable loss of popularity and prestige by both the president and the Congress, the basic parameters of the budget debate seemed set for several years, from 1991 to 1995. The sheer size and magnitude of the agreement—one thousand pages weighing twenty-four pounds and standing ten inches high—and the contentious and controversial issues that it tackled on the eve of an election emphasize that the budget is not some isolated bookkeeping or accounting document.

The budget is the result of the compromises made among the contending political and economic forces of the country. It is because of the diverse regions and innumerable interests of the nation that a budget agreement is so difficult to fashion. The public remains schizophrenic. It strongly favors action to reduce the deficit in general but opposes specific tax increases or spending cuts that apply to them.

The deficit cannot be eliminated with mirrors, gimmicks, or additional changes in "process." It is too big to "outgrow." Cutting out fat and waste, doing away with excess paperwork, or applying business efficiency can bring only minor changes in the totals. Only tough decisions to cut programs and benefits or to raise taxes, or a combination of both, can reduce the deficit.

In writing of the accomplishments of the Congress, David Broder, the most knowledgeable of American political commentators, stated that in the famous multiyear budget deal the Congress "made the first round of tough decisions and put in place an enforcement mechanism that will *compel* Congress to make further hard choices required to get the government on a pay-as-you-go basis."[50] If efforts over the past quarter of a century are any guide to the future, this may be a very optimistic conclusion.

NOTES

1. Presidential debate, 25 September 1988; as quoted in *The New York Times,* 26 September 1988, p. A18.
2. Ibid.
3. Ibid., 15 October 1988, p. A16
4. Ibid., 26 September 1988, p. A18.
5. *The Washington Post,* 11 February 1990, p. A6.
6. *Wall Street Journal,* 17 February 1989, p. A1.
7. *The Washington Post,* 26 February 1989, p. C1.
8. *Wall Street Journal,* 17 February 1989, p. A1.
9. *The New York Times,* 15 October 1988, p. A16.
10. *The Washington Post,* 16 April 1989, p. B1.
11. Ibid., 26 September 1989, p. A8.
12. For example, its extraordinarily useful table on the controllability of outlays, distinguishing between relatively uncontrollable outlays (75%) and relatively controllable outlays (25%), was missing. Also missing was the usual Special Analysis F, which detailed the direct loans, guaranteed loans, and loans by government-sponsored enterprises that in their totality equal the spending budget of the federal government.
13. *Budget of the United States Government: Fiscal Year 1991* (Washington, D.C.: U.S. Government Printing Office, 1990), sect. I-21.
14. *The Arizona Daily Star,* (Tucson), 29 December 1989, p. A6.
15. *The Washington Post,* 31 January 1990, p. A8.
16. Ibid.
17. Ibid., 2 February 1990, p. A2.
18. Ibid., 31 January 1990, p. A8.
19. Ibid., 11 March 1990, p. B1.
20. Ibid., 13 March 1990, p. A1.
21. Ibid.
22. Ibid., p. A4.
23. "Meet the Press," 18 March, 1990.
24. *The Washington Post,* 20 April 1990, p. A11.
25. Executive Office of the President, Office of Management and Budget, *Mid-Session Review of the Budget* (Washington, D.C.: 16 July, 1990), Table 7, p. 13.
26. *The Washington Post,* 7 November 1990, p. A18.
27. *Mid-Session Review,* Table 7, p. 13.
28. *Wall Street Journal,* 1 October 1990, p. A18.
29. *The Washington Post,* 4 October 1990, p. A12.
30. *New York Times,* 6 October 1990, p. 8.
31. *The Washington Post,* 6 October 1990, p. A1.
32. Ibid., 9 October 1990, p. A8.
33. Ibid., 7 October 1990, p. A1.
34. *USA Today,* 11 October 1990, p. A1.

35. *The Washington Post,* 11 October 1990, p. A1.
36. Ibid., 12 October 1990, pp. A1, A12.
37. Ibid.
38. *Congressional Record,* 16 October 1990.
39. *The Washington Post,* 14 October 1990, p. A6.
40. Ibid., 24 October 1990. p. A6.
41. Memorandum, Ed Rollins to Republican Members of Congress, 15 October 1990. National Republican Congressional Campaign (Committee) TOP CAMPAIGNS.
42. *The Washington Post,* 26 October 1990, pp. A1, A23.
43. I am indebted to the work of Edward Davis and Robert Keith of the Congressional Research Service of the Library of Congress in Washington, D.C., for their timely and accurate reports on the Budget Enforcement Act of 1990, at a time when accurate information concerning it was virtually nonexistent.
44. Lawrence J. Haas, "New Rules of the Game," *National Journal,* 17 November 1990, p. 2794.
45. House of Representatives, *Omnibus Budget Reconciliation Act of 1990, Conference Report,* 101st Cong., 2nd sess., Rep. 101–964, p. 1172.
46. Ibid., sec. 251(a)(7), and 252(d).
47. Ibid.
48. *The Washington Post,* 22 December 1990, p. A4.
49. *National Journal,* 17 November, 1990.
50. *The Washington Post,* 26 October 1990, pp. A1, A23.

A

Glossary of Federal
Budget Terms

ACCOUNT*

An item for which appropriations are made in any appropriations act and, for items not provided for in appropriations acts, such a term means an item for which there is a designated budget account identification code number in the president's budget.

APPROPRIATIONS ACT

A statute, under the jurisdiction of the House and Senate Committees on Appropriations, that generally provides authorization for federal agencies to incur obligations and to make payments out of the Treasury for specified purposes. An appropriations act, the most common means of providing

SOURCE: United States General Accounting Office, *A Glossary of Terms Used in the Federal Budget Process* (Washington, D.C.: U.S. Government Printing Office, 1981); Senate Budget Committee *Gramm-Rudman-Hollings: An Explanation* (Washington, D.C.: U.S. Government Printing Office, 1986, p. 32–6. Those terms marked by an asterisk are new definitions provided by Title XIII, Section 250, of the Budget Enforcement Act of 1990, and are essential to the understanding of the 1990 five-year budget agreement. Note especially the terms *direct spending* and *discretionary appropriations*.

budget authority, generally follows enactment of authorizing legislation unless the authorizing legislation itself provides the budget authority.

Currently, there are thirteen regular appropriation acts enacted annually. From time to time, the Congress also enacts supplemental appropriation acts (see also *Budget Authority*).

AUTHORIZING COMMITTEE

A standing committee of the House or Senate with legislative jurisdiction over the subject matter of those laws, or parts of laws, that set up or continue the legal operations of federal programs or agencies. An authorizing committee also has jurisdiction in those instances where back-door authority is provided in the substantive legislation.

AUTHORIZING LEGISLATION

Legislation enacted by Congress that sets up or continues the operation of a federal program or agency indefinitely or for a specific period of time. Authorizing legislation may place a cap on the amount of budget authority that can be appropriated for a program or may authorize the appropriation of "such sums as are necessary" (see *Budget Authority; Entitlements*).

BACK-DOOR AUTHORITY

Budget authority provided in legislation outside the normal (appropriations committees) appropriations process. The most common forms of back-door authority are authority to borrow (also called borrowing authority or authority to spend debt receipts) and contract authority. In other cases (e.g., interest on the public debt), a permanent appropriation is provided that becomes available without any current action by Congress. Section 401 of the Congressional Budget and Impoundment Control Act of 1974 (31 U.S.C. 1351) specifies certain limits on the use of back-door authority (see also *Authorizing Legislation; Appropriations* under *Budget Authority*).

BALANCED BUDGET

A budget in which receipts are equal to or greater than outlays.

BASE LINE, CURRENT POLICY

A set of projections showing the levels of spending and revenues that would occur for the upcoming fiscal year and beyond if existing programs and policies are continued unchanged, with all programs adjusted for inflation so that existing levels of activity are maintained (see *Current Services Budget*).

BREACH*

For any fiscal year the amount (if any) by which new budget authority or outlays for that year (within a category of discretionary appropriations) is above that category's discretionary spending limit for new budget authority or outlays for that year, as the case may be.

BUDGETARY RESOURCES*

With respect to budget year 1991, new budget authority, unobligated balances; loan guarantee commitments or limitations; direct loan obligations, commitments, or limitations; direct spending authority; and obligation limitations; or with respect to budget years 1992, 1993, 1994, or 1995, new budget authority, unobligated balances, direct spending authority, and obligation limitations.

BUDGET AUTHORITY (BA)

Authority provided by law to enter into obligations that will result in immediate or future outlays involving federal government funds; except the budget authority does not include authority to insure or guarantee the repayment of indebtedness incurred by another person or government. The basic forms of budget authority are appropriations, authority to borrow, and contract authority. Budget authority may be classified by the period of availability (one-year, multiple-year), by the timing of congressional action (current or permanent), or by the manner of determining the amount available (definite or indefinite).

Forms of Budget Authority

Appropriations An act of Congress that permits federal agencies to incur obligations and to make payments out of the Treasury for specified purposes. An appropriations act is the most common means of providing budget authority.

Borrowing Authority   Statutory authority that permits a federal agency to incur obligations and to make payments for specified purposes out of money borrowed from the Treasury, the Federal Financing Bank, or the public. The Budget Act in most cases requires that new authority to borrow must be approved in advance in an appropriation act.

Contract Authority   Statutory authority that permits a federal agency to enter into contracts in advance of appropriations. Under the Budget Act, most new authority to contract must be approved in advance in an appropriation act.

Balances of Budget Authority

Balances of budget authority result from the fact that not all budget authority enacted in a fiscal year is obligated and paid out in the same year. Balances are classified as follows:

Obligated Balance   The amount of obligations already incurred for which payment has not yet been made. This balance can be carried forward indefinitely until the obligations are paid.

Unobligated Balance   The portion of budget authority that has not yet been obligated. In one-year accounts, the unobligated balance expires (ceases to be available for obligation) at the end of the fiscal year. In multiple-year accounts, the unobligated balance may be carried forward and remain available for obligation for the period specified. In no-year accounts, the unobligated balance is carried forward indefinitely until (1) specifically rescinded by law; (2) until the purposes for which it was provided have been accomplished, or (3) in any event, whenever disbursements have not been made against the appropriation for two full consecutive years.

Unexpended Balance   The sum of the obligated and unobligated balances.

Determination of Amount

Definite Authority   The dollar amount of budget authority is contained in the law.

Indefinite Authority   The dollar amount of budget authority is not contained in the law; instead the law would provide "such sums as may be necessary."

Period of Availability

One-year Authority   Budget authority that is available for obligation only during a specified fiscal year.

Multi-year Authority   Budget authority that is available for a specified period of time in excess of one fiscal year.

No-year Authority   Budget authority that remains available for obligations for an indefinite period of time (until the objectives for which the authority was made available are attained).

Extensions of Budget Authority

Reappropriations   Congressional action to continue the obligational availability, whether for the same or different purposes, of all or part of the unobligated portion of budget authority that has expired or would otherwise expire. Reappropriations are counted as budget authority in the year for which the availability is extended.

Continuing Resolution   Legislation enacted by Congress to provide budget authority for federal agencies and/or specific activities to continue in operation until the regular appropriations are enacted. Continuing resolutions are enacted when action on appropriations is not completed by the beginning of a fiscal year. The continuing resolution usually specifies a maximum rate at which the obligations may be incurred, based on the rate of the prior year, the president's budget request, or an appropriation bill passed by either or both houses of the Congress.

Timing of Congressional Action

Current Authority   Budget authority enacted by Congress in or immediately preceding the fiscal year in which it becomes available.

Permanent Authority   Budget authority that becomes available as the result of previously enacted legislation (substantive legislation or prior appropriation act) and does not require current action by Congress. Authority created by such legislation is considered to be "current" in the first year in which it is provided and "permanent" in succeeding years (see also *Controllability*).

BUDGET DEFICIT

The amount by which the government's budget outlays exceed its budget receipts for a given fiscal year.

BUDGET RECEIPTS

Collections from the public (based on the government's exercise of its sovereign powers) and from payments by participants in certain voluntary federal social insurance programs. These collections, also called governmental receipts, consist primarily of tax receipts and social insurance premiums, but also include receipts from court fines, certain licenses, and deposits of earnings by the Federal Reserve System. Gifts and contributions (as distinguished from payments for services or cost-sharing deposits by state and local governments) are also counted as budget receipts. Budget receipts are compared with total outlays in calculating the budget surplus or deficit.

BUDGET SURPLUS

The amount by which the government's budget receipts exceed its budget outlays for a given budget/fiscal year.

CAPITAL BUDGET

A divided budget, with investment in capital assets excluded from calculations of the budget surplus or deficit, is often referred to as a capital budget. A capital budget provides for separating financing of capital or investment expenditures from current or operating expenditures.

The federal government has never had a capital budget in the sense of financing capital or investment-type programs separately from current expenditures. However, federal expenditures of an investment nature are presented in Special Analysis D of the *Special Analyses, Budget of the United States Government*.

CATEGORY*

For fiscal years 1991, 1992, and 1993, any of the following subsets of discretionary appropriations: defense, international, or domestic. For fiscal years 1994 and 1995, all discretionary appropriations. (The cost of Operation Desert Shield—Desert Sword shall not be counted within any category.)

COMPOSITE OUTLAY RATE*

The percent of new budget authority that is converted to outlays in the fiscal year for which the budget authority is provided and subsequent fiscal years, as follows: (1) for the international category, 46 percent for the first year, 20 percent for the second year, 16 percent for the third year, and 8 percent for the fourth year; (2) for the domestic category, 53 percent for the first year, 31 percent for the second year, 12 percent for the third year, and 2 percent for the fourth year.

CONCURRENT RESOLUTION ON THE BUDGET

A resolution passed by both houses of Congress but not requiring the signature of the president, setting forth, reaffirming, or revising the congressional budget for the United States government for a fiscal year.

A budget resolution is a concurrent resolution of Congress. Concurrent resolutions do not require a presidential signature because they are not laws. Budget resolutions do not need to be laws because they are a legislative device for the Congress to regulate itself as it works on spending and revenue bills.

The budget resolution for the upcoming fiscal year is to be adopted by the Congress by April 15. Additional concurrent resolutions revising the previously established budget levels may be adopted by Congress at any time before the end of the fiscal year. It is the usual practice for Congress to revise budget levels for the current fiscal years as part of the budget resolution for the upcoming fiscal year.

CONGRESSIONAL BUDGET

The budget as set forth by Congress in a concurrent resolution on the budget. By law the resolution includes:

- the appropriate level of total budget outlays and of total new budget authority;
- an estimate of budget outlays and new budget authority for each major functional category, for undistributed intergovernmental transactions, and for such other matters relating to the budget as may be appropriate to carry out the purposes of the 1974 Congressional Budget and Impoundment Control Act;
- the amount, if any, of the surplus or deficit in the budget;
- the recommended level of federal receipts;
- the appropriate level of the public debt; and
- the appropriate levels of total federal credit activity.

(See also *Concurrent Resolution on the Budget; President's Budget.*)

CONTINUING RESOLUTION

Appropriations legislation enacted by Congress to provide temporary budget authority for federal agencies to keep them in operation when their regular appropriation bill has not been enacted by the start of the fiscal year. A continuing resolution is a joint resolution, which has the same legal status as a bill.

A continuing resolution frequently specifies a maximum rate at which obligations may be incurred, based on the rate of the prior year, the president's budget request, or an appropriation bill passed by either or both chambers of the Congress.

A continuing resolution is a form of appropriation act and should not be confused with the budget resolution.

CONTROLLABILITY

The ability of Congress and the president to increase and decrease budget outlays or budget authority in the year in question, generally the current or budget year. Relatively uncontrollable refers to spending that the federal government cannot increase or decrease without changing existing substantive law. For example, outlays in any one year are considered to be relatively uncontrollable when the program level is determined by existing statute or by contract or other obligations.

Controllability, as exercised by Congress and the president, is determined by statute. In the case of Congress, all permanent budget authority is uncontrollable. For example, most trust fund appropriations are permanent, as are a number of Federal fund appropriations, and interest on the public debt, for which budget authority is automatically provided under a permanent appropriation enacted in 1847. In the case of the president, relatively uncontrollable spending is usually the result of open-ended programs and fixed costs (e.g., Social Security, Medicare, veterans benefits—outlays generally mandated by law), but also includes payments coming due resulting from budget authority enacted in prior years, such as entering into contracts (see also *Contract Authority* under *Budget Authority; Entitlements*).

CREDIT AUTHORITY

Authority to incur direct loan obligations or to incur primary loan guarantee commitments. Under the Budget Act new credit authority must be approved in advance in an appropriation act.

CROSSWALK

Also known as "committee allocation" or "Section 302 allocation." The means by which budget resolution spending totals are translated into guidelines for committee action on spending bills. The Budget Committees allocate the budget resolution totals among the committees by jurisdiction. Those committees in turn subdivide their allocations among their subcommittees or programs. Crosswalk allocations to the committees appear initially in Budget Committee reports on the budget resolution and finally in the joint explanatory statement accompanying a conference report on the budget resolution.

CURRENT ESTIMATES*

Budget estimates consistent with the underlying economic and technical assumptions when a budget is submitted by the Office of Management and Budget, or if submitted after a budget submission, estimates consistent with the most recently submitted president's budget.

CURRENT SERVICES BUDGET

A section of the president's budget, required by the Budget Act, that sets forth the level of spending or taxes that would occur if existing programs and policies were continued unchanged through the fiscal year and beyond, with all programs adjusted for inflation so that existing levels of activity are maintained (see *Base Line, Current Policy*).

DEBT, FEDERAL

There are three basic tabulations of federal debt: gross federal debt, debt held by the public, and debt subject to statutory limit (see also *Borrowing Authority* under *Budget Authority*).

Gross Federal Debt

Consists of public debt and agency debt and includes all public and agency debt issues outstanding.

Public Debt   That portion of the federal debt incurred when the Treasury or the Federal Financing Bank (FFB) borrows funds directly from the public or another fund or account. To avoid double counting, the FFB borrowing from the Treasury is not included in the public debt. (The Treasury borrowing required to obtain the money to lend to the FFB is already part of the public debt.)

Agency Debt   That portion of the federal debt incurred when a federal agency, other than the Treasury or the FFB, is authorized by law to borrow funds directly from the public or another fund or account. To avoid double counting, agency borrowing from Treasury or the FFB and federal fund advances to trust funds are not included in the federal debt. (The Treasury or FFB borrowing required to obtain the money to lend to the agency is already part of the public debt.) Agency debt may be incurred by agencies within the federal budget (such as the Tennessee Valley Authority) or by off-budget federal entities (such as the Postal Service). Debt of government-sponsored, privately owned enterprises (such as the Federal National Mortgage Association) is not included in the federal debt.

Debt Held by the Public

The part of the gross federal debt held by the public. (The Federal Reserve System is included in "the public" for this purpose.) Debt held by government trust funds (e.g., Social Security trust fund), revolving funds, and off-budget federal entities is excluded from the debt held by the public.

Debt Subject to Statutory Limit

As defined by the Second Library Bond Act of 1917, as amended, it currently includes virtually all public debt. However, only a small portion of agency debt is included in this tabulation of federal debt.

Under Public Law 96-78, approved September 29, 1979, an amendment to the Rules of the House of Representatives makes possible the establishment of the public debt limit as a part of the congressional budget process.

DEFERRAL OF BUDGET AUTHORITY

An action by the executive branch that delays the obligation of budget authority beyond the point it would normally occur. Pursuant to the Congressional Budget and Impoundment Control Act of 1974, the president must provide advance notice to Congress of any proposed deferrals. A deferral may not extend beyond the end of the fiscal year in which the president's message proposing the deferral is made. Congress may overturn a deferral by passing a law disapproving the deferral (see *Impoundment Resolution*).

DEFICIT

The amount by which total budget outlays exceed total revenues in a fiscal year.

DEFICIT FINANCING

A situation in which the federal government's excess of outlays over receipts for a given period is financed primarily by borrowing from the public.

DIRECT SPENDING*

Budget authority provided by law *other than* appropriations acts, entitlement authority, and the food stamp program.

DISCRETIONARY APPROPRIATIONS*

Budgetary resources (except to fund direct spending programs) provided in appropriations acts.

ENTITLEMENTS

Legislation that requires the payment of benefits (or entitlements) to any person or unit of government that meets the eligibility requirements established by such law. Authorizations for entitlements constitute a binding obligation on the part of the federal government, and eligible recipients have legal recourse if the obligation is not fulfilled. Budget authority for such payments is not necessarily provided in advance, and thus entitlement legislation requires the subsequent enactment of appropriations unless the existing appropriation is permanent. Examples of entitlement programs are Social Security benefits and veterans compensation or pensions. Section 401(b) of the Congressional Budget and Impoundment Control Act of 1974 [P.L. 93–344, 31 U.S.C. 1351(b)] imposes certain limits on the use of entitlements (see also *Authorizing Legislation; Controllability*).

EXPENDITURES OR OUTLAYS

With respect to provisions of the Antideficiency Act (31 U.S.C. 665) and the Congressional Budget and Impoundment Control Act of 1974 (P.L. 93–344, 31 U.S.C. 1301 note), the term expenditures has the same definition as "outlays" (see also *Outlays*).

FISCAL POLICY

Federal government policies with respect to taxes, spending, and debt management, intended to promote the nation's macroeconomic goals, particularly with respect to employment, gross national product, price level stability, and equilibrium in balance of payments. The budget process is a major vehicle for determining and implementing federal fiscal policy. The other major component of federal macroeconomic policy is monetary policy (see *Monetary Policy*).

FISCAL YEAR

A twelve-month accounting period. The fiscal year for the federal government begins on October 1 and ends on September 30. The fiscal year is designated by the calendar year in which it ends; for example, fiscal year 1995 is the year beginning October 1, 1994, and ending September 30, 1995.

FUNCTIONAL CLASSIFICATION

A system of classifying budget resources by major purpose so that budget authority, outlays, and credit activities can be related in terms of the national needs being addressed (e.g., national defense, health), regardless of the agency administering the program. A function may be divided into two or more subfunctions, depending upon the complexity of the national need addressed by that function (see *Budget Authority; Outlays*).

IMPOUNDMENT

Any action or inaction by an officer or employee of the United States government that precludes the obligation or expenditure of budget authority provided by Congress (see also *Deferral of Budget Authority; Impoundment Resolution; Rescission of Budget Authority*).

Impoundment Resolution

Section 1013(b) of the Congressional Budget and Impoundment Control Act of 1974 permits either chamber of Congress to adopt an impoundment resolution to veto a deferral of budget authority proposed by the administration. However, in 1983 the Supreme Court held that a one-house legislative veto is unconstitutional because it constitutes a legislative action without having been passed by both chambers of Congress and signed into law by the president (*INS v.Chadha,* U.S. [1983]). As a result, Congress now disapproves deferrals in appropriations laws.

MARK-UP

Meetings where congressional committees work on the language of bills or resolutions. At Budget Committee mark-ups, the House and Senate budget committees work on the language and numbers contained in budget resolutions.

MONETARY POLICY

Management of the money supply, under the direction of the Board of Governors of the Federal Reserve System, with the aim of achieving price stability and full employment. Government actions in guiding monetary policy include currency revaluation, credit contraction or expansion, rediscount policy, regulation of bank reserves, and the purchase and sale of government securities (see *Fiscal Policy*).

OFFSETTING RECEIPTS

Income from the public that results from sale of products or services rendered (such as sale of timber from federal lands or entrance fees for national parks). Offsetting receipts are deducted from total budget authority and outlays rather than added to federal revenues, even though they are deposited in the Treasury as miscellaneous receipts.

OUTLAYS (O)

Outlays are disbursements by the federal Treasury in the form of checks or cash. Outlays flow in part from budget authority granted in prior years and in part from budget authority provided for the year in which the disbursements occur.

The term "expenditures" is frequently used interchangeably with the term outlays (see *Budget Authority*).

PRESIDENT'S BUDGET

The document sent to Congress by the president in January of each year in accordance with the Budget and Accounting Act of 1921, as amended, estimating government receipts and outlays for the ensuing fiscal year and recommending appropriations in detail. Estimates for the legislative and judicial branches of the federal government are "transmitted without revision" (31 U.S.C. 11).

REAL ECONOMIC GROWTH*

With respect to any fiscal year, the growth in the gross national product during such year adjusted for inflation, consistent with Department of Commerce definitions.

RECONCILIATION

A process in which Congress includes in a budget resolution "reconciliation instructions" to specific committees, directing them to report legislation that changes *existing* laws, usually for the purpose of decreasing spending or increasing revenues by a specified amount by a certain date. The reported legislation is then considered as a single "reconciliation bill."

Gramm-Rudman-Hollings provides for an accelerated form of reconciliation in the Senate as the method for developing a congressional alternative to a presidential reduction order.

Reconciliation Bill

A bill, requiring enactment by both houses of Congress and approval by the president, making changes to legislation that has been enacted or enrolled.

Reconciliation Resolution

A concurrent resolution, requiring passage by both houses of Congress but not the approval of the president, directing the clerk of the House or the secretary of the Senate to make specified changes in bills or resolutions that have not yet reached the stage of enrollment.

RESCISSION OF BUDGET AUTHORITY

Cancellation of budget authority before the time when the authority would otherwise cease to be available for obligation. The rescission process begins when the president proposes a rescission to the Congress for fiscal or policy reasons. Unlike the deferral of budget authority, which occurs *unless* Congress acts to disapprove the deferral, rescission of budget authority occurs *only if* Congress acts within forty-five days of continuous session to enact the rescission (see *Deferral of Budget Authority; Impoundment*).

REVENUES

Collections from the public arising from the government's sovereign power to tax. Revenues include individual and corporate income taxes, social insurance taxes (such as Social Security payroll taxes), excise taxes, estate and gift taxes, customs duties, and the like.

SCOREKEEPING

Procedures for tracking the status of congressional budgetary actions. Scorekeeping data published by the Congressional Budget Office include status reports on the effects of congressional actions and comparisons of these actions to targets and ceilings set by Congress in budget resolutions.

SEQUESTER AND SEQUESTRATION*

That element of a presidential or congressional spending reduction order that occurs by reducing defense and nondefense spending by uniform percentages. For the 1990 Act, the cancellation of a budgetary resources provided by discretionary appropriations or direct spending law.

SNAPSHOT

The estimate of the projected deficit for the upcoming fiscal year made by the directors of the Congressional Budget Office and the Office of Management and Budget on August 15 under the provisions of the Gramm-Rudman-Hollings Act.

SUBSIDY

Generally, a payment or benefit made by the federal government for which there is no current charge. Subsidies are designed to support the conduct of an economic enterprise or activity, such as ship operations. They may also refer to provisions in the tax laws that provide certain tax expenditures and to the provisions of loans, goods, and services to the public at prices lower than market value, such as interest subsidies (see also *Tax Expenditures*).

SUPPLEMENTAL APPROPRIATION

An act appropriating funds in addition to those in the thirteen regular annual appropriations acts. Supplemental appropriations provide additional budget authority beyond the original estimates for programs or activities (including new programs authorized after the date of the original appropriations act) in cases where the need for funds is too urgent to be postponed until enactment of the next regular appropriations bill (see *Appropriations Act*).

TAX EXPENDITURES

Revenue losses attributable to provisions of the federal income tax laws that allow a special exclusion or deduction from gross income, or that provide a special credit, preferential tax rate, or deferral of tax liability.

Tax expenditures may be considered federal government subsidies provided through the tax system to encourage certain activities and to assist certain groups. For example, capital formation is encouraged by permitting businesses to claim some portion of the cost of an investment as a credit on their income taxes, and the unemployed are aided by excluding unemployment benefits from taxable income. Tax expenditures involve no transfer of funds from the government to the private sector. Rather, the U.S. Treasury Department forgoes some of the receipts that it otherwise would have collected, and the beneficiary taxpayers pay lower taxes than they otherwise would have to pay.

TRIGGER

If the August 15 estimate by the directors of the CBO and the OMB under the Gramm-Rudman-Hollings Act exceeds the maximum deficit amount for the coming fiscal year by more than $10 billion, this "triggers" potential action by Congress and the president by way of a joint resolution to reduce defense and nondefense spending by uniform percentages in order to meet the maximum deficit amount.

UNIFIED BUDGET

Describes the way the federal budget is currently displayed. This display includes revenues and spending for all regular federal programs and trust funds except Social Security, which was removed from budget totals beginning with fiscal year 1987. Prior to the creation of the unified budget in 1969, all trust funds were excluded from budget totals.

YEAR: BUDGET, CURRENT, AND OUTYEAR*

With respect to a session of Congress, "budget year" means the fiscal year of the government that starts on October 1 of the calendar year in which that session begins; "current year" means the fiscal year that immediately precedes that budget year; and the term "outyear" means any of the fiscal years that follow the budget year, through fiscal year 1995.

B

Concurrent Resolution on the Budget

| 101ST CONGRESS | | REPORT |
| 2d Session | HOUSE OF REPRESENTATIVES | 101–820 |

CONCURRENT RESOLUTION ON THE BUDGET—FISCAL YEAR 1991

OCTOBER 7, 1990—Ordered to be printed

Mr. PANETTA, from the committee of conference, submitted the following

CONFERENCE REPORT

[To accompany H. Con. Res. 310]

The committee of conference on the disagreeing votes of the two Houses on the amendments of the Senate to the concurrent resolution (H. Con. Res. 310) setting forth the congressional budget for the United States Government for the fiscal years 1991, 1992, 1993, 1994, and 1995, having met, after full and free conference, have agreed to recommend and do recommend to their respective Houses as follows:

That the House recede from its disagreement to the amendment of the Senate to the text of the resolution and agree to the same with an amendment as follows:

In lieu of the matter proposed to be inserted by the Senate amendment insert the following:

That the budget for fiscal year 1991 is established, and the appropriate budgetary levels for fiscal years 1992, 1993, 1994, and 1995 are hereby set forth.

MAXIMUM DEFICIT AMOUNTS

SEC. 2. The following levels and amounts in this section are set forth for purposes of determining, in accordance with section 301(i) of the Congressional Budget and Impoundment Control Act of 1974, as amended by the Balanced Budget and Emergency Deficit Control Act of 1985, whether the maximum deficit amount for a fiscal year has been exceeded, and as set forth in this concurrent resolution, shall be considered to be mathematically consistent with the other amounts and levels set forth in this concurrent resolution:

(1) The recommended levels of Federal revenues are as follows:

Fiscal year 1991: $1,172,900,000,000.
Fiscal year 1992: $1,260,800,000,000.
Fiscal year 1993: $1,349,800,000,000.
(2) The appropriate levels of total new budget authority are as follows:
Fiscal year 1991: $1,485,600,000,000.
Fiscal year 1992: $1,562,600,000,000.
Fiscal year 1993: $1,582,400,000,000.
(3) The appropriate levels of total budget outlays are as follows:
Fiscal year 1991: $1,236,900,000,000.
Fiscal year 1992: $1,269,300,000,000.
Fiscal year 1993: $1,305,000,000,000.
(4)(A) The amounts of the deficits are as follows:
Fiscal year 1991: $64,000,000,000.
Fiscal year 1992: $8,500,000,000.
(B) The amount of the surplus is as follows:
Fiscal year 1993: $44,800,000,000.

RECOMMENDED LEVELS AND AMOUNTS

SEC. 3. *(a) The following budgetary levels are appropriate for the fiscal years beginning on October 1, 1990, October 1, 1991, October 1, 1992, October 1, 1993, and October 1, 1994:*
(1) The recommended levels of Federal revenues are as follows:
Fiscal year 1991: $858,600,000,000.
Fiscal year 1992: $923,900,000,000.
Fiscal year 1993: $987,900,000,000.
Fiscal year 1994: $1,045,200,000,000.
Fiscal year 1995: $1,101,400,000,000.
and the amounts by which the aggregate levels of Federal revenues should be increased are as follows:
Fiscal year 1991: $14,700,000,000.
Fiscal year 1992: $24,300,000,000.
Fiscal year 1993: $26,900,000,000.
Fiscal year 1994: $30,700,000,000.
Fiscal year 1995: $30,300,000,000.
and the amounts for Federal Insurance Contributions Act revenues for hospital insurance within the recommended levels of Federal revenues are as follows:
Fiscal year 1991: $75,400,000,000.
Fiscal year 1992: $83,200,000,000.
Fiscal year 1993: $88,900,000,000.
Fiscal year 1994: $95,200,000,000.
Fiscal year 1995: $101,400,000,000.
(2) The appropriate levels of total new budget authority are as follows:
Fiscal year 1991: $1,174,700,000,000.
Fiscal year 1992: $1,230,100,000,000.
Fiscal year 1993: $1,229,600,000,000.
Fiscal year 1994: $1,216,000,000,000.
Fiscal year 1995: $1,266,000,000,000.

*(3) The appropriate levels of total budget outlays are as
follows:*
>   *Fiscal year 1991: $1,002,300,000,000.*
>   *Fiscal year 1992: $1,024,800,000,000.*
>   *Fiscal year 1993: $1,049,900,000,000.*
>   *Fiscal year 1994: $1,059,900,000,000.*
>   *Fiscal year 1995: $1,080,900,000,000.*

(4)(A) The amounts of the deficits are as follows:
>   *Fiscal year 1991: $143,700,000,000.*
>   *Fiscal year 1992: $100,900,000,000.*
>   *Fiscal year 1993: $62,000,000,000.*
>   *Fiscal year 1994: $14,700,000,000.*

(B) The amount of the surplus is as follows:
>   *Fiscal year 1995: $20,500,000,000.*

(5) The appropriate levels of the public debt are as follows:
>   *Fiscal year 1991: $3,369,600,000,000.*
>   *Fiscal year 1992: $3,540,900,000,000.*
>   *Fiscal year 1993: $3,676,700,000,000.*
>   *Fiscal year 1994: $3,766,900,000,000.*
>   *Fiscal year 1995: $3,827,600,000,000.*

*(6) The appropriate levels of total Federal credit activity for
the fiscal years beginning on October 1, 1990, October 1, 1991,
October 1, 1992, October 1, 1993, and October 1, 1994, are as
follows:*
>   *Fiscal year 1991:*
>>   *(A) New direct loan obligations, $21,000,000,000.*
>>   *(B) New primary loan guarantee commitments,
$106,800,000,000.*
>>   *(C) New secondary loan guarantee commitments,
$85,400,000,000.*
>   *Fiscal year 1992:*
>>   *(A) New direct loan obligations, $17,800,000,000.*
>>   *(B) New primary loan guarantee commitments,
$109,600,000,000.*
>>   *(C) New secondary loan guarantee commitments,
$88,700,000,000.*
>   *Fiscal year 1993:*
>>   *(A) New direct loan obligations, $18,200,000,000.*
>>   *(B) New primary loan guarantee commitments,
$112,100,000,000.*
>>   *(C) New secondary loan guarantee commitments,
$92,100,000,000.*
>   *Fiscal year 1994:*
>>   *(A) New direct loan obligations, $18,400,000,000.*
>>   *(B) New primary loan guarantee commitments,
$115,450,00,000.*
>>   *(C) New secondary loan guarantee commitments,
$95,600,000,000.*
>   *Fiscal year 1995:*
>>   *(A) New direct loan obligations, $18,600,000,000.*
>>   *(B) New primary loan guarantee commitments,
$118,100,00,000.*
>>   *(C) New secondary loan guarantee commitments,
$99,200,000,000.*

(b) The Congress hereby determines and declares the appropriate levels of budget authority and budget outlays, and the appropriate levels of new direct loan obligations and new primary loan guarantee commitments for fiscal years 1991 through 1995 for each major functional category are:

(1) National Defense (050):

Fiscal year 1991:

(A) New budget authority, $288,300,000,000.

(B) Outlays, $297,000,000,000.

(C) New direct loan obligations, $0.

(D) New primary loan guarantee commitments, $0.

Fiscal year 1992:

(A) New budget authority, $290,900,000,000.

(B) Outlays, $295,000,000,000.

(C) New direct loan obligations, $0.

(D) New primary loan guarantee commitments, $0.

Fiscal year 1993:

(A) New budget authority, $291,100,000,000.

(B) Outlays, $292,000,000,000.

(C) New direct loan obligations, $0.

(D) New primary loan guarantee commitments, $0.

Fiscal year 1994:

(A) New budget authority, $351,500,000,000.

(B) Outlays, $341,700,000,000.

(C) New direct loan obligations, $0.

(D) New primary loan guarantee commitments, $0.

Fiscal year 1995:

(A) New budget authority, $364,900,000,000.

(B) Outlays, $351,500,000,000.

(C) New direct loan obligations, $0.

(D) New primary loan guarantee commitments, $0.

(2) International Affairs (150):

Fiscal year 1991:

(A) New budget authority, $19,200,000,000.

(B) Outlays, $17,400,000,000.

(C) New direct loan obligations, $1,900,000,000.

(D) New primary loan guarantee commitments, $7,200,000,000.

(E) New secondary loan guarantee commitments, $400,000,000.

Fiscal year 1992:

(A) New budget authority, $19,800,000,000.

(B) Outlays, $18,000,000,000.

(C) New direct loan obligations, $2,000,000,000.

(D) New primary loan guarantee commitments, $7,200,000,000.

(E) New secondary loan guarantee commitments, $400,000,000.

Fiscal year 1993:

(A) New budget authority, $20,600,000,000.

(B) Outlays, $18,500,000,000.

(C) New direct loan obligations, $2,100,000,000.

(D) New primary loan guarantee commitments, $7,500,000,000.

        (E) New secondary loan guarantee commitments, $400,000,000.
    Fiscal year 1994:
        (A) New budget authority, $22,400,000,000.
        (B) Outlays, $19,700,000,000.
        (C) New direct loan obligations, $2,100,000,000.
        (D) New primary loan guarantee commitments, $7,700,000,000.
        (E) New secondary loan guarantee commitments, $500,000,000.
    Fiscal year 1995:
        (A) New budget authority, $23,800,000,000.
        (B) Outlays, $20,700,000,000.
        (C) New direct loan obligations, $2,200,000,000.
        (D) New primary loan guarantee commitments, $8,000,000,000.
        (E) New secondary loan guarantee commitments, $500,000,000.
  (3) General Science, Space, and Technology (250):
    Fiscal year 1991:
        (A) New budget authority, $15,200,000,000.
        (B) Outlays, $15,200,000,000.
        (C) New direct loan obligations, $0.
        (D) New primary loan guarantee commitments, $0.
    Fiscal year 1992:
        (A) New budget authority, $15,900,000,000.
        (B) Outlays, $15,700,000,000.
        (C) New direct loan obligations, $0.
        (D) New primary loan guarantee commitments, $0.
    Fiscal year 1993:
        (A) New budget authority, $16,500,000,000.
        (B) Outlays, $16,100,000,000.
        (C) New direct loan obligations, $0.
        (D) New primary loan guarantee commitments, $0.
    Fiscal year 1994:
        (A) New budget authority, $17,100,000,000.
        (B) Outlays, $16,800,000,000.
        (C) New direct loan obligations, $0.
        (D) New primary loan guarantee commitments, $0.
    Fiscal year 1995:
        (A) New budget authority, $17,700,000,000.
        (B) Outlays, $17,400,000,000.
        (C) New direct loan obligations, $0.
        (D) New primary loan guarantee commitments, $0.
  (4) Energy (270):
    Fiscal year 1991:
        (A) New budget authority, $6,400,000,000.
        (B) Outlays, $4,000,000,000.
        (C) New direct loan obligations, $2,000,000,000.
        (D) New primary loan guarantee commitments, $400,000,000.
    Fiscal year 1992:
        (A) New budget authority, $5,600,000,000.
        (B) Outlays, $4,400,000,000.

(C) New direct loan obligations, $1,600,000,000.
(D) New primary loan guarantee commitments, $0.
Fiscal year 1993:
    (A) New budget authority, $6,400,000,000.
    (B) Outlays, $5,000,000,000.
    (C) New direct loan obligations, $2,000,000,000.
    (D) New primary loan guarantee commitments, $0.
Fiscal year 1994:
    (A) New budget authority, $6,800,000,000.
    (B) Outlays, $5,300,000,000.
    (C) New direct loan obligations, $2,100,000,000.
    (D) New primary loan guarantee commitments, $0.
Fiscal year 1995:
    (A) New budget authority, $7,200,000,000.
    (B) Outlays, $5,200,000,000.
    (C) New direct loan obligations, $2,300,000,000.
    (D) New primary loan guarantee commitments, $0.
(5) Natural Resources and Environment (300):
Fiscal year 1991:
    (A) New budget authority, $18,800,000,000.
    (B) Outlays, $18,900,000,000.
    (C) New direct loan obligations, $100,000,000.
    (D) New primary loan guarantee commitments, $0.
Fiscal year 1992:
    (A) New budget authority, $19,900,000,000.
    (B) Outlays, $19,600,000,000.
    (C) New direct loan obligations, $100,000,000.
    (D) New primary loan guarantee commitments, $0.
Fiscal year 1993:
    (A) New budget authority, $20,500,000,000.
    (B) Outlays, $20,200,000,000.
    (C) New direct loan obligations, $100,000,000.
    (D) New primary loan guarantee commitments, $0.
Fiscal year 1994:
    (A) New budget authority, $21,200,000,000.
    (B) Outlays, $20,600,000,000.
    (C) New direct loan obligations, $100,000,000.
    (D) New primary loan guarantee commitments, $0.
Fiscal year 1995:
    (A) New budget authority, $22,000,000,000.
    (B) Outlays, $21,200,000,000.
    (C) New direct loan obligations, $100,000,000.
    (D) New primary loan guarantee commitments, $0.
(6) Agriculture (350):
Fiscal year 1991:
    (A) New budget authority, $18,000,000,000.
    (B) Outlays, $14,100,000,000.
    (C) New direct loan obligations, $9,000,000,000.
    (D) New primary loan guarantee commitments, $7,000,000,000.
Fiscal year 1992:
    (A) New budget authority, $22,600,000,000.
    (B) Outlays, $17,100,000,000.
    (C) New direct loan obligations, $8,800,000,000.

(D) New primary loan guarantee commitments, $7,300,000,000.
Fiscal year 1993:
    (A) New budget authority, $20,400,000,000.
    (B) Outlays, $16,000,000,000.
    (C) New direct loan obligations, $8,600,000,000.
    (D) New primary loan guarantee commitments, $6,600,000,000.
Fiscal year 1994:
    (A) New budget authority, $18,200,000,000.
    (B) Outlays, $15,300,000,000.
    (C) New direct loan obligations, $8,600,000,000.
    (D) New primary loan guarantee commitments, $6,700,000,000.
Fiscal year 1995:
    (A) New budget authority, $19,200,000,000.
    (B) Outlays, $14,600,000,000.
    (C) New direct loan obligations, $8,400,000,000.
    (D) New primary loan guarantee commitments, $6,800,000,000.
(7) Commerce and Housing Credit (370):
Fiscal year 1991:
    (A) New budget authority, $85,500,000,000.
    (B) Outlays, $87,000,000,000.
    (C) New direct loan obligations, $6,000,000,000.
    (D) New primary loan guarantee commitments, $63,300,000,000.
    (E) New secondary loan guarantee commitments, $85,000,000,000.
Fiscal year 1992:
    (A) New budget authority, $85,400,000,000.
    (B) Outlays, $81,400,000,000.
    (C) New direct loan obligations, $3,300,000,000.
    (D) New primary loan guarantee commitments, $65,500,000,000.
    (E) New secondary loan guarantee commitments, $88,300,000,000.
Fiscal year 1993:
    (A) New budget authority, $41,600,000,000.
    (B) Outlays, $39,700,000,000.
    (C) New direct loan obligations, $3,400,000,000.
    (D) New primary loan guarantee commitments, $67,800,000,000.
    (E) New secondary loan guarantee commitments, $91,700,000,000.
Fiscal year 1994:
    (A) New budget authority, $6,500,000,000.
    (B) Outlays, $9,200,000,000.
    (C) New direct loan obligations, $3,500,000,000.
    (D) New primary loan guarantee commitments, $70,300,000,000.
    (E) New secondary loan guarantee commitments, $95,100,000,000.

Fiscal year 1995:
    (A) New budget authority, $2,600,000,000.
    (B) Outlays, $3,200,000,000.
    (C) New direct loan obligations, $3,600,000,000.
    (D) New primary loan guarantee commitments, $72,100,000,000.
    (E) New secondary loan guarantee commitments, $98,700,000,000.
(8) Transportation (400):
  Fiscal year 1991:
    (A) New budget authority, $32,300,000,000.
    (B) Outlays, $30,700,000,000.
    (C) New direct loan obligations, $0.
    (D) New primary loan guarantee commitments, $0
  Fiscal year 1992:
    (A) New budget authority, $33,500,000,000.
    (B) Outlays, $31,900,000,000.
    (C) New direct loan obligations, $100,000,000.
    (D) New primary loan guarantee commitments, $0
  Fiscal year 1993:
    (A) New budget authority, $34,700,000,000.
    (B) Outlays, $33,100,000,000.
    (C) New direct loan obligations, $100,000,000.
    (D) New primary loan guarantee commitments, $0
  Fiscal year 1994:
    (A) New budget authority, $36,000,000,000.
    (B) Outlays, $34,300,000,000.
    (C) New direct loan obligations, $100,000,000.
    (D) New primary loan guarantee commitments, $0
  Fiscal year 1995:
    (A) New budget authority, $37,400,000,000.
    (B) Outlays, $35,500,000,000.
    (C) New direct loan obligations, $100,000,000.
    (D) New primary loan guarantee commitments, $0
(9) Community and Regional Development (450):
  Fiscal year 1991:
    (A) New budget authority, $9,200,000,000.
    (B) Outlays, $8,600,000,000.
    (C) New direct loan obligations, $1,200,000,000.
    (D) New primary loan guarantee commitments, $400,000,000.
  Fiscal year 1992:
    (A) New budget authority, $8,900,000,000.
    (B) Outlays, $8,600,000,000.
    (C) New direct loan obligations, $1,200,000,000.
    (D) New primary loan guarantee commitments, $400,000,000.
  Fiscal year 1993:
    (A) New budget authority, $9,000,000,000.
    (B) Outlays, $8,700,000,000.
    (C) New direct loan obligations, $1,200,000,000.
    (D) New primary loan guarantee commitments, $400,000,000.
  Fiscal year 1994:
    (A) New budget authority, $9,500,000,000.

 (B) Outlays, $8,900,000,000.
 (C) New direct loan obligations, $1,300,000,000.
 (D) New primary loan guarantee commitments, $400,000,000.
Fiscal year 1995:
 (A) New budget authority, $9,600,000,000.
 (B) Outlays, $9,200,000,000.
 (C) New direct loan obligations, $1,300,000,000.
 (D) New primary loan guarantee commitments, $400,000,000.
 (10) Education, Training, Employment, and Social Services (500):
Fiscal year 1991:
 (A) New budget authority, $43,000,000,000.
 (B) Outlays, $41,800,000,000.
 (C) New direct loan obligations, $0
 (D) New primary loan guarantee commitments, $12,500,000,000.
Fiscal year 1992:
 (A) New budget authority, $43,700,000,000.
 (B) Outlays, $43,000,000,000.
 (C) New direct loan obligations, $0
 (D) New primary loan guarantee commitments, $12,900,000,000.
Fiscal year 1993:
 (A) New budget authority, $44,400,000,000.
 (B) Outlays, $44,000,000,000.
 (C) New direct loan obligations, $0
 (D) New primary loan guarantee commitments, $13,200,000,000.
Fiscal year 1994:
 (A) New budget authority, $46,300,000,000.
 (B) Outlays, $45,400,000,000.
 (C) New direct loan obligations, $0
 (D) New primary loan guarantee commitments, $13,300,000,000.
Fiscal year 1995:
 (A) New budget authority, $48,100,000,000.
 (B) Outlays, $46,900,000,000.
 (C) New direct loan obligations, $0
 (D) New primary loan guarantee commitments, $13,400,000,000.
 (11) Health (550):
Fiscal year 1991:
 (A) New budget authority, $66,300,000,000.
 (B) Outlays, $65,500,000,000.
 (C) New direct loan obligations, $0
 (D) New primary loan guarantee commitments, $300,000,000.
Fiscal year 1992:
 (A) New budget authority, $73,900,000,000.
 (B) Outlays, $73,300,000,000.
 (C) New direct loan obligations, $0

    (D) New primary loan guarantee commitments, $300,000,000.
   Fiscal year 1993:
    (A) New budget authority, $81,300,000,000.
    (B) Outlays, $80,900,000,000.
    (C) New direct loan obligations, $0
    (D) New primary loan guarantee commitments, $300,000,000.
   Fiscal year 1994:
    (A) New budget authority, $89,600,000,000.
    (B) Outlays, $88,900,000,000.
    (C) New direct loan obligations, $0
    (D) New primary loan guarantee commitments, $350,000,000.
   Fiscal year 1995:
    (A) New budget authority, $98,500,000,000.
    (B) Outlays, $97,500,000,000.
    (C) New direct loan obligations, $0
    (D) New primary loan guarantee commitments, $400,000,000.
(12) Medicare (570):
   Fiscal year 1991:
    (A) New budget authority, $122,400,000,000.
    (B) Outlays, $104,900,000,000.
    (C) New direct loan obligations, $0
    (D) New primary loan guarantee commitments, $0
   Fiscal year 1992:
    (A) New budget authority, $133,500,000,000.
    (B) Outlays, $120,000,000,000.
    (C) New direct loan obligations, $0.
    (D) New primary loan guarantee commitments, $0.
   Fiscal year 1993:
    (A) New budget authority, $147,500,000,000.
    (B) Outlays, $134,400,000,000.
    (C) New direct loan obligations, $0.
    (D) New primary loan guarantee commitments, $0.
   Fiscal year 1994:
    (A) New budget authority, $161,900,000,000.
    (B) Outlays, $150,500,000,000.
    (C) New direct loan obligations, $0.
    (D) New primary loan guarantee commitments, $0.
   Fiscal year 1995:
    (A) New budget authority, $177,200,000,000.
    (B) Outlays, $168,000,000,000.
    (C) New direct loan obligations, $0.
    (D) New primary loan guarantee commitments, $0.
(13) Income Security (600):
   Fiscal year 1991:
    (A) New budget authority, $196,800,000,000.
    (B) Outlays, $160,500,000,000.
    (C) New direct loan obligations, $100,000,000.
    (D) New primary loan guarantee commitments, $0.
   Fiscal year 1992:
    (A) New budget authority, $205,200,000,000.

        (B) Outlays, $167,800,000,000.
        (C) New direct loan obligations, $100,000,000.
        (D) New primary loan guarantee commitments, $0.
    Fiscal year 1993:
        (A) New budget authority, $212,800,000,000.
        (B) Outlays, $175,300,000,000.
        (C) New direct loan obligations, $100,000,000.
        (D) New primary loan guarantee commitments, $0.
    Fiscal year 1994:
        (A) New budget authority, $223,500,000,000.
        (B) Outlays, $185,300,000,000.
        (C) New direct loan obligations, $100,000,000.
        (D) New primary loan guarantee commitments, $0.
    Fiscal year 1995:
        (A) New budget authority, $231,100,000,000.
        (B) Outlays, $192,200,000,000.
        (C) New direct loan obligations, $100,000,000.
        (D) New primary loan guarantee commitments, $0.
  (14) Income Security (650):
    Fiscal year 1991:
        (A) New budget authority, $3,800,000,000.
        (B) Outlays, $3,800,000,000.
        (C) New direct loan obligations, $0.
        (D) New primary loan guarantee commitments, $0.
    Fiscal year 1992:
        (A) New budget authority, $4,500,000,000.
        (B) Outlays, $4,500,000,000.
        (C) New direct loan obligations, $0.
        (D) New primary loan guarantee commitments, $0.
    Fiscal year 1993:
        (A) New budget authority, $4,900,000,000.
        (B) Outlays, $4,900,000,000.
        (C) New direct loan obligations, $0.
        (D) New primary loan guarantee commitments, $0.
    Fiscal year 1994:
        (A) New budget authority, $5,400,000,000.
        (B) Outlays, $5,400,000,000.
        (C) New direct loan obligations, $0.
        (D) New primary loan guarantee commitments, $0.
    Fiscal year 1995:
        (A) New budget authority, $6,000,000,000.
        (B) Outlays, $6,000,000,000.
        (C) New direct loan obligations, $0.
        (D) New primary loan guarantee commitments, $0.
  (15) Veterans Benefits and Services (700):
    Fiscal year 1991:
        (A) New budget authority, $31,900,000,000.
        (B) Outlays, $31,700,000,000.
        (C) New direct loan obligations, $7,000,000.
        (D) New primary loan guarantee commitments, $15,700,000,000.
    Fiscal year 1992:
        (A) New budget authority, $33,100,000,000.
        (B) Outlays, $32,700,000,000.

(C) *New direct loan obligations, $600,000,000.*
(D) *New primary loan guarantee commitments, $16,000,000,000.*
Fiscal year 1993:
    (A) *New budget authority, $34,100,000,000.*
    (B) *Outlays, $33,800,000,000.*
    (C) *New direct loan obligations, $600,000,000.*
    (D) *New primary loan guarantee commitments, $16,300,000,000.*
Fiscal year 1994:
    (A) *New budget authority, $35,100,000,000.*
    (B) *Outlays, $36,300,000,000.*
    (C) *New direct loan obligations, $500,000,000.*
    (D) *New primary loan guarantee commitments, $16,700,000,000.*
Fiscal year 1995:
    (A) *New budget authority, $36,100,000,000.*
    (B) *Outlays, $36,100,000,000.*
    (C) *New direct loan obligations, $500,000,000.*
    (D) *New primary loan guarantee commitments, $17,000,000,000.*
(16) *Administration of Justice (750):*
Fiscal year 1991:
    (A) *New budget authority, $13,300,000,000.*
    (B) *Outlays, $12,300,000,000.*
    (C) *New direct loan obligations, $0.*
    (D) *New primary loan guarantee commitments, $0.*
Fiscal year 1992:
    (A) *New budget authority, $14,400,000,000.*
    (B) *Outlays, $14,200,000,000.*
    (C) *New direct loan obligations, $0.*
    (D) *New primary loan guarantee commitments, $0.*
Fiscal year 1993:
    (A) *New budget authority, $15,000,000,000.*
    (B) *Outlays, $14,900,000,000.*
    (C) *New direct loan obligations, $0.*
    (D) *New primary loan guarantee commitments, $0.*
Fiscal year 1994:
    (A) *New budget authority, $15,600,000,000.*
    (B) *Outlays, $15,400,000,000.*
    (C) *New direct loan obligations, $0.*
    (D) *New primary loan guarantee commitments, $0.*
Fiscal year 1995:
    (A) *New budget authority, $16,200,000,000.*
    (B) *Outlays, $16,000,000,000.*
    (C) *New direct loan obligations, $0.*
    (D) *New primary loan guarantee commitments, $0.*
(17) *General Government (800):*
Fiscal year 1991:
    (A) *New budget authority, $11,700,000,000.*
    (B) *Outlays, $11,700,000,000.*
    (C) *New direct loan obligations, $0.*
    (D) *New primary loan guarantee commitments, $0.*

Fiscal year 1992:
   (A) New budget authority, $12,000,000,000.
   (B) Outlays, $12,000,000,000.
   (C) New direct loan obligations, $0.
   (D) New primary loan guarantee commitments, $0.
Fiscal year 1993:
   (A) New budget authority, $12,300,000,000.
   (B) Outlays, $11,800,000,000.
   (C) New direct loan obligations, $0.
   (D) New primary loan guarantee commitments, $0.
Fiscal year 1994:
   (A) New budget authority, $12,500,000,000.
   (B) Outlays, $12,000,000,000.
   (C) New direct loan obligations, $0.
   (D) New primary loan guarantee commitments, $0.
Fiscal year 1995:
   (A) New budget authority, $13,000,000,000.
   (B) Outlays, $12,400,000,000.
   (C) New direct loan obligations, $0.
   (D) New primary loan guarantee commitments, $0.
(18) Net Interest (900):
Fiscal year 1991:
   (A) New budget authority, $215,600,000,000.
   (B) Outlays, $215,600,000,000.
   (C) New direct loan obligations, $0.
   (D) New primary loan guarantee commitments, $0.
Fiscal year 1992:
   (A) New budget authority, $228,700,000,000.
   (B) Outlays, $228,700,000,000.
   (C) New direct loan obligations, $0.
   (D) New primary loan guarantee commitments, $0.
Fiscal year 1993:
   (A) New budget authority, $239,200,000,000.
   (B) Outlays, $239,200,000,000.
   (C) New direct loan obligations, $0.
   (D) New primary loan guarantee commitments, $0.
Fiscal year 1994:
   (A) New budget authority, $243,700,000,000.
   (B) Outlays, $243,700,000,000.
   (C) New direct loan obligations, $0.
   (D) New primary loan guarantee commitments, $0.
Fiscal year 1995:
   (A) New budget authority, $244,500,000,000.
   (B) Outlays, $244,500,000,000.
   (C) New direct loan obligations, $0.
   (D) New primary loan guarantee commitments, $0.
(19) Allowances (920):
Fiscal year 1991:
   (A) New budget authority, $0.
   (B) Outlays, −$95,400,000,000.
   (C) New direct loan obligations, $0.
   (D) New primary loan guarantee commitments, $0.
Fiscal year 1992:
   (A) New budget authority, $0.
   (B) Outlays, −$113,600,000,000.

(C) New direct loan obligations, $0.
(D) New primary loan guarantee commitments, $0.
Fiscal year 1993:
    (A) New budget authority, $0.
    (B) Outlays, −$86,600,000,000.
    (C) New direct loan obligations, $0.
    (D) New primary loan guarantee commitments, $0.
Fiscal year 1994:
    (A) New budget authority, $0.
    (B) Outlays, −$60,500,000,000.
    (C) New direct loan obligations, $0.
    (D) New primary loan guarantee commitments, $0.
Fiscal year 1995:
    (A) New budget authority, $0.
    (B) Outlays, −$76,400,000,000.
    (C) New direct loan obligations, $0.
    (D) New primary loan guarantee commitments, $0.
(20) Undistributed Offsetting Receipts (950):
Fiscal year 1991:
    (A) New budget authority, −$23,000,000,000.
    (B) Outlays, −$43,000,000,000.
    (C) New direct loan obligations, $0.
    (D) New primary loan guarantee commitments, $0.
Fiscal year 1992:
    (A) New budget authority, −$21,400,000,000.
    (B) Outlays, −$49,500,000,000.
    (C) New direct loan obligations, $0.
    (D) New primary loan guarantee commitments, $0.
Fiscal year 1993:
    (A) New budget authority, −$22,700,000,000.
    (B) Outlays, −$52,000,000,000.
    (C) New direct loan obligations, $0.
    (D) New primary loan guarantee commitments, $0.
Fiscal year 1994:
    (A) New budget authority, −$93,800,000,000.
    (B) Outlays, −$115,900,000,000.
    (C) New direct loan obligations, $0.
    (D) New primary loan guarantee commitments, $0.
Fiscal year 1995:
    (A) New budget authority, −$109,100,000,000.
    (B) Outlays, −$134,400,000,000.
    (C) New direct loan obligations, $0.
    (D) New primary loan guarantee commitments, $0.

RECONCILIATION

SEC. 4. (a) Not later than October 15, 1990, the committees named in subsections (b) and (c) of this section shall submit their recommendations to the Committees on the Budget of their respective Houses. After receiving those recommendations, the Committees on the Budget shall report to the House and Senate a reconciliation bill or resolution or both carrying out all such recommendations without any substantive revision.

HOUSE COMMITTEES

(b)(1) The House Committee on Agriculture shall report (A) changes in laws within its jurisdiction which provide spending authority as defined in section 401(c)(2)(C) of the Congressional Budget Act of 1974, sufficient to reduce outlays, (B) changes in laws within its jurisdiction which provide spending authority other than as defined in section 401(c)(2)(C) of the Act, sufficient to reduce outlays, or (C) any combination thereof, as follows: $1,022,000,000 in outlays in fiscal year 1991, $2,023,000,000 in outlays in fiscal year 1992, $3,214,000,000 in outlays in fiscal year 1993, $3,432,000,000 in outlays in fiscal year 1994, and $3,936,000,000 in outlays in fiscal year 1995.

(2) The House Committee on Banking, Finance and Urban Affairs shall report (A) changes in laws within its jurisdiction which provide spending authority as defined in section 401(c)(2)(C) of the Congressional Budget Act of 1974, sufficient to reduce outlays, (B) changes in laws within its jurisdiction which provide spending authority other than as defined in section 401(c)(2)(C) of the Act, sufficient to reduce outlays, or (C) any combination thereof, as follows: $1,507,000,000 in outlays in fiscal year 1991, $2,635,000,000 in outlays in fiscal year 1992, $2,812,000,000 in outlays in fiscal year 1993, $3,081,000,000 in outlays in fiscal year 1994, and $3,223,000,000 in outlays in fiscal year 1995.

(3) The House Committee on Education and Labor shall report changes in laws within its jurisdiction sufficient to reduce the deficit as follows: $215,000,000 in fiscal year 1991, $525,000,000 in fiscal year 1992, $760,000,000 in fiscal year 1993, $1,010,000,000 in fiscal year 1994, and $1,260,000,000 in fiscal year 1995.

(4) The House Committee on Energy and Commerce shall report (A) changes in laws within its jurisdiction which provide spending authority as defined in section 401(c)(2)(C) of the Congressional Budget Act of 1974, sufficient to reduce outlays, (B) changes in laws within its jurisdiction which provide spending authority other than as defined in section 401(c)(2)(C) of the Act, sufficient to reduce outlays, or (C) any combination thereof, as follows: $3,731,000,000 in outlays in fiscal year 1991, $6,822,000,000 in outlays in fiscal year 1992, $9,224,000,000 in outlays in fiscal year 1993, $10,988,000,000 in outlays in fiscal year 1994, and $12,956,000,000 in outlays in fiscal year 1995.

(5) The House Committee on Interior and Insular Affairs shall report (A) changes in laws within its jurisdiction which provide spending authority as defined in section 401(c)(2)(C) of the Congressional Budget Act of 1974, sufficient to reduce outlays, (B) changes in laws within its jurisdiction which provide spending authority other than as defined in section 401(c)(2)(C) of the Act, sufficient to reduce outlays, or (C) any combination thereof, as follows: $343,000,000 in outlays in fiscal year 1991, $400,000,000 in outlays in fiscal year 1992, $412,000,000 in outlays in fiscal year 1993, $425,000,000 in outlays in fiscal year 1994, and $438,000,000 in outlays in fiscal year 1995.

(6) The House Committee on Judiciary shall report (A) changes in laws within its jurisdiction which provide spending authority as defined in section 401(c)(2)(C) of the Congressional Budget Act of 1974,

sufficient to reduce outlays, (B) changes in laws within its jurisdiction which provide spending authority other than as defined in section 401(c)(2)(C) of the Act, sufficient to reduce outlays, or (C) any combination thereof, as follows: $91,000,000 in outlays in fiscal year 1991, $95,000,000 in outlays in fiscal year 1992, $99,000,000 in outlays in fiscal year 1993, $103,000,000 in outlays in fiscal year 1994, and $107,000,000 in outlays in fiscal year 1995.

(7) The House Committee on Merchant Marine and Fisheries shall report (A) changes in laws within its jurisdiction which provide spending authority as defined in section 401(c)(2)(C) of the Congressional Budget Act of 1974, sufficient to reduce outlays, (B) changes in laws within its jurisdiction which provide spending authority other than as defined in section 401(c)(2)(C) of the Act, sufficient to reduce outlays, or (C) any combination thereof, as follows: $222,000,000 in outlays in fiscal year 1991, $241,000,000 in outlays in fiscal year 1992, $249,000,000 in outlays in fiscal year 1993, $256,000,000 in outlays in fiscal year 1994, and $263,000,000 in outlays in fiscal year 1995.

(8) The House Committee on Post Office and Civil Service shall report (A) changes in laws within its jurisdiction which provide spending authority as defined in section 401(c)(2)(C) of the Congressional Budget Act of 1974, sufficient to reduce outlays, (B) changes in laws within its jurisdiction which provide spending authority other than as defined in section 401(c)(2)(C) of the Act, sufficient to reduce outlays, or (C) any combination thereof, as follows: $2,165,000,000 in outlays in fiscal year 1991, $2,140,000,000 in outlays in fiscal year 1992, $2,780,000,000 in outlays in fiscal year 1993, $3,545,000,000 in outlays in fiscal year 1994, and $3,720,000,000 in outlays in fiscal year 1995.

(9) The House Committee on Public Works shall report (A) changes in laws within its jurisdiction which provide spending authority as defined in section 401(c)(2)(C) of the Congressional Budget Act of 1974, sufficient to reduce outlays, (B) changes in laws within its jurisdiction which provide spending authority other than as defined in section 401(c)(2)(C) of the Act, sufficient to reduce outlays, or (C) any combination thereof, as follows: $42,000,000 in outlays in fiscal year 1991, $53,000,000 in outlays in fiscal year 1992, $53,000,000 in outlays in fiscal year 1993, $53,000,000 in outlays in fiscal year 1994, and $53,000,000 in outlays in fiscal year 1995.

(10) The House Committee on Science, Space, and Technology shall report (A) changes in laws within its jurisdiction which provide spending authority as defined in section 401(c)(2)(C) of the Congressional Budget Act of 1974, sufficient to reduce outlays, (B) changes in laws within its jurisdiction which provide spending authority other than as defined in section 401(c)(2)(C) of the Act, sufficient to reduce outlays, or (C) any combination thereof, as follows: $5,000,000 in outlays in fiscal year 1991, $5,000,000 in outlays in fiscal year 1992, $5,000,000 in outlays in fiscal year 1993, $5,000,000 in outlays in fiscal year 1994, and $5,000,000 in outlays in fiscal year 1995.

(11) The House Committee on Veterans' Affairs shall report (A) changes in laws within its jurisdiction which provide spending authority as defined in section 401(c)(2)(C) of the Congressional Budget Act of 1974, sufficient to reduce outlays, (B) changes in laws within

*its jurisdiction which provide spending authority other than as de-
fined in section 401(c)(2)(C) of the Act, sufficient to reduce outlays,
or (C) any combination thereof, as follows: $620,000,000 in outlays
in fiscal year 1991, $645,000,000 in outlays in fiscal year 1992,
$670,000,000 in outlays in fiscal year 1993, $695,000,000 in outlays
in fiscal year 1994, and $720,000,000 in outlays in fiscal year 1995.*

*(12)(A) The House Committee on Ways and Means shall report (i)
changes in laws within its jurisdiction which provide spending authority as defined in section 401(c)(2)(C) of the Congressional Budget
Act of 1974, sufficient to reduce outlays, (ii) changes in laws within
its jurisdiction which provide spending authority other than as defined in section 401(c)(2)(C) of the Act, sufficient to reduce outlays,
or (iii) any combination thereof, as follows: $3,320,000,000 in outlays
in fiscal year 1991, $9,245,000,000 in outlays in fiscal year 1992,
$11,870,000,000 in outlays in fiscal year 1993, $14,148,000,000 in outlays in fiscal year 1994, and $17,020,000,000 in outlays in fiscal year
1995.*

*(B) The House Committee on Ways and Means shall report
changes in laws within its jurisdiction sufficient to increase revenues as follows: $13,225,000,000 in fiscal year 1991, $24,135,000,000
in fiscal year 1992, $24,040,000,000 in fiscal year 1993,
$28,950,000,000 in fiscal year 1994, and $28,450,000,000 in fiscal
year 1995.*

*(C) In addition to the instructions in subparagraphs (A) and (B),
the House Committee on Ways and Means shall report changes in
laws within its jurisdiction sufficient to reduce the deficit as follows: $2,000,000,000 in fiscal year 1991, $3,000, '00,000 in fiscal year
1992, $4,000,000,000 in fiscal year 1993, $5,000,000,000 in fiscal year
1994, and $6,000,000,000 in fiscal year 1995.*

*(D) The House Committee on Ways and Means shall report
changes in laws within its jurisdiction which provides for an increase in the permanent statutory limit on the public debt by an
amount not to exceed $1,900,000,000.*

SENATE COMMITTEES

*(c)(1) The Senate Committee on Agriculture, Nutrition, and Forest-
ry shall report (A) changes in laws within its jurisdiction which
provide spending authority as defined in section 401(c)(2)(C) of the
Congressional Budget Act of 1974, sufficient to reduce outlays, (B)
changes in laws within its jurisdiction which provide spending authority other than as defined in section 401(c)(2)(C) of the Act, sufficient to reduce outlays, or (C) any combination thereof, as follows:
$1,000,000,000 in fiscal year 1991, and $13,473,000,000 in fiscal
years 1991 through 1995.*

*(2) The Senate Committee on Banking, Housing, and Urban Af-
fairs shall report (A) changes in laws within its jurisdiction which
provide spending authority as defined in section 401(c)(2)(C) of the
Congressional Budget Act of 1974, sufficient to reduce outlays, (B)
changes in laws within its jurisdiction which provide spending authority other than as defined in section 401(c)(2)(C) of the Act, sufficient to reduce outlays, or (C) any combination thereof, as follows:
$1,507,000,000 in fiscal year 1991, and $13,258,000,000 in fiscal
years 1991 through 1995.*

(3) The Senate Committee on Commerce, Science, and Transportation shall report (A) changes in laws within its jurisdiction which provide spending authority as defined in section 401(c)(2)(C) of the Congressional Budget Act of 1974, sufficient to reduce outlays, (B) changes in laws within its jurisdiction which provide spending authority other than as defined in section 401(c)(2)(C) of the Act, sufficient to reduce outlays, or (C) any combination thereof, as follows: $232,000,000 in fiscal year 1991, and $1,335,000,000 in fiscal years 1991 through 1995.

(4) The Senate Committee on Energy and Natural Resources shall report (A) changes in laws within its jurisdiction which provide spending authority as defined in section 401(c)(2)(C) of the Congressional Budget Act of 1974, sufficient to reduce outlays, (B) changes in laws within its jurisdiction which provide spending authority other than as defined in section 401(c)(2)(C) of the Act, sufficient to reduce outlays, or (C) any combination thereof, as follows: $36,000,000 in fiscal year 1991, and $364,000,000 in fiscal years 1991 through 1995.

(5) The Senate Committee on Environment and Public Works shall report (A) changes in laws within its jurisdiction which provide spending authority as defined in section 401(c)(2)(C) of the Congressional Budget Act of 1974, sufficient to reduce outlays, (B) changes in laws within its jurisdiction which provide spending authority other than as defined in section 401(c)(2)(C) of the Act, sufficient to reduce outlays, or (C) any combination thereof, as follows: $392,000,000 in fiscal year 1991, and $1,808,000,000 in fiscal years 1991 through 1995.

(6)(A) The Senate Committee on Finance shall report (i) changes in laws within its jurisdiction which provide spending authority as defined in section 401(c)(2)(C) of the Congressional Budget Act of 1974, sufficient to reduce outlays, (ii) changes in laws within its jurisdiction which provide spending authority other than as defined in section 401(c)(2)(C) of the Act, sufficient to reduce outlays, or (iii) any combination thereof, as follows: $3,015,000,000 in fiscal year 1991, and $55,883,000,000 in fiscal years 1991 through 1995.

(B) The Senate Committee on Finance shall report changes in laws within its jurisdiction sufficient to increase revenues as follows: $13,225,000,000 in fiscal year 1991, and $118,800,000,000 in fiscal years 1991 through 1995.

(C) In addition to the instructions in subparagraph (A) and (B), the Senate Committee on Finance shall report changes in laws within its jurisdicton sufficient (i) to reduce outlays, (ii) to increase revenues, or (iii) any combination thereof, as follows $2,000,000,000 in fiscal year 1991, and $20,000,000,000 in fiscal years 1991 through 1995.

(D) The Senate Committee on Finance shall report changes in law within its jurisdiction which provide for an increase in the permanent statutory limit on the public debt by an amount not to exceed $1,900,000,000,000.

(7) The Senate Committee on Governmental Affairs shall report (A) changes in laws within its jurisdiction which provide spending authority as defined in section 401(c)(2)(C) of the Congressional Budget Act of 1974, sufficient to reduce outlays, (B) changes in laws within its jurisdiction which provide spending authority other than

as defined in section 401(c)(2)(C) of the Act, sufficient to reduce outlays, or (C) any combination thereof, as follows: $2,165,000,000 in fiscal year 1991, and $14,350,000,000 in fiscal years 1991 through 1995.

(8) The Senate Committee on the Judiciary shall report (A) changes in laws within its jurisdiction which provide spending authority as defined in section 401(c)(2)(C) of the Congressional Budget Act of 1974, sufficient to reduce outlays, (B) changes in laws within its jurisdiction which provide spending authority other than as defined in section 401(c)(2)(C) of the Act, sufficient to reduce outlays, or (C) any combination thereof, as follows: $91,000,000 in fiscal year 1991, and $495,000,000 in fiscal years 1991 through 1995.

(9)(A) The Senate Committee on Labor and Human Resources shall report (i) changes in laws within its jurisdiction which provide spending authority as defined in section 401(c)(2)(C) of the Congressional Budget Act of 1974, sufficient to reduce outlays, (ii) changes in laws within its jurisdiction which provide spending authority other than as defined in section 401(c)(2)(C) of the Act, sufficient to reduce outlays, or (iii) any combination thereof, as follows: $120,000,000 in fiscal year 1991, and $2,640,000,000 in fiscal years 1991 through 1995.

(B) The Senate Committee on Labor and Human Resources shall report changes in laws within its jurisdiction sufficient to increase revenues as follows: $45,000,000 in fiscal year 1991, and $840,000,000 in fiscal years 1991 through 1995.

(10) The Senate Committee on Veterans' Affairs shall report (A) changes in laws within its jurisdiction which provide spending authority as defined in section 401(c)(2)(C) of the Congressional Budget Act of 1974, sufficient to reduce outlays, (B) changes in laws within its jurisdiction which provide spending authority other than as defined in section 401(c)(2)(C) of the Act, sufficient to reduce outlays, or (C) any combination thereof, as follows: $620,000,000 in fiscal year 1991, and $3,350,000,000 in fiscal years 1991 through 1995.

SALE OF GOVERNMENT ASSETS

SEC. 5. (a) It is the sense of the Congress that—

(1) from time to time the United States Government should sell assets to nongovernment buyers; and

(2) the amounts realized from such asset sales will not recur on an annual basis and do not reduce the demand for credit.

(b) For purposes of allocations and points of order under section 302 of the Congressional Budget and Impoundment Control Act of 1974, the amounts realized from asset sales or prepayments of loans shall not be allocated to a committee and shall not be scored with respect to the level of budget authority or outlays under a committee's allocation under section 302 of that Act.

(c) For purposes of reconciliation under section 310 of the Congressional Budget and Impoundment Control Act of 1974, the amounts realized from asset sales or prepayments of loans shall not be scored with respect to the level of budget authority, outlays, contributions, or revenues reconciled under a concurrent resolution on the budget.

(d) For purposes of this section—

(1) the terms "asset sale" and "prepayment of a loan" shall have the same meaning as under section 257(12) of the Balanced Budget and Emergency Deficit Control Act of 1985; and

(2) the terms "asset sale" and "prepayment of a loan" do not include asset sales mandated by law before September 8, 1987, and routine, ongoing asset sales and loan prepayments at levels consistent with agency operations in fiscal year 1986.

RESERVE FUND FOR CHILDREN

SEC. *6. (a) In the Senate, budget authority and outlays may be allocated to the Senate Committee on Finance for increased funding for children, including funding through tax credits, if the Committee on Finance or the committee of conference reports funding legislation that—*

(1) will, if enacted, make funds available for that purpose; and

(2) to the extent that the costs of such legislation are not included in this resolution, will not increase the deficit in this resolution for fiscal year 1991, and will not increase the total deficit for the period of fiscal years 1991 through 1995.

(b) Upon the reporting of legislation pursuant to subsection (a), and again upon the submission of a conference report on such legislation (if such a conference report is submitted), the Chairman of the Committee on the Budget of the Senate may file with the Senate appropriately revised allocations under section 302(a) of the Congressional Budget Act of 1974 and revised functional levels and aggregates to carry out this section. Such revised allocations, functional levels, and aggregates shall be considered for the purposes of such Act as allocations, functional levels, and aggregates contained in this resolution. The Committee on Finance shall report revised allocations pursuant to section 302(b) of such Act for the appropriate fiscal year (or years) to carry out this section.

And the Senate agree to the same.

That the Senate recede from its amendment to the title of the resolution.

LEON E. PANETTA,
RICHARD GEPHARDT,
Managers on the Part of the House.

JIM SASSER,
WYCHE FOWLER, Jr.,
Managers on the Part of the Senate.

JOINT EXPLANATORY STATEMENT OF THE COMMITTEE OF CONFERENCE

The managers on the part of the House and the Senate at the conference on the disagreeing votes of the two Houses on the amendments of the Senate to the concurrent resolution (H. Con. Res. 310) setting forth the congressional budget for the United States Government for the fiscal years 1991, 1992, 1993, 1994, and 1995, submit the following joint statement to the House and the Senate in explanation of the effect of the action agreed upon by the managers and recommended in the accompanying conference report:

The Senate amendment to the text of the resolution struck out all of the House resolution after the resolving clause and inserted a substitute text.

The House recedes from its disagreement to the amendment of the Senate with an amendment which is a substitute for the House resolution and the Senate amendment.

EXPLANATION OF CONFERENCE AGREEMENT

The following tables show the functional allocations and budget aggregates included in the conference agreement over five years for the total budget, the on-budget amounts and the off-budget amounts. In addition, a table is included which breaks out the credit amounts by function.

CONFERENCE AGREEMENT TOTAL BUDGET

[In billions of dollars]

	1991	1992	1993	1994	1995
Budget authority	1,485.6	1,562.6	1,582.4	1,593.4	1,668.4
Outlays	1,236.9	1,269.3	1,305.0	1,324.8	1,355.5
Revenues	1,172.9	1,260.8	1,349.8	1,433.3	1,511.7
Deficit (−) / surplus (+)	− 64.0	− 8.5	44.8	108.5	156.2
050 National Defense:					
Budget authority	288.3	290.9	291.1	351.5	364.9
Outlays	297.0	295.0	292.0	341.7	351.5
150 International Affairs:					
Budget authority	19.2	19.8	20.6	22.4	23.8
Outlays	17.4	18.0	18.5	19.7	20.7
250 General Science, Space and Technology:					
Budget authority	15.2	15.9	16.5	17.1	17.7
Outlays	15.2	15.7	16.1	16.8	17.4
270 Energy:					
Budget authority	6.4	5.6	6.4	6.8	7.2
Outlays	4.0	4.4	5.0	5.3	5.2
300 Natural Resources and Environment:					
Budget authority	18.8	19.9	20.5	21.2	22.0
Outlays	18.9	19.6	20.2	20.6	21.2
350 Agriculture:					
Budget authority	18.0	22.6	20.4	18.2	19.2

CONFERENCE AGREEMENT TOTAL BUDGET—Continued

[In billions of dollars]

	1991	1992	1993	1994	1995
Outlays	14.1	17.1	16.0	15.3	14.6
370 Commerce and housing credit:					
Budget authority	85.5	85.4	41.6	−6.5	2.6
Outlays	87.0	81.4	39.7	−9.2	−3.2
400 Transportation:					
Budget authority	32.3	33.5	34.7	36.0	37.4
Outlays	30.7	31.9	33.1	34.3	35.5
450 Community and regional development:					
Budget authority	9.2	8.9	9.0	9.5	9.6
Outlays	8.6	8.6	8.7	8.9	9.2
500 Education, training, employment and social services:					
Budget authority	43.0	43.7	44.4	46.3	48.1
Outlays	41.8	43.0	44.0	45.4	46.9
550 Health:					
Budget authority	66.3	73.9	81.3	89.6	98.5
Outlays	65.5	73.3	80.9	88.9	97.5
570 Medicare:					
Budget authority	122.4	133.5	147.5	161.9	177.2
Outlays	104.9	120.0	134.4	150.5	168.0
600 Income security:					
Budget authority	196.8	205.2	212.8	223.5	231.1
Outlays	160.5	167.8	175.3	185.3	192.2
650 Social security:					
Budget authority	339.5	367.0	396.2	427.5	460.9
Outlays	266.3	283.7	301.4	318.9	337.2
700 Veterans benefits and services:					
Budget authority	31.9	33.1	34.1	35.1	36.1
Outlays	31.7	32.7	33.8	36.3	36.1
750 Administration of justice:					
Budget authority	13.3	14.4	15.0	15.6	16.2
Outlays	12.3	14.2	14.9	15.4	16.0
800 General government:					
Budget authority	11.7	12.0	12.3	12.5	13.0
Outlays	11.7	12.0	11.8	12.0	12.4
900 Net Interest:					
Budget authority	194.4	201.9	206.2	203.8	197.0
Outlays	194.4	201.9	206.2	203.8	197.0
920 Allowances:					
Budget authority	0	0	0	0	0
Outlays	−96.6	−115.3	−88.3	−61.8	−77.4
950 Undistributed offsetting receipts:					
Budget authority	−26.6	−24.6	−28.2	−98.6	−114.1
Outlays	−48.5	−55.7	−58.7	−123.3	−142.5

CONFERENCE AGREEMENT ON-BUDGET ONLY

[In billions of dollars]

	1991	1992	1993	1994	1995
Budget authority	1174.7	1230.1	1229.6	1216.0	1266.0
Outlays	1002.3	1024.8	1049.9	1059.9	1080.9
Revenues	858.6	923.9	987.9	1045.2	1101.4
Deficit (−) / surplus (+)	−143.7	−100.9	−62.0	−14.7	−20.5
050 National defense:					
Budget authority	288.3	290.9	291.1	351.5	364.9
Outlays	297.0	−295.0	292.0	341.7	351.5
150 International affairs:					
Budget authority	19.2	19.8	20.6	22.4	23.8
Outlays	17.4	18.0	18.5	19.7	20.7

CONFERENCE AGREEMENT ON-BUDGET ONLY—Continued

[In billions of dollars]

	1991	1992	1993	1994	1995
250 General science, space and technology:					
Budget authority	15.2	15.9	16.5	17.1	17.7
Outlays	15.2	15.7	16.1	16.8	17.4
270 Energy:					
Budget authority	6.4	5.6	6.4	6.8	7.2
Outlays	4.0	4.4	5.0	5.3	5.2
300 Natural resources and environment:					
Budget authority	18.8	19.9	20.5	21.2	22.0
Outlays	18.9	19.6	20.2	20.6	21.2
350 Agriculture:					
Budget authority	18.0	22.6	20.4	18.2	19.2
Outlays	14.1	17.1	16.0	15.3	14.6
370 Commerce and housing credit:					
Budget authority	85.5	85.4	41.6	−6.5	2.6
Outlays	87.0	81.4	39.7	−9.2	−3.2
400 Transportation:					
Budget authority	32.3	33.5	34.7	36.0	37.4
Outlays	30.7	31.9	33.1	34.3	35.5
450 Community and regional development:					
Budget authority	9.2	8.9	9.0	9.5	9.6
Outlays	8.6	8.6	8.7	8.9	9.2
500 Education, training, employment and social services:					
Budget authority	43.0	43.7	44.4	46.3	48.1
Outlays	41.8	43.0	44.0	45.4	46.9
550 Health:					
Budget authority	66.3	73.9	81.3	89.6	98.5
Outlays	65.5	73.3	80.9	88.9	97.5
570 Medicare:					
Budget authority	122.4	133.5	147.5	161.9	177.2
Outlays	104.9	120.0	134.4	150.5	168.0
600 Income security:					
Budget authority	196.8	205.2	212.8	223.5	231.1
Outlays	160.5	167.8	175.3	185.3	192.2
650 Social Security:					
Budget authority	3.8	4.5	4.9	5.4	6.0
Outlays	3.8	4.5	4.9	5.4	6.0
700 Veterans benefits and services:					
Budget authority	31.9	33.1	34.1	35.1	36.1
Outlays	31.7	32.7	33.8	36.3	36.1
750 Administration of justice:					
Budget authority	13.3	14.4	15.0	15.6	16.2
Outlays	12.3	14.2	14.9	15.4	16.0
800 General government:					
Budget authority	11.7	12.0	12.3	12.5	13.0
Outlays	11.7	12.0	11.8	12.0	12.4
900 Net interest:					
Budget authority	215.6	228.7	239.2	243.7	244.5
Outlays	215.6	228.7	239.2	243.7	244.5
920 Allowances:					
Budget authority	0	0	0	0	0
Outlays	−95.4	−113.6	−86.6	−60.5	−76.4
950 Undistributed offsetting receipts:					
Budget authority	−23.0	−21.4	−22.7	−93.8	−109.1
Outlays	−43.0	−49.5	−52.0	−115.9	−134.4

CONFERENCE AGREEMENT OFF-BUDGET ONLY

[In billions of dollars]

	1991	1992	1993	1994	1995
Budget authority	310.9	332.5	352.8	377.4	402.4
Outlays	234.6	244.5	255.1	264.9	274.6
Revenues	314.3	336.9	361.9	388.1	410.3
Deficit (−) / surplus (+)	79.7	92.4	106.8	123.2	135.7
050 National defense:					
Budget authority	0	0	0	0	0
Outlays	0	0	0	0	0
150 International affairs:					
Budget authority	0	0	0	0	0
Outlays	0	0	0	0	0
250 General science, space and technology:					
Budget authority	0	0	0	0	0
Outlays	0	0	0	0	0
270 Energy:					
Budget authority	0	0	0	0	0
Outlays	0	0	0	0	0
300 Natural resources and environment:					
Budget authority	0	0	0	0	0
Outlays	0	0	0	0	0
350 Agriculture:					
Budget authority	0	0	0	0	0
Outlays	0	0	0	0	0
370 Commerce and housing credit:					
Budget authority	0	0	0	0	0
Outlays	0	0	0	0	0
400 Transportation:					
Budget authority	0	0	0	0	0
Outlays	0	0	0	0	0
450 Community and regional development:					
Budget authority	0	0	0	0	0
Outlays	0	0	0	0	0
500 Education, training, employment and social services:					
Budget authority	0	0	0	0	0
Outlays	0	0	0	0	0
550 Health:					
Budget authority	0	0	0	0	0
Outlays	0	0	0	0	0
570 Medicare:					
Budget authority	0	0	0	0	0
Outlays	0	0	0	0	0
600 Income security:					
Budget authority	0	0	0	0	0
Outlays	0	0	0	0	0
650 Social security:					
Budget authority	335.7	362.5	391.3	422.1	454.9
Outlays	262.5	279.2	296.5	313.5	331.2
700 Veterans benefits and services:					
Budget authority	0	0	0	0	0
Outlays	0	0	0	0	0
750 Administration of justice:					
Budget authority	0	0	0	0	0
Outlays	0	0	0	0	0
800 General government:					
Budget authority	0	0	0	0	0
Outlays	0	0	0	0	0
900 Net interest:					
Budget authority	−21.2	−26.8	−33.0	−39.9	−47.5
Outlays	−21.2	−26.8	−33.0	−39.9	−47.5
920 Allowances:					
Budget authority	0	0	0	0	0
Outlays	−1.2	−1.7	−1.7	−1.3	−1.0

CONFERENCE AGREEMENT OFF-BUDGET ONLY—Continued

[In billions of dollars]

	1991	1992	1993	1994	1995
950 Undistributed offsetting receipts:					
Budget authority	−3.6	−3.2	−5.5	−4.8	−5.0
Outlays	−5.5	−6.2	−6.7	−7.4	−8.1

CREDIT BUDGET FUNCTION TOTALS

[In billions of dollars]

	1991	1992	1993	1994	1995
Direct Loans	21.0	17.8	18.2	18.4	18.6
Guaranteed loans	106.8	109.6	112.1	115.5	118.1
Secondary guaranteed loans	85.4	88.7	92.1	95.6	99.2
050 Defense:					
Direct loans	0	0	0	0	0
Guaranteed loans	0	0	0	0	0
150 International affairs:					
Direct loans	1.9	2.0	2.1	2.1	2.2
Guaranteed loans	7.2	7.2	7.5	7.7	8.0
Secondary guaranteed loans	.4	.4	.4	.5	.5
250 General science, space and technology:					
Direct loans	0	0	0	0	0
Guaranteed loans	0	0	0	0	0
270 Energy:					
Direct loans	2.0	1.5	2.0	2.1	2.3
Guaranteed loans	.4	0	0	0	0
300 Natural resources and environment:					
Direct loans	.1	.1	.1	.1	.1
Guaranteed loans	0	0	0	0	0
350 Agriculture:					
Direct loans	9.0	8.8	8.6	8.6	8.4
Guaranteed loans	7.0	7.3	6.6	6.7	6.8
370 Commerce and housing credit:					
Direct loans	6.0	3.3	3.4	3.50	3.6
Guaranteed loans	63.3	65.5	67.8	70.3	72.1
Secondary guaranteed loans	85.0	88.3	91.7	95.1	98.7
400 Transportation:					
Direct loans	0	.1	.1	.1	.1
Guaranteed loans	0	0	0	0	0
450 Community and regional development:					
Direct loans	1.2	1.2	1.2	1.3	1.3
Guaranteed loans	.4	.4	.4	.4	.4
500 Education, training, employment and social services:					
Direct loans	0	0	0	0	0
Guaranteed loans	12.5	12.9	13.2	13.3	13.4
550 Health:					
Direct loans	0	0	0	0	0
Guaranteed loans	.3	.3	.3	.4	.4
570 Medicare:					
Direct loans	0	0	0	0	0
Guaranteed loans	0	0	0	0	0
600 Income security:					
Direct loans	.1	.1	.1	.1	.1
Guaranteed loans	0	0	0	0	0
650 Social security:					
Direct loans	0	0	0	0	0
Guaranteed loans	0	0	0	0	0
700 Veterans benefits and services					
Direct loans	.7	.6	.6	.5	.5
Guaranteed loans	15.7	16.0	16.3	16.7	17.0

CREDIT BUDGET FUNCTION TOTALS—Continued

[In billions of dollars]

	1991	1992	1993	1994	1995
750 Administration of justice:					
Direct loans	0	0	0	0	0
Guaranteed loans	0	0	0	0	0
800 General government:					
Direct loans	0	0	0	0	0
Guaranteed loans	0	0	0	0	0
900 Net interest:					
Direct loans	0	0	0	....	0
Guaranteed loans	0	0	0	0	0
920 Allowances:					
Direct loans	0	0	0	0	0
Guaranteed loans	0	0	0	0	0
950 Undistributed offsetting receipts:					
Direct loans	0	0	0	0	0
Guaranteed loans	0	0	....	0	0

RECONCILATION INSTRUCTIONS

The conference agreement includes reconciliation instructions directing twelve House Committees and ten Senate Committees to report legislation to achieve savings over fiscal years, 1991–1995. The House Committee instructions specify savings targets for each of the five years. The Senate Committee instructions specify targets for fiscal year 1991 and for total savings over the five years.

The conference agreement requires House and Senate Committees to report reconciliation recommendations to their respective Budget Committees not later than October 15, 1990.

CONFERENCE AGREEMENT RECONCILIATION BY HOUSE COMMITTEE

[Deficit reduction in billions of dollars]

Committee	Fiscal year—					5-year
	1991	1992	1993	1994	1995	
Agriculture: Mandatory/fee savings	−1.022	−2.023	−3.214	−3.432	−3.936	−13.627
Banking: Mandatory/fee savings	−1.507	−2.635	−2.812	−3.081	−3.223	−13.258
Education and Labor: Deficit reduction (DR)	−.215	−.525	−.760	−1.010	−1.260	−3.770
Energy and Commerce: Mandatory/fee savings	−3.731	−6.822	−9.224	−10.988	−12.956	−43.721
Interior: Mandatory/fee savings	−.343	−.400	−.412	−.425	−.438	−2.018
Judiciary: Mandatory/fee savings	−.091	−.095	−.099	−.103	−.107	−.495
Merchant Marine: Mandatory/fee savings	−.222	−.241	−.249	−.256	−.263	−1.231
Post Office: Mandatory/fee savings	−2.165	−2.140	−2.780	−3.545	−3.720	−14.350
Public Works: Mandatory/fee savings	−.042	−.053	−.053	−.053	−.053	−.254
Science, Space and Technology: Mandatory/fee savings	−.005	−.005	−.005	−.005	−.005	−.025
Veterans: Mandatory/fee savings	−.620	−.645	−.670	−.695	−.720	−3.350
Ways and Means:						
Mandatory/fee savings	−3.320	−9.245	−11.870	−14.148	−17.020	−55.603
Deficit reduction (DR)	−2.000	−3.000	−4.000	−5.000	−6.000	−20.000
Revenues (REV)	−13.225	−24.135	−24.040	−28.950	−28.450	−118.800
Committee total (DR)	−18.545	−36.380	−39.910	−48.098	−51.470	−194.403

CONFERENCE AGREEMENT RECONCILIATION BY HOUSE COMMITTEE—Continued

[Deficit reduction in billions of dollars]

Committee	Fiscal year—					5-year
	1991	1992	1993	1994	1995	
Total reconciled [1]	−24.307	−45.009	−50.921	−60.711	−65.258	−246.206
IRS enforce initiatives (REV)	−3.037	−1.835	−1.803	−1.488	−1.213	−9.376
Miscellaneous other mandatory entitlement/fees	−.600	−.600	−.600	−.600	−.600	−3.000
Total revenue increases and mandatory spending cuts (DR)	−27.944	−47.444	−53.324	−62.799	−67.071	−258.582

[1] Savings that may result from action by more than one committee due to joint jurisdiction are counted only once in the total.
Note.—All amounts are outlays unless specified as REV (revenues) or DR (deficit reduction—outlays or revenues).

CONFERENCE AGREEMENT RECONCILIATION BY SENATE COMMITTEE

[In millions of dollars]

		1991	5-year
Agriculture:			
Unspecified mandatory/fees	0	1,000	13,473
Banking:			
Unspecified mandatory/fees	0	1,507	13,258
Commerce:			
Unspecified mandatory/fees	0	232	1,335
Energy:			
Unspecified mandatory/fees	0	36	364
Environment:			
Unspecified mandatory/fees	0	329	1,808
Finance:			
Unspecified mandatory/fees	0	3,015	55,883
Unspecified revenues	REV	13,225	118,800
Unspecified rev or mandatory	DR	2,000	20,000
Subtotal, Finance	DR	18,240	194,683
Government Affairs:			
Unspecified mandatory/fees	0	2,165	14,350
Judiciary:			
Unspecified mandatory/fees	0	91	495
Labor:			
Unspecified revenues	REV	45	840
Unspecified mandatory/fees	0	120	2,640
Subtotal, Labor	DR	165	3,480
Veterans:			
Unspecified mandatory/fees	0	620	3,350
Total reconciled to committees	DR	24,307	246,206
IRS enforcement	REV	3,037	9,376
Miscellaneous mandatory/fees	0	600	3,000
Total	DR	27,944	258,582

Note: Savings that may result from action by more than one committee due to joint jurisdiction are counted only once in the total. Outlays are specified as "O," revenues as "REV," and deficit reduction as "DR."

BUDGET SUMMIT AGREEMENT

On May 6, 1990, the President and the bipartisan congressional leadership agreed to convene a special budget group. Five months later, the negotiators reached agreement. The budget summit agreement represents the largest deficit reduction plan ever agreed to, an estimated $500 billion during the next five years.

This conference agreement includes five-year reconciliation instructions and discretionary spending limitations that reflect the work of the budget summit. All caps for discretionary spending are upper limits on spending and not floors.

The conferees believe that the adoption and implementation of the conference agreement will hasten the achievement of a balanced Federal budget, reduce the demand on private credit markets, and enhance the long-run growth potential of the United States.

LEADERSHIP ENFORCEMENT OF CONFERENCE AGREEMENT

It is the intent of the conferees that the bipartisan leaders of the House and Senate work with the committees of Congress to assure that the deficit reduction amounts required by this conference agreement will be achieved and will result in real, permanent savings.

It is the intent of the conferees that the House-reported reconciliation bill should not contain provisions extraneous to the agreement.

Should legislation under consideration by any committee fail to comply with the conference agreement, the conferees intend that remedial efforts shall be made by all parties to achieve such compliance. Further, the conferees intend that the bipartisan leaders shall take steps to enforce the agreement.

ACHIEVEMENT OF UNSPECIFIED SAVINGS

The conferees urge that the joint leadership of Congress agree on a package of changes in laws that provide mandatory spending to achieve deficit reduction of $3,000,000,000 (in addition to the amounts reconciled in this concurrent resolution) and seek to include that package in the reconciliation bill pursuant to this concurrent resolution.

FUNDING FOR IRS COMPLIANCE

It is the intent of the conferees that the additional amounts requested by the President in the fiscal year 1991 budget for the IRS compliance initiative—$191 million in budget authority and $183 million in outlays in fiscal year 1991, $172 million in budget authority and $169 million in outlays in fiscal year 1992, $183 million in budget authority and $179 million in outlays in fiscal year 1993, $187 million in budget authority and $183 in outlays in fiscal year 1994, and $188 million in budget authority and $184 in outlays in fiscal year 1995—shall be provided by action of the Appropriations Committees in order to raise the assumed amounts of additional revenues from increased IRS compliance funding consistent with the budget summit agreement. The Appropriations Committees will be held harmless vis-a-vis the summit agreement's discretionary spending caps for increased funding in these amounts.

Budget Process Reform and Enforcement

To assure a $500 billion deficit reduction package is achieved and maintained, the conferees intend that the reconciliation act implementing this conference agreement include provisions to strengthen the budget process.

Costs of Operation Desert Shield

This agreement assumes the current costs for Operation Desert Shield represent emergency funding requirements not subject to the defense caps. Funding for Desert Shield will be provided subsequently through the normal legislative process and this agreement makes no assumptions as to the amount that may be required. Desert Shield costs should be accommodated through allied burden-sharing contributions, offsets within other non-Desert Shield accounts of the defense budget and/or subsequent appropriations Acts. Desert Shield costs mean those incremental costs directly associated with the increase in operations in the Middle East and do not include costs which would be experienced by the Department of Defense as part of its normal operations absent Operation Desert Shield.

Pay-As-You-Go for New Initiatives

The conferees do not intend to preclude the enactment of legislation providing for additional new initiatives. However, the conferees do intend that all new initiatives be paid for on a pay-as-you-go basis.

Deficit Reduction

The Managers expect that the legislative committees will maintain, to the greatest degree possible, the distribution of entitlement reductions and revenue increases in the bipartisan leadership agreement. The Managers expect that the shares of deficit reduction will closely parallel those of the summit agreement—36 percent discretionary, no less than 22 percent mandatory, no greater than 30 percent revenues, and 13 percent net interest. Further, the Managers expect that gross revenues would not exceed those assumed in the bipartisan budget summit agreement.

LEON E. PANETTA,
RICHARD GEPHARDT,
Managers on the Part of the House.

JIM SASSER,
WYCHE FOWLER, Jr.
Managers on the Part of the Senate.

Index